# Information Systems Transformation

## Architecture-Driven Modernization Case Studies

## Morgan Kaufmann OMG Press

Morgan Kaufmann Publishers and the Object Management Group™ (OMG) have joined forces to publish a line of books addressing business and technical topics related to OMG's large suite of software standards.

OMG is an international, open membership, not-for-profit computer industry consortium that was founded in 1989. The OMG creates standards for software used in government and corporate environments to enable interoperability and to forge common development environments that encourage the adoption and evolution of new technology. OMG members and its board of directors consist of representatives from a majority of the organizations that shape enterprise and Internet computing today.

OMG's modeling standards, including the Unified Modeling Language™ (UML®), Model Driven Architecture® (MDA), and Systems Modeling Language (SysML) enable powerful visual design, execution and maintenance of software, and other processes for example, IT Systems Modeling and Business Process Management. The middleware standards and profiles of the Object Management Group are based on the Common Object Request Broker Architecture® (CORBA) and support a wide variety of industries.

More information about OMG can be found at *http://www.omg.org/.*

### Morgan Kaufmann OMG Press Titles

*Distributed Systems Architecture: A Middleware Approach*
Arno Puder, Kay Romer, and Frank Pilhofer

*UML 2 Certification Guide: Fundamental and Intermediate Exams*
Tim Weilkiens and Bernd Oestereich

*Real-Life MDA: Solving Business Problems with Model Driven Architecture*
Michael Guttman and John Parodi

*Business Process Change: A Guide for Business Managers and BPM and Six Sigma Professionals*
Paul Harmon

*A Practical Guide to SysML: The Systems Modeling Language*
Sanford Friedenthal, Alan Moore, and Rick Steiner

*Master Data Management*
David Loshin

*Database Archiving: How to Keep Lots of Data for a Very Long Time*
Jack Olson

*SOA and Web Services Interface Design: Principles, Techniques, and Standards*
Jim Bean

*Information Systems Transformation: Architecture-Driven Modernization Case Studies*
William M. Ulrich and Philip H. Newcomb

# Information Systems Transformation

## Architecture-Driven Modernization
## Case Studies

**William M. Ulrich and Philip H. Newcomb**

AMSTERDAM • BOSTON • HEIDELBERG • LONDON
NEW YORK • OXFORD • PARIS • SAN DIEGO
SAN FRANCISCO • SINGAPORE • SYDNEY • TOKYO

ELSEVIER

Morgan Kaufmann Publishers is an Imprint of Elsevier

Morgan Kaufmann Publishers is an imprint of Elsevier.
30 Corporate Drive, Suite 400, Burlington, MA 01803, USA

This book is printed on acid-free paper.

**Library of Congress Cataloging-in-Publication Data**
Application submitted

**British Library Cataloguing-in-Publication Data**
A catalogue record for this book is available from the British Library.

ISBN: 978-0-12-374913-0

For information on all Morgan Kaufmann publications,
visit our Web site at www.mkp.com or www.elsevierdirect.com

Printed in the United States of America
10   11   12   13   14      5   4   3   2   1

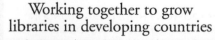

*I dedicate this book to my wife Kathy and children Cat and Max.*
**William M. Ulrich**

*I dedicate this book my wife Christine and children Arielle and Nicolas, parents Bob and Betty, and the brilliant and dedicated staff of The Software Revolution, Inc.*
**Philip H. Newcomb**

# Table of Contents

# Contributors

**Franck Barbier (Chapter 11).** Consultant, Netfective Technology, Professor, University of Pau, France

**Gabriel Barbier (Chapter 14).** MIA-SOFTWARE, Nantes, France

**Hugo Bruneliere (Chapter 14).** R&D Engineer at INRIA & EMN, Nantes, France

**Eric Cariou (Chapter 11).** Assistant Professor, University of Pau, France

**Robert Couch (Chapter 6 and 12).** Senior Scientist, The Software Revolution, Inc., Kirkland, WA

**Jerome DelaPeyronnie (Chapter 5).** Program Manager, FDP Product Manager, Thales Air Systems, Toulouse, France

**Bernhard Düchting (Chapter 13).** Technical Director of Modernization EMEA, Oracle Corporation

**Sylvain Eveillard (Chapter 11).** Netfective Technology

**Olivier Guitton (Chapter 11).** Netfective Technology

**Dru Henke (Chapter 6).** PowerBuilder Conversion Lead, NVISIA, LLC, Chicago, IL

**Frédéric Jouault (Chapter 14).** AtlanMod Team (INRIA & EMN) Nantes, France

**Mark Kramer (Chapter 10).** Senior Consultant, Target Systems

**Tom Laszewski (Chapter 7 and 13).** Technical Director Modernization, Oracle Corporation - Platform Technology Solutions

**Yves Lennon (Chapter 14).** Sodifrance, Nantes, France

**Jim LoVerde (Chapter 6).** Magna Conversion Lead, NVISIA, LLC, Chicago, IL

**Frédéric Madiot (Chapter 14).** MIA-SOFTWARE, Nantes, France

**Joyce McPeek (Chapter 8).** Northrop Grumman IT, Dayton, OH

**Vincent Morillo (Chapter 5).** FDP Senior Scientist, Thales Air Systems, Toulouse, France

**Luong Nguyen (Chapter 5, 6, and 8).** Operations Manager, The Software Revolution, Inc., Kirkland, WA

**Arnaud Perrier (Chapter 11).** Netfective Technology

**Mark Purtill (Chapter 5 and 8).** Senior Scientist, The Software Revolution, Inc., Kirkland, WA

**Ed Seidewitz (Chapter 9).** Vice President, Model Driven Architecture Services, Model Driven Solutions

**Michael K. Smith PhD, PE (Chapter 7).** Chief Technologist, Apps Modernization, EDS Office of the CTO, Hewlett-Packard

**Fakkhredine Trimech (Chapter 5).** FDP Senior Scientist, Thales Air Systems, Toulouse, France

**Kamal Youbi (Chapter 11).** Vice President R&D, Netfective Technology

# Preface

Much has been written and said about existing software systems over the past few years. Tools and solutions have come and gone as organizations have taken on and discarded numerous "silver bullet" strategies for addressing major business and IT challenges. Yet massive, aging software systems remain at the core of most every industry. Increasingly complex, yet fragile, software systems play a critical role in insurance and healthcare, banking and finance, defense and government, manufacturing and telecommunications, energy and utilities, transportation, retail, and other industries.

Executives have come to the stark realization that these systems can no longer be ignored, are not going to fade away, and must be dealt with proactively and not reactively. We agree, which is why we have written this book. We wrote this book to convey one message: Architecture-driven modernization (or simply "modernization") can play a strategic role in building a more agile, more competitive enterprise in the face of increasing internal and external pressures and demands. The following Gartner quote states the strategic value of modernization.

> IT modernization reinstates IT strategic planning at the heart of the CIO cabinet. Most CIOs will need to develop new skills and competencies in their management teams to deal with the significant challenges of IT modernization.
> **6 February 2008, ID Number G00154885, Andy Kyte and Dale Vecchio,**

Architecture-driven modernization provides an enterprise with a wide variety of options for understanding, evolving, and ultimately transforming critical software systems. Applying modernization options to existing software systems is no longer a tactical luxury or stop-gap measure for organizations. Rather, modernization now plays an essential and strategic role within an enterprise and serves as a vehicle for facilitating the alignment of IT with business strategy and business architecture. In addition, modernization opens up a variety of new options for executives as they consider the best way to leverage IT funding and avoid cost and project overruns common in many enterprises today.

To best convey the message of how modernization can address these needs, we offer this book as a testament to the fact that modernization provides real and quantifiable value to organizations. We included ten powerful modernization case studies that discuss how modernization solutions have been applied to a number of scenarios, across a wide variety of industries. In addition, we offer insights into why modernization is becoming more of a necessity as executives seek to find new and unique ways to leverage scarce resources yet still mobilize key enterprise initiatives.

Why architecture-driven modernization? We are frequently asked why the term "architecture-driven" is appended to term modernization. The answer is simple. For modernization initiatives and programs to gain long-term executive support so that the program remains successful and sustainable, modernization efforts must look at the broader impacts and benefits on the IT architecture and on the *business architecture*. We provide guidance on how to do this in Part I of this book.

Why a case study book? When we discussed writing a book with customers, clients, colleagues, and our publisher, one message came through loud and clear: Organizations want to learn how other organizations have applied modernization in practice, including hearing about the successes and the pitfalls of these projects. In seeking out these case studies, we felt that offering a diversified view of modernization was important. We believe that we achieved this diversification from a regional, industry, platform, and project approach perspective.

We also felt that any book on modernization case studies should present those case studies in a broader context. As a result, we have provided readers with a complete context and set of approaches for justifying, launching, and implementing modernization initiatives. In other words, this book not only serves as a basis for convincing your colleagues and management that modernization offers strategic value, but can also serve as an ongoing handbook that you will come back to again and again to continue to expand your understanding of modernization concepts and approaches.

In developing a book that included a number of contributions from additional authors for various case studies, we had an opportunity to see how modernization projects were evolving across international borders and industries. We hope you get as much value out of this book as we gained in writing and editing it.

# CONTENT OVERVIEW

Part I of this book provides a comprehensive overview of architecture-driven modernization. Chapter 1, Introduction to Architecture-Driven Modernization, is recommended for anyone who wants to understand why modernization is an essential element of one's IT and business strategy. It discusses how to avoid past project failures and build a sustainable modernization program; modernization benefits and cost justification; modernization as an alternative versus modernization as an augmentation option; how modernization supports business architecture/IT architecture alignment; assessment, refactoring, and transformation disciplines; and useful modernization principles. We hope you can draw from the various studies contained in this chapter to justify your modernization efforts.

Chapter 2, Modernization Technologies and Services, provides a comprehensive view of available tool, technology, service, and deployment options and when these options should be exercised. Chapter 3, Modernization Standards Roadmap, provides insights into the key role of standards in the evolution of tools, technologies, and the practice of modernization. Chapter 4, Modernization Scenarios, overviews how modernization fits into various project scenarios, many of which are incorporated into the case study section of the book in Part II.

Part II of this book provides ten case studies, each packaged into its own chapter. Modernization case studies cover a variety of industry sectors including insurance, banking, and finance; defense; private and public sector healthcare; education; tourism and travel; energy and geophysical services; federal government; air traffic control; and retail. Existing and target platforms varied but ranged from mainframe to specialty environments. In addition, we included stories from four different countries.

Case study projects addressed technology and platform migrations and transformations; hybrid solutions that incorporated commercial-off-the-shelf (COTS) packages with existing software architectures; migration to services oriented architecture (SOA); application and data architecture transformations, including database migrations; and transformation to model-driven architecture (MDA), which included the migration to UML-based environments. In addition, real-world examples of how to procure and maintain funding for modernization efforts provide excellent insights into how to launch these efforts and, just as important, how to sustain them.

Part III of this book contains a chapter entitled, Launching and Sustaining Modernization Initiatives. This chapter provides a list of modernization pitfalls — what to avoid; an expanded set of guiding principles; how to set up a center of excellence; a modernization tool/technology strategy; a modernization service provider strategy; and a guide for how to get started with a modernization initiative, including procurement strategies; and what to expect from modernization as time unfolds. Many times, books do not always offer the pitfalls associated with a given topic that authors may feel passionate about. However, we feel that it is important to understand when and how you can stumble in a modernization effort and how to avoid these situations.

## ACKNOWLEDGMENTS

The authors want to acknowledge a number of individuals and organizations as contributors to this book. First, we want to thank those executives and managers who have committed themselves and their organizations to the work involved in selling the concept of modernization to executives and finance teams that do not understand basic system concepts and the role of these systems within an enterprise. We also want to thank our contributing authors. Each chapter case study identifies the authors that contributed to that particular case study. We could not have written this book without their help.

We additionally wish to thank all of the in-house personnel, service providers, and vendors who worked on these projects. While there are too many to name on an individual basis, these hardworking individuals provided the management and technical skills necessary to deploy and deliver these projects. We would also like to make special mention of the tool vendors that continue to provide automation solutions to the modernization industry.

We must also thank the Object Management Group (OMG) on several counts. First, we want to thank the OMG Press (Morgan Kaufmann Elsevier) for having the foresight to request and support our work on this book. Specifically, we want to thank our editors, Greg Chalson and Heather Scherer and Production Manager, Paul Gottehrer. In addition, we want to thank Richard Solely, CEO of OMG, for his encouragement on this project. Finally, we want to thank the OMG Architecture-Driven Modernization Task Force for all of the work that it has performed on modernization standards. Again, there are too many ADM Task Force members to thank individually, but without their work on the ADM standards, modernization could have stagnated.

Finally, we want to thank our families and numerous other colleagues who have had to put up with us diverting our attention from other matters for the past year. We hope you enjoy reading this book as much as we enjoyed writing it.

**William M. Ulrich and Philip H. Newcomb**

# Authors' Biographies

**William M. Ulrich** is President of Tactical Strategy Group, Inc. and a management consultant. Fortune 1000 companies, government agencies, high-tech companies, and consulting firms have sought Mr. Ulrich's advice on business/IT architecture alignment. Mr. Ulrich is Co-Chair of the OMG Architecture-Driven Modernization Task Force, Co-Chair of the OMG Business Architecture Special Interest Group, Editorial Director of the Business Architecture Institute, and author of hundreds of articles and three books. Mr. Ulrich's last book was titled *Legacy Systems: Transformation Strategies* (Prentice Hall). In 2005 Mr. Ulrich was awarded the "Keeping America Strong Award" as seen on the Heartbeat of America for his work in the field of systems modernization.

**Philip H. Newcomb** is CEO of The Software Revolution, Incorporated (TSRI), and an internationally recognized expert in the application of artificial intelligence and formal methods to software engineering. He has published numerous papers and articles in technical journals and is a frequent presenter to national and international forums in his field. He has his MS degree in computer science from Ball State University in 1988 with graduate work towards this degree from Carnegie Mellon University and the University of Washington, and his BS degree in Cognitive Psychology from Indiana University in 1976. Over the course of 32 years, he has done groundbreaking research in the application of artificial intelligence, software engineering, automatic programming, and formal methods technology to industrial software problems, including 13 years at the Boeing Artificial Intelligence Center as a Principal Computer Scientist before founding TSRI in 1995. Mr. Newcomb formulated the conceptual product framework and led a team of computer scientists to develop the software transformation technology and products offered by TSRI.

# Contributing Author Acknowledgments

The authors of Chapter 5, Modernization of the Eurocat Air Traffic Management System (EATMS), would like to acknowledge Roger Knapp, Robert Couch, Francesca Anderson, Greg Tadlock, and Randy Doblar of The Software Revolution, Inc. for their contributions to the successful execution of the EATMS project.

The authors of Chapter 7, Modernization Case Study: Italian Ministry of Instruction, University, and Research, would like to acknowledge Alfredo Giorgi, SIDI project leader; Saverio Passaro, MIUR Application Development and Maintenance team leader; Massimo Rocchi, Hosting and Data Center team leader; and Francesco Mesto, EDS Applications leader for the SIDI project. This case study was compiled from presentations prepared by Francesco Mesto, Antonio Menghini, Corrado Fontanesi, and Alfredo Giorgi. Valuable suggestions were provided by the above team as well as Larry Acklin, Remo Denato, Fabio Valeri, and Aldo Tosti of HP.

The authors of Chapter 8, Modernization of Reliability and Maintainability Information System (REMIS) into the Global Combat Support System-Air Force (GCSS-AF) Framework would like to acknowledge Mel Meadows, Richard Micek, David McGuire, Karen Chambers, Patty Roll of Northrop Grumman IT, and Matthew Campbell, Francesca Anderson, Greg Tadlock, Roger Knapp, and Bob Couch, and Randy Doblar of The Software Revolution, Inc. for their contributions to the successful execution of the REMIS project.

The authors of Chapter 10, Legacy System Modernization of the Engineering Operational Sequencing System (EOSS), would like to acknowledge Matthew Campbell, Francesca Anderson, Greg Tadlock, Roger Knapp, Mark Purtill, Robert Couch, and Randy Doblar of The Software Revolution, Inc. for their contributions to the successful execution of the EOSS project, and Cdr. Rich Voter, NETWARCOM N63, Maryann Rockey, Deputy Chief Naval Operations,

Vice Admiral Richard Mayo, NETWARCOM, Admiral (Ret.) Archie Clemins, Commander in Chief of the U.S. Pacific Fleet for their management, oversight and sponsorship of the EOSS LSM project.

The authors of Chapter 12, Modernization of the Veterans Health Administration's MUMPS Modernization Pilot, would like to acknowledge the following TSRI personnel for their contributions to the MUMPS conversion pilot: Matthew Campbell, Francesca Anderson, Greg Tadlock, Roger Knapp, and Randy Doblar. The authors would also like to thank the following personnel at the VHA for their support for the MUMPS conversion pilot: Robert N. McFarland, Assistant Secretary for Information and Technology; Craig B. Luigart, Associate Deputy Assistant Secretary for Policy, Portfolio Oversight and Execution, Office of Information and Technology; Robert M. Kolodner, M.D., Acting Deputy Chief Information Officer for Health and Acting VHA Chief Health Informatics Officer; Jim Demetriades, Chief Health Information Architect of the Veterans Health Administration's Office of Information; The authors would also like to thank the following SAIC personnel to their contributions to the MUMPS conversion pilot: Larry Peck, President, Enterprise and Infra Solutions Group; Dr. Stephen Rockwood, Special Executive Staff; Robert McCord, Senior Vice President and Health Solutions Business Unit General Manager; Dr. Marv Langston, Senior Vice President and SPAWAR Account Manager; Pamela Graff, Vice President and Director of Business Development; Dennis Eisenstein, Vice President and Operations Manager, George Hou, Assistant Vice President and VA Account Manager; Bruce Custis, Assistant Vice President and Acquisition Manager Conversion Pilot; Alex Bravo, Project Manager.

The authors for Chapter 13, Delta Lloyd Deutschland Data Migration Case Study, would like to acknowledge the following people. First, Bernhard Duchting who is a member of the Oracle Modernization Solutions team in Europe. He was the Oracle Modernization trusted technical advisor for this project. In this function he leads application portfolio and detailed assessment phases of the project and provides technical assistance for the life of the modernization effort. He also provides recommendations for legacy modernization based on database migration and integration, as well as application porting and rehosting.

The Consulting project was led by Ulrich Buck. He is a senior principal consultant based in Hamburg and has a strong background in mainframe modernization. Ulrich was involved in similar projects in Germany, Switzerland, UK, and the United States. Ulrich is authoring a case study about the DLD project and has provided invaluable assistance and input to this chapter.

FreeSoft is a modernization partner based in Budapest. They started to invest in migrating Ingres and Informix environments in 1990. This included database migration, ESQL conversion, and replacing dialog systems (i.e., Informix 4GL) by Oracle Forms and HTML. Their X2O conversion technology for porting applications is based on a runtime emulation with minimal change to the source programs. Recently, FreeSoft added the same capability for DB2 environments, both on mainframe and distributed platforms.

UC4 is a leading provider of solutions for workflow automation. The UC4 job scheduler was used in the project to map the job scheduling from IBM mainframe to the target platform.

Finally, credits go to Tom Laszewski from the Oracle Modernization Solution Team for his continued support, guidance, contribution to the content, and proofreading during the creation of this chapter. Tom has authored many articles on modernization, and also co-authored the book *Oracle Modernization Solutions* published by PACKT.

The authors of Chapter 14, MoDisco, a Model-Driven Platform to Support Real Legacy Modernization Use Cases, would like to acknowledge the European Commission, which funded the EU FP 6 project Modelplex; the work presented in the MoDisco Case study has been carried out in the context of the EU FP 6.

# Architecture-Driven Modernization

# CHAPTER 1

# Introduction to Architecture-Driven Modernization

**William Ulrich**

For decades, Information Technology (IT) organizations and the businesses and government agencies they support have been struggling with an ever-growing installed base of software systems. These systems control virtually all automated aspects of a given business or government entity. While maintained out of necessity, these same systems have grown into black-box behemoths of business logic and data representations that continue to stifle organizational agility and the ability of enterprises to move into increasingly competitive markets.

For the vast majority of organizations, these systems have been anchors that dragged them down as they attempted to meet growing competitive and economic demands. IT organizations, driven by the need to control their own internal costs, have responded by outsourcing systems to third parties, building add-on software that replicates aspects of the old systems, plugging in commercial-off-the-shelf (COTS) software packages or enterprise resource planning (ERP) systems, and wrapping systems with middleware. The results have delivered far less than anticipated in many cases.

Every IT and business situation is unique, yet there are numerous parallels in the challenges facing most enterprises today. These issues include:

- Application and data architecture silos that reflect historic partitions in business structures that no longer apply in today's environment
- Extensive replication and inconsistency of data definitions and functional logic across application silos
- Layers of middleware that have wrapped aging architectures only to mask the need to unravel and modernize these architectures
- Systems and user interfaces that are totally out of sync with business processes that require extensive manual effort and countless user-developed, desktop shadow systems (e.g. spreadsheets, Access databases, etc.)

## CONTENTS

- Diminishing level of expertise capable of managing, changing, or even understanding application and data architectures
- Little or no documentation as to how these environments are constructed or function
- A lack of understanding by executive teams regarding the impact of these issues and the actions that can be taken to address them for the betterment of the business environment

This last point is probably the most disconcerting aspect of the challenge facing organizations with a significant installed base of existing software systems. Considering the complexity and interwoven nature of many existing systems, this is not a big surprise. Yet, when one considers the criticality of these systems to the continuity and survivability of the enterprise, it is of great concern that software and data assets are largely a mystery to management and planning teams.

The general feeling is that these systems cannot be salvaged or otherwise rehabilitated, so why make an effort to understand them? This belief is so ingrained in organizational thinking that organizations march almost in lockstep toward traditional solutions that have become increasingly ineffective. These traditional solutions involve Greenfield replacement, COTS deployment, and wrapping old architectures with middleware. The historical inadequacy of these traditional approaches to the software challenges facing organizations today will be discussed in more depth in the section entitled "Business and IT Challenges."

Organizations do have an option when it comes to creating more agile and business friendly IT solutions to respond to ongoing shifts in the "business architecture." Business architecture is defined as "a blueprint of the enterprise that provides a common understanding of the organization and is used to align strategic objectives and tactical demands."[1] It is called architecture-driven modernization or simply "modernization." Architecture-driven modernization is defined as "a collective set of tool-enabled disciplines that facilitate the analysis, refactoring and transformation of existing software assets to support a wide variety of business and IT-driven scenarios."

The Object Management Group (OMG) defines architecture-driven modernization as the "process of understanding and evolving existing software assets for the purpose of software improvement; modification; interoperability; refactoring; restructuring; reuse; porting; migration; translation; integration; service-oriented architecture; and model-driven architecture™ transformation.[2]

The OMG laundry list of modernization topics boils down to three general categories: assessment, refactoring, and transformation. These three high-level categories or stages of modernization disciplines may be mixed and matched to address a wide variety of business and technical objectives.

The concept of modernization has been around for many years. However, the automation capabilities and supporting motivations to deploy modernization projects to support a wide variety of business scenarios have evolved to the point where every organization attempting to understand, evolve, or replace existing application and data architectures now has an alternative to traditional IT strategies. At a minimum, management can augment traditional IT strategies with various modernization options and techniques.

The increasing interest and demand for the capabilities delivered through modernization projects are driven by the fact that organizations are now seeking alternatives to historic IT approaches. Historic approaches — Greenfield development, COTS package deployments, and middleware proliferation — have not delivered the business value many organizations originally anticipated.

While succeeding modestly in some cases, many IT initiatives have failed to meet business objectives, encountered major cost or schedule overruns, or delivered significantly reduced value over what was originally anticipated. In most cases, the IT solutions have been interwoven into complex and often convoluted software architectures and only served to add more redundancy and complexity to those architectures.

This chapter discusses the business and IT challenges facing most organizations: the difficulties enterprises have encountered in trying to address these challenges, the benefits of modernization as an augmentation strategy or as an alternative to traditional approaches, and the basic tasks associated with modernization. This includes tracing historic failures of the past as well as looking at how modernization can be used to address a variety of critical business and technical initiatives required by the 21st century enterprise.

## BUSINESS AND IT CHALLENGES

Senior executives often think that complex business and IT challenges can be addressed by rebuilding applications from scratch, licensing COTS packages, or tying systems together using middleware-based solutions. While these options continue to play a role in ongoing IT strategies, projects applying these approaches have been plagued with problems.

Corporations and government agencies increasingly find it more and more difficult to address complex information-related challenges. Organizations have spent considerable time, effort, and capital on IT projects with little to show for it. While IT projects in general have been challenged, there are numerous failure stories in the industry. A few of these are cited in this list.

- Cigna's $1 billion IT overhaul suffers a false start, causing the health insurer to acknowledge customer defections.[3]
- The Hershey Foods ERP system implementation failure led to massive distribution problems and a loss of 27% market share.[4]

- The FoxMeyer Drug ERP system implementation failure led to the collapse of the entire company.[5]
- A new IRS system allowed $200 million in bogus refunds to slip through and had to be deactivated.[6]
- The Oregon DMV conversion to new software took 8 years to complete and public outcry eventually killed the entire project.[7]
- State of Florida welfare system was plagued with numerous computational errors and $260 million in overpayments.[7]
- AMR Corp, Budget Rent A Car, Hiltons Corporation, Marriott "confirm" project crumbled having spent over $125 million over 4 years.[7]
- A £456 million IT system (from EDS) implemented at the Child Support Agency in UK worked less effectively than the system it replaced.[8]
- An IRS project, expected to cost $8 billion when completed, was already 40% over budget with less than $1 billion of work done to date.[9]
- "Science Applications International Corp. (SAIC), in San Diego, delivered 700,000 lines of code so bug-ridden and functionally off target that this past April the bureau had to scrap the US $170 million project, including $105 million worth of unusable code."[10]
- U.S. Federal Agency cancels $70 million SAP implementation.
- An international telephone company canceled a major systems replacement project at a loss of more than $80 million.

These last two examples are not sourced to protect the anonymity of the organizations.

Industry research shows just how challenging it is to undertake major IT projects. For example, IT project overruns are commonplace. The latest Standish Group research shows that IT projects are late 72% of the time — a marked improvement over figures from prior years.[11] Additionally, certain risk factors are reflected in the Standish Group research related to project waste on IT projects. Out of the $364 billion spent on IT projects for 2006, only $204 billion of this amount was considered to have delivered organizational value while $160 billion in IT spending was considered waste.[11]

A related Standish Group finding showed that of all the IT projects analyzed for 2006, only 35% of those projects were considered to have succeeded. This study found that 19% were outright failures (again a marked improvement over prior years) while 46% were considered "challenged."[11] Note that "challenged" means "the project is completed and operational but over-budget, over the time estimate, and offers fewer features and functions than originally specified."[12]

These studies demonstrate that anytime IT undertakes a major project, management should be suspect of the ability to deliver the project on time and on budget in a way that satisfies business requirements as set forth at the onset of that project. To further illustrate the challenges facing organizations with a significant dependence on a large installed base of software systems, we consider the issues associated with Greenfield replacement, COTS deployment, and middleware utilization.

## Greenfield Replacement Issues

Greenfield replacement involves designing, developing, and deploying one or more new application systems from scratch to either replace one or more existing mainframe application systems and/or to automate existing manual processes. It should be made clear that Greenfield replacement, by definition, does not draw on business logic or data descriptions contained within existing application and data architectures. When a project does rely on existing systems as input to the specification and development process, then the project has morphed into a modernization initiative.

Greenfield replacement requires: determining and analyzing business and systems requirements, designing a solution to meet those requirements, designing and developing the actual software to be implemented, testing that new software in the appropriate business environment, and moving the new system into a production-ready state so that business people can use it. The Greenfield approach also requires business people to re-specify and programming teams to re-create years of complex, highly evolved and fairly intricate business knowledge — knowledge that these people are unlikely to command.

Greenfield replacement projects, in our experience and based on industry analysis, commonly result in a combination of project delays, unhappy business users and customers, missing or misinterpreted business functionality and data, and costs that far exceed initial projections.

A Greenfield approach to rewriting application systems takes a significant amount of time, investment, and human capital. Further, the risks associated with omitting critical business functionality that was buried in the old application system and never included in the new system are substantial. The series of industry studies and citations discussed next show how cost, time, and risk-related factors constrain organizations from successful deployment of software systems using Greenfield development.

The costs incurred, per line of code, on Greenfield replacement projects demonstrate the expensive nature of application system rewrite projects. The studies cited provide a range of replacement costs for deployed application systems. The general approach for calculating these costs, based on our experience, involves dividing the lines of software deployed by the total cost of the entire project. These studies provide a useful way to determine the historic cost of Greenfield replacement but are not intended to serve as a project-estimating tool on a project-to-project basis.

Studies have cited line of code replacement costs at $18–45 per line of fully delivered, debugged production software. For example, one cost per line figure that is based on extrapolation of the COCOMO II model is $18 per line of code.[13] A second source cited the cost per line range for developing fully functioning software as $30–40 per line of code.[14] A third study put the cost of developing fully functioning software within the range of £20–25 per line of new code.[15] The pound estimate reflects a Greenfield development cost of $34–43 per line of code. This last citation, which is based on research work using a combination of estimating models, brings the line of code development cost figure to the upper range of the scale — close to $45 per line of code.[16]

Using these numbers, a small company with 2 million lines of software would estimate its portfolio replacement costs using Greenfield replacement in the range of $36 million ($18 per line) to $90 million ($45 per line). In our experience, these costs in practice can even exceed the high end of this cost range.

While costs are a major consideration, the time frames associated with Greenfield replacement can also be unacceptable to organizational management. Rebuilding a system from business requirements using the Greenfield approach takes significant amounts of time. One common statistic is that the productivity generally seen over the life of a project is approximately 10 to 15 lines of new software per person, per day.[17]

Assuming that an organization is planning to rewrite a 1-million line application system using the Greenfield approach, and further assuming this same organization plans to assign 30 people to that project and that each person delivers 3,000 lines of code per (200 work-day) year, it would take those 30 people[18] more than 11 years to complete this project. Note that even if a replacement project team employs computer languages, tools, and techniques that cut this time in half, (which is unlikely) this still represents a 5.5-year project.

These numbers are typically dismissed by programmers who claim to be able to write hundreds of lines of code per day. But these individuals overlook the fact that these industry statistics represent delivered production software from inception to production status. To deliver software to a production ready state, project teams must expend many hours of analysis, design, development testing, and deployment activities. Overall, the numbers revert to the 10–15 lines per day figure even with the advent of new tooling. Much of the real work involves analysis and testing, not just coding.

According to the Standish Group, large projects fail more often than small projects. "Only 3% of projects that cost $10 million or more succeed."[11] A 1-million line rewrite project cited previously would take 330 person-years. At $50,000 per person per year, this equates to $16.5 million and, according to the failure percentage of large projects as cited by Standish in its "Chaos Summary 2008" report,[11] this effort would have a 97% chance of not succeeding.

Based on prior Greenfield replacement per line cost figures, replacing a small system of 1 million lines of software could quickly move into the aforementioned 97% failure rate range. In other words, based on this calculation almost any Greenfield replacement project is too risky to pursue.

Even if projects are delivered eventually (late and over budget), but deliver less than promised because they omit critical functionality from the delivered system, those systems are not useful to the business people they were meant to serve. These projects generally deliver requirements that are dated and only partially fulfilled.

## COTS Software Limitations

Executives may believe that COTS packages or ERP software is the answer. Yet experience shows that most organizations acquire multiple, overlapping packages that are partially deployed and poorly integrated.

The COTS acquisition and deployment alternative involves licensing and deploying application software from third party vendors. Using this approach involves finding a third party package that meets your business requirements such as converting in-house data to the format used by the new system, retraining all business users, decoupling all system and data interfaces from the old system, parallel testing the old and new systems, deactivating and retiring the old system, and activating the new COTS system.

Several studies over the past decade found that deploying COTS solutions, particularly those projects that have targeted replacing older, complex applications systems, have failed more often than they have succeeded. In 2006, I was involved in performing a survey on the success of COTS projects in association with Cornell University and Cutter Consortium. The findings of the Cutter Survey determined that the success of COTS deployment projects is never guaranteed and far from easy.

This survey involved 76 respondents from a wide range of industries, government agencies, and non-profit centers.[19] The demographics of the participants varied widely and included a number of small-to-medium sized organizations.[20]

The Cutter Survey also found that 98% of package users were forced to change business practices. This is significant because it meant that business people who would benefit from these COTS packages had to change the way they did their jobs. In my experience, this type of disruption in an enterprise can cause discontinuity in the quality of operations while creating a disruptive atmosphere among employees. This forced change in business practices extended to respondents ranging from small to medium to large.

Application packages were only fully implemented 28% of the time according to the Cutter Survey. This means that 72% of the time the licensed application software was only partially implemented. This finding challenges the cost benefit justifications typically associated with the licensing and deployment of COTS packages as an overall strategy and further contributes to the cost-related constraints inherent in the COTS alternative.

The Cutter Survey found that 81% of respondents had to expend a great deal or at least some effort to connect the COTS packages with existing data while 77% of respondents had to expend a great deal or at least some effort to connect COTS packages with existing application systems. This meant that even small-to-medium-sized organizations had to expend effort to connect the COTS packages with their existing applications and data. Increased effort results in an increase in costs, time, and risks.

Another Cutter Survey finding showed 61% of business users favored the existing legacy applications over the new package. This means that the people who were supposed to use the COTS package did not want to use it. When this occurs, it means that the COTS package will be rejected or it will drive up costs and time associated with its implementation. This rejection by users also drives up the risk of project acceptance by the business.

Additionally, the Cutter Survey found that 40% of respondents reported that realizing benefits had been quite difficult or extremely difficult while only 18% reported that it was easy to realize benefits. In other words, most of the respondents, even the small-to-medium-sized organizations, found it challenging to realize benefits from a COTS package approach of replacing one or more application systems. A lack of realization of benefits as well as the time it takes to gain those benefits further increase the risk of rejection of the COTS package.

Another COTS-related study by the Standish Group found that the COTS projects are expensive and rarely succeed. Findings from this report include the following citations. "The average purchase price for a single ERP application is $1.3 million, with the cost to implement averaging at 6.4 million."[21] In addition, "The cost to implement is, on average, 5 times the purchase price."[21] This study further demonstrates that the costs of using package solutions can far outweigh the benefits and be beyond management expectations. In addition, according to the Standish Group, "…less then [than] 10% of ERP implementations actually succeed."[21] Failure is a project risk and can take the form of out and out rejection of the COTS package by the business, missing data, missing functionality, lost revenues, lost customers, and a host of other factors. This Standish Group statistic further demonstrates how implementing a COTS package as a means of addressing business and IT challenges is highly constrained by the risks of outright failure.

Combining the Standish Group findings with the Cutter Survey shows that COTS projects are not only expensive and rarely succeed, but they are also very difficult to implement and the business users who are supposed to benefit from these projects are not always pleased with the results. These studies demonstrate the constraints associated with deploying COTS packages and also show that the executive who thinks that packaged software is an easy answer to their IT and business requirements is often incorrect.

## Middleware Deployment Challenges

One way organizations have attempted to address these failures is by treating existing applications as a black box and using non-invasive integration technology to retool user front-ends. However, middleware tools stop at the user interface. Unfortunately, the user interface is where most IT and business solutions must begin, not end! As a result, non-invasive integration has helped in the short-term but has also made the situation more problematic. Consider the results of the following IBM study:

> …recent advances in integration middleware technology have provided some relief by making it possible for financial institutions to move customer information across channels. But in many cases the technology has been laid over flawed legacy architecture and has merely created more duplication.[22]

Middleware itself is not the problem. Rather, it is the poorly architected use of middleware that becomes an issue as stated in the previous study. When middleware deployment is coupled with an examination and streamlining of business processes and used to deploy first stages of a modernization initiative by driving business requirements back into core architectures via modernized front-end architectures, then middleware serves as a part of the overall solution within the modernization toolkit.

# MODERNIZATION BENEFITS

For a large number of organizations, the need to modernize application and data architectures is triggered by a wide variety of requirements and the fact that their information systems do not provide effective support for those requirements. Modernization provides the means to address these requirements using a measured approach that is both sustainable and risk averse. Key benefits that can be achieved by applying modernization concepts to existing application and data architectures are based on the following concepts.

- Expose and untangle inherent application and data architecture complexities in a way that allows more people with less experience to evolve and modernize those systems in accordance with business demands.
- Build a basis of understanding of existing application and data architectures to establish more intelligent IT planning concepts in line with business and technical demands.

- Facilitate a business' ability to consolidate, streamline, and automate business processes in operational performance or customer facing areas.
- Provide immediate business productivity benefits by aligning user interfaces with business processes while laying a foundation for aligning business capabilities with applications and, ultimately, services.
- Incrementally deploy and deliver essential business requirements by aligning backend application and data architectures with business capabilities.
- Augment and improve ROI on programs and projects that directly interface with or impact existing software systems and data structures.
- Eliminate unwanted, non-standard, and obsolete technologies in a manner aligned with business and technical requirements.
- Achieve IT-related objectives, such as services oriented architecture (SOA) migration and cloud computing, in a way that concurrently aligns IT architecture with business architecture.
- Extend the useful life of existing applications while reducing the risks associated with Greenfield replacement, COTS package deployment, and front-end integration projects.

## IT Versus Business Value: The Real Benefits of Modernization

Over the years, modernization tool and service vendors have promoted modernization benefits based on helping the IT organization save money. This has been a well intended, yet highly misdirected approach to promoting modernization benefits. IT costs represent a relatively small percentage of an enterprise's overall budget. A relatively small IT organization typically supports thousands of business people. Viewing it from this perspective, modernization has a much greater potential ROI benefit for business units and customers through cost reduction and revenue generation than it has on IT cost savings.

Consider that, at many organizations, IT has already squeezed as much as it can get out of limited skills sets. There is the rare IT organization that has not undergone streamlining in recent years and modernization could certainly benefit in these cases. But in most circumstances, many systems have either been outsourced, are only maintained by a small handful of aging experts, or have been turned into inaccessible black boxes that no one is allowed to touch because no one understands them or has confidence that they can change them. None of these situations is ideal and modernization allows the workings within and across these black-box environments to once again become transparent so that they can be reincorporated back into the strategic enterprise ecosystem.

Management should refocus IT as a revenue-generating and operational efficiency-enabling force within the business as opposed to decimating IT to the point where it becomes ineffectual. Modernization can help meet this goal by exposing IT architectures and providing insights into how and where business capabilities and processes rely on various aspects of the IT architecture. For example, consider a situation where all business capabilities and processes related to a certain product line must be modified to incorporate a new set of products from a merger. These capabilities rely on certain data and application systems and the processes interact with various user interfaces, which in turn invoke various programs across applications and subsystems. Determining the impact of these changes on applications and data establishes the basis for driving a practical, incremental modernization strategy. Management can also determine where new functionality is required and develop approaches for either building or leasing that functionality and incorporating it into the modernized architecture.

Another important step in using modernization as an ROI enablement tool requires that management values a system in terms of the business capabilities it supports. In this way, management can determine the value of evolving the systems in question based on the criticality of those business capabilities and on the agility and depth of functional quality of the systems that support those capabilities and processes. This is a key step in terms of evaluating options for evolving, deactivating, replacing, or modernizing these systems. Consider these questions when evaluating strategic systems options:

1. If a given application system disappeared tomorrow, how much would it cost to replace that application?
2. If this same application system is eliminated, what are the immediate and long-term impacts on our business?

The answer to the first question is based on historical application replacement costs; costs that have previously been cited as ranging from $18–45 per line of debugged, production-ready software. If the business goals can be achieved through a modernization-based approach that costs less and lowers the risk of the overall effort, then modernization becomes a viable option based *on the needs of the business* as a key driver.

A Standish Group study found that less than 30% of the code in a given application contained business logic, while the remaining source code supported infrastructure-related activities.[23] This means that replacing only the business logic while ignoring the infrastructure logic would lower replacement costs by a factor of 70%. Assuming the environmental logic could be largely, but not fully, handled through modern languages, frameworks, and architectures, then a very conservative estimating technique for application replacement costs could be stated as:

■ Total existing system lines of code * .30 (percent business logic) * $18 (lower cost per line replacement cost from industry studies) = absolute lowest replacement cost achievable.

- Using this equation, which applies the absolute best case/lowest cost scenario, a 1 million line application would cost, at a bare minimum, $5.4 million to replace.

If the cost estimates associated with a modernization project can outperform the costs estimates associated with a Greenfield replacement effort, then modernization can and should be used as either an alternative or minimally as a way to supplement the reuse of existing data and system functionality under the targeted environment.

The answer to the second question, which referred to the impact on a business of eliminating a given system, is situation dependent. Consider a billing system that services 10,000 customers and collects $100 million annually. If the system disappeared or failed, a typical company would likely have to quadruple user headcount and would still lose a significant percentage of annual billing revenue.

When viewing a system from a pure business value perspective, the project justification and ROI analysis associated with any planned initiative becomes much clearer. Consider an alternative situation where a $250,000 project is employed to streamline business processes; eliminate manual and spreadsheet-related tasks; align user interfaces with processes; and refactor data structures and application logic and results in business user headcount reductions while increasing billing collections and decreasing payment time.

This investment lowers user personnel and associated costs by several hundred thousand dollars annually while increasing collectible revenue by 5%. The ROI in this type of modernization project can be measured in less than a year — a window that represents only a fraction of the time spent on a Greenfield or COTS-based project to meet similar goals. This approach to ROI analysis can and should be used to drive modernization projects.

Most commercial environments are too large and intertwined to accommodate a "big bang," single project transformation. The exceptions to this might be found in real-time environments or smaller organizations where an application is isolated and therefore can be migrated into a new architecture in its entirety. Any large initiative, however, that involves actual transformation of multiple applications, data structures, and related user interfaces will typically require a phased approach to assess, refactor, consolidate, and transform selective systems and related data structures, and incrementally apply changes to any related applications and data structures.

Make no mistake about the fact that each of these individual projects, within a larger initiative, delivers incremental degrees of value to the business and to IT. The value proposition of the phased modernization approach has not been clearly articulated to executives or business sponsors who believe in a big bang approach to achieving business and IT-related goals. The all or nothing approach usually yields the latter — nothing.

## Modernization Mitigates Risks

Risk can be even more important than time and cost issues for many organizations. Most enterprises cannot afford a major failure of inventory, claims, procurement, order processing, or other mission critical system. As a result, management is reluctant to invest in major changes to core applications.

"Risk" is any potential threat to the delivery of a quality product.[24] Attempting to re-specify fundamental business logic using a Greenfield approach introduces risk. Similarly, deploying a COTS package without requisite analysis and mapping of existing architectures introduces significant risk to a project.

Using modernization tools and techniques, on the other hand, to expose data usage, functional logic, and cross-functional discrepancies as an essential part of the project can lower the risks of failure. This is because modernization builds on the fundamental cornerstone of robust production systems. Modernization minimizes risks in two important ways.

1. Understanding existing systems from a variety of perspectives facilitates the reuse, integration, and/or decommissioning of existing application and data architectures in an incremental, low-risk fashion. In this way, the fallback position of any modernization project is a viable, functioning system. This is not the case in a typical Greenfield or COTS project where investments are significant, time frames long, and existing systems erode rather than evolve.

2. Reuse of viable data definitions, business logic, and related abstractions in the specification and deployment of replacement architectures reduces the risk of deploying systems that do not, at a minimum, meet today's critical business requirements.

In other words, analysts can reuse proven functionality that already exists in production systems to spawn modernized services and systems that become the foundation for the new target architecture. Using this approach, which shuns the blank slate thinking that has dominated management mindshare for decades, enterprises can draw on a wealth of functionality that serves as software building blocks for the future. This is the real risk mitigation approach inherent in the modernization concept.

## Modernization: Augmentation or Alternative

The response from IT to failing projects often defies reason. The first response is to double, triple, or quadruple project resources, funding, and time allotted to complete the project. When the project is canceled, it is normally written off, buried, or, in a worst-case scenario, restarted with new personnel using the same approach. The argument in this last case is that better people will be put on the next project than were on the last project.

When the project fails the second and third time using the same approach, management reacts by reverting to the same old approaches of throwing more money at the project or canceling it. Yet this vicious cycle of project failures continues in countless corporations and government agencies over and over again. Clearly, examining different options is warranted and modernization offers an alternative to traditional IT strategies as well as an effective way to augment historical IT strategies.

Modernization can either augment or serve as an alternative to existing IT approaches and strategies. Serving as an alternative means that modernization, in the form of a pure platform, language, and/or data transformation project, becomes a fourth alternative to traditional replacement or integration options. Serving as an augmentation option means that modernization analysis, refactoring, and reuse concepts are incorporated into Greenfield replacement, COTS package deployment, and middleware integration projects.

Modernization provides a variety of options for refactoring and transforming core application and data architectures. When coupled with traditional IT solutions, modernization can lower risks, drive down overall costs, streamline delivery time frames, and increase the success of these projects. The degree of the role of modernization activities in any IT project is driven by the need to understand the existing IT architecture and the depth of the role that these existing applications and data structures will play in the target solution.

Consider these issues related to augmenting Greenfield replacement and COTS package deployment:

- Greenfield replacement must be phased in from a practical perspective and accommodate IT environments that are interwoven with business processes across the organization.
- Greenfield replacement projects cannot rely solely on top-down, blank slate design and development because such projects omit essential functionality embedded in existing application and data architectures.
- Users do not have the ability to fully envision and articulate critical business functionality, therefore, Greenfield projects should leverage production-tested functionality embedded in existing systems as a source of how the business functions today.
- Packages rarely align cleanly with entrenched business processes and, as a result, require custom alignment with existing application and data architectures.
- Packages are rarely fully deployed and typically end up being woven into the fabric of existing data and software environments.
- Adapting packages into existing, complex information architectures is usually undertaken with little understanding of underlying application and data architectures and related user environments.

■ Data architecture consolidation and migration are typically undertaken without the requisite rationalization and reconciliation of existing business semantics and systems data stores.

Modernization can address each of the aforementioned Greenfield and COTS issues. Organizations that apply modernization-based efforts to analyze, decompose, reuse, refactor, and/or transform existing application and data architectures are well-positioned to augment and succeed in pursuing Greenfield replacement and COTS deployment initiatives. Modernization projects may be viewed as an alternative to traditional IT strategies, but can be even more effective as an augmentation vehicle when coupled with traditional IT strategies.

## AN ARCHITECTURAL VIEW OF MODERNIZATION

We have been discussing application, data, and technical architectures from an IT perspective and business architecture from a business perspective, but these architectures have a mutual dependence on one another. Pursuing a modernization strategy, therefore, must recognize these dependencies, otherwise, business and IT can get out of sync. One may be modified or deployed and the business cannot adapt or the systems and data cannot support change. It is important, therefore, to understand where and how these architectures interact.

The technical architecture is an abstract representation of the platforms, languages, and supporting technological structures that provide the "plumbing" that keeps the environment functioning. This includes SOA and related communication structures. The application architecture is an abstract representation of the applications, subsystems, services, and orchestration structures and their relationship to each other and to the data. The data architecture is an abstract representation of the data files, databases, and relationships to the application architecture. These three views create the IT architecture and modernization impacts each in unique ways.

Similarly, the business architecture has its own set of artifacts and abstractions. These include organization units, capabilities, process, semantics, and rules at the most basic level. Business and IT architectures live in separate yet related domains (commonly referred to as the 'enterprise architecture'). Figure 1.1 shows the business and IT domains of an organization. Business architecture describes the business domain while IT architecture describes the IT domain. The business architecture relies on the application and data architecture, which in turn relies on the technical architecture as shown in Figure 1.1.

**FIGURE 1.1**

*Business versus IT architecture domains.*[25]

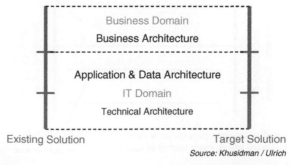

| Business Domain |
| Business Architecture |
| Application & Data Architecture |
| IT Domain |
| Technical Architecture |

Existing Solution                          Target Solution

*Source: Khusidman / Ulrich*

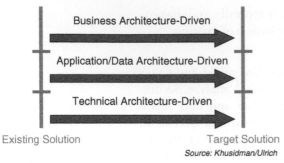

**FIGURE 1.2**
*Modernization drivers and trajectories.*[25]

Figure 1.1 also shows the existing (as-is) solution to the left and the target (to-be) solution to the right. As business and IT architectures evolve, the existing solution morphs into the target solution. The challenge facing most enterprises is that the business environment continues to evolve beyond IT's ability to keep application and data architecture synchronized with business requirements. Modernization disciplines allow IT to evolve the as-is IT architecture in a way that keeps it synchronized with business changes and requirements.

Figure 1.2 illustrates how certain business and technical factors drive movement from the as-is to the to-be business and IT architectures. Business architecture is driven by the business and this should be the overriding consideration as executives consider how IT architecture must evolve. Business requirements have a direct bearing on the evolution of data and applications. This means that IT must respond to an evolving business ecosystem and drive corresponding changes to data and application architectures. Understanding IT requirements means understanding existing and target business architectures and mapping the impacts of the changing business to the as-is IT architecture. IT can then identify the modernization plan to move from the existing to the target IT architecture.

Figure 1.3 shows that there are many paths to moving from an as-is to the to-be business and IT architectures. One common path followed by IT is to focus on the technical architecture. This physical transformation shown in Figure 1.3 represents a "lift and shift" concept where the technical architecture is transformed and data and application architectures remain largely intact. While the cost of this approach is lower and project duration shorter, there is almost no impact or value to the business.

**FIGURE 1.3**
*Modernization domain model.*[25]

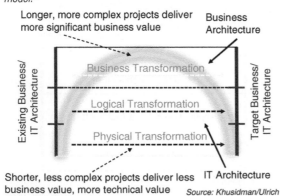

A modernization effort that seeks to provide value to the business, on the other hand, would need to change the application and data architecture, which in turn would rely on an analysis of requirements stemming from shifts to the business architecture. These types of projects are of a longer duration, require more investment, and deliver significantly more value to the business. In Figure 1.3 this means traveling up the "horseshoe" into the application and data (i.e. logical) architecture and into the business architecture.

It is important to understand that IT has been selling technical architecture transformation via concepts like SOA and model-driven architecture (MDA) to executives, and management has invested millions of dollars in pursuit of these architectures. The impact on business, however, has been inconsequential. To really deliver business value, SOA and MDA must be driven by business requirements that drive application and data architecture transformation. Unfortunately, this has not been the case in most IT organizations.

If executives believe that IT will deliver significant business value through a technical or physical route to SOA or MDA, they will be shocked to find out that their investments have been ill-advised and poorly spent. Therefore, when planning a modernization effort, consider the concepts in Figure 1.3 and the impact to the overall architectural environment from a business perspective.

There are a wide variety of disciplines that fall under the modernization umbrella and are used to enable various modernization scenarios. Modernization disciplines, which are a collection of tool-enabled tasks, can be summarized and categorized into three major categories: assessment, refactoring, and transformation.

Disciplines defined within each of these categories are mixed and matched together in a way that creates a specialized solution for a given business and IT situation. These solutions will be generalized into project scenarios in Chapter 4. An overview of assessment, refactoring, and transformation phases of modernization provide the requisite background for planning teams that base their efforts around the scenarios and case studies that are presented in subsequent chapters.

## MODERNIZATION ASSESSMENTS

Modernization assessments are geared toward exposing aspects of existing technical, application, and data architectures from a wide variety of perspectives. Projects can expose 50,000-foot views of these architectures that examine the overall enterprise perspective or they can drill down a number of levels into the detail required to launch or complete a given project. Assessments can support strategic IT planning or an individual project. The objective drives the depth and breadth of coverage of a given assessment.

Assessment-related tasks include exposing application architectures and interrelationships; analyzing system source code and documenting processes flows, structure, complexity, and anomalies; assessing data usage and data architecture; examining and exposing semantic business rules buried within systems; and tying each of the exposed IT architecture artifacts, as required by a given scenario, back to the business architecture.

In a modernization project, management must seek to strike a balance between too little and too much analysis. Many organizations are leery of spending too much time in front-end assessment efforts and even loathe the task of exposing the as-is architecture. However, ignoring front-end analysis on any IT project that impacts existing IT architectures can result in false starts, poorly coordinated projects, haphazard architectures, wasted time, and misplaced resources. We would argue that many of the project failures cited earlier in this chapter are a direct result of not having understood the existing application and data architectures impacted by those projects. As SEI's Watts Humphrey said: "If you don't know where you are, a map won't help."

Whether modernization is positioned to augment a Greenfield, COTS, or middleware effort, or serve as a complete alternative as would be the case with a platform and language migration or transformation scenario, an understanding of business and IT requirements *and* the existing environment is essential. The as-is IT architecture provides a view of the way things work today as input to planning and executing a variety of projects and can even serve as the basis for creating straw man candidates for evolving target architectures.

In general, assessments rely on tool-enabled, analyst-assisted examination of application systems and data-related artifacts along with discussions with subject matter experts. The benefits and related tasks for various levels of assessment are discussed in the next section.

## Assessment Benefits

If you plan to maintain, improve, migrate, transform, or otherwise modify software systems, knowledge of those systems is essential. Just as a surgeon would never operate without obtaining X-rays and other diagnostic results, a project team working on software systems must similarly obtain an understanding of those systems. Modernization assessments provide this essential understanding at a multitude of levels.

The benefits of performing an assessment vary based on the type of project involved. The larger the project, the greater the benefit derived from the assessment. An assessment allows project teams to streamline implementation tasks and delivery time frames while increasing project success rates.

A second benefit of performing an assessment is the provision of highly useful technical and functional documentation to project teams. Assessment-generated documentation supports portfolio analysis, outsourcing plans, ongoing enhancements and improvements, and, of course, modernization projects.

Another assessment benefit involves confirming the viability of a proposed approach. Often, management engages a project and has little understanding of the existing IT architecture. This leads to a lack of understanding of the depth of functionality that is to be integrated or replaced. For example, management may plan to replace three systems with a package. The assessment step may discover, however, that these systems are intertwined with two other systems. As a result, management must adjust its plan to salvage and integrate these other two systems into the package environment. Skipping the assessment phase of any project involving existing systems is like taking a journey with no knowledge of your current location.

The assessment approach, level of effort, and deliverables vary based on the depth and breadth of a given assessment. The depth and breadth of the assessment is driven by the type of project and related requirements. While there are a number of hybrid approaches and nuances for various situations, two common assessment types have emerged in practice: the enterprise assessment and the in-depth or project-level assessment.

## Enterprise Assessment

The main goal of enterprise assessment is to determine the scope and viability of a given strategy or set of proposed projects. Enterprise assessments can also be used to help fulfill portfolio management requirements. Deliverables include a systems inventory, summary of the technical environment, cross-reference of systems and data structures, a functional overview of systems and subsystems, a statement of scope, and a risk evaluation and cost/benefit analysis.

The enterprise assessment involves greater breadth and less depth of analysis. As scope is important to project goals and expectations, the breadth and depth must be recognized and planned for accordingly; otherwise, project teams can end up digging too deep into a subset of systems without understanding the big picture. There have been a number of circumstances where scope and objectives were poorly articulated and the project team did not know when they should have stopped or how far they needed to go.

Executing the enterprise assessment first helps analysts ascertain individual project scope and boundaries. Individual project teams tend to have difficulty carving out project scope due to a lack of planning capacity, authority, and cross-functional insight. In other words, projects involving existing IT architectures are at a major disadvantage if they do not have a comprehensive view of how those projects impact or are impacted by other business units, applications, subsystems, data, and projects.

A sample scenario highlights this concept in practice. Consider an initiative to replace a billing application. An enterprise assessment identifies interfacing and overlapping systems, examines high-level data flow into and out of the system, and determines relationships to surrounding applications. These deliverables, which are typically mapped to aspects of the business architecture, provide management with the big picture view of IT transformation issues and options. This is information required to build a viable plan on how to proceed with a variety of project scenarios.

If applicable, the enterprise assessment can deliver a high-level mapping to target requirements to clarify the role of current data and functionality within the target environment. For example, if billing data architecture and functionality are obsolete, a package option may be the best path forward. If, on the other hand, the system is functionally sound and merely running on an obsolete platform, refactoring and platform migration may make more sense. All too often these decisions are made in a vacuum, resulting in failed or ill-advised projects.

Determination of a final approach, such as using COTS over a migration/integration project, can be made once an assessment is completed. In practice, management often makes a decision on a system replacement effort prior to understanding all of the facts. This leads to many of the failures cited in the prior Standish Group studies.

The tasks involved in an enterprise assessment vary based on the business needs of the organization. Project scenarios drive the specifics of a given assessment effort. These tasks are included in a typical enterprise assessment:

- Requirements analysis and scope setting: Determines assessment requirements, sets breadth and depth of analysis, finalizes the deliverable list, and sets the overall scope of the analysis.
- Strategic planning and target architecture definition: Identifies the scope and objectives of the assessment based on the objectives of the scenario driving the analysis.
- Current applications and data inventory: Provides a high-level view of the current systems and general attributes of those systems.
- Existing application and data architecture analysis: Maps applications and subsystems to business capabilities, applications and subsystems to major data stores, and major data stores to business semantics.
- Current-to-target architecture mapping: Provides current functional, information, and technical architectures to target architectures and requirements — given that target architectures and requirements have been articulated.
- Strategy and proposed project definition: Identifies ROI-driven projects or project stages to meet management requirements set forth at the onset of the assessment.

The goal of an enterprise assessment is to deliver maximum value with minimal effort. This requires being selective when determining which enterprise assessment tasks and subtasks should be applied to a given situation.

## In-Depth/Project-Level Assessment

Project-level assessments are an extension of the enterprise assessment and the initial stage of an implementation project. In the billing system example discussed earlier, analysts would build upon prior assessment deliverables and drill down into specific data usage, functionality, process flow, usage scenarios, user interfaces, and other aspects of the billing environment.

At this stage, project teams require more granular, highly targeted analyses about execution flow, data definitions, business rules, and user interfaces. Typical deliverables include artifact cross-reference maps; data definition mappings; business rule extractions; detailed system interface identification; extracted logical models of data, processes, and systems; gap analysis between current and target architectures; and a plan on how to proceed with the implementation phase or phases of a project.

In-depth, project-level assessment deliverables and the level of corresponding effort are project dependent. A simple platform migration may only require an inventory, data usage analysis, and execution flow analysis while a systems consolidation project would require significantly more analysis and include the business architecture. The following assessment activities are commonly performed as a part of a project-level assessment.

## Technical Assessment

The technical assessment lays a foundation for the architectural and functional assessments. The three tasks comprise the technical assessment:

- Environmental Analysis: Inventories and cross-references application artifacts that define an application and related data structures. This step serves as a baseline for subsequent analysis steps.

- Data Definition Analysis: Provides group-level, cross-system analysis of persistent and non-persistent data usage. This includes data grouping analysis essential to the rationalization and normalization of existing data structures.

- Program Process Flow Analysis: Identifies program or module structure, defects and complexity that hinder efforts to modularize, migrate, refactor, or modify systems. (Note that this does not imply business process analysis.)

## Architectural Assessment

Architectural assessment exposes the implicit and explicit organization of user interfaces, execution flow, data structures, and external and internal interfaces. Major tasks include:

- Online/Batch Workflow Analysis: Exposes online transaction flows, including determination of actual user dynamics essential to understanding user interaction, transaction flow, and application functionality. This step also analyzes batch execution flows to expose how applications run and interact from a background perspective.

- Data Architecture Analysis: Provides derived diagrammatic depictions of persistent data structures, which include relational, hierarchical, or network diagrams as well as other file structure derivations.

- User Interface Analysis: Critical to mapping the IT architecture to the business architecture for any project involving changes to business processes or the business workflow. Business user interface analysis is an essential step to aligning existing software assets to streamlined business processes.

- System Interface Analysis: Identifies all data interfaces between systems and subsystems included in the assessment as well as interfaces to external systems or entities.

## Functional Assessment

Functional assessment examines the business-specific data usage and logic within the current architecture. Major tasks within the functional assessments include:

- Functional Decomposition: Decomposes system-related business capabilities and maps these capabilities to the modules that implement them. This step also includes a mapping of business processes to system workflow and user interfaces.

- System Data/Business Semantics Mapping: Maps business data usage to previously extracted system data definitions and reconciles potentially problematic discrepancies across systems and business areas.

- Current-to-Target Function/Data Mapping: Maps current data, application, and/or technical architectures to the target environment assuming that the scenario requires this analysis step and provides target architecture as a mapping baseline.

## Implementation Phase Planning

Creation of the modernization plan is a process that examines all relevant assessment information to inform a best approach to the project requirements. The modernization plan must be aligned with business requirements and overall project plans that may include elements of package deployment or new development.

## REFACTORING

Refactoring makes existing systems more malleable and adaptable while allowing for a streamlined set of business semantics and rules to be transformed into target architectures. Refactoring tasks allow project teams to rationalize structure, realign, modularize, or otherwise retool existing application data usage and source code. Stabilization and refactoring streamlines systems in preparation for business rule extraction and reuse; application consolidation; and migration to SOA, MDA, and other modernization scenarios.

## Benefits of Refactoring

Refactoring provides near- and long-term value to an enterprise. For example, if project teams intend to leverage existing systems in redesign or replacement initiatives, rationalizing and standardizing application logic and data will streamline these efforts.

Further, the use of application and data refactoring delivers major benefits to migration, upgrade, or enhancement projects as well as creating systems more conducive to SOA migration and reuse under target architectures. Refactoring may include the following tasks based on the scenario driving the project.

## Program Structuring and Design Improvement

There are several ways to improve a program while keeping the program or module intact as a functioning unit of code. These include:

- Anomaly/Flaw Removal: Identifies and removes program-level flaws including runaway logic, recursion, modular programming violations, and semantically and syntactically dead code. This step is important if the code is to be reused in target architecture.

- Program Structuring: Refactors poorly written or "unstructured" source code and transforms it into a source code that uses accepted, easily understood programming logic. This step has value if portions of the software are transformed and reused in the target architecture and provide for the separation of business, user access, and data access logic.

- Program Design Improvement: Corrects program-level design issues by optimizing data usage, program constructs, or control structures to help expose functional intent; reduce redundancy; clean up module names; create tables or arrays; externalize logic into data structures; shrink inefficient code structures; and eliminate spurious logic.

## Data Definition Rationalization and Standardization

Data usage in existing systems can be a very valuable clue to discovering how systems work and provide a basis for code reuse and transformation projects. Because data spans program, application, and enterprise boundaries, this rationalization and standardization task requires unique disciplines. The assessment phase of the project and related scenario surfaces requirements for upgrading application data definitions and includes aligning program data names with business semantics. Specific tasks included in this category are

- Data Definition Rationalization: Reconciles redundant and inconsistent, code-based data grouping definitions, making each individual representation unique and explicit. This includes business semantic mappings, which ultimately support the creation or validation of a target data model.

- Literal Externalization: Externalizes, consolidates, and incorporates embedded business data constants or literals into appropriate tables, rule structures, or other formats.

- Field and Record Attribute Standardization: Reconciles field sizes across a system or systems. Examples include amount fields, total fields, bar codes, and other data.

## Software Modularization

Reaggregating large, complex, or convoluted modules along functional boundaries is driven by specific business and technical objectives. For example, if a project wishes to migrate existing software to an SOA, the modularization concept is essential. The three variations are

- Code Slicing (or splitting): Involves moving select data and procedural logic from one source module into a new source module. Code slicing benefits include eliminating code that no longer has business value; segregating business, user access, and data access logic; and allowing large modules to be ported to a distributed platform.

- Application Reaggregation: Applies code-slicing concepts to create functionally cohesive source programs, essentially extending the slicing concept in a more sophisticated fashion.

- Application Consolidation: Extends the reaggregation concept, but with the added task of consolidating functionality across multiple applications of highly cohesive modules or services. This third aspect of modularization becomes essential to SOA migration.

## User Interface Refactoring

User interface refactoring can involve middleware deployment, alignment of user interfaces with streamlined business processes, replacement of multiple "green screen" interfaces with Web-enabled front-end, automation of manual steps, and the elimination of "shadow systems." Note that shadow systems include spreadsheets and other desktop business tools that may have "trapped" data or created non-transparent process flows.

Refactoring can offer significant benefits to organizations seeking to streamline and modernize existing code bases. In this sense, refactoring has been underutilized.

Refactoring is rarely performed as a stand-alone activity. Rather, it is typically interwoven into architectural transformation projects as discussed in the Transformation section.

## Lift and Shift Platform and Language Migration

One additional category involves a concept called "lift and shift" platform and language migration. Lift and shift migration involves applying minimal changes to a system, moving that system to a distributed target platform such as .NET or UNIX, and redeploying the system using emulation software to support the previous environment's compiler, middleware, and data environment. Lift and shift is a transliteration process that falls under the domain of refactoring.

This process is useful if an organization has a near-term need to eliminate the old technology platform. Yet this concept applies minimal if any modernization value and can even lead to making larger, more comprehensive transformation solutions more difficult by scattering subsystems to multiple platforms. The argument for this type of project is that a system, once moved to a newer platform, can be transformed more effectively within the confines of that platform.

There is little evidence that any of the lifted and shifted systems have been taken through additional refactoring or transformative steps once moved. In fact, executives looking to save incremental hardware costs tend to see lift and shift as an end-game solution. In many cases, it can be a dead-end solution.

## TRANSFORMATION

The transformation phase of modernization includes tasks related to reusing the "essence" of the existing application and data architecture in a new target application and data architecture. Target architectures change over time. Years ago, target architecture may have been considered a C or C++-based client server environment, although this was a highly code-centric versus model-driven environment.

Today, target architecture likely refers to a combination of SOA, MDA, cloud computing, or whatever comes next. While targets shift over time, the concept of using modernization to achieve those architectures is constant.

One thing should be clarified at this point. When IT people talk about target architecture, they typically are thinking in technical terms. For example, IT technical architects tend to focus significant time on the underlying "plumbing" that makes SOA and MDA viable. As a rule, significantly less attention is given to the application and data architecture. This predisposition results in poorly articulated target application architectures and data architectures resulting in poorly thought out solutions that do not meet business demands.

Transformation must ultimately focus on the alignment of existing application and data architectures with strategic requirements. For example, if you are planning an assessment to review options for migrating existing application functionality and data to a target environment, you have to understand the capabilities, business services, and business processes to be automated and/or replaced. This provides a baseline target that analysts can use to assess scope and transformation options when assessing the existing application and data architecture.

In other words, if you plan on moving to SOA, MDA, or any other target architecture, teams must articulate the business architecture to be supported within this new target. The relationship between modernization, IT architecture, and business architecture will be discussed further in Chapter 2.

While transformation to these model-driven ideals requires articulation of what is to be deployed in the target, there are other types of transformations that can be performed that do not rely heavily on a top-down, target architecture definitional approach. For example, consider a situation where a project team has a system that is running in one environment and wishes to move it to another environment. The existing architecture becomes the baseline for the target. The validity of this approach depends on the circumstances and requirements at hand.

## Transformation Benefits

The benefits of transformation are centered on the ability to capture and transform critical business data representations and business logic and redeploy that functionality in a new target architecture. Transformation benefits include the:

- Ability to increase the effectiveness, lower the costs, and reduce the risks associated with major IT initiatives.
- Value of streamlining Greenfield and COTS projects using incremental, low risk approaches, lower deployment costs.
- Ability to align application and data architectures with shifting or new business capabilities and information requirements.
- Capability of aligning business interfaces and system workflows with new or streamlined business processes.
- Capacity to expedite the elimination of obsolete or non-standard IT environments and redeploy proven business functionality in new target architectures.
- Ability to facilitate a wide variety of project scenarios for IT.

## Transformation Basics

Architecture transformation extends the previously discussed assessment concepts into the detailed capture, reuse, redesign, and redeployment of existing data and business rules.

The general goal, which varies based on a given scenario, is to extract and redesign existing application and data architectures. Extracted as-is representations can be used to document the existing architecture, validate target design models, and establish the foundation for logically redesigning and reconstructing existing data architectures.

## Language and Platform Transformation

Transforming older, procedural languages such as COBOL, C, PLI, or FORTRAN to object-based languages such as Java or C# is a transformative process. Design and implementation paradigms used to create and deploy these object-based languages differ from those used to create and deploy procedural languages.

The transformative process must accommodate this shift along with related platform and technology changes. Note that a transformative approach to language and platform migration is different from the concept of lift and shift discussed in the Refactoring section. Major language and platform transformation tasks, which are highly but not fully automated include:

- Application Encoding: Transforms the entire set of system artifacts into an intermediate representation to facilitate refactoring and transformation. This allows the system to be refactored and transformed in a formal environment.

- Application Refactoring and Transformation: Applied to consolidate redundancies or clean up anomalies that should not be transformed into the new target architecture. This step applies necessary system transformations to achieve a new object-based system.

- Application Redeployment: Produces the new system in the new target environment. This portion of the process takes the modernized application and reproduces it in a newly transformed language and architectural environment.

The application redeployment approach is useful for single system transformations, but does not facilitate multi-application and multi-data architecture consolidation and transformation of multiple stand-alone system architectures and data structures. In addition, this approach does not tie in business architecture issues as a rule. To accomplish this, additional tasks need to be applied across these systems as described in the following transformation tasks.

## Data Architecture Derivation and Transformation

Data architecture is a very important aspect of any transformation project because aging data architectures are redundant, intractable, and poorly aligned with business requirements. This transformation phase generally focuses on bottom-up extraction, mapping, and redesign of refactored data definitions. Major tasks include:

- Application Data Definition Extraction: This serves as the baseline step for creating a bottom-up view of existing application data. These data definitions should have been semantically rationalized and standardized as part of the refactoring phase of a project because most systems have highly redundant, cryptic, and inconsistent data definitions.

- Logical Data Derivation: Provides a first cut view of a new logical data model using existing definitions as the source. This first cut can then be used for various steps to refine or merge existing data with business data definitions.

- Logical Data Model Validation: Involves a combination of merging the bottom-up data model with a top-down business model or refining the bottom-up model based on business semantics. The approach varies based on availability of business semantics expertise and the target data model as well as the degree of new versus existing data to be incorporated into the target architecture.

- Physical Data Architecture Deployment: Deploys transformed data into the new target environment, which completes the cycle of modernization. Migration of the physical data would need to be timed by system and within the much bigger context of the project scenario.

## Systems Workflow Transformation

One thing that is least apparent yet highly important is how application user work flows. While assessment efforts can expose the workflows with good documentation approaches, the use of these workflows within a modernization effort are very important because they allow application analysts to map and align system workflows with business processes.

The difference with this transformation task and other aspects of core architecture transformation is that workflow transformation provides business insights into backend modernization that is based on incremental approaches meeting business needs. As workflows are transformed, they move IT toward the ideal orchestration model that SOA advocates have been promoting. The two main aspects of workflow modernization are

- Online Workflow Modernization: Involves mapping existing user interfaces and workflows to streamlined business processes, deploying incremental versions of Web-based interfaces that align with these processes and eliminate manual steps and shadow-systems, and ultimately migrating these retooled workflows into SOA-based orchestrations or other formats.

- Batch Workflow Modernization: Similar to online workflow modernization, but there tends to be more batch functionality within an enterprise. Much of the batch processing may need to be retained, only in a new architectural format. There may, however, be a significant amount of batch functionality that could be taken into an interactive user environment.

## Business Rule Extraction and Transformation

The business rule extraction and transformation process involves capturing, filtering, packaging, analyzing, and redeploying business logic. Once program logic is extracted, it must be filtered, packaged, and analyzed by subject matter experts before it can be called a business rule. The key aspect of this process involves using tools to find and distill vast amounts of functionality so that subject matter expertise can be leveraged more effectively.

The value and objectives for business logic reuse must be determined prior to beginning such a project, and the effort must be very focused on a specific set of business functions and related semantics. In addition, it is critical that prior assessment and data definition analysis work precede logic extraction to ensure that the results are well defined and focused. The tasks associated with business rule extraction and transformation are as follows.[26]

- Business Rule Extraction: An extension of the previously discussed functional decomposition at a more specific and more granular level. Business logic extraction abstracts logic directly from program source code and presents it in various formats to analysts for analysis, packaging, and reuse. This task is supported by tools and is not practical in the absence of tools on any scale. Analysis at this level performs a first round of filtering to exclude inactive, spurious, and similarly non-useful logic.

- Business Logic Packaging: An extension of the logic extraction process that extends the analysis process by creating business or analyst friendly views of the logic so it may be considered for reuse. At this point, logic is transformed into rules through certain transformation techniques that may include event diagrams or other machine-readable structures.

- Business Rule Consolidation and Transformation: Takes the packaged rules and moves them into the new target architecture. This may include UML models, rule engines, or other structures that can take advantage of the business rules extracted from the existing systems.

## Architecture Transformation and Reconstruction

The concept of current-to-target model mapping and deployment is iterative and occurs over the life of a given project, depending on the modernization scenario and business objectives. This section highlights the specific concepts of transforming into two common industry architectures: SOA and MDA.

- SOA Mapping and Redeployment Requires refactoring of data definitions and systems as well as the transformation of data structures, business logic, and system workflows into target services and orchestration. The degree of SOA to be achieved varies from organization to organization, but the phasing, reuse, interim states, and decommissioning strategies are driven by business requirements. The issue of data architecture transformation is also important yet often ignored.

- MDA Mapping: Requires mapping existing data and business logic into a multitude of logic representations such as those found in UML. This mapping process is dramatically simplified by the refactoring and transformation techniques discussed thus far.

Whereas transforming extracted data and business logic into SOA structures or various models is becoming increasingly tool-enabled, it is important to note that wholesale loading of inconsistent, redundant, and highly fragmented software architectures into models without refactoring will yield unusable results. This has been done over the years and continues to be an ill-advised approach to transformation.

# BASIC MODERNIZATION PRINCIPLES

Aging, convoluted data and application architectures are an entrenched reality in organizations and inextricably intertwined with enterprise business models. Few organizations, however, have a strategy that reconciles the limitations of entrenched IT architectures with high-priority, time-critical business requirements. Ultimately, an organization's ability to remain agile can be severely impacted by entrenched, unresponsive IT infrastructures.

Consider this real-world example of how architectural challenges hindered business agility. A major insurance company had an old mainframe Assembler system that was processing the main customer file on a nightly basis. The file structure was sequential, yet had many record types, which made the data architecture very complex. This system was surrounded by numerous COBOL applications, a myriad of Java applications, and a large and growing middleware environment. IT felt that migrating these applications to more modern languages and platforms would address their requirements. However, numerous interviews with frontline users found that they could not get the information they needed in the form they needed it and in the time frame required.

This lack of availability of critical and timely information impacted the ability of users to respond to customers. All the middleware, language conversion, or platform migration projects in the world would not correct this problem. Core applications, along with the surrounding systems and middleware architecture, were essentially slaves to the archaic data architecture. This highlights the fact that business requirements must drive modernization or organizations can spend a lot of money and not provide bottom-line business value. The following modernization principles are a good guide to follow to avoid this situation.

- Modernization projects should be deployed incrementally and based on phased ROI and deliverables.
- Do not apply solutions until you understand the underlying problem or requirement.
- Business requirements and related ROI must be the major driver in modernization initiatives.
- Business units, including frontline users, must play an ongoing and active role in creating and reviewing business requirements, incremental deliverables, and ROI.
- Modernization initiatives should target core architecture issues raised by the business community where applicable.

These principles should serve as guiding factors for any organization intent on pursuing modernization work. Any organization with an entrenched IT architecture that is hindering organizational agility should consider modernization. A more complete set of modernization principles are provided in chapter 15.

## SUMMARY

This chapter is an introduction to modernization that included a discussion on business and IT benefits; the failures of traditional, non-modernization-based projects; an overview of basic modernization disciplines and tasks; and a summary of the principles that management can use to govern modernization efforts. Subsequent chapters provide an overview of modernization standards, modernization project scenarios, modernization technologies, and, of course, modernization case studies. This foundation will provide a good backdrop for the case studies in this book.

## REFERENCES

1. Business architecture is defined as a blueprint of the enterprise that provides a common understanding of the organization and is used to align strategic objectives and tactical demands. See http://bawg.omg.org.
2. Object Management Group. see www.omg.org.
3. Berinato S. A Rash of IT Failures. *CIO Magazine*. 2003; http://www.cio.com/archive/061503/tl_health.html.

4. Koch C. Supply Chain: Hershey's Bittersweet Lesson. *CIO Magazine*. 2002; http://www.cio.com/article/31518/Supply_Chain_Hershey_s_Bittersweet_Lesson.

5. *Rocky Road*. 1999: http://www.thespot4sap.com/articles/Rocky_Road.asp.

6. McCoy K. How the IRS Failed to Stop $200 million in Bogus Refunds. *USA Today*. 2006; http://www.usatoday.com/money/perfi/taxes/2006-12-04-irs-bogus-refunds_x.htm.

7. Rain L. A Recipe and Ingredients for ERP Failure. *Purchasing Link*. 2005; Contributing Editor — http://www.articlesbase.com/software-articles/a-recipe-and-ingredients-for-erp-failure-124383.html.

8. Child Support Agency Head Quits Over Massive IT Failures. 2004; http://www.publictechnology.net/modules.php?op=modload&name=News&file=article&sid=2087.

9. Johnston DC. *At I.R.S., a Systems Update Gone Awry*. 2003; http://www.cs.usfca.edu/~parrt/course/601/lectures/IRS.software.late.html.

10. Goldstein H. *Who Killed the Virtual Case File?* http://www.spectrum.ieee.org/sep05/1455.

11. Chaos Summary 2008. The 10 Laws of Chaos, Standish Group, 2008.

12. The Standish Group Report. Chaos, Standish Group, 1995; http://net.educause.edu/ir/library/pdf/NCP08083B.pdf.

13. Wheeler D. Counting Source Lines of Code (SLOC), 2001; http://www.dwheeler.com/sloc/.

14. *DoubleCheck Static Analysis Tool.* http://www.ghs.com/products/doublecheck.html.

15. Whitehead J, Coveney D. *How Much Does Code Cost?* 2008; http://liverpoolwebdesigner.com/2008/06/01/how-much-does-code-cost/.

16. Boehm B, Abts C, Chulani S. *Software Development Cost Estimation Approaches — A Survey1*. 2000; http://sunset.usc.edu/publications/TECHRPTS/2000/usccse2000-505/usccse2000-505.pdf.

17. STE 6221 Sanntidssystemer Vår 2005 — Øving 7, http://ansatte.hin.no/pjn/fag/sanntid/oving7.pdf and ACM Forum. 1981;24(7).

18. A 1 million line system will take more than 11 years to be replaced by 30 people working full time if each person delivers 3,000 lines of production-ready code per year (15 lines per day in a 200 day year).

19. Ulrich W. Application Package Software: The Promise vs. Reality. 2006;6(9).

20. Twenty-six percent had more than 5,000 employees, 24% had between 1,000 and 5,000 employees, 33% had between 100 and 1,000 employees, and the remaining organizations had 100 or fewer employees. Twenty-four percent had annual revenues of more than US $1 billion, 20% have annual revenues between $100 million and $1 billion, 38% had annual revenues between $10 million and $100 million, with the remainder having annual revenues less than $10 million. See Report in Appendix E.

21. *The Cost of ERP*. 2002; http://www.standishgroup.com/chaos/beacon_243.php.

22. Hess H. Aligning Technology and Business: Applying Patterns for Legacy Transformation. *IBM Systems Journal*. 2005;44(1); http://www.research.ibm.com/journal/sj/441/hess.pdf.

23. *The Internet Goes Business Critical*. Standish Group white paper [online].

24. Gotterbarn D. Reducing Software Failures Addressing the Ethical Risks of the Software Development Lifecycle. *Australian Journal of Information Systems*. 2002.

25. Khusidman Dr V, Ulrich W. *Architecture-Driven Modernization: Transforming the Enterprise*. http://www.omg.org/docs/admtf/07-12-01.pdf.

26. Ulrich W. Extracting Business Rules from Existing Systems. *BPM Strategies Magazine*. 2005; http://www.systemtransformation.com/IT_Arch_Transformation_Articles/arch_extracting_business_rules.htm.

# CHAPTER 2

# Modernization Technologies and Services

William Ulrich

Software tools and services enable a wide variety of modernization tasks. Much of the technology needed by IT professionals is available for use on projects today and new capabilities are emerging on an ongoing basis. Some of the technologies are available as licensed tools while other technologies are controlled by certain service providers. Identifying and leveraging modernization technologies and services are critical to the success of a modernization initiative.

In practice, organizations have not even come close to leveraging modernization technologies and services on modernization projects. This is due to a lack of knowledge of modernization capabilities, related techniques, and deployment options. This chapter discusses how to set up a technology and service strategy based on particular modernization requirements. It also provides an overview of the kinds of tool features and functions that support modernization projects.

## CREATING A MODERNIZATION TECHNOLOGY STRATEGY

Before selecting and procuring modernization technologies and services, it is important to have a modernization technology strategy based on your unique enterprise requirements. Management, architecture teams, and modernization specialists should identify the types of planned and ongoing projects that require modernization and craft a technology plan based on these requirements.

One option that supports the creation and deployment of such a strategy involves setting up a modernization center of excellence. This center would include people that either understand or can research how to apply modernization within an enterprise. The center of excellence — working with project planning teams — will assess requirements, determine technology and service needs, and identify in-house or third-party technologies to fill these requirements. This team would also identify service options as required.

## Strategy Drives Technology and Service Requirements

Before determining a modernization tool strategy, management must assess what they are trying to accomplish, related objectives, and the role of modernization technology and services within the context of those objectives. Management may have one specific project in mind or may want to establish a comprehensive program. The following four categories represent the range of modernization deployment options available to management and project teams. Each option is considered within the context of situations where it would best be applied.

- Tool-centric modernization involves licensing one or more tools, training in-house staff, and delivering in-house modernization projects with internal staff. This approach does not preclude the use of vendor training but is largely an in-house driven, in-house controlled approach. This approach works well in situations in which:

  - Multiple systems and application areas require analysis and modernization
  - Management has a clear set of objectives and areas targeted for analysis and modernization
  - A series of ongoing assessment and refactoring projects are planned across a large application software portfolio
  - The enterprise has established a modernization center of excellence to provide in-house mentoring and deployment support

- Service supported modernization is performed in-house and involves licensing one or more tools, but engages outside support to work with in-house teams. This approach is useful when:

  - A specific, multi-phased project is envisioned and the enterprise lacks in-house modernization expertise
  - There is a lack of in-house expertise or an ability to build the expertise required to staff modernization project teams
  - Ongoing modernization work will be transferred to in-house staff at a later time
  - Executives want to jump-start projects to prove that modernization can deliver value to the enterprise

- In-sourced modernization shifts project ownership to an external service provider, but is still an in-house delivered project. Tooling in these situations is typically provided by the service provider staffing and managing the project. This approach works well when:

  - A single project is planned that requires specialized expertise that will not be required for other projects

- The enterprise cannot staff, nor can they manage, a modernization project on their own
- The service provider brings software to the project that is not licensed to third parties but must be used by the service team
- Specialized rule extraction or related transformation work is required that in-house personnel are not positioned to perform

- Outsourced modernization involves shipping software off-site to have it refactored and/or transformed within a third-party environment. This approach still requires in-house coordination and validation testing and may be combined with any of the first three approaches. The outsourced modernization approach works well for situations in which:

  - The project is very specialized and requires complex, one-time transformations to a given system or systems
  - There is no in-house expertise available and it is impractical to attempt to develop such expertise to perform a given set of modernization tasks
  - A service provider has a unique set of refactoring and transformation technologies that it will not license to IT organizations for any of a variety of reasons

A couple of points are worth noting as modernization technology and deployment options are examined. If management has determined that there are numerous assessment and refactoring projects that can help streamline and realign applications to accommodate various business and IT requirements, the in-house and service-supported options make the most sense.

On the other hand, if application transformation from existing platforms and languages is required, this is a skill that is unlikely to be in place and impractical to establish at a bank, insurance company, manufacturing firm, or government agency. Complex, one-time transformations are ideally suited for outsourcing. Note that in all cases the oversight and acceptance of a project must remain the responsibility of in-house management.

One last point involves the accessibility to in-house analyst and business skills. This is required for business rule extraction and analysis projects, which should be performed in-house and not off-site.

## Modernization Technology/Service Strategy Guidelines

Based on the following guidelines, management can assess their overall technology and service requirements and use these requirements to establish an overall tool strategy. General guidelines for developing this strategy include:

- Establish a center of excellence as the coordination point for modernization projects, technologies, and services to ensure that investments are leveraged as broadly as possible.

- Assess overall modernization project requirements to determine the need for various technologies and services.
- Build a consensus on the need for certain modernization projects from an enterprise perspective.
- Based on project type, duration, and repeatability requirements, identify in-house, service-supported, in-sourcing and/or outsourcing options.
- Based on the overall set of modernization requirements, determine the need to bring in certain assessment tools that can be used to support the anticipated in-house and/or external modernization work.
- Determine if any of the required tools are already available in-house and verify that software product licenses are current or update them accordingly.
- Incorporate third-party consulting and outsourcing vendors into these discussions to augment and leverage available consulting tools as required.
- Focus on tool integration and incorporate tools, if possible, into a workbench environment where applicable.
- Monitor modernization activities to ensure that lessons learned are shared accordingly.

## MODERNIZATION TOOL CATEGORIES

Over the past several years, modernization technologies have advanced to the point where there is an expectation of a fundamental baseline set of capabilities for any given toolset. This includes code parsing capabilities for a variety of software environments that lay the foundation for a wide variety of analyses from a variety of perspectives. These perspectives include structural views, execution views, data architecture views, application architecture views, and the ability to map information between IT architecture and business architecture.

Beyond these baseline capabilities, there are a wide variety of refactoring and transformation features and functions that are available for different languages, platforms, environments, and objectives. The following workbench description provides the fundamental features and functions that are commonly embodied in a baseline set of modernization tools.

### Modernization Workbench

Fundamental workbench functionality should be embodied in a tool called a modernization workbench. Such a workbench would include parsing tools to analyze the artifacts that define the IT architecture, the ability to load and represent these artifacts in a standard tool repository, a comprehensive set of relationship definitions among the artifacts within this repository, and a query and reporting facility that allows analysts to produce on-demand analysis results for that captured set of artifacts.

A modernization workbench should contain static analysis capabilities at the program and system level. The foundation for the workbench is the underlying repository, which defines attributes and relationships for each software artifact. The repository should

- Be flexible enough to allow an enterprise to specify any physical or logical object type required
- Represent any physical or logical artifact within the repository model
- Allow analysts to define additional artifacts or attributes for artifacts as required
- Have standards-based import and export capabilities, which will be expanded upon in Chapter 3
- Recognize and update only modified components to avoid a complete reload when repository updates are required

A modernization workbench may be an off-the-shelf product, a toolkit that is carried by service providers when they provide an in-sourced modernization project, or an off-site tool that is only available to service providers through an outsourced modernization project. Regardless of the packaging and accessibility of a given workbench, it should have the following basic capabilities:

- Parsing Technology: Statically performs syntactic analyses on source code artifacts, including relevant program files, macros definitions, workflow artifacts (e.g., JCL, CICS definitions, ECL, WFL, Shell Scripts, etc.), data definition artifacts, table definitions, and any additional artifacts that comprise the application and data architecture. Dynamic analysis (while the system is running) can augment static analysis, but is typically within the domain of a different and unique toolset. The result of a parsing step is a populated repository with missing artifacts identified or accounted for.

- System-Wide Analysis: Capabilities that provide an inventory of all captured artifacts, maintain a cross-reference of all physical system artifacts, have the capacity to represent a wide variety of related system flows and dependencies through online views and reports, assess system-level complexities via metrics, and summarize this information in various ways.

- Program Level Analysis Capabilities: Analyze program logic paths, recognize program structural diagnostics, graph out the overall program map; assess program complexity, provide the foundation for generating path flow diagrams, and provide the baseline for various program complexity metrics.

- System Workflow and Presentation Analysis: Analyzes job control, online table definitions, and screen definitions; depicts batch job flows; diagrams online system transaction flows; and incorporates automated screen and report mock-ups. This analysis is highly useful for mapping business processes to the application architecture via user interfaces and also augments business process analysis by representing the automated portions of transaction flows across a system. It also serves as a baseline for performance streamlining and functional redesign.

- Data Definition Analysis: A specialized form of system-wide analysis that represents a cross-reference of system data definitions and relationships; highlights semantic inconsistencies and redundancies; identifies rationalization and standardization opportunities based on discrepancies related to size, attribute definition, control transfers, naming standards, and group data definitions; summarizes this information in the form of data definition metrics; and provides planning information into data architecture redesign and migration.

- Metric Analysis: This was mentioned in other tool feature descriptions but requires special mention. Metrics drive project estimating models and are desirable for each system and program level analysis category found within a workbench.

## Refactoring and Transformation Tool Features and Functions

With a repository-based foundation established in the modernization workbench, a number of tools additionally provide refactoring and transformation automation capabilities. While most commercially licensed tools are not full-blown workbenches, service-based workbenches have a more fluid approach to systems refactoring and transformation within the workbench environment because they are built to transform systems.

This is where workbench categories can veer into two groups. The first workbench category is typically found in commercial tools that can be licensed for in-house use, are repository-based, and provide user-initiated refactoring and transformation with the intent of allowing analysts to selectively use or import certain code or model-based outputs into a target environment. There is no intent or underlying capacity, however, for automatically reproducing a logically equivalent application in the new target architecture.

The second workbench category transforms the system into an intermediate work environment, allows analysts to tune the workbench to support various refactoring and transformation requirements, and produces a logically equivalent application within the target architecture. This second category is a more specialized tool that is focused on transforming applications from one platform, language, and environment into a target platform, language, and environment. Workbench category one and two can overlap in terms of features and functions, although the second category is typically used in outsourced modernization projects. General features and functions include:

- Source Program Editor: Facilitates manipulating source views of a system. The editor is used for modernization work that tools cannot perform automatically. The assumption is that the tool is working against the tool repository representations of the system and not the actual source code, even though the editor may appear to be editing source code.

- Language/Platform Migration: Converts source code to comply with either the requirements of a newer version of the same language or an entirely different language. Converting source code does not change functionality. This approach, which supports lift and shift products, represents a transliteration approach versus a transformational approach. For example, a language that has been transliterated from PLI to COBOL would largely be a line-for-line translation. This is not to be confused with the concept of a procedural to object-based language transformation (which may move COBOL code into Java or C++, for example).

- Program Structuring: Determines all possible program logic paths and creates a functionally identical version of the program in a structured format. The resulting source program is functionally equivalent, is reconstructed using single entry/single exit modules, has I/O structures consolidated and isolated, and conforms to the basic precepts of structure or modular programming rules.

- Code Modularization: Facilities code slicing to carve out segmented functions of a source program and turn the original program into a main program and series of sub-programs. Code slicing is based on multiple criteria that can be established as parameters within the tool. Options include the ability to slice along a data usage path, conditional path, or a control-based path. Such a tool would also support the concept of aggregating programs, which combines sliced modules into common routines and uses a combination of slicing and clone analysis approaches. This feature isolates logic and consolidates business, data access, and user access logic to form components that support services oriented architecture (SOA) and other types of migrations.

- Data Definition Rationalization: Builds composite records, segments or tables from redundant I/O area groupings; facilitates analyst-driven semantic name standardization and field expansion; propagates the new composite source code definitions back into source programs; renames program level data element names to the new composite names; and creates a foundation for systems consolidation, reuse, and target architecture migration.

- User Interface Migration: Transforms and integrates older system interfaces into Web-based or GUI interfaces. Given that this transformation task can be automated but also typically requires business input and alignment with business processes, such a feature should support analyst interaction. While a one-to-one conversion falls into a refactoring category, a true transformation would need to be aligned with a coordinated business process alignment and/or an application transformation effort.

- Language/Platform Transformation: Supports the transformation of procedural languages to object-based languages (e.g., Java, C#) to take advantage of the new target architecture. This concept differs from the transliteration approach because of the ability to utilize pattern recognition in moving from one paradigm (e.g., procedural) to another (e.g., object-based). Note that this concept is inherent in the aforementioned workbench category two.

- Data Reverse Engineering: Redesigns cross-system data definitions with the intent of deriving or augmenting a logical model from the existing environment. Some tools attempt to do this by evaluating the physical data as well as system artifacts. The results of such an effort produce an entity relationship (ER) model for the new data architecture. Certain tools support the partial automation of the normalization process as well. Note that this works best when rationalized data structures are used as input.

- Business Rule Capture and Consolidation: Statically (or dynamically) analyzes and slices out source code logic based on various user selection criteria across module or even system boundaries. This tool feature selectively filters out implementation-dependent logic, stores the extracted rules, extracts against previously extracted rules, displays rules in analyst-friendly formats, and transforms extracted rules into reusable formats. Different options exist in different tools. For example, a tool may allow an analyst to interactively select, trace, capture, tag, and migrate business rules. Certain tools are better than others at discerning that various data elements define the same business data as other data elements, in spite of naming variations. Finally, certain tools may facilitate the migration of selected logic to models and object-based languages.

- Modeling Tool Exportation: A general-purpose concept that transforms code-based representations into model-based representations. The model-based targets can vary but are generally considered to be UML representations. Capabilities are also emerging to support the creation of model-driven business rules and processes in various formats. Where tools can support code-to-model transformations, caution should be taken because there is a risk associated with moving poorly constructed, implementation-dependent software architectures into models that will not or cannot be fixed once the models have been derived. Systematic approaches to model derivation are much preferred over wholesale system migrations to models.

## Technology Capability/Needs Alignment

When looking at modernization technology options, it is important to define your needs within a broad-based view of enterprise requirements. Too many times we find tools have been deployed in companies and very few people are aware of their existence. Companies end up buying similar tools when they already own a tool that meets their needs.

This stems from project-driven tool acquisition and deployment, which involves one area justifying and using that tool on a single project. If the project is canceled, the tool is shelved — even though many other areas of the enterprise could use the tool. In other cases, a tool has one user who leaves the organization and the tool is likewise shelved. This happens all too frequently and costs an organization in lost opportunities and real dollars.

One last needs-alignment issue involves what the project requires versus what the tool can actually do in contrast to how a vendor promoted the product. Many times, companies license a tool with one idea in mind but the vendor pushes the tool's canned solutions onto the project team and as a result project goals and customer plans are derailed. This happened at one company that licensed a product to streamline and improve their existing COBOL environment. Yet once the vendor came in and helped install the tool, the only thing they ended up doing was trying to eliminate dead code and reduce a complexity metric that did not need lowering. As a result, the tool delivered suboptimal value to the system, to the project, and to the organization.

The bottom line is that organizations must stay focused on their real needs and not let a tool or a vendor derail their plans.

## SERVICE PROVIDER STRATEGY

Service providers mirror the modernization deployment options outlined at the beginning of this chapter. These include tool-centric, service-supported, in-sourced, and outsourced approaches to deploying modernization projects. Many times management creates a strategy based on a preexisting relationship with a service provider and this may be a bad strategy. For example, management may feel comfortable with a certain firm that always in-sources modernization work — a scenario under which the service provider completely owns the project, brings in their own tools, and does not provide skills transfer to the client. This may not be appropriate if there are a number of projects or areas that could benefit from assessment, refactoring, or transformation-related activities on an ongoing basis.

This situation is more common than one would think, but it can be avoided by stepping back and understanding what is to be accomplished. For example, if an organization has large volumes of COBOL code on a mainframe and no immediate need to move that code off of the mainframe, the focus is more likely to be on an assessment and refactoring strategy if a business case is in place to drive such a plan. The business case in this situation, for example, might require a plan to clean up, streamline, and consolidate a series of redundant applications and return those systems to the existing platform. This "consolidation scenario" would drive the modernization plan.

Under this scenario, management should craft a strategy that couples the in-sourced project option with the service-supported option. A specialized or high-priority project could be in-sourced, where an outside firm owns the project, while other projects can be jump-started using the service-supported deployment option. This second option should incorporate a rollout program that includes technology and skills transfer to enterprise employees. Over time, the tool-centric approach could be rolled out to various projects across the enterprise.

Another example involves an enterprise where systems were deployed under a highly decentralized management structure for decades. This resulted in numerous systems running on a wide variety of unsupported platforms, using unsupported technologies. In this case, the outsourced option could be selectively pursued to transform those environments into standard languages, running on a standardized platform. As this program evolves, a service-supported approach could be deployed to further consolidate and transform these migrated environments into common data and application architectures.

Executives should not jump into an approach randomly or based on personal relationships with a given firm. Rather, services strategies should follow a consistent philosophy that makes good sense for the business.

## SUMMARY

One of the biggest issues that has stymied modernization is a lack of education about the tools and services available. Building this knowledge base provides organizations with a much broader set of options when planning their system strategies. It also helps avoid many potential missteps along the way.

# CHAPTER 3

# Modernization Standards Roadmap

William Ulrich

Architecture-driven modernization has a long history, but it has faced many challenges as it has been deployed and redeployed at numerous organizations. Any time there is a lack of standards within a given industry, it opens the door to confusion, and this has a direct bearing on the adoption rate of a given set of solutions. This is particularly true in the case of modernization.

While an executive buyer or even casual deployment team of modernization solutions is unlikely to spend much time thinking about standardization issues, standardization does matter. Having seen companies go through modernization efforts over the decades and across various organization units, one can quickly see that the lack of synergy, coordination, and interoperability across modernization tools results in silo-based projects that cannot cross individual project or organizational boundaries. Numerous issues have complicated adoption of modernization over the years that can be tied directly back to the historic lack of industry standards such as:

- No consistent message from modernization service and tool providers as to the breadth of capabilities that modernization can provide.
- Conflicting and often wrong-headed value propositions in terms of what modernization can deliver to the enterprise bottom line.
- Lack of a clear understanding of the disciplines and the specific role of tools in various stages of modernization projects.
- Inability to perform assessments beyond the bounds of an individual system because tools cannot interoperate with other tools that support different platforms and languages.
- Repeated start-up and assessment efforts every time a new project team or business unit begins a modernization effort.
- Inability to muster any momentum for modernization programs due to the fragmented concepts and strategies that dominate the marketplace.

## CONTENTS

The bottom line is that the historic lack of standards has been responsible for proliferating misinformation and the inability of management to create a cohesive modernization strategy. Fortunately, a task force was formed under the international, not-for-profit standards body called the Object Management Group (OMG). The OMG is responsible for the creation and maintenance of a number of standards including UML, BPMN, and a host of other standards in a variety of technical and business domains.

Standards are created by member organizations that submit a standard in response to a task force request. Members then evaluate the submissions and pass them as a standard. Various levels of oversight and review are involved and, in a number of cases, the work is coordinated with other standards groups such as the Open Group or International Organization for Standardization (ISO). The modernization standards discussed in this chapter involve current standards, work in progress, and planned standards as defined by the OMG modernization roadmap.

## MODERNIZATION STANDARDS OVERVIEW

In 2003, the OMG Architecture-Driven Modernization (ADM) Task Force was formed by a number of companies including major hardware suppliers, systems integrators, independent software providers, and customer organizations. The ADM Task Force crafted and issued a multi-stage modernization roadmap that established a plan for a series of modernization standards.[1]

OMG standards focus on creating a common view of information or metadata that a given tool gathers, manipulates, and shares with and through other tools. Within the context of modernization, this means defining a common view of all of the artifacts that comprise existing software environments. Because every modernization tool gathers and stores information about existing software environments in different ways, there is no expectation that every vendor has to change every tool repository to conform to a common metamodel.

When it comes to exchanging or sharing this information with other tools, however, a common view of existing systems metadata becomes very important, and this is what the ADM standards are meant to address. For example, consider project planning that requires an analysis of several large systems containing overlapping functionality. These systems are running on a mainframe and several distributed environments. They are written in COBOL, IBM Assembler, C, and Java using different data structures and user interfaces. Two tools have been brought in to examine these systems, compare overlapping data usage and business logic, and create a consolidation plan.

Traditionally, several approaches have been used to accomplish this analysis. One involved running a tool across as much as the tool could read and reviewing the rest of the systems manually. This time-consuming approach resulted in incomplete and inaccurate results. A second approach involved running the same tool and totally ignoring the rest of the applications as out of scope. This second approach created an incomplete view of the problem and the solution, leading to a failed or canceled project. The last approach involved running two separate tools and attempting to reconcile reports and inquiries manually, across highly incompatible views of these systems. Each approach was time consuming, incomplete, and error prone.

The OMG ADM standards now in place and being created by the ADM Task Force are meant to address the challenges facing modernization analysts who have had to struggle around piecemeal solutions to significant IT architecture challenges. These standards allow tools to share captured information, which benefits organizations looking for alternatives to traditional IT strategies or seeking to use modernization to augment those strategies. Consider that:

- Analysts and project planning teams can gain a comprehensive view of the overall application and data architecture to ensure that an accurate understanding of the as-is architecture is incorporated into strategic plans.
- Projects may not be able to rely on a single tool where they span application areas, organizational units, or even business boundaries.
- One tool cannot analyze every platform or language.
- Non-IT (e.g., desktop) systems can be examined using specialty tools, and this information can be incorporated into the bigger planning picture.
- Visualization features in one tool can be used on information captured by another tool.
- Additional tools can be applied to visualize application and data architectures in new and unique ways that could include simulations or other advanced analysis techniques.
- Existing IT architecture metadata can be imported into refactoring and/ or transformation tools and, ultimately, into forward engineering tools to help automate redesign and redeployment.
- Modernization standards allow organizations to begin modernization projects knowing that tool interoperability across vendors provides migration options should a given vendor tool be removed from the market.
- Standards provide organizations with assurance that they are investing not just in individual tools but in a coordinated industry approach.

OMG standards enable tool interoperability across languages, platforms, vendor organizations, business units, and IT disciplines. One beneficiary of this interoperability concept is the enterprise that must leverage these tools to modernize IT environments and synchronize these modernization efforts with the evolution of business models and forward engineering paradigms. Collectively, these standards create a set of building blocks for modernization-based alignment of business and IT architectures.

Figure 3.1 shows the role of various OMG standards across business and IT domains. A number of standards support the evolution and transformation from existing business and IT architectures to target business and IT architectures. As more organizations understand the need to synchronize transformation efforts across multiple architectures, the demand will grow for vendor tools to interoperate across business and IT domains, as-is and to-be architectures, and the various tools that function within and facilitate the evolution and transformation of these environments.

The backdrop for Figure 3.1 is the modernization domain structure introduced in Chapter 1. Figure 3.1 depicts several metamodels within the IT domain that build upon each other in terms of their ability to reflect different views of the existing IT architecture. The Abstract Syntax Tree Metamodel (ASTM) standard provides the most granular view of the IT architecture and supports the highly automated transformation from existing languages and platforms to target languages and platforms. This type of transformation can be accomplished with limited or no involvement of the business architecture, although we recommend engaging business teams to ensure that you built support and funding for these projects.

The Knowledge Discovery Metamodel (KDM) standard is a multipurpose metamodel that represents all aspects of the existing IT architecture. The KDM is the baseline interchange metamodel and facilitates tool interoperability for any tool that captures or utilizes information about the existing IT architec-

**FIGURE 3.1**

*Business/IT standards in modernization environment.[2]*

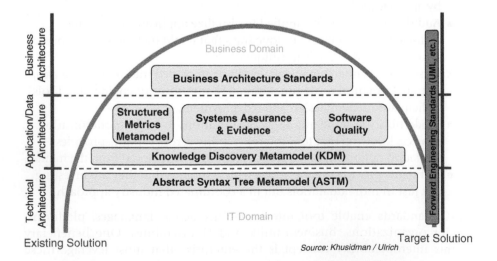

ture. While the KDM can leverage information captured by the ASTM, both the KDM and the ASTM can exist as stand-alone metamodels.

Additional modernization standards that provide different views of the existing IT architecture include the Systems Assurance Evidence Metamodel (SAEM), the Pattern Recognition Metamodel, and the Structured Metrics Metamodel (SMM). These standards will be explained in more detail throughout the remaining sections of this chapter. Basing each of these subsequent ADM standards on a common metamodel view of existing IT architectures eliminates reanalysis and misinterpretation of existing IT environments throughout iterative assessment and modernization project cycles.

Modernization paths through application, data, and business architectures require synchronization of IT and business domain, and this has been historically absent from modernization tools and projects. The goal is to enable highly coordinated transformations of business and IT architectures and ensure that business effectively drives change through IT application and data architectures.

Figure 3.1 shows how business modeling standards, which continue to evolve just as modernization standards evolve, support the mapping across business architectures and between business and IT architectures. For example, there have been selective mappings established between the existing software artifacts within KDM and rule definitions defined within the OMG Semantics for Business Vocabulary and Rules (SBVR) standard. SBVR defines business semantics and the rules associated with those semantics. While this is an important interface, it is not a complete picture of the business architecture. Business units, capabilities, processes, customers, partners, and value chains, along with semantics and rules, collectively define the business architecture.

The standards needed to fully represent the business architecture, along with how these standards interrelate, are still evolving through active efforts by the OMG Business Architecture Working Group.[3] As business standards evolve, modernization standards can be synchronized to ensure that business architectures and IT architectures evolve in a synchronized fashion so that IT can be more responsive to short- and long-term business requirements.

As IT architectures undergo modernization, part of that evolutionary process is to transform existing architectures into target architectures that are typically defined using a different set of disciplines and paradigms than were used on existing application and data architectures. For example, target architectures are now being crafted using a Model-Driven Architecture® (MDA), as defined by the OMG. According to the OMG Web site, MDA "provides an open, vendor neutral approach to the challenge of business and technology change."[4]

MDA is supported through the use of the Unified Modeling Language (UML), another OMG standard. According to OMG,

UML, along with the Meta Object Facility (MOF), also provides a key foundation for OMG's Model-Driven Architecture®, which unifies every step of development and integration from business modeling, through architectural and application modeling, to development, deployment, maintenance, and evolution.

UML has been widely deployed in development tools and is an ideal target for standards-based mapping between as-is and to-be IT architectures through the alignment of ADM-based standards and MDA and UML. Note that we are not advocating the use of UML as a key communication tool for business but only as a requirement and specification facility.

Mapping between the modernization standards, business standards, and forward engineering standards addresses a significant industry problem. In the past, the forward engineering industry largely ignored existing software assets and this has resulted, in part, in the industry failures highlighted in Chapter 1. There is a gap between modernization and Greenfield- and COTS-based initiatives. Interoperability across modernization, business and development standards, and paradigms breaks down these barriers and facilitates increased automated tool support for business architecture/IT architecture alignment efforts.

In the absence of modernization standards and tools, there is no glue in place to synchronize the transition across business and IT domains and as-is and to-be architectures. This gap, along with the historic absence of an integrated set of business modeling standards, has placed an impossible burden on organizations that need to address business and IT challenges while dealing with aging and complex architectures.

Therefore, modernization interoperability standards, which have been developed by the ADM Task Force and deployed in commercial modernization tools, are essential to the successful adoption of forward engineering paradigms such as MDA and the ability to align existing IT architectures with evolving business modeling paradigms. The next sections describe the ADM standards that have been deployed, are being deployed, or are in various planning stages.

## KNOWLEDGE DISCOVERY METAMODEL

The KDM established a metamodel that allows modernization tools to exchange application metadata across applications, languages, platforms, and environments. This metamodel provides a comprehensive view of as-is application and data architectures, but was not intended to represent systems at the most granular levels possible. (The ASTM, on the other hand, addresses detailed metadata below the procedure level.)

The KDM describes representations of the as-is application and data architecture along with information that can be derived from an as-is view. The KDM was developed based on a number of key requirements and

- Represents principal artifacts of existing software as entities, relationships, and attributes
- Is restricted to the artifacts of the existing software environment
- Maps to external artifacts with which the software interacts through other standards and metamodels
- Consists of a platform- and language-independent core but is extensible to support other languages and platforms
- Defines a single unified terminology for knowledge discovery of existing software assets
- Is represented using UML class diagrams
- Utilizes an XMI interchange format for vendors to import and export tool-specific metadata out of and into their toolsets
- Supports every type of platform and language environment through various means and describes the physical structure of software architectures and the logical structures where appropriate
- Facilitates tracing artifacts from a logical structure back to physical artifacts

Figure 3.2 identifies each of the varying views of the existing IT architecture represented by the KDM. For example, Figure 3.2 shows how KDM depicts an "execution" perspective as well as a "build" perspective of applications. The execution perspective exposes software artifacts from a runtime view to depict how the system flows, how transactions are triggered, and how execution artifacts interact. The build view, on the other hand, depicts system artifacts from a source, executable, and library viewpoint. Other perspectives include design, conceptual, data, and scenario views.

The KDM offers a vehicle for modernization teams, armed with standards-based technologies to establish and maintain a complete and comprehensive view of application and data architectures. This ability provides an enhanced capability to understand, refactor, and transform these environments.

KDM supports a variety of languages, database structures, middleware, tele-processing monitors, and platforms in a common repository. Where a certain technology cannot be represented, a tool vendor can extend KDM to include language- or platform-specific entities and relationships. A special mention should be made of the portion of the KDM called "Micro KDM." The Micro KDM allows vendors to exchange statement-level representations of software programs.

KDM tool compliance can be achieved by a vendor tool at multiple levels as shown in Figure 3.2. One important point regarding compliance with KDM and other ADM standards is that for tools to be KDM compliant, they do not

**FIGURE 3.2**

*KDM domains of artifact representation.*[5]

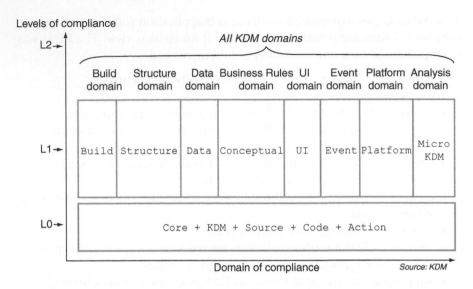

need to apply any internal changes to their products or to tool repositories. The KDM is an external representation that can be imported into and exported from using the agreed-upon standard XMI formats. Compliance, therefore, is a matter of mapping internal tool repository representations to the KDM format for purposes of importing or exporting metadata to or from another toolset. This is also the case for other ADM standards.

KDM was adopted as an OMG standard in 2007 and has undergone revisions since that time. KDM is also slated to be adopted as an ISO standard in early 2010. ISO[6] works with the OMG on various standards. KDM, along with ASTM as described in the next section, is the foundation for various other modernization standards. When an organization considers various modernization technologies or tools, they should ask about KDM compliance.

## ABSTRACT SYNTAX TREE METAMODEL

This ASTM was established to represent software at a very granular level of procedural logic, data definition, and workflow composition. ASTM can provide this granular level of information to KDM to augment the KDM view of a system. As a standard, ASTM can stand alone and supports tools geared at the complete, functionally equivalent refactoring and transformation of a system from one platform and language environment to a target platform and language environment.

Some background on the concept of the abstract syntax tree (AST) helps clarify the purpose of the ASTM. ASTs are models of software that represent software artifacts using data structures that represent the types of language constructs, their compositional relationships to other language constructs, and a set of direct and derived properties associated with each language construct. The AST is derived by analyzing software artifacts and provides a way to create a representation of those software artifacts.

An AST is an extensible, formal representation of the syntactical structure of software that is amenable to formal analysis techniques. It is possible to traverse the AST and reconstruct the "surface syntax" of the system or reconstitute it in textual form from the abstract structures. While the use of AST structures for the abstract representation of the structure of software has become an accepted practice for modeling software, the format of AST structures and the mechanisms for representation and interchange of AST models were not standardized prior to the formalization of the ASTM.

AST interchange, via the ASTM, facilitates exchanging software models in standard formats among tools. The ability to freely exchange software models between tools provides organizations with the ability to use advanced model-driven tools for software analysis and modernization. The ASTM has these attributes:

- ASTM is language and platform independent, but can be extended as needed.
- ASTM uses XMI formats for tool-based metadata exchange.
- Generic Abstract Syntax Tree Metamodel (GASTM) represents a generic set of language modeling elements common across numerous languages. Language Specific Abstract Syntax Tree Metamodel (SASTM) represents particular languages such as Ada, C, FORTRAN, and Java.
- Proprietary Abstract Syntax Tree Metamodel (PASTM) expresses ASTs for languages such as Ada, C, COBOL, etc., modeled in formats inconsistent with MOF, the GSATM, or SASTM.

Figure 3.3 represents the structure of the ASTM, including the SASTM, GASTM, and PASTM.

The ASTM standard, which was officially adopted as a standard in 2009, will continue to evolve as it expands to support more languages and environments. It will also support the evolution of other ADM standards as they change and mature.

## PATTERN RECOGNITION

The Pattern Recognition Metamodel (PRM) is a work-in-progress effort by the ADM Task Force and is initially focused on structural, architectural, and design patterns and anti-patterns that provide essential information about software. Patterns and anti-patterns provide qualitative information about existing software systems, but this concept can also be extended into the business domain of standards because the PRM is being established as a generic standard.

**FIGURE 3.3**

*ASTM modeling framework.[7]*

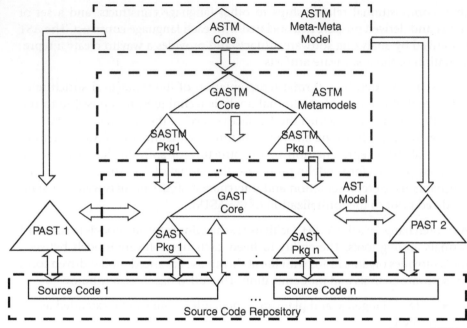

Source: ASTM

Patterns and anti-patterns are based on the analysis and abstraction of the metadata initially represented by the KDM, ASTM, or alternative sources where applicable. The PRM standard will include

- Pattern libraries describing structural, architectural, and design patterns that define opportunities to retain or transform aspects of the existing IT architecture
- Anti-pattern libraries describing structural, architectural, and design anti-patterns that signal certain refactoring and/or transformation scenarios
- A metamodel capable of representing the patterns and anti-patterns defined within the patterns library

Initial use of the PRM will be in the area of software quality and systems assurance. In either case, a given pattern or anti-pattern may signal that a system is of high or low quality. Patterns also signal that the software or business structures have desirable qualities that should be retained or reused in target architectures. For example, if an application contains viable, reusable business logic that is identifiable, segregated, and reusable, planning teams may determine that this system is an ideal candidate to be directly transformed into a UML-based environment with little or no refactoring.

A second patterns example involves highly rationalized, clearly defined data definitions, shared across several applications, that could serve as a basis for extracting and deriving a baseline data model that reflects the business data required to move to the target data architecture. In this example, little or no refactoring of redundant, inconsistent data definitions is required and the existing data definitions can be directly transformed using data transformation and modeling technologies and techniques. This pattern may also be reflected in metrics that signal high-quality software.

Anti-patterns, which are admittedly more likely to arise in existing software systems, include structural, architectural, or design-based patterns that are problematic or minimally questionable from a variety of qualitative perspectives. Anti-patterns are signs of poor software quality. Examples of anti-patterns include:

- Cloned or redundant data structures that are inconsistently defined across a system or multiple systems
- Cloned or redundant business logic, distributed across a system or systems
- Syntactically inactive source code (can never be executed)
- Semantically inactive source code (cannot be activated based on conditional logic)
- Diagnostically defective logic that violates modular programming standards and likely works in unanticipated ways including:
  - Unintended recursive structures
  - Logic that runs past the end of the program
  - Logic that exits from a routine prematurely, leaving active addresses that could trigger an unintended return to another address
  - Buffer overflows or data area overlays that could wipe out program data unintentionally
- Business logic that is highly intertwined with implementation-dependent logic
- Highly coupled data access patterns that provide input to target data architecture redesign efforts or performance tuning of existing structures
- System workflow and execution patterns that expose portions of business process flows

Note that identification of a given pattern or anti-pattern could result in triggering multiple actions. For example, highly coupled data access patterns could trigger a performance tuning effort in the near-term and a data architecture redesign effort over the long term. The pattern and anti-pattern libraries will likely continue to grow over time.

A major benefit of the PRM is that it provides the vehicle through its pattern and anti-pattern libraries to standardize terms for problematic software and business issues inherent in IT and business architectures. It is often difficult to articulate if a system is in good shape or bad shape, or whether modernization options could make a difference. In addition, if a system does have useful and valid functional logic, which could be determined by recognizing a pattern that links software logic occurrences to business capabilities, then reuse of that logic could be valuable under certain modernization scenarios.

Structural views, as represented within the KDM or ASTM, provide some insights into modernization requirements. The KDM and ASTM as a foundation for deriving patterns and anti-patterns, however, can provide much more significant insights into refactoring and transforming IT architecture. When KDM is mapped to certain business models, these insights into potential transformation opportunities expand even further.

Finally, patterns and anti-patterns defined in a given PRM patterns library, whether related to IT architecture, business architecture or a collective view of both architectures, can be described in several ways. One way to communicate these patterns is through a direct mapping to the Structured Metrics Metamodel (SMM) standard that the ADM Task Force has developed.

## STRUCTURED METRICS METAMODEL

One of the best ways to quantify various aspects of existing IT architectures is the use of metrics. In our experience, what organizations do not know about their application and data architectures could fill volumes. Executives and most managers are not very interested, however, in looking at reports or diagrams of their IT environment. Yet these individuals are the ones who must understand, buy into, and fund IT projects. They also have the power to incorporate and drive modernization disciplines into traditional IT projects. The use of metrics can provide project teams and management with the hard facts needed to gain executive attention, build executive support, and procure funding for modernization projects.

Historically, software metrics have focused on a very narrow slice of the IT architecture. For example, the McCabe Cyclamate Complexity metric, which is useful when attempting to determine program testing and maintenance difficulty, provides somewhat limited strategic value to modernization architects and planning teams.

A second metric that has been emphasized *to a fault* is the amount of syntactically inactive source code within a system. This overemphasis on this simple construct is, in our opinion, due to the limited imaginations of tool providers and service teams. Most modernization tools can find and handle this type of dead code whereas other constructs are harder to analyze, identify, and address. This has led tool builders to focus on this single metric, which in turn has taken the focus off of a much larger set of issues that need to be addressed including system level anti-patterns; poor design; and fragmented, redundant architectures.

At a program or module level, a more useful metric would be the number of occurrences and the whereabouts of semantically inactive code, which indicates that there is convoluted logic embedded within an application that should *not* be transformed wholesale into target architectures but should be selectively extracted, analyzed, and either discarded or reused accordingly.

Consider some of the other metric categories that have been ignored but provide valuable insights into architecture and planning teams. These include basic environmental counts such as job steps, system-wide data definition replication, program-to-program nesting levels, percentage of batch versus online interfaces, number and percentage of business capabilities in a current system that map to a target architecture, or the mapping of data usage between the current and target architecture. These are just a few examples of useful metrics that are mostly ignored in practice during assessment projects. This gap can be attributed to the lack of agreed-upon foundation "metrics library" to support quality analysis, modernization assessment, planning, and deployment.

Using metrics such as these, a wide variety of modernization scenarios can be more effectively planned and estimated, staffed accordingly, and deployed with a higher degree of confidence. Software metrics are required to assess the qualitative and quantitative aspects of systems and serve as a foundation for scoping and estimating modernization projects. Metrics can also provide a much broader set of benefits. The SMM, which was officially adopted in 2009, is the vehicle for supporting software quality, systems assurance, green computing, and business architecture. The SMM enables interchange of metric metadata and helps define representative metrics as metadata or metadata attributes within various models. The SMM standard is based on:

- A metrics metamodel that enables the interchange of measures across a wide spectrum of domains
- Metric libraries that support selective domain categories including modernization, systems assurance, business domain analysis, and other areas

The metamodel is in place and will likely be adjusted as it is deployed into the marketplace. Similarly, the metrics libraries will continue to evolve based on the usage of the SMM standard.

Figure 3.4 depicts a summary-level view of the SMM where a measure is the thing numerically identified and a measurement is the result of the process to quantify a given measure. An observation represents contextual information such as the time of the measurement and the identification of the measurement

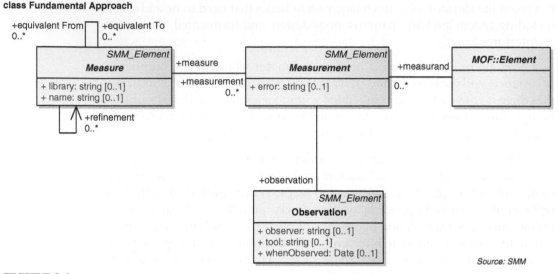

**FIGURE 3.4**
*Structured metrics metamodel approach.*

tool. This structure provides a way for various tools that produce or utilize metrics to import and export those metrics across a wide variety of domains. These domains are defined by the metric libraries to be associated with the SMM over time.

The SMM has established an initial framework of metric categories to be incorporated into the modernization metrics library. These categories support software quality analysis and modernization planning. They include

- Environmental Metrics (e.g., number of screens, programs, lines of code.)
- Data Definition Metrics (e.g., number of data groups, overlapping data groups, unused data elements.)
- Program Process Metrics (e.g., Halstead, McCabe.)
- Architecture Metrics (e.g., number of batch workflows, number of discreet online workflows, and depth of hierarchical database hierarchies.)
- Functional Metrics (e.g., capabilities supported by a given system, business data as a percentage of all data, capabilities in current system that map to capabilities in target architecture.)
- Quality/Reliability Metrics (e.g., failures per day, meantime to failure, meantime to repair.)
- Performance Metrics (e.g., average batch window clock time, average online response time.)
- Security/Vulnerability (e.g., breaches per day, vulnerability points.)

These metric categories represent a comprehensive set of proven industry metrics that provide analysis, planning, and deployment support for modernization projects.[8] These are subset examples of one view from a modernization metrics library that is posted on the Internet.[9] Additional metrics libraries will continue to emerge for software assurance, development standards, business modeling, and other domains that arise within the standards community. The SMM metamodel was designed to be flexible enough to provide a foundation for these and future metric libraries.

Views of the existing architecture, as defined within KDM or ASTM models, provide the baseline for a foundational set of ADM metrics. KDM provides a good source for a wide variety of structural metrics. The previously identified environmental metrics category is a good example of the kind of metrics that can be easily derived from the KDM. Other standards will ultimately serve as an additional source of potential metrics. The ADM Pattern Recognition initiative at OMG, in particular, will provide another level of metrics that support more qualitative analysis of existing IT environments. Several of the previously discussed metric categories, such as the architectural metrics, reflect patterns and anti-patterns. The SMM will serve as the foundation for these new standards as they evolve.

To raise the degree of sophistication and support that metrics can provide to modernization projects, we must seek to derive metrics not just from one standard, but from a combination of standards. For example, one previously referenced metric category was called functional metrics. Within this category, the ability to derive the number of capabilities supported by existing systems that need to be retained within the design of the target architecture requires metamodel mapping between ADM and business domain standards. Business metamodel mappings are being considered through the efforts of the OMG Business Architecture Working Group.[10]

We anticipate that the SMM will be used to support business domain and other standards through the use of domain-specific metrics libraries for business architecture, green computing, SOA, and other topical areas. In addition, the OMG ADM Task Force will work to ensure that pattern and anti-pattern libraries defined in conjunction with the PRM will be synchronized with corresponding SMM metric libraries.

Finally, the SMM metrics can be plugged into various project-estimating models for various modernization projects, which offer project planning teams powerful, quantitative and qualitative measures that can be used to establish project timelines and funding. For example, data definition redundancy metrics would facilitate estimating efforts for a scenario to migrate from flat file structures to a relational database. These estimating models for modernization scenarios will continue to evolve as they are deployed internally and in conjunction with modernization tool and service providers.

## ADM VISUALIZATION

KDM, ASTM, PRM, and SMM establish an excellent foundation of information about existing IT architectures. Yet the means of visualizing this vast and potentially powerful cross-section of metadata is not addressed in any of these standards. Rather, individual tool vendors define what is to be visualized and how it is to be presented. As a result, there is no consistency in how one tool versus another tool depicts the same information to the users of those tools.[11] One appropriate definition of "visualization" as it applies to the concept of ADM metadata is as follows.

> Visualization is the process of representing abstract business or scientific data as images that can aid in understanding the meaning of the data.[12]

An ADM Visualization standard would allow vendors to exchange metadata geared at enriching the visualization of complex, yet essential, relationships and derived analysis buried inside of various ADM metamodel views. Visualization provides the link for modernization analysts between the four baseline standards (i.e. KDM, ASTM, PRM, and SMM), refactoring, and transformation. With no set way to visualize existing IT architecture, modernization analysts could potentially ignore or sidestep issues that need to be addressed in existing systems. A lack of visualization definitions and consistency ultimately leads to project teams ignoring or neglecting the need to address this particular issue, buried within existing systems. This is a common practice within modernization projects.

Ignoring visualization of existing systems metadata handicaps analysis and planning efforts associated with modernization initiatives by propagating inconsistent, misleading, or conflicting views of this important information. ADM Visualization addresses this issue by providing a consistent set of visualizations across platforms, languages, and tools. ADM Visualization, which is only at the discussion stages as of this writing, would support various artifact representations that either exist or will emerge from ADM and related standards. These include, but are not limited to, the following concepts:

- System-to-system interface mappings
- General architectural artifact mappings between various KDM views
- Data-store-to-data-store mappings
- Data redundancy visualizations
- Batch and online workflows
- Data definition mappings at various levels
- Functional decompositions and mappings
- Call and related invocation structures
- Current to target technical, data, and application architecture mappings
- Other mappings and views as may be applicable

ADM Visualization plays an important role in bridging the gap between the current set of understanding-based ADM standards and the refactoring and transformation standards discussed in the following sections. Early research into visualization of existing architectures suggests that there are various 3D and dynamic representations that will ultimately provide new and unique ways to view not only as-is IT architectures but also business architectures.

## ADM REFACTORING

As discussed in Chapter 1, "refactoring is any change to a computer program's code which improves its readability or simplifies its structure without changing its results."[13] Recognizing refactoring as a unique collection of tool-enabled disciplines isolates the underlying "model transformation" requirements without adding the complexities of architectural transformation to the equation. Model-to-model transformations may be specified within OMG standards.

We should provide some background on the concepts of model transformation to help position the refactoring and transformation discussions that follow. Johan den Haan defines an eight-step approach that includes concepts such as transformation rules, rule application scope, source and target relationships, and other factors.[14] OMG has expressed approaches for this but these transformations generally define moving from an MDA platform-independent model to a platform-dependent model, which is inherently part of the MDA forward engineering concepts.[15] Forward engineering has applied this concept within the standards community; modernization can similarly apply it too.

For example, model transformation in the case of refactoring would involve source-model-to-target-model transformations where the source would involve poorly rationalized data definitions (i.e., highly redundant, inconsistent) and the target would involve rationalized data definitions. Taking this into a standards framework provides modernization teams the ability to use one tool to gather relevant application metadata and, if required, apply a second tool to refactor those representations. It also supports the idea of refactoring across language and platform domains. There are several reasons for isolating the refactoring standard model transformations from the transformation standard model transformations.[16]

1. Refactoring is a bounded, well-defined set of disciplines that are well understood and provide value without radical architecture changes.
2. The complexity of building all modernization options into a single package is impractical based on the diversity and complexity of the transformations involved.

3. While some applications will be transformed to new target architectures, many more will merely require incremental improvements, retaining their application and data architectural integrity.
4. Addressing refactoring as a separate set of disciplines creates options for project teams and tool vendors as to how and when they wish to refactor applications versus transform those applications to new target architectures.
5. Treating refactoring as a separate discipline will reduce the tendency of modernization teams to migrate flawed architectures into new target environments.

Refactoring can be enabled through metamodel transformations. The process involves defining the model-to-model transformations that would occur to certain KDM, ASTM, or other ADM metamodels as necessary to achieve different refactoring tasks. Consider the following points:[16]

- Populated KDM and ASTM models represent views of the existing IT architecture.
- Programs and systems represented by the populated models are, as a general rule, typically riddled with poor structure, diagnostics, and convoluted logic.
- Flaws include a high degree of inconsistency and redundancy, monolithic (vs. modular) programs, spurious logic, or poorly implemented solutions and other factors too long to list here.
- Structural, diagnostic, and design flaws should be corrected if software or the essence of that software is to survive in current or target architectures.
- Moving flawed systems directly into MDAs without refactoring will propagate these issues into those environments.
- A series of transformational passes between views of these populated models would have the capacity to produce refactored results that could generate refactored applications.
- Model transformation-based refactoring provides a powerful, standardized approach to extending the life of countless millions or billions of lines of software while establishing a baseline for subsequent transformation.

The ADM Refactoring standard is still in the discussion stages within the OMG ADM Task Force.

## ADM TRANSFORMATION

The ADM Transformation standard defines model transformations between the KDM, ASTM, and target architecture paradigms. These target models include, for example, UML, SOA, and other potential representations. Deployment of this standard will complete ADM Task Force efforts in providing a modernization bridge between existing systems and target architectures.

ADM Transformation defines an encoding set of transformational mappings between other ADM standard metamodels and various target architectures. Model transformations, as it applies to the transformation stage of modernization, is already being pursued through research work and related project initiatives. One such effort explored the transformation of domain-specific models to MDA.[17] Even though this approach was limited to the transformation of Web engineering paradigms to MDA, the general applicability of the concept can be expanded into a more generalized form.

For example, KDM is a language- and platform-independent representation of existing IT architectures. This means that several language environments and platform-specific collections of artifacts may be represented within the KDM. Assuming that the target architecture is MDA, using various UML representations, a series of model transformations would be defined to populate UML-based target architecture representations.

Work along these lines has already been pursued by a consortium of organizations from Europe (MODISCO) that moved C and Java applications into a KDM representation, which was transformed into UML2 representations. This was called the MODELPLEX scenario.[18] These types of efforts are becoming more common; however, transforming existing software environments into target architectures — in the absence of refactoring — will merely result in moving problematic architecture and design constructs into new target paradigms, which will propagate serious architectural problems into UML and other MDA target architectures.

The ADM Task Force is responsible for ensuring that these models are synchronized in such a way that vendors can utilize them in a coordinated fashion. This approach will be beneficial to the organizations pursuing modernization projects. The ADM Transformation standard has no set target date.

## SUMMARY

A cross-section of software tool vendors and service providers has emerged to enable the modernization of existing systems. Unfortunately, users and vendors have been working in isolation, often reinventing the wheel. Standardization of modernization metamodels, along with related ADM patterns and metrics libraries, provide vendors, service providers, and the enterprises deploying modernization solutions with a clear roadmap for delivering projects. Standardization of the software modernization process will help businesses reduce the risk of undertaking software improvement initiatives by lessening the time, risk, and cost of software modernizations, improving the effectiveness of modernization tools and extending the ROI on software development projects.

# REFERENCES

1. Architecture-Driven Modernization Standards Roadmap, 12/5/2007, http://adm.omg.org/ADMTF%20Roadmap.pdf.
2. Khusidman Dr V, Ulrich W. Architecture-Driven Modernization: Transforming the Enterprise. http://www.omg.org/docs/admtf/07-12-01.pdf.
3. Business Architecture Working Group. http://bawg.omg.org.
4. http://www.omg.org/mda/.
5. Knowledge Discovery Metamodel Standard. http://www.omg.org/docs/formal/08-01-01.pdf.
6. International Organization for Standardization. http://www.iso.org/iso/home.htm.
7. Abstract Syntax Tree Metamodel. OMG. http://www.omg.org/cgi-bin/doc?admtf/07-09-02.
8. Ulrich W. *Legacy Systems: Transformation Strategies*. Prentice Hall; 2002:221–223.
9. Software Metrics Guide, http://www.comsysprojects.com/SystemTransformation/tmmetricguide.htm.
10. Business Architecture Working Group. Work-in-progress page, http://www.omg-wiki.org/bawg/doku.php.
11. Ulrich W. ADM Visualization White Paper. http://www.omg.org/docs/admtf/08-06-08.pdf. 2008.
12. Bitpip.com Web site, http://www.bitpipe.com/tlist/Data-Visualization.html.
13. Wikipedia online encyclopedia, http://www.wikipedia.org/.
14. Haan J. Classification of model transformation approaches. http://www.theenterprisearchitect.eu/archive/2008/02/18/mda-and-model-transformation. 2009.
15. Model transformation approaches in the MDA. http://www.theenterprisearchitect.eu/archive/2008/02/18/mda-and-model-transformation. 2009.
16. Ulrich W. ADM Refactoring White Paper. http://www.omg.org/docs/admtf/08-06-09.pdf. 2008.
17. Brambilla F, Tisi. A Metamodel Transformation Framework for the Migration of WebML models to MDA. http://ftp.informatik.rwth-aachen.de/Publications/CEUR-WS/Vol-389/paper07.pdf.
18. Modeling solution for complex software systems, Co-funded by the European Community under the Information Society Technology Program. http://www.omg.org/docs/admtf/08-06-13.pdf.

# CHAPTER 4

# Modernization Scenarios

**William Ulrich**

In Chapters 1 through 3 we introduced the disciplines, technologies, and standards needed to deliver architecture-driven modernization solutions. Experience has shown, however, that the majority of managers and IT project teams do not have a wealth of experience in planning and deploying modernization projects. Many teams are unaware of how to articulate project benefits and how to determine the best approach. To address these requirements, modernization solutions should be prepackaged in a way that communicates the power and the applicability of modernization to the IT planning and project teams.

The most effective way to prepackage modernization solutions is in the form of modernization scenarios. Scenarios allow executives to see where and how modernization can be applied to various businesses and IT challenges. Scenarios also provide planning teams with project planning templates and estimating models. In addition, scenarios provide deployment teams with a roadmap of the disciplines required to achieve the benefits of a given scenario.

A modernization scenario can be defined as an ongoing initiative such as portfolio management, a project such as migrating from one platform to another, or a series of project phases (i.e., a super project). The super project is deployed in many major phases. This would be the case, for example, when consolidating, redesigning, and redeploying an application in a model-driven architecture.[1] This chapter provides an overview of the modernization scenario concept, guidelines for crafting scenarios, and an overview of selected modernization scenarios.

## SCENARIOS FORM BASIS FOR MODERNIZATION ROADMAPS

Disciplines, technologies, and standards provide three corners of the four-cornered foundation of modernization. Modernization disciplines, which break down into a series of discreet tasks and subtasks under the assessment,

## CONTENTS

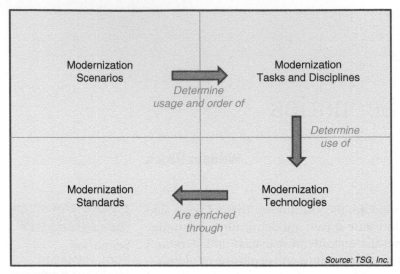

Source: TSG, Inc.

**FIGURE 4.1**

*Four corners of modernization.*

refactoring, and transformation stages of modernization, are used to construct the project plan. This can be done from scratch but it is more effective if there are project planning templates that teams can use to jump-start their efforts. Figure 4.1 shows the relationships between modernization scenarios, modernization tasks and disciplines, and the relationship between disciplines, modernization technologies, and modernization standards.

Figure 4.1 summarizes the four corners of modernization. You can think of various assessment, refactoring, and transformation disciplines as a series of tasks and subtasks that fit into one or more project planning templates. These tasks and subtasks can be assembled in many ways, depending on the applied scenario. In some cases a task may not be required and sidestepped entirely. For example, a data architecture project requires assessing data definitions and data structures, rationalizing those representations, porting these into a data modeling facility, refining data designs, refactoring application data accesses, migrating physical data structures, and redeploying the new data architecture and related application. A data architecture migration scenario would omit, however, a number of other modernization tasks. This scenario would, for example, exclude business rule extraction, workflow mapping and migration, and migration to a services-oriented architecture (SOA) because they are not needed to meet the data related objectives such a project.

Once tasks required to deploy a given scenario have been identified using a scenario planning template, analysts must then determine how each task and subtask can be automated using various modernization tools. The relationship between tasks and technologies, shown in Figure 4.1, dictates that the project task drives the choice of modernization tooling. For example, if a project team needs to analyze data definition usage and data structure composition, analysts would need to identify a tool that fits these requirements. Ideally, a general purpose modernization workbench would have most of the required features for a given project and related project tasks.

An all-too-common mistake made by project teams is that they reverse the direction of the arrows in Figure 4.1 and let tools drive the tasks to be performed. Analysts further compound this mistake by allowing tool-driven tasks to determine the selection and alignment of tasks within the project roadmap and plan. The result is that business objectives take a backseat to tool-based deliverables and activities. When this occurs, and it is alarmingly common, the project's focus is lost and the effort ends in failure.

Reversing this trend is the key to success in modernization projects and this can be accomplished through the use of modernization scenarios that are driven by objectives and are deliverable and results focused. If this does not occur, project teams will continue to struggle with trying to build retroactive justification for the actions that they have taken, which leads to a high percentage of canceled modernization projects.

## BENEFITS OF SCENARIO-BASED MODERNIZATION

A scenario-based approach to modernization has a number of benefits. One important benefit is that scenario-based project templates help those individuals who are unfamiliar with modernization envision where and how to apply modernization concepts in response to a given set of business and IT demands. For example, management does not immediately think of modernization-based refactoring as a vehicle for incrementally moving to an SOA. The SOA migration scenario, however, provides a roadmap to SOA with a focus on application and data architecture refactoring and transformation. The SOA migration scenario, which can take multiple paths, helps analysts determine the modernization tasks and tools necessary for deploying an SOA migration effort.

Scenarios additionally provide templates for outlining program objectives, project plans, roles, and staged deliverables. This in turn dramatically reduces the time to build, estimate, and justify project plans for modernization initiatives. Templates help define modernization tasks and subtasks within a project plan and specify the roles and skills required to plan and execute a project. For example, a language conversion or transliteration scenario would not involve redesigning application data structures. Therefore, no data architect would be required for such a project.

Similarly, a data architecture migration scenario, which redesigns and redeploys existing data structures into cohesive, relational data architecture would not require language conversion tasks and not require language conversion specialists. Scenarios not only identify which tasks are required to meet a given set of business and IT objectives but also allow analysts to determine which modernization tasks can be omitted from a given project because they do not contribute to the project's business and IT objectives.

Ultimately, the use of project planning templates is a useful way to rapidly determine where and how modernization can be applied to various projects. Not only are project planning windows reduced, but the process of communicating the role of modernization to executive and management teams can be streamlined through the use of project templates, estimating guidelines, task and tool identification, and role definition.

## MODERNIZATION SCENARIOS: RELATIONSHIP TO BUSINESS & IT ARCHITECTURE

Modernization scenarios fall along a spectrum when viewed from an architectural perspective. In Chapter 1, we examined how business and IT architecture can be modernized from an existing to a target architecture, either independently or through phased synchronization. We also examined how some initiatives impact the technical architecture while other initiatives additionally impact the application and data architecture. Different modernization scenarios similarly impact the business and IT architectures to varying degrees.

In Figure 4.2, initially introduced in Chapter 1, we superimpose business and IT project scenarios over the migration model representing the paths that can be taken between the existing business and IT architecture to the target business and IT architecture. The superimposition of these scenarios sets the context for related projects, role definitions, tasks, and expectations.

Consider, for example, a replacement or rewrite project that combines aspects of Greenfield development and modernization tasks. Such a scenario would require an analysis of and mapping between business architecture and IT

**FIGURE 4.2**

*Scenarios mapped against business and IT architecture modernization paths.*

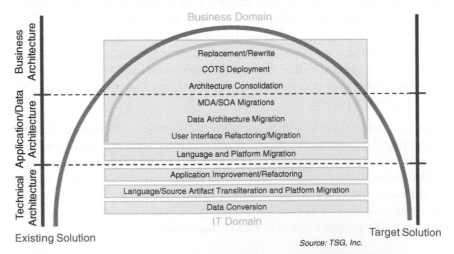

architecture. In this scenario, the path to a new system must travel through the business architecture as well as the IT architecture. As a result, this scenario would require mapping the as-is IT architecture to the as-is business architecture, determining the to-be view of the business architecture, crafting a business transformation roadmap, assessing the impact of the business transformation roadmap on the as-is IT architecture, driving to-be business representations into the to-be IT architecture view, and developing the transition strategy between the as-is and to-be IT architecture.

This approach establishes the broad framework for this scenario and clearly differentiates it from the traditional Greenfield/top-down approach to systems replacement. As this framework is driven down to subsequent levels of details, the modernization tasks and subtasks required emerge and form into an assessment, refactoring, and transformation plan. This approach works for any scenario, as long as that scenario meets business and IT objectives.

A stark contrast to the previous replacement scenario is the Language/Source Artifact Transliteration and Platform Migration. This scenario moves from the as-is technical architecture to the to-be technical architecture with very little impact on the application, data, and business architecture. The business people who use the systems undergoing migration may not even know that it happened. A scenario such as this would be primarily driven by IT technical requirements versus business requirements.

The scenario template for the transliteration scenario and resulting deployment plan would differ radically from the replacement/rewrite scenario. As-is IT architecture analysis is limited to a technical assessment and target architecture mapping is limited to the target technical architecture requirements. Business architecture analysis and mapping is not required and there would be limited analysis of the existing application and data architecture, because those architectures remain unchanged from a business perspective. The roles of application architects, data architects, and subject matter experts are limited while the roles of business architects and subject matter experts are not required at all. In addition, there is typically a significant role for outside expertise, because migration work is normally outsourced to a service provider.

Placing modernization projects in context using scenarios, driven by business and/or IT requirements, provides a clear roadmap for all participants. If one party feels that there are inconsistencies with a given set of project goals, business and IT sponsors and project owners could use an alternative template to drive their requirements into a modernization plan. One issue we caution against is the risk of applying a low-level (i.e., technical architecture) scenario and expecting that the approach will yield benefits normally associated with a more far-reaching (i.e., business level) scenario. This is shockingly common and results in cancelled projects and angry project sponsors. This is where the concepts in Figure 4.2 help position one's thinking and ensure that all parties are on the same page with project objectives, realistic benefits, and the approach for achieving those objectives and benefits.

## UNDERSTANDING THE USE AND STRUCTURE OF MODERNIZATION SCENARIOS

There are several ways to draft a modernization project plan. One approach involves creating the plan from scratch based on business and IT requirements. This approach requires knowledge of how to apply modernization disciplines within the context of an overall set of requirements; knowledge of the modernization tasks, subtasks, and related project dependencies and deliverables; the ability to derive and apply various metrics to estimating models; a clear concept of role definitions; and an understanding of when to leave out unnecessary tasks while incorporating essential tasks. Pursuing this option requires a unique understanding of modernization that is not common in a given project management office (PMO) or elsewhere within the enterprise.

A second approach involves handing project ownership off to a third-party service provider. This reduces the need to fully understand all aspects of a modernization project, yet can also yield problematic results because you have handed off all aspects of the modernization effort, even portions that require in-house participation. Management justifies this approach by signifying that these projects are evaluated by results and not by the process used by the service provider. But even under this approach, management may not find out that the results are unacceptable until it is too late to correct the situation.

In-house management, therefore, cannot sidestep its responsibility for understanding and managing modernization-based projects. For example, a systems integrator was chartered with performing an extensive business rule extraction project for a financial institution. The integrator bypassed several essential prerequisite analysis steps that resulted in elongating project time frames, driving up project costs, and devaluing project deliverables. Fortunately, the integrator called in a third party to catch this problem. The client, however, was totally oblivious to the fact that this project was spiraling into a chasm of failure. Even more problematic was the fact that the entire set of tasks was unlikely to meet the majority of project objectives. We contend that organizations that outsource or in-source modernization projects must have a fundamental understanding of the work to be done — within the context of a given modernization scenario — to determine the validity of the overall project plan, time frames, and expected returns on investment. They must also be able to clearly associate the work performed with overall business and IT objectives.

A third and more practical approach involves starting with a scenario template as a guide to verifying that the approach matches symptoms and requirements; identifying tasks, subtasks, and related dependencies; and working from a baseline understanding as to what needs to be accomplished from a project perspective. The project planners must also clearly tie intermediate and long-term deliverables to business and IT goals.

Certain commercial templates are available from service providers and other sources to support this third approach to modernization planning. For example, commercially available modernization scenarios have been around for many years in the form of methodologies and methodology templates. One such methodology template is based on the Transformation and Integration Methodology (TIM),[2] which was originally called The Systems Redevelopment Methodology (TSRM).[3] The TSRM-built scenarios are a predefined set of tasks and subtasks, metrics, estimating models, and work plan building tools. The TIM retains and provides access to the publicly posted templates, but public access to task and subtask details and estimating models is restricted.

In other cases, scenarios have been provided in certain publications[4] as well as in work by standards committees. The ADM Task Force drafted a white paper on modernization scenarios that is used as a benchmark for the need and viability of various modernization standards as they move through the standards roadmap.[5] In addition, professional service firms use project planning templates based on the specific scenario pursued.

Unless a modernization scenario is unique enough to have never been performed or attempted before, project planning teams should leverage preexisting scenario templates as the basis for modernization project planning. Whether drafting a scenario from scratch or transforming an existing scenario into a customized plan, there are certain basics that a project planning team should understand.

## Attributes of a Modernization Scenario

A modernization scenario has a number of structural attributes that allow planning teams to create project plans. These include:

- Symptoms: Provide management with insights that this scenario may play a role in addressing a given set of business and/or IT issues. For example, consider a situation where there are several claims processing teams for different product lines. These redundancies are a symptom that would point to the architecture consolidation scenario. Other symptoms might include business costs associated with multiple teams, inconsistency in claim processes across product lines involving the same customer base, or difficulty in managing related customer calls across product lines. Identifying and matching symptoms to scenarios is the first step toward scenario identification.

■ Requirements: Define the business and IT needs or demands that would address certain symptoms. Certain requirements would, for example, emerge as a result of the prior example involving the redundant claims units. Management wants to consolidate business teams and how they function. This may start with business process or capability alignment, but will ultimately result in an application and data architecture consolidation. The requirements in this example might include aligning application and data architectures to the to-be view of consolidated organizational units, business capabilities, business processes, and business semantics. These requirements would further draw project planning teams into using some form of the architecture consolidation scenario.

■ Work Task Breakdown: Provides the task and subtask structure of a given scenario. Modernization scenario templates and projects are normally phased into assessment and planning efforts and subsequent implementation tasks. Assessment tasks may include cross-architectural analysis as well as more detailed analysis steps. Implementation tasks rely on the scenario and selected approach and may be heavily oriented toward refactoring, transformation, or a combination of both.

Consider the sample tasks and subtasks in Figure 4.3 that have been extracted from the assessment phase of a consolidation scenario. The environmental and data definition analysis tasks and related subtasks are a portion of the project-level assessment that would be required to support consolidation efforts. Each subtask ties back to an overall methodology that provides the detailed guidelines and related tool usage recommendations required to complete a given subtask.[6]

Figure 4.3 represents only a small cross-section of an assessment and implementation scenario. The scenario slice represented in Figure 4.3 contains 13 subtasks within two tasks. The overall scenario actually contains hundreds of subtasks across scores of tasks. Each subtask, in turn, breaks down into a series of steps or detailed guidelines. Decomposing a project in this manner allows management, planning teams, sponsors where appropriate, and implementation teams to agree on the overall roadmap and approach.

A modernization architecture consolidation program based on the scenario template depicted (in part) in Figure 4.3 would be expanded significantly as it is turned into a multi-phased project with interim deliverables. Consider a situation, depicted in Figure 4.4, where there are three claims units, three sets of unique business processes, three sets of user interfaces, three backend

**Assess IS Application Infrastructure**

**Environmental analysis**

Identify and Categorize Physical System Components

Identify and Categorize External System Components

Inventory and Cross Reference Mainframe Components

Review and Refine Environmental Analysis Results

Produce Environmental Counts and Scores

Produce Environmental Analysis Narrative Summary

**Data definition analysis**

Perform System-Wide Data Definition Analysis

Perform Physical Data Analysis

Assign Data Definition Metric Counts

Calculate Data Definition Metric Scores

Produce Data Definition Narrative Summary

Review Data Definition Analysis Results

Assess Multi-System Data Definition Usage

Source: Comsys, Redundant Systems Consolidation
Scenario/Selected Assessment Tasks

**FIGURE 4.3**

*Partial slice of a consolidation scenario — selected assessment tasks.*

applications, and three customer databases — all of which support claims across multiple product lines and with overlapping customers.

The situation shown in Figure 4.4 requires multiple levels of assessment. An initial enterprise assessment would fully scope each environment, system-to-system interfaces, business interfaces, business process impacts, capability and application mappings, the overall data architecture, and other aspects of the business architecture/IT. Based on the findings of this assessment, a series of project-level assessments would be enacted to determine the exact mappings across applications, interfaces, and data structures.

The results of this staged analysis drive various consolidation deployment projects. Based on the target architecture, this is likely to involve a series of refactoring and transformation tasks, with each stage of the effort delivering a new target application and data architecture that is synchronized with the evolving business

**FIGURE 4.4**

*Example of business/
IT situation-driving
consolidation scenario.*

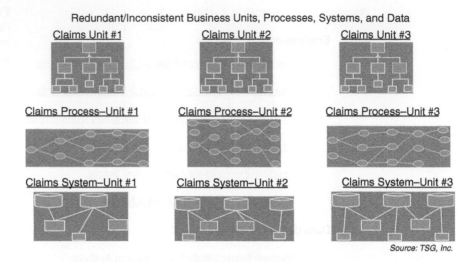

architecture. Ultimately, scenario templates provide an excellent starting point for a project plan and — when coupled with project management tools, metrics, and estimating guidelines — go a long way toward demystifying the work involved in crafting modernization strategy and project plans.

## COMMON MODERNIZATION SCENARIOS

The following scenario descriptions overview several sample modernization scenarios, why one would pursue such a scenario, and the benefits of performing that scenario. Subsequent chapters provide case study examples that show how these scenarios have been applied in practice. While there are many potential modernization scenarios, we have provided a brief list of the scenarios as depicted in Figure 4.1. In addition, we have added one additional scenario to address the issue of IT portfolio management, a goal that numerous organizations have established as a way of managing IT portfolios from a more strategic perspective.

We describe each scenario as a way to establish the kinds of modernization projects that organizations can pursue. These generic templates provide a backdrop for the case studies presented in subsequent chapters.

### IT Portfolio Management

As organizations seek to optimize and align IT environments with business capabilities, processes, and requirements, the issue of IT portfolio management has taken a much higher profile. IT portfolio management is an initiative, as opposed to a one-time project, and should be recognized as an ongoing program. IT portfolio management is defined as the "application of systematic management to large classes of items managed by enterprise IT." Examples include planned initiatives, projects, and ongoing IT services (such as application support)."[7]

This definition is project-based and omits IT assets such as systems, data structures, and other artifacts that define the IT environment. This is problematic from our perspective since the projects and services are temporary, whereas the assets are permanent. In addition, a given project or series of services could cease for a period of time and have varying degrees of impact, but the systems must continue to work without interruption. IT artifacts must be incorporated into the portfolio management definition and this scenario assumes that this is the case.

Although there is a perceived need for IT portfolio management, the practice has been defined too narrowly to only providing transparency into temporal organizational structures — projects and initiatives. Management should rightly include projects into this scenario, but should also include a mapping of IT assets to those initiatives and to the business capabilities, processes, and organizational units that rely on connecting related artifacts defined within IT assets. This business mapping process relies on connecting related artifacts defined within the IT architecture and business architecture. A quick guide to setting up a modernization-based view of IT portfolio management is as follows.

- Establish a foundational accounting of IT assets, initially at a high level, to create an inventory of IT artifacts.
- Map the application to business capabilities within the business architecture.
- Drive high-level asset analysis into more detailed artifact mappings, based on related requirements for assessing or modernizing different portions of the portfolio.
- Map ongoing IT and business projects and initiatives to IT assets.
- Manage the portfolio mapping to support project planning, prioritization, evaluation, and ongoing management.

The IT portfolio management scenario relies on many of the enterprise and project-level assessment techniques discussed in Chapter 1. The depth of analysis begins at a very high level, using the enterprise assessment concepts, and drills down to deeper levels of analysis as follow-on scenario requirements emerge. Artifact management requires repository-based tooling.

## Replacement/Rewrite Scenario

A replacement/rewrite scenario assumes that executives have a reason to replace one or more existing applications with a new application in some target architecture. The assumption is that there is enough dissatisfaction with the current set of applications that management has decided to move to a significantly different architecture application and data. This scenario also assumes that a decision as to how to proceed is still pending.

In other words, a rewrite, commercial-off-the-shelf (COTS) package deployment, migration and redesign, or automated transformation options are all on the table. This scenario examines available options and recommends one or a combination of modernization scenarios, possibly coupled with new development and/or COTS options. "The nature of this scenario establishes and tests a multitude of hypotheses as the basis for the new system."[8] A summary of the approach is as follows.

- Determine or obtain high-level business and IT requirements from all relevant and affected parties, and craft a vision for what they collectively want to achieve.

- Establish a series of hypotheses that would fulfill the requirements for the new replacement environment. This typically includes some combination of a rewrite and selective modernization, a pure rewrite, COTS with selective reuse of the current architecture, aspects of data redesign and migration, or various migration and/or transformation-based scenarios.

- Perform an enterprise assessment on the portions of the IT architecture that are to be replaced.

- Assess the as-is business architecture that relies on the portion of the IT architecture being replaced and map business capabilities to be replaced to the as-is IT architecture.

- Review strategic and tactical business plans related to the aforementioned capabilities. This establishes the to-be business architecture.

- Determine the impacts of business requirements on existing business and IT architectures and create target business and IT architectural views that satisfy these requirements.

- Test each hypothesis against the transition requirements between the as-is and to-be business and IT architectures. This includes synchronizing IT changes with business changes, examining general COTS options, and assessing the amount of reusable business functionality that exists within the as-is IT architecture.

- Identify which hypothesis makes most sense by establishing one or more project plans, comparing cost/benefits of each plan, and selecting the best approach.

This scenario may be formally or informally deployed. It may only take a short period of time to determine that the amount of functional reuse in the current system dictates a high degree of modernization and reuse. Conversely, a 45-day assessment of the existing business, application, data, and technical architectures may determine that the amount of reusable business value contained in the existing applications is low and a heavy rewrite or COTS focus is warranted.

Note that this process is generally sidestepped by management and planning teams because "they already know which approach is best." The high degree of IT project failures cited in Chapter 1 would suggest that executives may not always know what is best "in their gut" and the replacement/rewrite scenario should be applied more formally. This scenario will direct planning teams to one of the scenarios described in the following sections where varying degrees of new development work may be incorporated into the SOA, model-driven architecture (MDA), or consolidation scenarios.

## COTS Package Deployment Scenario

Deploying a COTS package is highly invasive to existing business, application, and data architectures. Deployment teams must assess the current environment, determine overlap and uniqueness between the package and the existing environment, map and redesign the existing data architecture to the package data architecture, save and integrate existing application functionality into the new architecture, and deactivate existing functionality. In addition, business and IT architects and analysts must map as-is business processes and capabilities to the application architecture to support transition planning.

The modernization aspects of such a project include multiple levels of assessments, existing application reuse and migration; user interface retooling; data architecture redesign and migration; and selective application deactivation. Major phases of this scenario include:

- Creating a high-level map of existing application and data architectures and mapping these architectures to the business capabilities supported by the proposed COTS solution.

- Systematically comparing the functionality of various packages against target requirements and the functionality running in the existing application environment. This assessment provides the foundation for selecting the appropriate COTS package.

- Determining which portions of the existing application architecture should be retained, retired, or integrated into the target COTS architecture. This involves business capability and process mapping, retooling of user interfaces in conjunction with shadow systems and business processes, and the extraction and reuse of unique functionality from the existing application architecture.

■ Performing data mapping, integration, and migration. Existing data tends to be defined inconsistently and redundantly, making it difficult to move cleanly into the target data architecture. Data definition rationalization, redesign, and data migration efforts ensure that existing data is migrated accordingly.

The statistics related to COTS deployment failure, as well as our experience in this area, point to the fact that organizations have not analyzed existing IT and business architecture and requirements adequately when selecting and deploying a COTS package. Using the assessment and selected refactoring and transformation tasks defined under the modernization umbrella, organizations can streamline these efforts and ensure that the package is deployed in a systematic fashion.

## Architecture Consolidation Scenario

The architecture consolidation scenario — used as an earlier example of how a scenario ties back to various modernization tasks — is a common, yet often ignored, modernization opportunity. There is a definite need for architecture consolidation given that "as much as 60% to 80% of the functionality in silos may be redundant or duplicated in other parts of the business."[9] As depicted in Figure 4.4, redundancies across the business and IT architecture must be dealt with accordingly. The to-be architecture, whether it is SOA, MDA, or even a code-based environment, dictates the target paradigm while the target business architecture defines the functional alignment required. The approach to assessing and consolidating existing application functionality, data definitions, and data is summarized in the following list.

■ Determine the business capability, process, user interface, application logic, data definition, shadow systems, and related redundancies to be used as candidates for consolidation.

■ Create a cross-silo, cross-functional consolidation roadmap based on current architecture assessment and requirements analysis.

■ Select a baseline application and data architecture that will be used as a mapping target for the other application and data architectures targeted for consolidation. Alternatively, select and deploy an approach where the new target architecture is used as the baseline and populated with consolidated functionality from each existing, redundant application and data architecture.

■ Phase in the deployment over a window of time using various refactoring and transformation disciplines.

There will likely be aspects of redundancy consolidation found in most strategic migrations to SOA or MDA. The approaches and lessons in this scenario, therefore, should be carried over to these other scenarios. These types of projects should be phased in carefully and only with full cooperation and commitment from the business. One caution must be given regarding this scenario: If the business architecture cannot be consolidated because business professionals have no appetite for consolidation-based benefits, then IT will not be able to drive this effort forward by itself. We have seen this attempted and it has failed miserably.

## MDA Migration Scenario

Transforming code-based software architectures into MDAs requires a series of phased activities that involve significant refactoring and transformation. The first rule is to not assume that there can be a direct, one-for-one transformation of code-based artifacts into a UML or other model-driven representations. Hand-crafted software systems, particularly systems that have been heavily modified over many years, contain a large degree of functional redundancy, inactive logic, fragmented design structures, and implementation-dependent logic.

These architectural weaknesses can be addressed by either refactoring these structures and/or using sophisticated data definition and business rule extraction tools and techniques to selectively realign and populate reusable functionality into the new target architecture. A summary of the approach is as follows.

- Assess the existing business capabilities and related application systems that are to be replaced by the new applications.
- Solidify the target architecture to support major business capabilities and subject areas.
- Determine the degree of reuse desired; for example, some projects may focus on actually transforming code to models while other projects focus on validating and streamlining strategic design models.
- Incrementally migrate existing business functionality and data definitions to ensure that target architectures reflect actual business data and critical business functionality.
- Selectively and incrementally deactivate existing application functionality as the new architecture comes online.

One approach used to accomplish incremental migration was employed at a government agency. A complex application performed three unique functions and only one function was deployed in the first version of the MDA. The existing application had to remain intact during this transition, but the data was diverted to the new replacement application. This effectively "starved" the existing application of data for one of its three functions, while retaining the integrity of external data interfaces that needed to remain intact.

As time progressed, the old application would ultimately not be processing any data and the new architecture would take over. This particular example focused very heavily on design verification of data usage and business rules and focused less on the actual reuse of existing systems functionality within the new architecture.

## SOA Transformation

The transformation to an SOA is performed in stages. Much of the work to date on SOA has focused on establishing the technical aspects of the architecture as well as smaller deployments related to add-on systems and functionality. Moving to SOA on any scale, however, must incorporate existing application and data architectures and use modernization-based approaches.

The SOA transformation approach involves moving from redundant, stove-pipe application and data architectures to business specific components, derived from existing application functionality, which have been refactored and aligned accordingly. The following high-level steps provide the basis for a modernization-based SOA transformation scenario.

- Determine which business capabilities should be focused on as the basis for identifying business services.

- Map existing application architecture to business architecture with a focus on mapping capabilities to applications, business processes to user interfaces, and business processes to system workflows.

- Establish a migration strategy that determines the target architecture, such as J2EE, and prioritize migration of business capabilities and related application artifacts. Note that capabilities should be decomposed at least to level three.

- Focus early phases of the migration on user interface/business process mapping, refactoring, and transformation. This approach will create initial services and related orchestration based on the automation of manual tasks, elimination of shadow systems, and decoupling of user interface logic from business logic.

- Map existing capabilities and processes to application functionality, interfaces, and workflows. This provides a foundation for filling in the new SOA. This requires the refactoring and segregation of business logic from user interface and data access logic as well as the transformation of that functionality to the target architecture.

- Identify data architecture migration requirements as required to support the overall SOA transformation approach.

- Continue a phased program of SOA migration as priorities and business benefits warrant.

SOA is a long-term goal and beneficial conceptually to reduce the inconsistency and redundancy deployed across today's silo architectures. As business streamlining and consolidation continues to drive requirements, IT can use SOA to streamline processes and capability deployment for the business.

## Data Architecture Migration Scenario

The data architecture migration scenario transforms existing data structures from redundant, cumbersome, and non-relational structures to a data architecture that mirrors the needs of the business. Pitfalls include ignoring business requirements, sidestepping relational design techniques, not incorporating related or redundant data in the project, not utilizing qualified data analysts, and treating the project as a straight conversion effort. The approach should focus on:

- Determining strategic data requirements within the context of other initiatives and business requirements.
- Assessing the data definitions and data structures related to the target data architecture migration.
- Rationalizing data definitions of interest into a consistent set of data definitions based on business semantics, and feeding these definitions into bottom-up and top-down data modeling efforts.
- Deploying target data structures and performing incremental migrations from the current set of data structures.
- Optionally, creating a data bridge to facilitate the transformation process.
- Isolating, consolidating, and reconciling data access logic within the existing applications that are impacted by the data migration.

## User Interface Refactoring Scenario

User interface refactoring and transformation (this scenario addresses both refactoring and transformation) should be driven by business process streamlining and consolidation, along with near-term business productivity and cost-reduction objectives. This approach ensures that the work performed on user interfaces will drive long-term modernization efforts, establish a foundation for certain types of user oriented services, and provide a gateway toward other modernization scenarios. Major categories of work include:

- Mapping relevant business processes and user interfaces that trigger system-related activities.
- Streamlining and consolidating business processes as a driver toward new user interface design and deployments.

- Developing and deploying new front-ends to automate manual business processes, replace shadow systems, and consolidate backend "green screen" and other older front-ends. (This is done using agile design and development techniques that deliver rapid returns in days, weeks, or months.)

- Evolve front-end architectures into more mature services over time and transition to additional modernization scenarios based on the evolution of these front-end environments.

## Language/Platform Migration Scenario

Moving systems from one language environment and platform to another is driven by technological obsolescence and the desire to standardize applications to an organizational standard. This scenario does not involve any functional or data redesign beyond that which is essential to the platform migration. This scenario is marked by a high degree of automation, coupling of refactoring and transformation, and migration from procedural source code environments to object-based source code environments.

This particular scenario performs a one-for-one transformation from an existing system to a new system under the target architecture and does not involve complex consolidations as discussed in other scenarios. Major tasks include:

- Highly automated analysis of the existing environment with a focus on aligning the current system to target architectural requirements.
- Refactoring and transformation through modernization workbench environments to achieve a one-for-one transformation to the new target (typically Java, C#, or similar object-based environments).
- Redeployment of the application in the new target environment.

## Application Improvement Scenario

The application improvement scenario is comprised of several sub-scenarios, all of which address "in-place" refactoring of applications. This scenario is used in situations where there is no immediate need to move to a new target architecture or the situation dictates a measured migration where the system is cleaned up then ported to the target architecture.

The goal of this scenario is to improve the robustness, integrity, quality, consistency, and/or performance of applications. Activities include the correction of program or system flaws (e.g., recursion), source code restructuring, data definition and source code rationalization, field size standardization, or other system refactoring tasks. Major tasks, which may be performed independently or collectively, are as follows.

- Remove structural diagnostics from the code including syntactically and semantically inactive code, violations of structured coding protocols, runaway logic, recursion, violations of storage protocols, and similar diagnostics.
- Rationalize and standardize data definitions across a system or set of related systems.
- Restructure the code to conform to structured coding standards.
- Slice up large modules into functionally aligned subroutines.
- Reaggregate source code to segregate business, data access, and user interface logic into separate routines or modules.

## Language/Source Artifact Transliteration and Platform Migration Scenario

This "lift and shift" scenario involves converting one or more information systems from one language to another language. It is typically driven by the need to eliminate a given platform, language, or related technology. The scenario involves no architectural changes and, as a rule, the language remains constant while the code is adjusted to work under a new compiler. Platform migration is generally coupled with and a main goal of this effort. Major tasks include:

- Converting an existing language to a target compiler.
- Converting related system artifacts as required.
- Deploying the system on a new platform.

Note that this lift and shift concept was discussed in Chapter 1. This is a technological migration and is almost always driven by IT operating cost reductions. These cost reductions do not always come to pass and the nature of this scenario is that it typically creates an emulation environment that has become a dead-end architecture for application and business areas which have performed this work on selected applications. In other words the long-term risks of this approach can outweigh the near-term cost benefits.

## Data Conversion Scenario

Data conversions have been performed for many years. This is a conversion from one data structure to another, but does not involve architectural redesign. For example, this scenario may involve converting one set of indexed files on one platform to another set of indexed files on another platform. Unfortunately, this process is used when a more business-driven transformation should be warranted. Tasks include:

- Identifying and analyzing the files to be converted.
- Determining the indexed or related changes required.
- Performing the physical data migration.
- Adjusting the source code data access as required.

# SELECTING AND COMBINING MODERNIZATION SCENARIOS

The previously discussed sample modernization scenarios do not represent an exhaustive list of potential modernization project options. Most companies have a long list of project requirements that involve existing application and data assets. Most of these projects will combine aspects of common modernization scenarios as well as aspects of Greenfield replacement and COTS deployment. The hybrid nature of modernization projects means that management, analysts, and project planning teams must be creative in terms of structuring and proposing solutions to business and IT issues.

Consider a situation where executives know that they have inconsistencies in the data aggregated from multiple financial centers across the enterprise. They also know that there are certain redundancies in customer information and financial data across these same areas. Each area has its own set of systems and data. There is no clear understanding, however, of the degree of functional overlap across these areas, nor is there an agreed-upon approach for addressing these issues. More information is required to make an intelligent assessment of the situation and craft a solution. This is where a modernization assessment would come into play.

The situation we just described requires that executives not jump to a solution when the problem remains undefined and the situation remains cloudy. Yet this is done far too often. In many organizations, executives look at this situation and dictate a COTS package, Greenfield replacement or other solution — even when such a move has very little chance of delivering value and may be a huge waste of money. In a difficult economic climate, a small series of steps, each of which deliver incremental value, is a much more prudent approach. Determining the value of proposed end-game solutions and the series of steps needed to achieve those solutions requires an assessment of the existing IT architecture and, as a general rule, business architecture.

## Getting Started with an Assessment

Determining the combination of enterprise and project-level assessment tasks to be performed, as a way to uncover a roadmap going forward, requires some degree of modernization analysis skills coupled with the ability to bring clarity and transparency to business and IT architectures. Arguments against these assessments are common. Management says "we understand the current environment and do not need any additional analysis of the as-is architecture." If this were true, the IT project failure rates and wasted IT investment dollars cited in Chapter 1 would not be so significant and the alignment of new projects and aging architecture would have a better track record.

We always ask executives a simple question when this arises: Would a responsible surgeon begin operating without conducting a series of increasingly detailed diagnostic tests? The answer is no. So why would you let your IT organization perform the equivalent of replacing every organ in your body without any analysis whatsoever to determine what really needs to be accomplished. These assessments provide the foundation for building a scenario-based modernization roadmap to address the true needs of the enterprise and may be applied to projects or initiatives of any size or scope.

While a given scenario may seem apparent, the situation can change once an assessment is completed and the entire picture is exposed. So even in situations where a given scenario is assumed, management should keep an open mind regarding the ultimate approach. IT projects are characterized by too many false starts, the belief in silver bullet solutions, wasted investment money, and major failures to claim that assessment efforts are a waste of time. The result of these efforts will create the basis for selecting the right combination of tasks and subtasks to address the needs of the enterprise.

## Combining Scenarios

When seeking solutions to various business and IT issues, management should be creative and look at a mix-and-match approach that addresses their requirements. Any given project is likely to require some type of hybrid solution. All situations are unique, yet most projects can draw from the common modernization scenario templates outlined in this chapter.

Consider, for example, that many projects can leverage aspects of the user interface refactoring scenario and the code improvement scenario. These two scenarios play an important role in SOA transformation and numerous other projects driven by business process realignment. Having well-articulated requirements and a clear understanding of the as-is architecture provide the basis for selecting the right creative mix-and-match modernization solutions.

In one instance a situation may dictate a partial COTS, partial rewrite, and partial modernization approach. We have worked on projects where a package was partially deployed (only 25% of the overall functionality) and additional functionality needed to be developed to replace existing systems functionality. The modernization portion of the project required multiple levels of assessment, data definition analysis, business rule extraction, and selectively slicing away portions of old subsystems as new functionality was brought online.

When deploying a mix-and-match approach, unique solutions may need to be crafted as interim solutions. Such is the case when large data structures are to be migrated that cross several application environments. This may involve temporary bridges or interfaces that would be deactivated later. Any interim solution should be viewed with appropriate caution because funding on a project could be cut at any point based on difficult economic climates. This includes bridge-based solutions, temporary front-end applications or partially migrated or partially deployed applications, or data structures. Therefore, deployed interfaces and other structures should be reasonably robust solutions.

The mix-and-match approach, assuming that the prerequisite assessments have been performed, requires combining tasks from various scenarios into an overall initiative that provides interim deliverables and value while continuing to work toward an overall vision and long-term target architecture. Depending on in-house project management approaches, each phase of a given initiative or program may be packaged into a given project.

Different project phases may also utilize different approaches. For example, an initial project phase may use an outsourced approach to migrate selected applications to a common environment. Once systems have been moved to the shared technical architecture, additional consolidation may proceed using an in-source or in-house approach. This approach makes sense if most of the targeted systems are already in the target technical architecture. In other situations, where the applications of interest reside on a mainframe, the order of this work may be reversed. Each case requires careful analysis to ensure that the right approach is pursued at the correct point in an overall initiative and to ensure that business and IT architectures remain synchronized through the transition process.

## SUMMARY

Scenarios offer real-world approaches for applying modernization tasks and subtasks, tools, and services to business and technical challenges. The scenarios discussed in this chapter are the most common modernization options. Scenarios also support a mix-and-match approach to building in-house strategies and project plans. The most important thing to remember is that scenarios, customized around business and IT requirements, drive modernization solutions whereas modernization tasks, subtasks, services, and tools play a supporting role in these efforts.

## REFERENCES

1. Architecture-Driven Modernization Scenarios. http://adm.omg.org/ADMTF_ Scenario_White_Paper(pdf).pdf. 2006:2.
2. Comsys Transformation & Integration Methodology (TIM) Scenarios. http://www. comsysprojects.com/SystemTransformation/TMscenarios.htm.
3. HCL James Martin, Inc. announces TSRM 6.0. *Business Wire*. 1996; http://findarticles. com/p/articles/mi_m0EIN/is_1996_April_3/ai_18151103.

4. Ulrich W. *Legacy Systems: Transformation Strategies.* Prentice Hall; 2002:114–128.
5. Architecture-Driven Modernization Scenarios, 2006, http://adm.omg.org/ADMTF_Scenario_White_Paper(pdf).pdf.
6. Comsys Transformation & Integration Methodology (TIM). http://www.comsysprojects.com/SystemTransformation/TMethodology.htm.
7. Wikipedia, http://en.wikipedia.org/wiki/IT_portfolio_management.
8. Application Replacement Scenario, Comsys. http://www.comsysprojects.com/SystemTransformation/usrm_replacement.htm.
9. Aligning Technology and Business: Applying Patterns for Legacy Transformation. *IBM Systems Journal.* 2005;44:1.

# Modernization Case Studies

# CHAPTER 5

# Modernization of the Eurocat Air Traffic Management System (EATMS)*

Jerome DelaPeyronnie, Philip H. Newcomb, Vincent Morillo, Fakkhredine Trimech, Luong Nguyen, and Mark Purtill

## ABSTRACT

This case study describes the modernization methods, technology, and processes employed by Thales Air Systems S.A., a leading major global provider of air traffic management systems and The Software Revolution, Inc. (TSRI), an industry leader in automated legacy system modernization, to modernize hundreds of thousand lines of several variants of Thales' Eurocat, is an air traffic management system (ATMS) used at 280 airports worldwide.

Safety evidence, demonstrating the transformation process of Eurocat to be *non-distortive* of original functionality, convinced Thales customers to accept Eurocat modernization by means of a metrics-guided architecture-driven modernization process and technology that achieved 100% automated code transformation accompanied by iterative semi-automated re-engineering to adapt Eurocat to meet the rigorous and exacting performance and architecture requirements of the *next generation* EATMS.

A twofold improvement in code and design quality metrics as measured by key design metrics was achieved during the transformation of Eurocat system software from mission-critical Ada 83 into high-performance, real-time Java. Today, the Java Eurocat system has been officially accepted by major ATMS customers, and will commence operation at the end of 2010 at airports all across Europe and Asia.

## INTRODUCTION

With operations in 50 countries and 68,000 employees, Thales is a world leader in the development, operation, and maintenance of mission-critical information systems for the aerospace, defense, and security markets. Thales' Eurocat air traffic management system, written in Ada 83, is a fully proven air traffic management system that has demonstrated its operational capabilities in 16 European countries (Sweden, Denmark, Ireland, Finland, Belgium, Hungary, Croatia…), Australia, Asia (Taiwan, Singapore), and Africa (Egypt, South Africa, etc.). Building on proven capabilities in large and complex software systems, Eurocat is suited for applications ranging from the management of single approach on tower to complex en route control in transcontinental, oceanic, or very high-density environments.

This system is composed of several CSCIs and its development principles are derived from the DOD2167A. In Europe Eurocat must comply with the safety requirements of Eurocontrol (ESARR6) mandates governing SoftWare Assurance Levels (SWAL assessment required for ground applications). Thales has supplied Eurocat to 280 air traffic control (ATC) centers worldwide, all designed to comply with international standards and meet customers' requirements for enhanced air traffic safety and security.

Eurocat modernization was undertaken as part of the European Air Traffic Management System (EATMS) modernization initiative. Underway since at least 1995, with broad participation of industry and government throughout Europe, EATMS is designed to ensure that European air traffic capacity can continue to grow in European air space as new technology and new initiatives are introduced, including satellite navigation and communication, and preparations for the introduction of Automatic Dependent Surveillance (ADS). From a technology point of view, transition from and partial incorporation of proven existing legacy systems is an essential factor in the transition to EATMS from existing systems.

EATMS is the key starting element of the Single European Sky ATM Research (SESAR) project, the European initiative equivalent to the FAA project "Next Gen" (NGATS), defining new concepts in avionics and air traffic management to cope with expected traffic growth and safety requirements at the 2025 horizon.

This case study describes the specific modernization technology and processes employed by Thales to modernize its air traffic management systems into EATMS from 2005 through 2008. The systems discussed in this chapter commenced with an initial pilot project in 2005 that modernized 17,000 lines of code to assess the transformation validity and determine whether real-time Java or C++ would be the preferred target language. The pilot was followed by a series of projects that ultimately modernized nearly 1.7 million lines of three variants of Thales' Eurocat, which were originally implemented in Ada 83. The modernization tools, technology, processes, and services used to achieve this transformation were supplied by TSRI, an industry leader in automated legacy system modernization.

Thales' Automatic Dependent Surveillance-B (ADS-B) is adapting airspace surveillance and management to non-radar airspace. It is very often coupled with the Controller Pilot Data Link Communications (CPDLC) capability that exchanges messages between aircraft and ground systems. Aircraft periodically broadcast data such as identification, position, altitude, velocity, intent, and status, which can be received and processed by other aircraft or ground systems equipped with ADS-B for use in improved situation awareness, conflict avoidance, and airspace management. ADS-B is installed in Australia at 28 sites as part of The Australian Advanced Air Traffic System (TAAATS), where it is the first such nationwide system in the world. Under contract with ITT Corporation, Thales is integrating ADS-B as a key component of the FAA's Next Generation Air Transportation System (NGATS).

Established in 1995, TSRI has its roots in projects at the USAF Knowledge-Based Software Assistance Program and the Boeing Artificial Intelligence Lab. The company's JANUS™ technology is used in legacy modernization projects to transform existing applications written in a variety of procedural languages into object-oriented software written in Java/J2EE, C++, or C# /NET. TSRI has completed more than 60 modernization projects, mainly for customers in government and the defense industry. TSRI undertakes modernization projects using the JANUS™ technology to achieve a highly automated iterative modernization process, which includes documentation, transformation, refactoring, redesign, re-architecture, and Web-enablement into modernized systems.

JANUS™ parses source code into an abstract syntax tree (AST) that is then used to populate a language-neutral Intermediate Object Model (IOM) of the application. Conversion to an object-oriented design is driven by automated pattern-based transformation rules and semi-automated, human-directed refactoring plans, which are developed through iterative refinement to remove dead code, consolidate redundant code, and refine and improve the resulting design and architecture of the modernized system.

JANUS™ is typically used for modeling and transforming systems in their entirety through a series of adaptive and perfective refinement iterations of transformation rules and executable refactoring specifications. The source and target AST representations provide detailed "as-is" and "to-be" documentation that supports multiple design methodologies including Unified Modeling Language (UML), Object-Oriented Analysis, and Object-Oriented Design (OOA/OOD), Business Rule Modeling (BRM), and Structured Analysis and Design (SASD).

TSRI technology and process achieve fully automated transformation of the software and platform adaptation, as well as fully machine-mediated iterative perfective refinement to optimize code structure, design, and architecture. The code achieved generally exceeds human software in quality (as measured by key quality metrics), correctness (as measured by incidence of errors), and producibility (speed, accuracy, and completeness). TSRI offers engineering and testing services to adapt and tailor its services and products to the specific needs of individual projects. TSRI is a member of the Mainframe Migration

Alliance, the Architecture-Driven Modernization group at OMG, the Enterprise Re-Architecting Consortium, and the Natural Modernization Strategies Information Forum (NAMS-IF).

## EATMS OVERALL PROJECT OBJECTIVES

Thales determined that replacement of the outdated Ada 83 programming language in which the core components of Eurocat systems were originally written was critical to the successful migration of these systems to meet the complex requirements necessitated by the Single European Sky initiative, the European EATMS, and FAA NGATS initiatives. The core function of this system, the Flight Data Processing (FDP) system, is the most complex function of the Eurocat system and the one that is deemed to change dramatically for the next generation of ATC systems that will gradually transition from radar-based systems to flight plan trajectory based systems. The FDP transformation was the main project undertaken by Thales and TSRI. The key business drivers of these initiatives included

1. Management of the obsolescence of the Ada software language and recruitment of software engineers
2. Modernization of development method and tools
3. Improved code safety and quality owing to code rejuvenation
4. Code-based consolidation and preparation for a migration to next generation Eurocat, which includes CORBA-based middleware (CARDAMOM) and Java-based, model-driven development tools for the evolution of these systems

**FIGURE 5.1**

*Real-time language usage application history.*
*Source: Aonix.*

The transformation strategy allowed a faithful code replacement of the Ada FDP system with perfect functional "replication" in Java. The replication of the existing application in new language and platform was undertaken in advance of any operation and functional changes with the primary objective of cleanly separating all risks of technological changes from the developmental risks associated with functional evolution. After considering the alternatives of *manually rewriting* or *redevelopment from scratch* of FDP, Thales decided on *automated modernization* into real-time Java as the most effective approach for meeting these objectives.

The rapid ascendance of Java as the most widely used object-oriented programming language is depicted in Figure 5.1. The ascendance and dominance of Java factored heavily into Thales' preference to migrate its

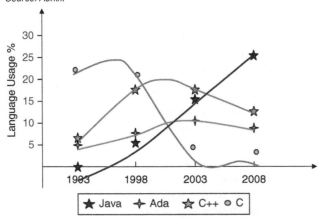

applications into real-time Java, but not before Thales and TSRI performed a detailed pilot to evaluate the relative viability of C++ and Java as real-time target languages.

## EATMS MODERNIZATION PILOT PROJECT

To begin the EATMS modernization process, Thales undertook a pilot project with TSRI in early 2005 to investigate the feasibility of automated language transformation and assess the quality and performance of the generated code. Key objectives of the pilot project were to

1. Assure functional equivalence between the produced Java/C++ code and the original Ada legacy code
2. Assure that the generated code complied with coding safety rules and established coding standards
3. Assure that the documentation produced by the tools allowed detailed comparison between the source and target code
4. Assess whether Java or C++ could meet EATMS performance objectives
5. Define refactoring strategies for code transformation and optimization
6. Assess chances of success for the full transformation of the FDP process

The target system selected for the pilot project was a high-performance, real-time Ada 83 application called the Trajectory Prediction Manager (TPM) which consisted of 17,000 lines of code. TPM is a piece of FDP not too closely linked to the rest of the software. It is representative of the FDP application algorithmic complexity (predictions of speed laws and vertical evolution of the aircraft), its CPU demand, and has a key functional role in the Eurocat system. TPM's symbolic functional role is enforced by the fact that it is based on aircraft models provided by Eurocontrol Base of Aircraft Data (BADA). For the pilot project, TSRI transformed TPM into C++ as well as into Java to compare behavior and performances (see Figure 5.2) in these two languages.

The initial phase of the pilot completed in five weeks included adaptation of TSRI process to translate TPM code into C++, generation of the Transformation Blueprint™ of the *as-is* and *to-be* system to support code and design inspection, and engineering support during the testing process. The transformed C++ code was visually inspected and determined to be easy to read and easy to modify.

During performance testing, the C++ code was integrated with the existing FDP Ada processes, integration tested, and within a few days found to be functionally equivalent in the full Eurocat test environment. Critical performance testing included invocation of the C++ TPM as library calls from legacy Ada, and demonstration that trajectories generated by the C++ TPM were identical to those produced by the Ada TPM. Graphical display of trajectory outputs allowed a quicker and easier comparison of the two sets of sources (see Figure 5.2).

**FIGURE 5.2**

*Comparison of Ada to C++ for TPM.*

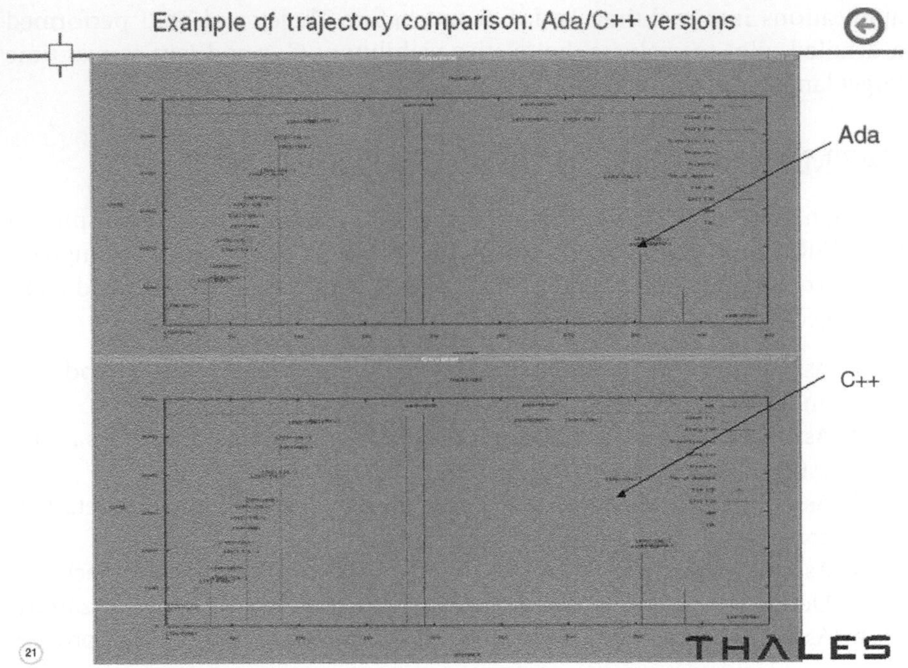

Example of trajectory comparison: Ada/C++ versions

Ada

C++

THALES

Eight C++ APIs are used in the FDP Ada library, and the ability to load parameters files data (modeling aircraft performances with the BADA model) was demonstrated. Five bugs were detected in the translated C++ due to translation errors. These bugs were corrected by modifying the transformation rules, and the Ada code was retranslated into C++ and delivered by TSRI to Thales. TSRI subsequently adapted the transformation process to generate the Java version of TPM from Ada 83 in two weeks, delivering the Java version of TPM and the TSRI as-is and to-be Transformation Blueprint™ upon completion of the transformation.

After assessment of the TPM software in C++, Thales contracted with TSRI to transform TPM into Java. The Java version of TPM was produced in 3 weeks after the delivery of the C++ version of TPM. Since integration between Ada with Java and C++ modules within the FDP test bed was not yet seamless at the time of the pilot, both the Java and C++ versions of the TPM module were tested using stubbed flight plan routes and ATC constraints for two different kinds of aircraft and tested in the Eurocat test environment. During testing, trajectories were found to be identical between Java TPM and Ada TPM. Only 10 bugs were detected in the Java translation — slightly more than with C++ — with the difference attributable to the Ada to C++ transformation rules being slightly more robust by virtue of having been used on a greater number of previous projects at the time the pilot was undertaken. As with the C++ TPM, the bugs in the Java TPM were corrected by modifying transformation rules and the TPM was retranslated and retested to demonstrate a 100% automated bug-free transformation.

The transformation from Ada 83 into C++ and Java resulted for both languages in fewer than 0.1% incidence of errors in the initial transformation and 100% error-free transformation after correction of the transformation rules. When an error was detected, TSRI engineers corrected the deficient C++ or Java transformation rules, re-transformed the Ada code, and delivered the updated code within a 24-hour period. TSRI's ability to perform problem identification and resolution within a 24-hour window during the pilot engendered confidence that TSRI's technology and process could support the full Eurocat conversion.

## Key Findings

Both the C++ and the Java transformations of TPM produced faithful replicas of the original Ada 83 TPM implementation. There was no functional distortion of TPM (i.e. no difference in expected functional behavior). The initial transformed code was not fully object-oriented; however, this was expected due to the absence of refactoring during the TPM pilot. The TPM code was assessed to identify the kinds of refactoring steps and operations that would subsequently be incorporated into refactoring specifications developed for the full conversion.

The as-is and to-be Transformation Blueprint™ design documentation was deemed excellent as delivered. The as-is and to-be Transformation Blueprint™ permitted Thales engineers to carry out detailed inspections of the code-level translation permitting line-by-line comparison of the Ada and the C++, and design-level comparison between graphical data element tables, structure charts, control flow, state machine, and cause-effect models of the hypertext code model of the Ada, the Java, and C++.

A representative set of Thales-specific Java coding standards rules was defined, and the TPM pilot code was visually inspected using the Transformation Blueprint™ documentation to verify that the transformation process had correctly implemented them.

## TPM PERFORMANCE ASSESSMENT BEFORE CODE OPTIMIZATION

Assessment of the performance of the translated C++ and Java code was a key objective of the TPM project and a core adoption concern, especially for Java because its runtime architecture and reputation (slower runtime and erratic response times) had raised red flags about the suitability of the language for air traffic management applications within the ATC community. The TPM pilot project was thus a unique opportunity to obtain a definitive benchmark of comparison between the Ada, C++, and Java languages. At the time the pilot was initiated, the target language of the EATMS project was still C++ due to performance concerns regarding Java.

The test computer used in the pilot project was a LINUX P4 3 GHz processor. During the test, 27 flight plans were created and tested successively. A full profile computation was undertaken, but only the duration of the TPM services "Compute Climb/Cruise/Descent" was measured in each of these tests. The original Ada TPM response time was used as the indicator of the flight plan complexity. All TPM flight tests were conducted and measured in the Eurocat test environment. The duration of TPM flight plan creation was identical each time the test was performed and CPU consumption was deterministic. The initial benchmark compared Ada TPM and C++ TPM performance. Java code was compiled with JDK 1.5.

During the initial performance tests of the C++ TPM prior to code optimization, performance was ten times slower than the Ada TPM. A probe package was used to pin-point areas of the C++ code requiring optimization. One significant but very simple optimization was found and implemented for the C++ TPM. Following this optimization the C++ TPM performed three times better than the original non-optimized Ada. The same optimization was then performed on the Ada, following which the optimized Ada TPM outperformed the optimized C++ TPM, but by a reduced 1.66 to 1 performance ratio. The Ada optimization was applied only to the TPM module. The rest of the Eurocat Ada code was not optimized. The response time of the optimized Ada TPM module was improved by a factor of three compared to the original.

In a second series of tests, two flight plans were created for two aircraft types, one modeled by BADA and one not modeled by BADA, with four combinations of flight plans and aircraft types. During this stand-alone test, only the Compute Climb/Cruise/Descent test sequence of the TPM was invoked and measured. Each of these four combinations was computed and the computation sequence was repeated 100 times during each of these test scenarios.

For both sets of test sequences the overall Java TPM and C++ TPM performance times were similar, but there were notable differences in the performance profiles of Java and C++ during repeated calls of the test sequences conducted before any form of code optimization was undertaken. The initial call time of the Java TPM was very lengthy and the Java TPM response time was unstable throughout the test sequence. Of greatest concern was the Java startup time, which was much greater than the C++ startup time. This time disparity was attributed to C++ precompilation. Another concern was the unstable response times of the Java TPM, which were attributed to Java garbage collection. Both these original performance characteristics were deemed unacceptable for ATC applications, and became the primary focus of the performance optimization study.

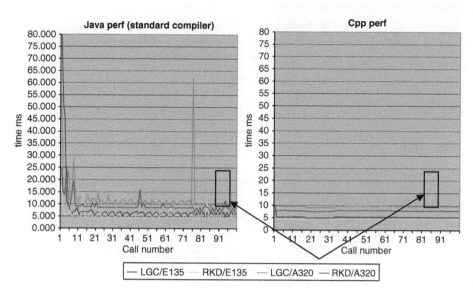

**FIGURE 5.3**

*Non-optimized performance call duration times.*

Figure 5.3 shows the performance measured in call duration for each invocation of the TPM module for a series of 100 calls for all 4 test scenarios for both the resultant Java and the C++ languages.

## Performance After Code Optimization

To address the Java startup and response time instability, the Java TPM was optimized using the Excelsior JET compiler. The JET is a compliant Java SE 6 technology implementation with an ahead-of-time (AOT) compiler and deployment kit. Java optimization with JET required a skilled software engineer one day to obtain and learn the tool and a week to optimize the Java code. The objective of Java optimization was to reduce the startup time and decrease the impact of the Java garbage collection mechanism to stabilize response times.

Upon completion of this optimization effort, the optimized Java code achieved performance comparable to the optimized C++, and both the optimized Java and the optimized C++ achieved overall performance time superior to the original Ada. Both Java's excessive startup time and excessive variability in response time were eliminated. The time performance ratio of the optimized C++ TPM to the optimized Java TPM was 1 to 1.09. Although Java's intermittent variability in response times remained due to incremental garbage collection, as shown in Figure 5.4, controls imposed on garbage collection behavior enabled the Java TPM to achieve performance levels superior to the non-optimized Ada TPM that were acceptable to the FDP function. With optimized compiler and garbage collection settings (GC and AOT compiler) the real-time Java gave comparable performance to the C++ and provided acceptable response time dispersion.

**FIGURE 5.4**

*Optimized performance call duration times.*

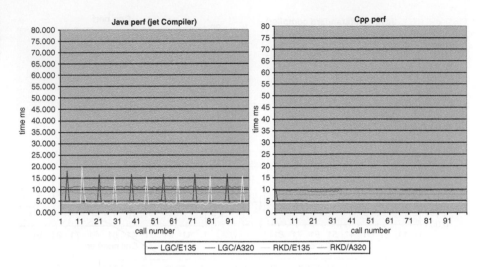

## Performance Factor

The final time performance comparison between the original Ada and the optimized Ada, C++, and Java is shown in Table 5.1.

When considering these performance results it is important to recognize that the TPM code was designed for the Ada language. As a consequence there were many code-level decisions made in the implementation of TPM that favored the Ada language over the C++ or Java languages. For example, Ada uses fixed length arrays while both the C++ and Java used resizable arrays implemented as dynamic vectors or lists. When performance was measured on 200 copy operations applied to points (x, y), the static Ada array implementation outperformed the dynamic C++ vector implementation by a ratio of 2.2. Another example occurred in the choice regarding storage representation of floating point numbers.

The Ada 32-bit float was translated into the Java 64-bit double. This would result in floating point operations computations with twice the precision in Java as in Ada, but the time performance of floating point operations would double as would the times for storage allocation and retrieval. While correctable, these translation choices were decided by the default behavior of the

**Table 5.1** Final Language-Based Time Performance Ratios

| Language | Optimized Ada | Optimized C++ | Optimized Java | Original Ada |
|---|---|---|---|---|
| Time performance ratios | 1 | 1.66 | 1.81 | 3 |

translation. Subsequent phases of the Java FDP (JFDP) project addressed many of these low-level translation choices by modifying transformation rules to optimize the choice of code-level representation.

## Memory Utilization and Optimization

The memory utilization ratio of Java to C++ was 4 to 1 as shown in Figure 5.5. It should be noted when considering the Java memory performance that inconsistent time performance response and high initial levels of memory utilization were corrected by tuning during optimization.

Before optimization, the use of a Just-in-Time (JIT) Java compiler was used. This resulted in long response times preceding the first call to any function for compilation. By transitioning to the use of an AOT compiler, this up-front time performance degradation was eliminated altogether. The impact of garbage collection was the primary cause of inconsistent response time. After a long garbage collection, response time decreased.

On a unary processor, the garbage collector would block all other activity when it was running. The way memory is utilized and the way garbage collection is invoked influence performance tuning. Java objects in memory are either Young (recently affected objects), Tenured (objects with long lifetimes), or Permanent (static objects with indefinite lifetimes). Young generation

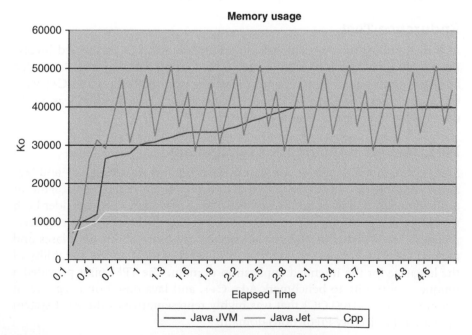

**FIGURE 5.5**

*Memory utilization ratio.*

recollection is fast (a few milliseconds) and frequent. When an element of the Young list is still referenced during the garbage collection, it is moved to the Tenured list. Tenured generation recollection is slow (requiring at least 50 ms) and sparse. Parameters affecting garbage collection behavior include the heap size, collection size, and the frequency of explicit garbage collection calls. It is possible to set the minimum heap size to avoid useless garbage collection on objects that cannot be reclaimed. The larger a collection size is, the longer it takes to fill, the lower the garbage collection frequency, and the longer it takes to empty (high garbage collection impact).

The application can explicitly call a garbage collection. Explicit garbage collection calls are expensive as they launch a full garbage collection. Explicit garbage collection can be done during idle times, but should not be done during periods of intense computation. These were the primary properties monitored during garbage collection performance testing:

1. Type of garbage collection (Young/Tenured/Permanent)
2. Overall time doing garbage collection
3. Method computation time without garbage collection
4. Average garbage collection duration
5. Number of calls out of standard time by 20%

With a good Young collection size, the Tenured collection should not grow and Tenured recollection can be completely avoided. The garbage collector is tunable, thus the response time dispersion can be greatly reduced with tuning.

## Endurance Test

As a final pilot project benchmark, an endurance test was performed involving 14,000 invocations of TPM (Figure 5.6). During this benchmark, the list of calls with response time superior to average was +30%. Java and C++ were observed to have similar performance dispersion behavior which was attributed to LINUX daemons stealing CPU cycles.

## Performance Benchmark Conclusions

Many conventional language comparison benchmarks involving C++ and Java are made using code and algorithms that have no relevance or bearing on the air traffic domain. It is important when evaluating benchmarks to consider both the choice of algorithms and applications as well as the biases of the engineers preparing the benchmark. Benchmarks often say more about the biases and preferences of the engineer conducting the benchmark than the suitability of the language for the intended application domain. The TPM pilot provided a unique opportunity to benchmark Ada, C++, and Java based on a significant amount of code (16KLOC) that was highly representative of the ATM system operations (Trajectory Prediction) domain.

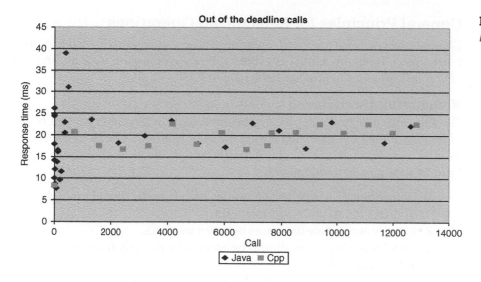

**FIGURE 5.6**
*Endurance test results.*

A key objective of the pilot was to benchmark the performance and suitability of C++ and Java using code that was sufficiently representative of the ATC systems operations to support the choice of language for Eurocat modernization that would meet all application performance requirements as well as EATMS and FAA NGATS directives regarding software quality assurance, tools and methods, and project objectives to improve code quality, sustainability, and maintainability.

The TPM pilot was undertaken at the time of a choice between C++ and Java for future FDP applications (EATMS projects). The TPM outputs proved that the Java language could be used for FDP types of applications, provided application performance was monitored and tuned to meet performance requirements. A key conclusion of the TPM project was that there was a need to select an appropriate Java Virtual Machine (JVM) compatible with performance requirements. The transformation rules should also be adapted to introduce code-level optimizations tuned to the target language to improve the target language response time. In addition, for each application, specific GC tuning was found to provide the best results, and any significant modification in an application should be assumed to require new garbage collection adjustments. A key finding of the pilot regarding the Java garbage collection was with tuning — response time dispersion could be optimized, and functional performance of tuned Java was well within constraints for application in the ATC domain.

An outcome of the pilot was the selection of Java for the Eurocat modernization and the selection of Java as the primary language for use in new ATC applications.

## General Principles for Refactoring Operations

General principles of the transformation process were identified during the pilot project. From the pilot TPM project the general program built around the FDP transformation to Java has been named JFDP.

### Refactoring Guidelines

The following ten guidelines were developed regarding refactoring as a result of reviews of the code generated during the pilot project. These guidelines were used to guide preparation of the Refactoring Specification employed as the Eurocat systems were modernized:

1. Define high- and low-level modules with consistent content and limited inter-module dependencies.
2. Identify and isolate interfaces between modules.
3. Middleware interfaces should be accessed separately from core application code.
4. Types and procedures should be grouped consistently and the visibility of objects minimized to improve object-oriented design.
5. Memory occupancy and performances should be optimized.
6. Dead code should be identified and potentially eliminated, unused entries should be stubbed and potentially eliminated, and redundant code should be identified and potentially consolidated.
7. Structure of FPL record will be set consistently with modules.
8. Global variables should be eliminated to allow multi-threading.
9. Procedures and classes should be recomposed into smaller units to improve code quality metrics and decrease code defect counts.
10. Java code should be refactored after raw transformation to improve code quality and readability.

Several key principles of the modernization approach were identified and incorporated as guiding principles for the definition of the refactoring specification.

1. Any refactoring operation must be repeatable for any new release of the Ada version of the original software throughout the life cycle of the modernization project. This was necessary because during the JFDP project life the FDP function development was going on (new functionalities were being added and deficiencies corrected).

2. Post transformation manual modification of resulting target Java code should be limited as much as possible. All modifications to the code were to be made through modification of transformation and refactoring rules. Only when no other choice was possible would manual patches be allowed, but nearly all were duly identified and eventually corrected using rules.

**3.** Thales (the client) was completely responsible for defining all refactoring: schedule, tasks, specifications, and inputs. TSRI was completely responsible for implementing all refactoring specifications and generating all code and reports.

The high-level refactoring process was defined this way:

1. Thales updated the configuration input files for refactoring
2. Thales updated the Ada code if necessary
3. TSRI transformed accordingly the code into Java with the new configuration
4. The Java code was sent back to Thales together with updated reports and TSRI outputs
5. Thales proceeded to automated test verification for major releases

Configuration input files contain a detailed model of how code items should be refactored or re-allocated. TSRI reports indicate requested data flows, dependencies, and code characteristics of all the code in a highly detailed code map for each Java version generated by the TSRI tools. These code maps were analyzed by the Thales team and used to update the configuration input files for a new transformation cycle until a satisfactory status was reached. Thus operations 1 though 5 in the above refactoring process were repeated as many times as needed until the code generated through all the iterations achieved the code construction, composition, and system design objectives.

## FULL EATMS PROJECT MODERNIZATION OBJECTIVES AND CONSTRAINTS

After Thales and TSRI completed the pilot project, the team undertook the modernization of the Thales FPL system. A key objective of the transformation of Eurocat was to achieve exact functional replication of the FDP system's original Ada 83 code into real-time Java code. Perfect functional replication of JFDP at the code level was needed to assure that the FDP software specifications System Segment Specification/Software Requirements Specification (SSS/SRS) were unaffected by the transformation and remained strictly identical to the original. This requirement ruled out a human translation as the consistency of a human translation could not be guaranteed. The use of automated rule-based transformation guaranteed both uniformity of the translation, as well as a high level of assurance that deficiencies, when detected, would be uniformly corrected.

To assure the consistency of translation between all language elements of the source Ada 83 and target Java code, it was essential that the translated code be obtained by employing a highly automatic process in which at least 99.5% of code could be translated fully automatically. In addition to code translation, code refactoring was employed to improve code quality and the software design to meet EATMS design requirements so that the modernized code would serve as a foundation for future system enhancement. These objectives were achieved through the use of model-based transformation technology from TSRI that would ultimately achieve a 100% automation level by encoding the entire translation and refactoring process as rules in TSRI's rule engine.

Another key requirement was for the interfaces of Java FDP with other systems to remain strictly identical to the original Ada 83. This was essential for the Eurocat baseline, which involved integration of Eurocat and ADS/CPDLC functionalities. In particular, there could be no change to the interfaces of the FPL system with other Eurocat systems. The introduction of JFDP in Eurocat was to be done smoothly at no cost for other CSCIs. The UNIX-Based System Software (UBSS) (see the abbreviation on page 131) version introducing Java APIs to its services was used to allow proper running of the FPL process in Java on UBSS nodes. Additionally, the JFDP had to interface with other existing libraries, in particular the C libraries (kinematics) that were called through JNI, preserving legacy Ada interfaces and the data and parameters files prepared off-line that are widely used for FPL processing.

## JFDP Wrappers Guidelines

Definition of JFDP wrappers was an important aspect of the transformation process. Definition of wrappers facilitated seamless interfacing between FDP and the rest of the Eurocat system. The middleware UBSS allowed proper dynamic communication between Eurocat CSCIs via shared memory between remote nodes or point-to-point buffers. UBSS gives access to services for Ada, C, and Java applications.

JFDP wrappers are Java functional prototypes with encoding and decoding byte buffers for receiving data through UBSS Java APIs. Wrappers are based on a set of Perl tools that Thales used for preparing JFDP interfaces. The JFDP wrappers definition process required that wrappers be adapted to the new Ada baseline and the process for wrapper creation be made generic and automated. Wrappers were available for the FDP parameters files to read, available for buffers transported through UBSS services, and performances were optimized so that wrapper invocation, and the encoding and decoding of parameterized data, was as fast as possible to minimize overhead at the interfaces.

Finally, the following were key JFDP refactoring constraints that had to be met by the modernization project:

1. JFDP code and inner interfaces needed to be restructured, while preserving functional behavior
2. JFDP needed to easily be adapted to new interfaces
3. JFDP must be able to load any dataset distributed on the system

4. JFDP must interact with other Ada processes as if JFDP was written in Ada

5. JFDP needed to be monitored, restarted, and switched just like in Ada

6. FPL Xtermlogs (traces) of JFDP must be identical to the original logs

An automated transformation followed by an automated and repeatable incremental refactoring process was vital to achieving technological change while preserving full Eurocat functionalities. Early in the project manual re-coding was investigated and quickly discarded as a long, expensive, and error-prone process. Feasibility studies and pilot projects undertaken in 2005 proved automatic transformation to be the most promising way to produce JFDP, and most satisfactorily met needs pertaining to fine-tuning the process and technology used in the project. Incremental refactoring was combined with transformation achieving a step-by-step iterative process that could be repeated as often as needed, and that would validate each step of that process through the use of automated CSCI tests.

As the success of automation was confirmed, additional tools were developed by Thales to achieve automation of the manual processes that were originally outside the scope of the original transformation and refactoring process. A tool called FANTOM was developed to define wrappers. A tool called REFACTOR was used to insert Ada fake-blocks. A tool called AIRSPACE was also developed to automate testing at the CSCI level.

The main technical refactoring objectives were defined during the TPM pilot projects and they are listed in the section on Refactoring Guidelines (above).

## Full EATMS Modernization Approach

To accomplish the automated transformation of Ada 83, Thales contracted with TSRI to modernize the 1.7 million lines of outdated Ada 83 programming language in which the core components of Eurocat systems were originally implemented into modernized real-time Java. TSRI provided a highly automated flexible modernization service that could be easily tailored to the specific needs of Thales. TSRI's specific services included: (1) legacy as-is documentation, (2) Ada 83 to a real-time Java code transformation, (3) automatic refactoring, (4) semi-automatic refactoring, (5) system integration and test support, and (6) final to-be documentation. The effort included extensive refactoring to meet precise, mission-critical coding standards that would require tailoring of TSRI technology and processes to meet Thales' coding specifications.

In addition, TSRI tuned the JANUS™ grammar systems and transformation rules engine to address the legacy Ada 83 code of several versions of the FPL process, Minimum Safe Altitude Warning System, and Air-Ground Data Processor modules of EATMS. Thales also contracted with TSRI to (1) provide additional engineering support to a determined minimal set of code used that needed to be transformed, (2) generate dependency analysis reports to support Thales in decisions regarding refactoring, and (3) tune the transformation to tailor and optimize the transformation scheme and refactoring patterns for many language constructs and programming idioms to meet Thales' exacting specifications.

## Full EATMS Modernization Process Overview

While existing industry-standard certifications (CMMI, ISO, etc.) do not yet address cutting-edge automated modernization technologies such as the JANUS™ toolset or their application to legacy system modernization, TSRI's industrial toolsets have achieved a high-quality, automated, multi-source, multi-target, model-driven, rule-based technology framework that is highly illustrative of the 'best practices' promoted by the OMG's Architecture-Driven Modernization (ADM) initiative. As a platform member of the OMG, TSRI participates in the definition of standards and specification for the OMG's ADM Task Force (ADM-TF), and its JANUS™ tool suite partially implements OMG's Abstract Syntax Tree Metamodeling, Knowledge Discovery Metamodel, and Structured Metric Metamodel specifications emerging from the ADM-TF.

The methods and practices employed by Thales and TSRI for the EATMS project are good examples of several of the ADM-TF architecture-driven modernization scenarios, specifically (1) portfolio management, (2) language-to-language (L2L) modernization, (3) platform-to-platform (P2P) modernization, (4) component consolidation and reuse, and (5) architecture-driven transformation.

TSRI's legacy system modernization process is configuration controlled through the use of CVS configuration control over all input files, generated code, and all generated reports and documentation. All project deliverables and incremental versions of tools are tagged with version control at all critical milestones and major deliverables. Virtually all changes are accomplished by the application of model-based transformation rules to software models. Manual modifications of code are very rare, but if required, manual modifications are rigorously integrated with the automated transformation by automatically applying CVS controlled merging techniques immediately following each model-based, rule-driven target code regeneration cycle. Eventually all "hand-fixes" are retrofitted into the rule-driven process. Quality is assured and process replication is achieved by exercising regression tests prior to any major deliverable/release.

## Full EATMS Project Modernization Process

Three tools supported the full EATMS modernization process:

1. JANUS™ from TSRI was used for the code transformation, automated refactoring, and to execute domain-specific refactoring specifications produced using Klocwork Architecture™. JANUS™ was used for parsing

and executing refactoring specification and regenerating Java code after applying refactoring operations.

2. Klocwork Architecture™ was used by Thales to graphically refactor the Java code, creating new code items and re-allocating packages, classes, methods, and fields to proper modules.

3. REFACTOR, a Thales-built Perl tool, automated the tagging blocks of Ada, called fake-blocks, code to detect blocks of code that belong to a particular FPL module. REFACTOR was applied to tag Ada code to be refactored into methods before transformation to improve the scope of modules. JANUS™ transformed the tagged blocks of Ada code into Java methods and allocated them automatically to components in the target Java according to an allocation specification given to TSRI by Thales.

Figure 5.7 depicts the iterative modernization process employed by Thales and TSRI.

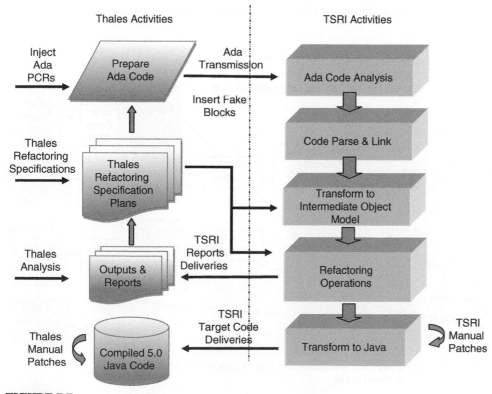

**FIGURE 5.7**

*Iterative automated legacy system modernization.*

## EATMS Transformation and Refactoring Process

TSRI's legacy system modernization technology process is shown in Figure 5.8. JPGEN™ is TSRI's technology for generating parsers that process code to generate AST models and printers that generate code from AST models from a grammar specification for a computer language. JTGEN™ is TSRI's technology for automatically recognizing patterns in ASTs and transforming AST models. TSRI employs JPGEN™ and JTGEN™ in a highly disciplined process that transforms the entire legacy application into an IOM upon which a sequence of transformation and/or refactoring operations are applied before target code is generated from the model.

During the EATMS transformational process the EATMS software was represented in three related AST models. It was represented first as a Legacy Ada 83 AST, then as an IOM AST, and finally as a target Java AST. The transformation into the Legacy Ada 83 AST model was carried out by a parser generated by JPGEN™ and a constrainer generated by JTGEN™. The transformation between the Legacy Ada AST model and the IOM AST model is carried out by Ada2IOM transformation rules generated by JTGEN™. The transformation between the IOM and the target Java AST is carried out by the IOM2Java transformation rules generated by JTGEN™.

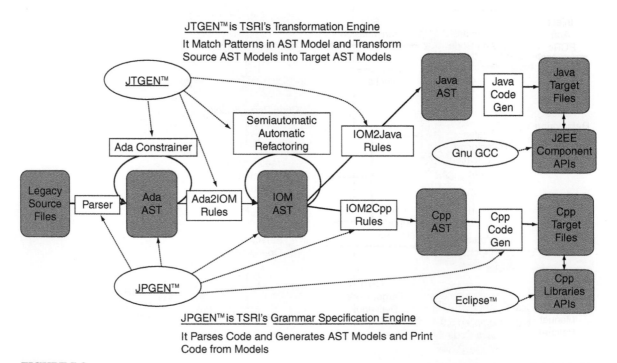

**FIGURE 5.8**

*TSRI's JANUS™ technology modernization process.*

Refactoring is the process of changing a software system so that it does not alter the function of the code yet improves its internal structure. When carried out manually, refactoring is applied directly to the source code itself, and is generally a labor-intensive, ad hoc, and potentially error-prone process. In contrast to conventional manual refactoring, TSRI has achieved a highly automated refactoring process characterized by the application of pattern-based transformations to a model of the software rather than to the source code itself. This approach allows refactoring to be applied reliably and safely on a massive scale as a rigorous disciplined multi-level automated and machine-mediated process.

Automated and semi-automated refactoring is accomplished by transformation rules generated by JTGEN™ that are applied to the IOM AST model to improve its structure before transformation into the target Java AST model. Refactoring operations vary greatly in their granularity and scope. Some refactoring operations are atomic and limited in scope, while others are more complex, composed by applying many more finely grained refactoring operations to accomplish a larger grained restructuring objective. The order of refactoring operations is crucial to assuring their proper application. Some refactoring operations must be done prior to others to establish the appropriate state of the software model for subsequent refactoring operations. Many refactoring operations are application domain-neutral and are applied whenever transforming between any procedural and any object-oriented language. Others are language-pair specific and are applied only when transforming between a particular source and target language.

The iterative transformation and refactoring process employed by TSRI for all projects, and that used on the EATMS project for Thales, is shown in Figure 5.9.

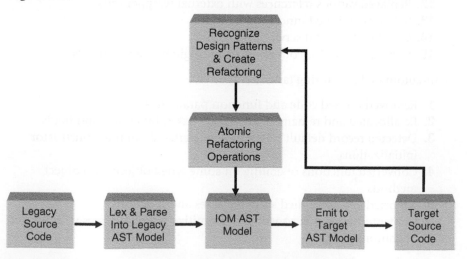

**FIGURE 5.9**

*TSRI iterative transformation and refactoring process.*

Domain- or application-specific refactoring operations such as those used during the EATMS project are strongly dependent upon the specific design objectives of a project. In a very large and complex modernization project, domain-neutral and domain-specific refactoring operations are generally combined and require the order and sequence of their invocation to be choreographed by means of a refactoring process specification.

A partial summary of the major automated and semi-automated refactoring operations performed by TSRI using its JANUS™ toolset for the EATMS project is shown in the following list.

Automated refactoring tasks:

1. Generic Ada packages to Java-generic classes
2. Packages to non-instantiable classes with static members
3. Record types and exceptions to instantiable classes
4. Ada package with inner types to Java Package containing corresponding classes
5. Variant records to Java classes with inner classes and additional members and methods to manage variant values and types
6. Ada Enumerations refactored into Java Enum
7. Arrays to string, list, or EnumMap based on index and value types
8. Ada overloaded operators resolved and transformed into Java methods
9. Aggregated initializations transformed into simple assignments in Java
10. Named associations to positional function parameters and class attributes
11. Managed package initialization
12. Replaced various references with external wrapper calls
13. Split or combined function parameters
14. Generated external service interfaces
15. Generated Javadoc comments from original Ada comments

Semi-automated refactoring tasks:

1. Removed unused code and function parameters
2. Re-allocated and re-named packages, classes, functions, and fields
3. Detected record default values and converted them into constructor initializations
4. Converted functions operating on some typed objects into object methods
5. Reported and combined similar classes and functions
6. Converted some Ada constrained primitive types in classes with proper operations

## Refactoring Process Specifications and Plan Development

The purpose of developing the JFDP refactoring process specification was to define and document all refactoring operations required to reach JFDP technical objectives. The refactoring process specification structured the sequence of applications of all refactoring operations and provided a framework for monitoring progress in the definition of the rule-sets and the execution of refactoring specifications. In addition, it enabled formal verification of the refactoring operations when applied to code.

The JFDP refactoring specification defined a uniform process to be applied to each new Ada baseline throughout the duration of the project. Sixty-three refactoring requirements were implemented for the first JFDP transformation. Fourteen additional refactoring requirements were defined for the second JFDP instantiation transformation based upon actions and safety analysis feedback. The definition of these refactoring operations was driven from several sources, including analysis of defects raised by dependency reports that identified poorly structured types and poorly located procedures.

To supplement the work of the analysts, the Klocwork tool Architect™ was used in an iterative fashion to analyze successive iterations of the Java applications generated by JANUS™ to construct a graphical visualization of the architecture of the JFDP and define refactoring plans specifying the restructuring of the application to improve intra- and inter-component dependencies between packages, classes, and methods. Architect™ output, such as the example shown in Figure 5.10, allowed a user to quickly define the project's refactoring plans.

This diagram corresponds to one of the FPL process level 1 modules, called PRO, which is sub-divided in level 2 packages (tpm, proManager, etc.). The light blue boxes (proIo, tpm …) depict Java packages. Red boxes depict Java classes (ExternalServices). Arrows indicate the real software dependencies ("import xxx") and the numbers indicate the actual numbers of lines of code where this dependency occurs. External dependencies of each item are depicted by arrows pointing towards the boundaries of the enclosing rectangle.

For instance, the proManager package uses the ctrm package 28 times, and tpm uses proManager twice. In this latter case it means that in reality there is one statement for method calls, plus one statement for the Java import. In this example, circular dependencies have been reduced to a minimum; however, some code-level defects remain that cannot be resolved by automatic refactoring that still require hand patches, either to the target Java code or source Ada code. For instance dual dependencies between tpm and proManager, volm and cotrm, volm and rtem, or volm and proManager will be resolved through manual modifications of code. The low number of unwanted dependencies

**FIGURE 5.10**
*Klocwork Architect™ refactoring plan output example.*

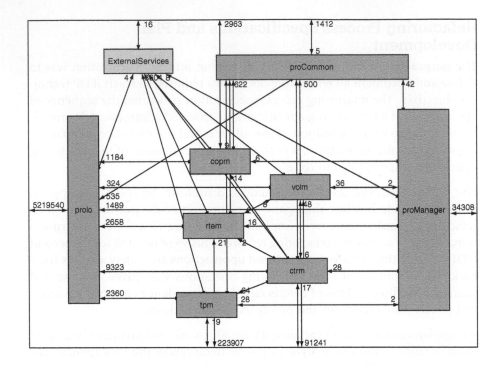

(occurrences <6 ) indicates that manual modification of the code inside the body of class or method is required because the unwanted dependencies cannot be resolved solely by means of atomic level refactoring operations that manipulate the compositional relationships between components (see Table 5.3). Manual code-level modifications can be made either to the original Ada code or a CVS controlled patch following transformation of the application into Java.

This output illustrates the general nature of a refactoring plan:

- Isolate functional modules (ctrm, tpm, volm) in a consistent way
- Decrease dependencies between functional modules as much as possible
- Avoid circular dependencies between modules
- Identify and isolate interfaces between functional modules to reduce dependencies between packages
- Concentrate external modules into classes created automatically by refactoring operations into external services.

Klocwork reports depict the actual detailed dependencies as they are implemented in code algorithms, while classic UML diagrams usually stay at the design level, and do not show all of the implementation details.

Applying the Thales-derived domain-specific refactoring plans for the JFDP project consisted of executing a sequence of atomic refactoring operations such

**Table 5.2** EATMS Refactoring Plan Excerpt

| Operation | Entity | Kind | Source: Legacy System Model | Target: New System Model |
|---|---|---|---|---|
| Move | getCharPointName | Method | com/ComDummyClass_3/getCharPointName | com/FPL_DATA_TYPES/LimitPoints/getCharPointName |
| Move | pointNameLength | Field | com/ComDummyClass/pointNameLength | com/FPL_DATA_TYPES/LimitPoints/pointNameLength |
| Delete | GridMngCInterface | Class | com/GridMngCInterface | |
| Move | IAC_RDP_TO_FDP_TYPES | Package | com/IAC_RDP_TO_FDP_TYPES | com/IO_DATA/IAC_RDP_TO_FDP_TYPES |
| Add | COM_FDPS_DEFINITION | Package | | comFdps/COM_FDPS_DEFINITION |
| Delete | ProConstIo | Class | pro/PRO_IO/ProConstIo | |
| Move | calibratedPointListDef | Field | pro/PRO_COMMON/ExtractionFormat/calibratedPointListDef | pro/PRO_IO/SpeedToReach/calibratedPointListDef |
| Move | SpeedKind | Enumeration | pro/PRO_COMMON/ExtractionFormat/SpeedKind | pro/PRO_IO/SpeedToReach/SpeedKind |
| Delete | TpConstraint | Class | pro/PRO_IO/TpConstraint | |
| Move | extractionProcessingBlk2 | Method | pro/ProDummyClass_8/extractionProcessingBlk2 | pro/RTEM/SidStarProposal/extractionProcessingBlk2 |
| Rename | PRO_TRIGGER | Package | pro/PRO_TRIGGER | pro/PRO_MANAGER |

as those depicted in Table 5.2. The plan shown is excerpted from a 2,800+ step refactoring plan that is one of many applied to the project code. Atomic operations, such as create package, move class to package, move method to class, delete class, and rename method are executed by a refactoring plan interpreter by Janus™. Execution of such a plan is considered to be a semi-automated refactoring process because while the steps in the refactoring plan are carried out by automation they are explicitly specified by human-constructed specifications.

## Refactoring Drivers and Execution

Using the derived methodology defined above, the Thales/TSRI modernization approach addresses the following key refactoring drivers of the JFDP modernization project:

**Extract a new architecture from FPL library by isolating modules with limited dependencies and consistent definition**: This breakdown was mainly driven by functional considerations but also obtained by analysis of TSRI reports that supported this process.

**Group types definitions and their instantiations for computation**: The design rationale for allocating types to packages was driven by the object-oriented design principle that states (1) operations on data belong with the types (classes) the operations manipulate, (2) similar types and operations on types belong in the same class or package, (3) redundant definitions of types and redundant operations on types should be avoided, (4) superfluous operations on types should be avoided, and (5) the set of operations on types should be restricted to the minimal set necessary. As a general rule, the implementation of refactoring operations to achieve these object-oriented design principles eliminated bad dependencies and achieved a more coherently structured JFDP in which data of the same types were computed in the same classes and packages.

**Prohibit or limit the use of external types for internal FPL processing**: Elimination of the use of external components inside FPL avoided the risks of intrusive code inside FPL, achieved independence from external I/F, and avoided the risk of incorrect external dependencies. One of the isolated modules contained the precise definition of external interfaces of JFDP.

**Prohibit coupling FPL types or processing to external CSCIs**: The elimination of intrusive code from references to external components inside FPL reduced the scope of the translation and simplified translation by eliminating references to types and operations that were not defined within the Ada source to be translated. The elimination of intrusive code eliminated the risk of incorrect references to types external to the FPL due to change in external CSCIs. Many useless code items implemented for other CSCIs and indirectly referenced in Ada for FPL code were removed during the refactoring operations.

**Structure the code with deeper package hierarchy, with smaller classes, and smaller methods whenever possible**: The implementation of smaller code items and the decomposition of large and complex Ada packages and procedures into structured Java packages with smaller classes and methods, markedly improved code metrics by reducing the dependency between modules. That effort also reduced type conflicts during code merging, and the splitting off and isolation of necessarily co-dependent code into separate modules for realignment with other modules with which they shared greater affinity. Splitting dependencies facilitated re-allocation of components between modules to improve the structural coherence of modules. Refer to Figure 5.13 for evidence of this principle.

**Prohibit global variables**: The prohibiting of global variables avoids hidden dependencies between modules that are a safety risk to multi-threaded applications. Global variables are code safety hazards because they have universal scope and may be altered without restriction. Code quality and safety is improved by converting global variables into members of types and using attributes to control their scope. Encapsulation of global variables as member variables improves code readability by making their access and update as qualified members of a class or package clearly apparent. Indeed one of the major refactoring operations eliminated two large global variables that were heavily referenced throughout the FPL software.

**Prevent poor inter-module dependencies**: Prevention of poor inter-module dependencies can be achieved by careful structuring of types to place data and algorithms into packages and classes according to functional relationships and dependencies. For example, flight profile computation, flight coordination, and SSR codes allocation belong to separate modules because they are functionally dissimilar. Designing functionally cohesive types from the beginning prevents bad dependencies between modules from the outset and reduces the need for downstream refactoring adjustments. Good packaging from the outset decreases the number of public services and reduces bad (ad hoc) inter-module dependencies. Detailed refactoring rules allowed or disallowed type-to-type dependencies, method-to-method dependencies, or method-to-type dependencies. Detailed rules are now automatically checked in JFDP projects using the Klocwork tool.

**Prevent poor module performance**: While the design of algorithms is a vast and complicated subject area, a number of simple precautions can be taken to improve algorithm performance. These include, but are not limited to, (1) avoiding looping over the complete range of large indexes, (2) avoiding looping over heavy processing algorithms (e.g., compute trajectory), (3) preferring "renames" for large objects to copies, (4) avoiding unnecessary heavy weight computations such as the re-computation of a profile more than once during the same computation cycle, (5) avoiding multiple accesses to external systems or shared external data, and (6) decreasing memory consumption by downsizing the memory resident modules.

**Restrict use of middleware (UBSS) services**: The first driving principle that isolates consistent modules has been precisely instantiated relative to usage of UBSS middleware in the FPL system. One module called FDS (see the definition on page 131) has been extracted as the only module permitted to use UBSS services. It is a module dedicated to reception of external messages, internal timers, and transmission of FPL outputs. Its applicative content has been limited as much as possible. The other FPL modules contain business code and are all prohibited from using UBSS services. This design objective complies with target EATMS architecture principles that cleanly separate technical software (FDS or Façade) from applicative software (Trajectory Computation, Coordination, etc.).

**Do not implement applicative code inside FDS (FPL Interface Module):** This rule is a direct derivation of the one listed previously: FDS application code shall be restricted to a minimum and there should be no "call backs" to FDS service from other parts of the code. The JFDP architecture should converge to allow later splitting of FPL into several processes as designed for the EATMS project. However, full implementation of this rule cannot be reached solely by current automatic refactoring technology and its implementation was done manually.

Figure 5.11 shows the detailed refactoring plan for the EATMS modernization project. The overall process contains operations that are fully automated as well as others that are semi-automated (human-guided or specified). Data flows and analysis reports are omitted from the process flow diagram to condense this discussion. The refactoring process depicted in Figure 5.11 contains refactoring operations that are unique to the JFDP and the specific systems to which they are applied, as well as refactoring operations that are generic that could be applied in the context of any Ada to Java refactoring project.

## Refactoring Process Verification

Refactoring plans of the complexity employed on the EATMS project require rigorous verification procedures. A process for verifying the refactoring specifications was, therefore, defined to assure that every refactoring requirement was applied correctly to all code items to which they were applicable. Some of the steps in the previous refactoring plan involved the application of thousands of complex refactoring operations applied to the code automatically. The process for verifying the accuracy of individual refactoring operations and the refactoring plan were guided by the project's Java Refactoring Specification Verification (JRFSV) document. The JRFSV stipulated an inspection test be designed to verify every refactoring operation specified in the Refactoring Specification.

Refactoring is an inherently iterative process that required many kinds of inspection procedures, including direct visual code inspection, analysis run by scripts, analysis in Klocwork reports, and evidence of compliance gathered by dependency reports and metrics. Through this iterative process of refactoring and testing followed by more refactoring, the design of a complex application is gradually evolved to improve compositional coherence of individual components, and bad

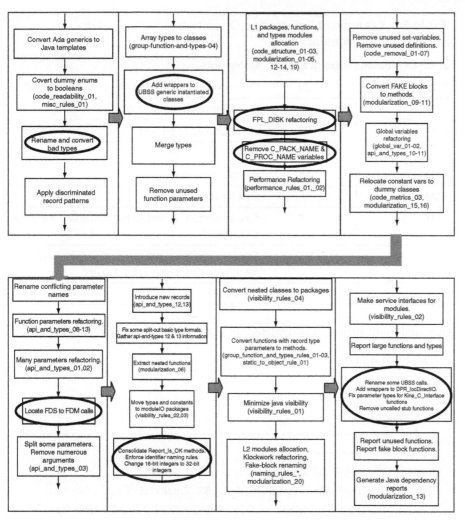

**FIGURE 5.11**

*EATMS-specific refactoring plan.*

inter-module dependencies between modules are eliminated. Inspection reports and dependency analyses were actively interleaved with the refactoring process to guide, adapt, and optimize each refactoring cycle in the process.

This verification process was also done to provide evidence of safety and provide quality assurance justification in support of the integration of the JFDP software into actual ATC projects as well as to gather metrics to provide evidence of the JFDP transformation benefits. This JRFSV document was part of a global Justification Document of JFDP in an audit carried by major Thales customers.

Some examples of the refactoring outputs are given in Table 5.3, which lists the JFDP level 1 modules and their size in actual KLOC. Wrappers and interfaces to UBSS and C libraries are excluded from this count.

**Table 5.3** Example of Refactoring Operation: FPL_DISK Type Structure Improvement

| JFDP L1 Module | Size in KLOC | Comments |
|---|---|---|
| COM | 29 | Common basic types and services of the system |
| IODATA | 27 | Define external interfaces of JFDP system |
| ENV | 60 | Define access to environment data of the system |
| PRO | 45 | Functional module |
| DAD | 45 | Functional module |
| FDM | 50 | Functional module |
| SSR | 4 | Smaller functional module but with sharp expertise and scope |
| TFM | 0.6 | Smaller functional module introduced for strategic reasons (will get larger in the future). |
| FDS | 70 | Technical module |

An actual flight plan that is depicted in Ada by the following record type:

Extract of Ada file FPL_BASE_MNG.ADS:

```
"….
494 type FPL_DISKS is
  495 records
  497 -----------------------------------------------
  -------------------------
  499 CDC_FIX_LIST_LENGTH :
IAC_FLIGHT_PLAN_TYPES.FIX_LIST_LENGTH_T;
  500 VERSION_NUMBER : STANDARD_TYPES.NATURAL_8;
  501 CDC_MODIFICATION_TIME_FPL :
ARTTS.ARTTS_TIME.TC_TIME_UNIVERSAL_TIME;
  502 CDC_MODIFICATION_TIME_COORD :
ARTTS.ARTTS_TIME.TC_TIME_UNIVERSAL_TIME;
  503 ICAO : FPL_DATA_TYPES.ICAO;
  504 ICAO_ORIGIN : FPL_DATA_TYPES.ICAO;
  505 EET_FROM_FIELD_18 : HHMM_TIME_MNG.HHMMS;
….
707 MANUALLY_CREATED : Boolean;
  708 VFL : FPL_DATA_TYPES.LEVEL_AND_UNITY_T;
  709 AETX : HHMM_TIME_MNG.HHMMS;
  710 FTEXT : IAC_FLIGHT_PLAN_TYPES.FTEXT_T;
```

```
 711 NON_COUPLING_WARNING_STATUS : Boolean;
 712 DATA_LINK_EQUIPMENT :
IAC_FLIGHT_PLAN_TYPES.EQUIP_STATUS_T;
 713 ADS_C_EQUIPPED : IAC_FLIGHT_PLAN_TYPES.
EQUIP_STATUS_T;
 714 end record;
 ...``
```

In this record more than 200 fields were listed at the same level without any sub-structures indicating the function the field is related to.

To improve the design of this code, a refactoring strategy was employed that used reverse engineering on the corresponding `fplDisks.java` to introduce intermediate structures for the following set of first-level modules of JFDP: aircraftAddress, `fplFdm`, `fplFds`, `fplPro`, `fplDad`, `fplSsr`, `fplComFdps`, `FplMemorys`, `FplDisks`.

An example of such an Associations definition for the fplFdm class is shown below:

- undefined: (0–1) as undefined to `FplFdm` (0–*) `fplFdm` as {JavaNoAccessor}

This refactoring scheme was applied in a recursive way to successive intermediate sub-structures. For instance, the `FplPro` data structure is also re-structured, as illustrated by the following UML diagram extracted by reverse engineering from the generated JFDP code.

The defined associations correspond to second level functional components that were illustrated in the previous Klocwork screen snapshot of the PRO module (Figure 5.12). For instance, FplProRtem data (attributes or other associations) are defined because RTEM is defined as a level 2 module of PRO, and the refactoring strategy calls for the computations associated with this data to be associated with the RTEM package as methods the package.

We can see that the refactoring strategy reorients the flat procedurally-oriented design into a more structured and modular design. When this strategy is followed systematically the previously object-based application design of the original Ada code of the FDP trends toward a much more object-oriented design for the JFDP.

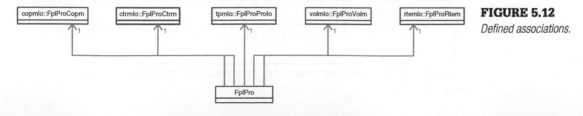

**FIGURE 5.12**
*Defined associations.*

### Example of Refactoring Operation: Elimination of DISK Global Variable

There are numerous occurrences of FPL_OBJECT.DISK global variable that were referenced in read or write operations throughout the Ada code. Here is an extract of PROCESS_XFL_SECTOR procedure (located in FDM level 1 module):

```
"...

FPL_OBJECT.DISK.TRANSITION_TABLE.LIST
(TRANS_INDEX).DIRECT_FILTER):= False;
```

Here we had direct "patch" of the global variable contained in FPL_OBJECT package.

In Java it gives:

```
fdsGlobalArg.disk.fplDad.fplDadCoordDataBld.
transitionTable.list.get(transIndex -
1).getEntryFirExitFirIntersectorDiscr().
directFilter)= false;
```

The reference to DISK global variable is now replaced by a reference to fds-GlobalArg given as argument of the method:

```
public static boolean fdmProcessXflSector(…,

    FdsGlobalVar fdsGlobalArg)
```

Since the DISK type has been restructured as explained in the previous example, the data contained in the transitionTable are now clearly indicated as part of the fplDad.DadCoordDataBld structure.

### Example of Refactoring Operation: Method Issued from Fake-Block

Inside procedure PROCESS_FORCE_ACT_SECTOR two fake-blocks are inserted automatically by the Thales REFACTOR tool, one for FDM and one for the DAD module. This procedure was flagged in the input configuration file as belonging to the FDS module.

```
"procedure PROCESS_FORCE_ACT_SECTOR...

   ...

$<BLK1><BEGIN><FDM><EXTRACTION_PROCESSOR><PROCESS_
FORCE_ACT_SECTOR>
```

```
... DAD fake block consisting of 280 lines od
Ada code
```

```
$<BLK1><END><FDM><EXTRACTION_PROCESSOR><PROCESS_FORCE_
ACT_SECTOR>

   ...
```

```
420    end if;
...”
```

The focus of this fake-block resolution refactoring strategy is to demarcate otherwise undifferentiated code to guide automated refactoring operations to segregate the code into methods of methods that adhere to the coding and design practice. In this example Java method derived from the fake-block will be an FDM method exported in its fdmIo package. This fake-block is created to separate the technical part of the code (FDS) from the applicative processing (FDM). Then a second fake-block for DAD, encapsulated in FDM, is created automatically by the tool, because the code inside this block manipulates objects or triggers routines that are owned in the configuration by the DAD module. This DAD fake-block represents 280 lines of Ada code.

In Java for an FDS package, a very simple method corresponding to the legacy Ada without the fake-block has been extracted from the surrounding code of the block and encapsulated in the Java as a method of the FDM package:

```
“public static void processForceActSector(final
IcaoMessages message, final MmiToFdpMessage mmiMessage,

    final ReportsE report, Inouts buffer, FdsGlobalVar
fdsGlobalArg) {

    FlightPlan cdcRecord = new FlightPlan();

    ...

ExternalServices.fdmServices.fdmProcessForceActSector
(message, cdcRecord, coordRecord,

    ...

    }”
```

> Call to external FDM service issued from FDM fakeBlock

In the FDM package a very simple method is introduced that implements the corresponding FDM fake-block:

```
public static boolean fdmProcessForceActSector(final
IcaoMessages message, FlightPlan cdcRecord,

    ...

ExternalServices.dadServices.dadProcessForceActSector
(message, reportMessage,

    ...

return doPostUpdateUpdate;

    }
```

> Call to external DAD service issued from DAD fakeBlock

This example illustrates a few of the many refactoring strategies and mechanisms that were used to define interfaces between JFDP modules and formalize the calls to external modules that are exported through the xxxIo packages.

## EATMS Refactoring Quality Metrics

Significant improvements in quality and safety aspects in the code were achieved due to refactoring-related modularization of the JFDP code: Removal of dead code and global variables produced smaller, easier to maintain procedures and classes. Refactored modules achieved consistent content and produced modularized code that was easier to read and understand. Inter-module dependencies were reduced, thereby decreasing side effects that must be considered when analyzing modules. Transformation of global variables into members of classes achieved localization of global variable definitions and made their behavior more easily understood.

Impact analysis was simplified, reducing the analysis time and costs associated with Engineering Change Requests (ECRs) and Problem Correction Reports (PCRs). Implementation of code modifications was better controlled due to improvements in quality metrics and integration of UML models into maintenance tools and procedures. In addition, the technical sophistication of tools improved through the use of Eclipse, Junit, Jprofiler, Emma, Checkstyle, findBugsKlocwork, and the use of design documentation (Transformation Blueprints™) and code from TSRI. These tools were significant improvements over the Ada-oriented tools logiscope and rulechecker, which they replaced.

These transformation benefits and the tools built around Java have been key elements in convincing the ATC community of the value of Java for operational ATC applications.

Figure 5.13 documents an average factor of two improvements on the key code quality metrics that was achieved by the modernization of EATMS into Java.

## JFDP MODERNIZATION TEST STRATEGY

### Test Strategy Principles

The main goal of the JFDP test strategy was to ensure the faithfulness of the transformation process applied to the Ada code from a functional point of view, and assure that the real-time requirements of the FDP system, as well as its integrity and degree of service, were maintained when FDP was re-implemented from Ada into Java. In the absence of any intended functional change, the focus of regression testing is system-wide testing to achieve a wide scope of coverage under a broad set of realistic test conditions rather than unit level testing to achieve deep

| Ada Metrics (FDP) | | Java Metrics (JFDP) | |
|---|---|---|---|
| Number of unwanted module dependencies | ~ 1000 | Number of module dependencies | 80 |
| Number of CSCs levels in hierarchy | 2 | Number of package levels in hierarchy | 4 |
| Number of ada packages: | 1006 | Number of Java classes: | 1976 |
| Average lines of code per package: | 500 | Average lines of code per class | 195 |
| Number of Ada sub-programs | 3511 | Number of Java methods | 15669 |
| Average lines of code per procedure | 52 | Average lines of code per method | 25 |
| Number of large Ada packages | 1500+ lines of code: 57 violations | Number of large Java classes | 1500+ lines of code: 28 violations |
| Number of large Ada procedures | 150+ lines of code 269 violations | Number of large Java methods | 150+ lines of code 121 violations |

**FIGURE 5.13**

*Post-modernization code quality metrics comparison.*

validation of individual units of the system. Unit testing is indicated when functions are being developed for the first time and the full range of required behaviors must be exercised and validated. The JFDP modernization scenario functions did not involve any changes to FDP functionally, therefore stand-alone unit-level testing, which segregates the focus of the validation effort on repeated executions of the same lines of code, is not a sensible use of testing resources. An advantage of Java technology is the wide availability of a range of tools that enable better code quality, control, and testing. One such tool, EMMA, allows test coverage measurement. EMMA is able to produce a report detailing which package/class/method/lines have been executed under a given series of tests thus allowing unit-level code coverage metrics to be achieved during system level testing. EMMA can be executed with unit tests, CSCI tests, and system tests without requiring specific coding instrumentation. Results are aggregated and summarized in an html report.

Four major steps of the JFDP qualification testing were performed:

1. CSCI tests, involving only the FDP function in a stand-alone mode addressing functional requirements testing
2. Integration tests, involving complete system platform focusing on FDP interfaces, system behavior, and performances
3. Validation tests, involving complete system platform focusing on functional requirements testing
4. Shadow tests, involving customer tests in live ATC environment and real controllers

## CSCI Tests Principles

A high level of automated testing was achieved for JFDP modernization and tightly coupled with the transformation and refactoring processes. The

Eurocat FDP test bed provided the means to exercise both the Ada and Java code in complete ATC simulations using data from live airspace FDP environments. Following every major transformation and refactoring cycle, 12 distinct test datasets were used to simulate execution of JFDP under a battery of rigorous flight scenarios using data captured from live and simulated FDP scenarios.

A tool named AIRSPACE allowed the automatic live replay of existing FDP test scenarios built to test functional requirements of the FPL system. Then another AIRSPACE module was designed to extract the JFDP outputs and allow a smart difference between two distinct runs of the same scenario. In a full test cycle, 272 CSCIs were unit-tested using an 8 hour integrated system test of the modernized system. Detailed functional and time performance comparisons were made using the test performance log files that permitted side-by-side comparison of Ada and Java. The exact same test sequences were performed for both the Ada and the Java, and each Java test sequence output was compared to the Ada test reference sets to assure non-functional distortion between the Ada FDP and JFDP. This set of CSCI tests combined with automatic comparison of the outputs of Ada and Java test runs was the key to achieving confidence in the transformation process and providing evidence of the rigor of the process to external auditors.

The functional status in Ada during these tests was known and referenced. Sometimes erroneous behaviors were noted in the Ada FDP. These legacy bugs were referred to the legacy Ada FPD project teams, but the CSCI test process for JFDP was structured to verify that the same erroneous behavior observed in Ada was also observed in Java. Replication of known faults was proof of functional equivalence.

## Integration Tests Principles

Integration tests for the legacy FDP system were selected and run both in Ada and Java on a system platform. These system integration tests were selected with the following criteria:

- Specific impact of the translation on interfaces: test wrappers around JFDP interfaces
- Assurance that interactions with other CSCIs are still running correctly, in particular tests for safety requirements
- Degraded mode tests
- Performances tests (load test, time to start, time switch)

Test wrappers were used around JFDP interfaces. A set of wrapper scenario-specific tests were performed to ensure all JFDP wrappers were executed for all transformed modules, and that they were interoperable with Ada modules in the test environment. A complete range of interface tests was performed to assure that all CSCIs would run and interact with JFDP correctly.

## System Validation Tests

In addition to CSCI and integration testing, additional validation system tests were selected to extend the range of testing to functional areas that were not covered by the live data simulation testing by using outputs of EMMA tool after CSCI tests run. Results were used to design CSCI-specific tests and to create JFDP system tests required for safety analysis. Validation tests that were relative to requirements flagged "safety" were also selected in priority.

These tests were run first on the system platform in Ada and then in Java.

Combining live data simulation with specially designed CSCI-specific validation tests facilitated rapid convergence on all transformation and refactoring issues. Test results brought a high level of confidence to the Java transformation and refactoring processes, confirming the expectations of the pilot project. This disciplined process combined a well-structured refactoring plan along with a rigorous automated validation process that facilitated rapid identification and correction of any issues resulting from each iteration and asymptotic issue incidence throughout the 10-month duration of the project on the initial Eurocat baseline.

Test status results on the initial Eurocat baseline were as follows:

- 100% tests OK for 272 automatic tests
- 100% tests OK on 27 integration tests
- 100% tests OK on 99 validation test procedures

As shown in Figure 5.14, the total number of bugs (85) was very small for a project that eventually involved the transformation of 1.7 million lines of code, a near phenomenal per line-of-code LOC error incidence of 0.00005%.

After presentation of these positive results there was a decision made to launch the ultimate step of JFDP qualification: testing it with live air traffic data with real controllers acting as if they were controlling the airspace with the system. This is called shadow testing in the ATC world. The objective of live operational tests is twofold:

**FIGURE 5.14**

*Test results — bug reporting.*

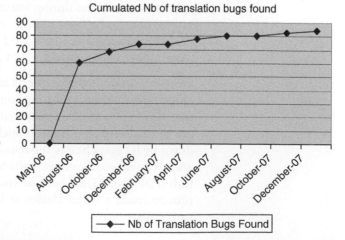

1. Ensure the non-functional distortion proved in the laboratory was also proved in live testing on customer site

2. Observe the system behavior with long-term running and proceed to endurance tests to prove that Java technology was able to cope with real-life air traffic control environment

These steps were key to preparing the safety folder for certification authorities and ensuring that both the refactoring process and Java technology could be used for ATC operations. The JFDP system was installed for several months and tested by some customer experts performing particular specific functional and performance tests. Along with these test procedures, controllers of several countries were invited to work with the system in a two-day shadow session.

The results of these live tests met expectations and proved that both the JFDP system and Java technology were usable. Only three transformation bugs were raised (just in the first couple of days) and only two problems were due to Thales wrappers. There was no crash, no loop occurrence, and no problem linked to the JVM. Thousands of hours of JFDP running were performed in a 5 day, non-stop usage. The two days of shadow testing managed 2,700 flight plan creations and allowed 7 controllers to use the system as if it were in Ada. There were no response time performance issues due to Java.

## EATMS HARDWARE PERFORMANCE EVALUATION

The current trend in hardware is toward many core and multi-processor CPUs. The modernized JFDP architecture and design provided much better multi-threading benefits and multi-CPU hardware than the original Ada. Multi-threading was a key enhancement required to support Coopans' scalability requirements.

A key focus of the EATMS project was to assure JFDP software performance satisfaction of Eurocat's strict runtime performance requirements. To date there have been no JVM crashes, no crashes in the Java code, and no performance/response time issues during testing. The times to start, restart, and switch the system were far below 1 minute, 99% of FDP responses times are below 1 second even during load tests, and the highest CPU consumption is approximately 30–35% for Dual Core PC.

More important Java side effects associated with garbage collection, JIT compilation, and memory consumption have been mastered, and it has been proved that JFDP software complies with all Eurocat performance needs. The margin of final response times is such that even initial processing that is slowed down by JIT stays below the required limit. In the same manner the duration and frequency of garbage collection did not preempt CPU enough to disturb JFDP processing, because memory size was optimized and because JFDP process loads a lot of classes at initialization, which optimizes the memory variations.

The fact that garbage collection and JIT compilation effects were still below the requirements contradicted the initial fears raised during the pilot project. The following section justifies the eventual choice of the Sun JVM for EATMS applications. This point has been confirmed by the live tests performed in customer sites. Use of Java technology requires more careful handling of performances and optimization of memory, but there is unarguable evidence that it is possible to operate a central core server like FDP in a real ATC environment.

## JVM Evaluation

Two JVMs were evaluated for use in the EATMS project: Sun JDK 1.5 and Aonix PERC-Ultra. The JVM provides platform independence and a runtime architecture that greatly simplifies programming by eliminating memory management, but it does so at a cost in runtime performance and non-control-determinism in memory utilization.

JVM performs byte-code interpretation, garbage collection, exception handling, thread management, initialization of variables, and type definition. The industry-wide default standard at the time of the project was Sun's JDK 1.5. Sun's JIT compiler generates byte code that runs in the JVM as interpreted byte code rather than as platform-specific, machine-level instructions.

For real-time applications, the garbage collector can be tuned, but if full garbage collection operation is required, the garbage collector will preempt processing. Through performance tuning, Sun's JVM non-determinist effects were mastered satisfactorily to meet Eurocat and Coopans requirements. Full garbage collection occurs only 0.2% of the time, therefore, 99% of all FDP response times stay below 1 second. Initial input response times always stay below 1 second, and when the response time exceeds 1 second it stays reasonably low (<5 seconds). Therefore the Sun JVM complies with performance requirements for the FDP system. The key performance requirements (restart, reboot, switch-over times) on which the JVM 1.5 was tested were verified through extensive and exhaustive performance tests.

No JVM problems were raised with Sun's JDK 1.5 in 6,500 hours of Java tests of the JFDP from factory CSCI tests to live shadow tests. The conclusion is that the current Sun JVM is reliable.

Sun JVM was first released in 1995. It is validated internally by Sun and also by the Java open source community. The interface of JVM is stable and it is widely used. This also explains its reliability.

Previous analysis showed that the Sun JVM is also compatible with EATMS safety objectives. This is key information for the decision to use Java in ATC systems.

The other JVM evaluated for potential EATMS use was the Aonix PERC-Ultra whose JVM is specifically designed for real-time systems. PERC provides more options to tune the garbage collector, and its garbage collector operations do not preempt the CPU. Unlike Sun's JDK 1.5, PERC can provide either AOT or JIT compilation. However, at the time of performance assessment (2007) the Sun JVM was consistently 2.5 times faster than the fastest PERC-Ultra configuration. At the time of evaluation, the PERC-Ultra product did not support optimal usage of multi-CPU hardware. This was a show-stopper for this option, and the Sun JVM was chosen to be the best option for the EATMS projects.

## PROJECT CONCLUSIONS

The EATMS Ada to Java modernization project was an exceptionally sophisticated and highly disciplined application of automated transformation and semi-automated refactoring against a high-performance, mission-critical software application. Key to the success of the EATMS modernization project was the tuning of the software technical and management processes to achieve a metrics-guided modernization process that maximized the utilization of skills and technology from all members of the team. This included continuous perfective adaptation of the tools and methods to achieve and maintain a high level of automation in all phases of the project. Detailed attention to process, methods, and technology permitted re-application of modernization methods and tools that achieve high economies of scale when applied to multiple related systems in Thales' Eurocat product lines.

Another significant output of this project, which has been continuously driven to support an industrial application and a final integration in operational projects, is the possible usage of Java technology adapted to air traffic management real-time requirements. This key evidence would not have been so clearly identified without this project.

### Acronyms and Definitions for Eurocat Systems

- **ADS: Automatic Dependent Surveillance**. Surveillance system based on aircraft data downloaded to the ground system. In ADS-B stations are scattered in the controlled ADS-B airspace to populate a network with aircraft positions and reports.
- **BADA: Base of Aircraft Data**. Aircraft Performance database allowing modeling of commercial aircraft managed by ATC applications.
- **Dataset**. Set of parameters and data files that are produced by an off-line application for online usage in the Eurocat system. It contains both parameters used to tune the system behavior and operational data that adapt the Eurocat system to a particular airspace.

- **FDP: Flight Data Processing**. Eurocat CSCI that manages all aspects of the flight plan data, including FDP, ground-to-ground messages, environment data, etc.
- **JFDP**. Java image of the FDP core function (FPL).
- **FPL system**. Core functionality of the FDP CSCI (64% of code and requirements). The FPL is the heart of the future evolutions brought by EATMS projects.
- **FPL record**. Record of flight plan data stored or computed by FDP in a disk database.
- **FDS: Flight Data Server**. Module that interfaces an FPL process with the rest of the Eurocat system via UBSS services.
- **TPM: Trajectory Prediction Manager**. Piece of software that computes the vertical evolution of the aircraft trajectories.
- **UBSS: UNIX-Based System Software**. Thales Middleware for ATC systems, running on top of UNIX/LINUX OS.

# CHAPTER 6

# PowerBuilder/4GL Generator Modernization Pilot*

### Philip H. Newcomb, Dru Henke, Jim LoVerde, William Ulrich, Luong Nguyen, and Robert Couch

## INTRODUCTION

This case study describes a pilot modernization project at a major US company and includes a description of the modernization methods, technologies, and processes employed in this project. The software environment was written in PowerBuilder and COBOL that was generated by a fourth generation language code generator (4GL). The entire environment was deployed on an IBM mainframe. The pilot project encompassed the investigation, planning, and a proof of technology test to move (or retire) applications from the technology stack using an iterative, phased approach that encompasses multiple methods of conversion.

Although this was technically considered a pilot project, the intent from the beginning and throughout the work effort was to deploy a production-ready application at the end of the pilot phase and deactivate the corresponding mainframe software that was being migrated. The effort began in 2007 and various implementation tasks are continuing as of this writing. The overall effort involved an analysis of options and approaches, development of certain target architecture technologies to support the migration, on-site system preparation and packaging, off-site software conversion, on-site software validation and user acceptance testing, and final deployment.

### External Project Participants

NVISIA, LLC is an advanced development and architecture advisory firm providing custom development, architectural planning, and integration solutions in a wide range of industries. NVISIA's role was to work with in-house staff to develop the future state architecture and develop transformation specifications as input to the TSRI toolset. Additionally, NVISIA provided analysis and integration services specific to the semi-automated processes.

TSRI specializes in automated legacy system modernization services for the military, federal and commercial business sectors. Established in 1995, the company transforms existing applications written in a variety of procedural languages into object-oriented software written in Java/J2EE, C++, or C/C# .NET. The company undertakes modernization projects using a highly automated iterative modernization process, which includes documentation, transformation, refactoring, redesign, rearchitecture, and Web-enablement. The company's low-cost, low-risk perfective modernization services are made possible by advanced artificial intelligence-based technology that achieves 100% automation of most modernization scenarios.

## PILOT PROJECT OVERVIEW

This case study describes the modernization methods, technologies, and processes employed in the pilot project to mitigate the risks associated with the replacement and retirement of the PowerBuilder- and 4GL-based applications. Because the PowerBuilder and 4GL technologies are the foundation of several of the larger core business applications, modernizing these systems required mitigation of risk through careful planning and execution of a risk-reduction pilot.

The company sought to migrate the PowerBuilder and 4GL generated COBOL applications to a standardized technology platform and architecture. There were numerous systems within the overall application suite that collectively managed a portion of the customer tracking environment. The particular system selected for the pilot was a small subset of this customer tracking system.

There were a number of additional applications that were targeted for migration, assuming the pilot project met certain goals. One key goal of the project was to prove the cost savings of an automated conversion effort versus a manual rewrite. The timeframe for the proof of automatic conversion viability was the end of 2007 with the commencement of actual systems migration in 2008.

The pilot project encompassed the investigation, planning, and proof of technology test of effort required to move (or retire) applications from the technology stack using an iterative, phased approach that incorporated multiple methods of conversion. It required the development of two highly automated architecture-driven modernization technologies and processes to transform, refactor, Web-enable, and fully document the PowerBuilder and 4GL sample applications. The target environment would be a Java system that was compatible with the company's application architecture, which was built upon several popular open source frameworks as well as proprietary, in-house frameworks. The project is an example of architecture-driven, language-to-language and platform-to-platform modernization scenarios.

# The 4GL and PowerBuilder Challenge

The two main technologies involved in this project were the PowerBuilder and 4GL generated COBOL computing language environments. These two environments were used to create a large cross-section of in-house applications. Each of these technologies presented their own challenges.

The 4GL was an application generator that uses a custom COBOL-like language to generate COBOL service programs that operate under the control of IBM's CICS online transaction environment. The 4GL also uses a DBMS-based metadata repository and includes Windows client applications for development purposes. The software vendor that created the 4GL terminated operations years before and the 4GL has since been maintained only out of necessity by an external service provider. The lack of industry support for this 4GL code generator motivated the search for alternative technology solutions for the applications under consideration for this pilot and any subsequent project work.

PowerBuilder, on the other hand, was a common online development environment that exploded onto the scene in the late 1980s and early 1990s. The issue with PowerBuilder is that it represents highly proprietary technology from a single vendor. PowerBuilder has switched hands over the years as well. Being a proprietary technology (as opposed to an open technology such as Java), PowerBuilder customers are totally beholden to the vendor. In addition, PowerBuilder is likely to reach an end-of-life situation at some point.

While the business users and customers were reasonably satisfied with the 4GL and PowerBuilder based applications, the technologies continued to create obstacles for IT as they tried to support future business growth. The issues presented by the 4GL and the PowerBuilder technologies to the company's overall architectural strategy were numerous:

- Language Obsolescence: The languages do not leverage the newest performance and security features of the modern Web-facing platform technologies the company had adopted.
- Increasing Operational Risk: Migration to new operating system versions would become impossible as the current operating systems reach end of life.
- Increasing Maintenance Cost and Risk: The existing PowerBuilder and 4GL source code is difficult to maintain without harming its efficiency.
- Expanding Technology Gap: The existing PowerBuilder and 4GL environments cannot leverage contemporary reuse capabilities such as services oriented architecture (SOA) and Portal.
- Workforce Retention and Recruitment Risk: Recruitment of top-notch programmers to use PowerBuilder and obsolete 4GL technologies is becoming increasingly difficult.

## Modernization Benefits

Because the PowerBuilder and 4GL applications are functioning, valuable software assets, a total rewrite of these applications makes little economic sense. In addition, these applications provide unique business value and have been customized accordingly over a period of many years. Therefore, it makes little sense to seek an ERP or commercial-off-the-shelf (COTS) package solution because these options will not provide the same business functionality that is already built into these existing applications.

In other words, migration of these applications to a standardized, open technology is the preferred and only sensible approach because this approach retains the rich, underlying business functionality of the existing application environment. By attacking the migration issue aggressively, the company seeks to accrue these following additional benefits through their modernization:

- Streamline Deployment of New Business Requirements: React more quickly to business needs as enhanced reuse allows applications to be extended more easily and eventually allow applications to be assembled from existing parts.

- Eliminate Dependence on Aging Technology: Reducing dependence on technologies that have reached or are reaching end of life provides a more robust foundation for delivering improved value to the company's business and to its customers.

- Facilitate Future Enhancements: Streamline the applications and ready them to be refactored to support SOA and Portal capabilities, thus allowing for the creation of more efficient and more extensible code. Ultimately, the business will gain significant benefits as application teams will be able to deploy more functionality, more quickly across more environments.

- Leverage New Technologies: Leverage newer, better tools and methods for development, testing, and tuning. This will open up many more options for the business and IT support teams as new technologies can be integrated into the environment more seamlessly.

## Migration Strategy

The overall migration strategy requires an assessment of the long-term objectives and feasibility analysis of short-term maintenance requirements. This includes definition of a migration roadmap to guide the phasing and staging of the overall pilot effort. These action items are discussed below.

- Long-Term Strategy: Determining cost and feasibility of modernization would be essential before commencement of the

modernization of the 2.5 million lines of code that comprised
the core applications to be modernized as part of this project. To
manage these risks, a series of risk-reduction efforts were undertaken,
commencing with a risk mitigation pilot that played a crucial role
in determining the viability of automated and/or semi-automated
conversion. Modernization performance factors derived from the
risk mitigation pilot established the cost and timeline profiles on
the pace of migration that are key determining factors in defining
the migration roadmap and timeline for migrating all systems to the
standard Java-based development platform.

- Short-term Maintenance Strategy: To ensure continuity of business
  operations, the existing systems will continue to be maintained
  within the 4GL and PowerBuilder environments until the risk
  mitigation project is accepted and signed off. In-house teams
  responsible for ongoing maintenance changes will continue to
  maintain the existing applications. To ensure that migrated software
  incorporated ongoing changes, the on-site team worked out a multi-
  pronged approach. First, software batches sent off for migration
  will represent the latest version of the software. In addition, batch
  sizes would be kept to a reasonable size so there was no unnecessary
  elongation of the migration and validation testing cycle. Maintenance
  changes would be minimized wherever possible on the software
  undergoing migration. Finally, emergency changes would be
  retrofitted into migrated software batches upon completion of a
  given batch validation testing cycle.

- Migration Roadmap: A high-level migration roadmap, produced
  during the pilot using global dependency analysis, was generated
  using the automated migration toolset. The resulting analysis was
  used to identify the various application module interdependencies to
  determine the proper order in which to migrate various application
  modules so as to absolutely minimize impacts on business
  operations. In addition, the on-site team assessed its ability to
  validate and gain system owner acceptance of each batch of migrated
  software so as to streamline the phasing and staging roadmap
  accordingly.

## Pilot Objectives and Constraints

Additional concerns would be addressed by the pilot in order for the final
solution to meet and satisfy modernization, security, non-functional and
architectural objectives, and non-traditional architectural objectives and
constraints as identified in the tables in Figures 6.1–6.3.

| 1. 4GL Modernization | 2. Non-Functional Requirements |
|---|---|
| a. **Conversion** - Must automatically convert at least 95% of existing 2.5 million lines of 4GL code.<br><br>b. **Standards Adherence** - Generated code must adhere to internal standard Java architecture and frameworks. | a. **Usability** - The ease with which a user can learn to operate, prepares inputs for, and interprets outputs of a system or component. The application(s) will need to follow internal standard usability requirements for internal users.<br><br>b. **Accessibility** - The ease with which different facets of the system are exercised. The application(s) will need to follow internal standard accessibility requirements for internal users. |
| **3. Security Requirements**<br><br>a. **Security Permissions** - Must be able to automatically migrate the existing security permissions to the new model/repository.<br><br>b. **Service Level Security** - Must provide service-level security. | c. **Aesthetics** - The aesthetic quality of the user interface. The application(s) will need to follow internal standard aesthetic requirements for internal users.<br><br>d. **Consistency** - The consistent use of mechanisms employed in the user interface. This applies both within the system, and with other systems. The application(s) will need to follow internal standard consistency requirements for internal users. |

**FIGURE 6.1**

*Modernization, security, and non-functional requirements.*

## Application Architecture Modernization

The legacy application architecture (depicted in Figure 6.4) is a complex composite of languages and platforms with its applications written in PowerBuilder, 4GL generated COBOL, natively developed COBOL, and Java. The CICS COBOL, PowerBuilder, and 4GL applications support a composite client–server and mainframe-based architecture that was developed in the 1980s and 1990s. The older legacy applications and architecture now coexist, compete, and conflict with the newer Web-facing Java platform technologies. In addition, they pose increasing operational and maintenance cost, recruitment issues and workforce retention risks that are largely related to technology obsolescence.

### Existing High-Level Application Architecture

These categories of applications can be found in the existing architecture:

- Java Web Applications: Using a server-side custom Java to 4GL generated COBOL access library that uses the Java CICS transaction gateway to invoke the generated mainframe CICS COBOL services, which in turn interact with DB2.
- PowerBuilder Clients: Using a custom DLL to invoke the generated mainframe CICS COBOL services that interact with DB2.
- CICS Online Applications: The CICS COBOL applications invoke the generated CICS COBOL services directly.
- COBOL Batch Programs: The application also includes a separately generated, batch mode version of the COBOL 4GL code that interacts with DB2.

## 4.    Architectural Concerns

a.    **Reliability** - The ability of a system or component to perform its required functions under stated conditions for a specified period of time. The application(s) will meet internal reliability requirements.

b.    **Accuracy** - Accuracy of any calculations performed. The application(s) will meet internal accuracy requirements.

c.    **Availability** - The degree to which a system or component is operational and accessible when required for use. The application(s) will need to meet internal availability requirements.

d.    **Restorability** - The restoration of a system, program, database, or other system resource to a prior state following a failure or externally caused disaster; for example, the restoration of a database to a point at which processing can be resumed following a system failure. The application(s) will follow internal standard recoverability requirements for internal applications.

e.    **Performance** - Performance refers to the responsiveness of the system - the time required to respond to stimuli (events) or the number of events processed in some interval of time. Performance qualities are often expressed by the number of transactions per unit of time or by the amount of time it takes to complete a transaction. The new system will be required to support and average response time for service requests at least equal to the existing COBOL-based system. Note that this is on average. Some individual requests may take longer and others may be quicker.

f.    **Efficiency** - The amount of resources used and the duration of such use in performing its function. For example: CPU Time; Disk Time; # of active threads at the high watermark level of usage. Knowing the efficiency should lead to a solid understanding of the overall system capacity. The application will follow internal efficiency requirements for internal applications.

g.    **Recovery** - The time to recover from a system failure. The application(s) will follow standard internal application recovery time requirements.

h.    **Response** - The time for the system to provide a response (i.e., elapsed time).The end-user experience for Web page interaction should generally fall into the time-ranges indicated below:

- Typing, cursor motion, mouse selection: 50 to 150 milliseconds
- Simple frequent tasks: 1 second
- Common tasks: 2 to 4 seconds
- Complex tasks: 8 to 12 seconds

i.    **Shutdown time** - The time for the system to shut down. The application(s) will follow internal standard shutdown time requirements.

j.    Start-up time - The time for the system to start up. The application(s) will follow internal standard startup time requirements.

k.    **Throughput** - The capacity of the system to support a given flow of information. Often discussed in terms of volume. The application(s) will meet or exceed throughput requirements.

l.    **Supportability** - Supportability is the inherent quality of a system - including design for reliability and maintainability, technical support data, and maintenance procedures - to facilitate detection, isolation, and timely repair/replacement of system anomalies. The application(s) will meet internal supportability requirements.

m.    **Adaptability** - The ease with which the system is adapted to new environments. The system will be able to adapt to future usage scenarios in a service-oriented environment.

n.    **Auditability** - The ease with which the system provides audit trails of its execution. The application(s) will meet internal auditability requirements.

o.    **Compatibility** - The compatibility of this system with previous versions of the system. The migrated system will need to have interoperability flexibility with existing versions of the system in the following ways:

    i.    **Support for parallel operation** - The migrated systems need to be able to operate in a parallel environment alongside the legacy system during a transition period.

    ii.    **Seamless existing Java compatibility** - There are numerous Java Web applications in production today. Replacement API will be provided that minimizes the effort to port these Java applications to the new Java Web services implementation converted from the 4GL.

    iii.    **Legacy COBOL compatibility** - The migrated code will need to be able to be invoked from legacy COBOL code.

p.    **Configurability** - The ease with which the system is configured. The migrated system will conform to intern configuration options, such that changing between the CICS and Web service implementation of a converted 4GL service will require only change to a configuration.

q.    **Installability** - The ease with which the system is installed. The target applications should be deployed as standard Java EAR files to the standard internal WebSphere Java application server environment.

r.    **Localizability** - The level to which the system supports multiple human languages. There are not currently any localizability requirements. The chosen implementation should not preclude the potential future use of standard Java localization mechanisms.

s.    **Maintainability** - The ease with which the system is maintained. Ease of maintenance of the migrated applications is extremely important.

    i.    To the greatest extent possible, the solution must use pre-existing internal standard frameworks and patterns.

    ii.    To the greatest extent possible, maintenance of the migrated applications should be identical to the maintenance of a clean room developed Java application.

    iii.    Additionally, tools must be provided to enable developers familiar with the legacy PowerBuilder and 4GL code to locate the corresponding code and functionality in the migrated Java system.

t.    **Scalability** - The ease with which the system can scale in terms of data volumes and users. The target applications must support user base in the millions. Actual 4GL-based COBOL call volumes in the millions of transactions per day.

u.    **Testability** - The ease with which the system is tested.

    i.    The target application environment will support tracing and testing services calls as other metrics such as timing information.

    ii.    In addition, the migrated system must provide templatized JUnit-based test scaffolding that can be used by developers to create data-driven unit and regression tests to further improve the testability of the migrated applications.

    iii.    Finally, the migrated system must be tested in comparison to the legacy applications to ensure the correctness of the migrated code.

**FIGURE 6.2**

*Architectural concerns.*

**5. Additional Architectural Concerns**

This section provides additional information that doesn't fit into the typical non-functional requirements categories and generally represents constraints.

a. **Design Requirements** - A design requirement, often called a design constraint, specifies or constrains the options for designing a system. For example, if you specify that a relational database is required, that's a design constraint. There should be no schema or data changes required to the legacy application databases by the migrated applications. Any new data requirements must be kept to an absolute minimum.

b. **Implementation Requirements** - An implementation requirement specifies or constrains the coding or construction of a system. Examples include required standards, implementation languages, and resource limits. The migrated code should follow internal Java coding standards.

c. **Interface Requirements** - An interface requirement specifies an external item, with which a system must interact, or constraints on formats or other factors used within such an interaction.

d. **Physical Requirements** - A physical requirement specifies a physical constraint imposed on the hardware used to house the system - shape, size, or weight, for example.

**FIGURE 6.3**

*Additional non-traditional architectural concerns.*

**FIGURE 6.4**

*Existing application architecture.*

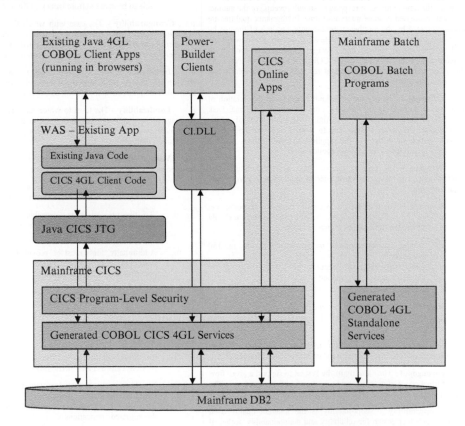

## New High-Level Application Architecture

In the new architecture, 4GL generated COBOL and PowerBuilder services will be implemented in automatically generated Java using standardized frameworks including Spring and Hibernate (see Figure 6.5).

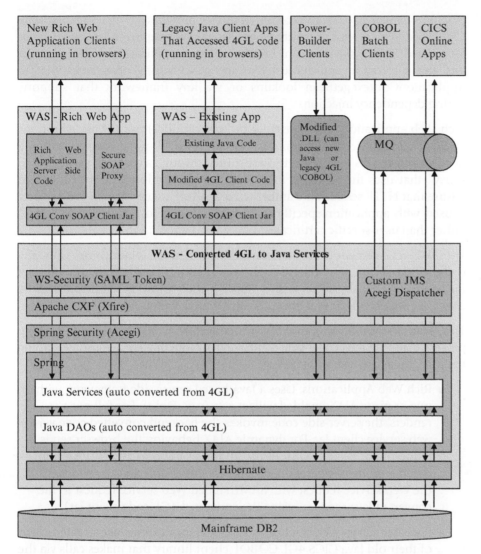

**FIGURE 6.5**
*New application architecture.*

This new architecture functions as follows. For security purposes, the Spring code uses the Acegi framework, which isolates the code from how the authentication and authorization actually occurs. There are at least two types of Acegi interceptors, one for WS-Security and another to establish the credentials from incoming JMS/MQ messages. Finally, the Spring services are remotely enabled as Web services using the Apache CXF framework (which is the new version of XFire).

Note that the converted services are exposed as standard Web services secured by WS-Security using the SAML Token authentication. This means that they are accessible to any Web service client or framework (e.g., Axis1, Axis2,

JAXB-WS/Glassfish, etc.). The converted service provides a prepackaged Apache CXF-based Web service client that exposes the Web service client interface as a standard Spring service bean. From the client application code's perspective, the application appears just like any other Spring bean accessible via ApplicationContext.getBean lookups or via any framework that supports Spring dependency injection.

Rich Web applications (i.e., currently in PowerBuilder) use the asynchronous JavaScript and XML (AJAX) communication facility. Browser controls with the need for direct calls to 4GL services are routed through a custom "Secure SOAP Proxy" that uses the standard in-house Web application security context to ensure that HTTP sessions are authenticated. SAML token form of WS-Security is used with application-specific certificates (similar to managed ID's today) rather than user-specific certificates.

The 4GL replacement Web services establish a trust relationship with any request signed with one of these application certificates to ensure that the user ID passed by that signed request is valid (if the request is tampered with by changing the user ID, it will invalidate the digital signature).

This results in the following application architecture, which drives the conversion process mapping into target-side components. Note that we are also describing the transition state where applicable.

- Rich Web Applications: Uses a Java-based server-side framework with one or more AJAX-enabled widget sets (e.g., Dojo). For full page renders, the server-side code invokes the backend converted code via a web service client jar. For dynamic AJAX behavior, the browser sends a request to a "Secure SOAP Proxy" that uses the normal HTTP session-based security to ensure the user is authenticated and then wraps the Web service request with SAML signed Web service request to the converted Java services (using the converted 4GL code client jar).

- Preexisting Java Web Applications: These applications use a replacement of their old Java CICS 4GL COBOL client library that makes calls via the new SAML signed Web services instead of the old CICS approach. The existing API uses static methods and exposes some CICS level details that may require some manual migration efforts beyond dropping in a replacement library.

- PowerBuilder Clients: Via a data bridge, these applications use a modified DLL that has both the old capability to invoke the mainframe CICS COBOL 4GL services that interact with DB2 database as well as the capability to invoke the new SAML signed Web services. This can be configured on a call-by-call basis. (Note: This data bridge is a temporary solution until all of the PowerBuilder applications are migrated.)

- CICS Online Applications: These applications will invoke the converted CICS COBOL 4GL services directly and submit requests via secure JMS/MQ queues. The Java services container listens for requests, dispatches them to the converted Java services, and puts the response on a response queue.

- COBOL Batch Programs: The architecture will include a separately-generated set of COBOL 4GL code that interacts with DB2 on a case-by-case basis. They may be able to use the JMS/MQ-based approach used by the COBOL online applications. In some situations conversion of a COBOL-based batch program to Java will be necessary.

## New Application Environment Components Overview

The target Java environment for the converted 4GL framework is based on the company's internal Java starter app platform. This starter app framework is an internally-developed compilation of preferred open source frameworks and ideal techniques for utilizing those frameworks. Some of the key open-source frameworks that make it up are XDoclet, Struts 1.x, Spring, Hibernate, Derby, JUnit, Apache Commons, Log4J, XFire for Web service support, and Acegi for security.

Several internal frameworks are incorporated into the platform as well. The "starter app" platform is the preferred environment for all current and future Java development efforts. As such, the Java code converter makes every effort to generate target code that operates within this starter app environment. The principle components in the internal Java/JEE framework are described briefly in the following list.

- Spring Framework: An open source application framework for the Java platform and the .NET framework.

- Acegi Security System for Spring: Spring Security, using Acegi, provides powerful and flexible security solutions for enterprise applications developed using the Spring Framework.

- Apache Struts: This is an open source Web application for developing Java EE Web applications that uses and extends the Java Servlet API to encourage developers to adopt a model-view-controller (MVC) architecture.

- Apache Commons: This is a set of Java components that have minimal dependencies on other software libraries so that components can be deployed easily. Common components keep their interfaces as stable as possible.

- Dojo Toolkit: This is an open source, modular JavaScript library (i.e., JavaScript toolkit) designed to ease the rapid development of cross platform, JavaScript/AJAX-based applications, and Web sites. AJAX is a group of interrelated Web development techniques used to create interactive Web applications or rich Internet applications. With Ajax, Web applications can retrieve data from the server asynchronously in the background without interfering with the display and behavior of the existing page.

- Hibernate: An object-relational mapping (ORM) library for the Java language that provides a framework for mapping an object-oriented domain model to a traditional relational database. Hibernate solves object-relational impedance mismatch problems by replacing direct persistence-related database accesses with high-level object handling functions.

- JUnit: This is a unit testing framework for the Java programming language.

- Log4J: This is a Java-based logging utility.

- Spring Data Access Object (DAO; specifically the Hibernate and JDBC implementations): This access object provides an abstract interface to a *database* or persistence mechanism and provides data access operations, without exposing details of the database. This isolation separates the concerns of which data accesses the application needs.

- Xdoclet: This is an open source code generation library that enables attribute-oriented programming for Java via insertion of special JavaDoc tags. It comes with a library of predefined tags that simplify coding for various technologies.

- XFire: A next-generation Java SOAP framework that makes service-oriented development approachable through an easy-to-use API and its support for standards. It also performs well because it is built on a low memory StAX-based model.

## Architecture Conversion

To achieve the new architecture, the 4GL-based business logic and data services will both be converted to equivalent Java applications and linked to replacement services available in Spring and Hibernate.

### Business Services Conversion

There are two types of services supported by the existing 4GL environment: business and data services. The general approach taken for both types of services is to generate a Java interface, a Java implementation of that interface, a JUnit test case, and for data services a DAO interface and DAO implementation.

- 4GL based Business Services: These are exposed as Web services that communicate with the "legacy" application through the legacy application interface until replaced by the Java application and Java interface.

- 4GL based Application Data Services: These interact with the underlying DB2 database via Java objects that map to the DB tables. This concept follows a traditional DAO-based approach (using Hibernate to map the objects to the appropriate tables/columns).

### Transaction Management Conversion

The existing system manages transactions using CICS's transaction management capabilities, including the automatic transaction behavior upon calling a CICS service as well as explicit calls to the CICS transaction API. In the migrated applications, these same transactions are handled by the Spring transaction manager. For converted code that explicitly performs commits and rollbacks, the base service class provides a convenience method for the generated code to do this using the Spring transaction manager API.

### Security Management Conversion

The migrated codebase uses the Acegi framework API for security purposes. Using Acegi allows for a standard security API across all application layers and comes with numerous preexisting adapters to plug in authentication and authorization contexts in different operating environments (e.g., Web clients vs. Web services vs. stand-alone/asynchronous batch applications).

## TRANSFORMATION AND REFACTORING TECHNOLOGY

The 4GL and PowerBuilder application code conversion for the pilot was accomplished using TSRI's JanusStudio™ modernization framework for information system transformation, JanusStudio™ which supports architecture-driven modernization as an automated model-based, rule-driven managed process that includes automated documentation, transformation, refactoring, and Web enablement as depicted in Figure 6.6 and outlined in the following steps.

**Step 1:** Assessment and documentation captures and documents the 4GL and PowerBuilder as-is and to-be code structure and related architecture, to provide a detailed evaluation of the existing target system's design. This step also helps identify the baseline metrics that will support the transformation business case.

**Step 2:** Transformation rewrites the legacy 4GL and PowerBuilder software into object-oriented Java code and accurately couples that code to Hibernate and Spring services, ensuring accurate conversion of all system internal and external interfaces.

**FIGURE 6.6**
*JanusStudio™*
*transformation framework.*

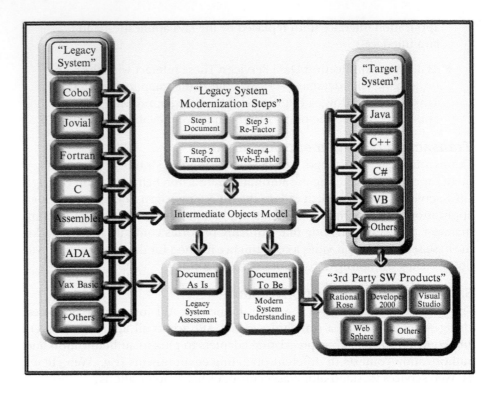

**Step 3**: Refactoring reengineers the resulting Java code, along with the Spring and Hibernate components, to improve system structure, performance, and maintainability. Internal subject area experts developed detailed specifications for automated refactoring. These were applied to optimize the structure of the generated Java code and to optimize the interface with Spring and Hibernate services with the new target architecture.

**Step 4**: Web-enablement transforms the legacy applications into the requisite language to take advantage of J2EE Spring and Hibernate components, while the derived components are segregated to operate on the client or server side of the application. The rich GUI features of PowerBuilder were replaced by equivalent services of Dojo/AJAX browser interface services of the target Spring architecture.

## Standards Adherence

The JanusStudio™ modeling transformation framework adheres to practices of the Object Management Group (OMG) architecture-driven modernization initiative. This initiative advocates that modeling, analysis, visualization, transformation, translation, and refactoring of the design and architecture be accomplished as operations performed on platform-independent models with generators for platform-specific implementations. The modernization framework internal Intermediate Object Model (IOM) also conforms to the OMG Abstract Syntax Tree Metamodel (ASTM), Knowledge Discovery Metamodel (KDM), and Structured Metrics Metamodels (SMM) standards specifications.

## Summary of High-Level Specification Languages

The 4GL and PowerBuilder transformation required some degree of tool customization. The 4GL used by this company, in particular, is not a common technology and PowerBuilder has not been transformed in any volume. Therefore, the company needed to ensure that the pilot project did not require a significant amount of customization that would drive up costs and extend project timeframes. To this end, a technology was required that would meet these goals. At the core of the transformation framework are three high-level platform-independent specification languages, JPGEN™, JTGEN™, and JRGEN™:

- JPGEN™ for defining grammar system and language models. Defines compact and efficient grammar systems for mapping application source code into model bases.

- JTGEN™ for defining transformations between these models. Defines the complex rewrite rules that map between these model bases to ensure that the semantics within a source language are accurately re-expressed within the semantics of a target language.

- JRGEN™ for model manipulation and analysis that supports first order logic and predicate calculus as well as 3GL and 4GL language constructs. Communicates between model bases and alternative representations such as design, documentation, software metrics, and visual presentations.

Language conversion involves model-based transformations, which are applied to abstract syntax and semantic graph representations of the source code of one language to generate the abstract syntax and semantic graph representations of the target language.

## Intermediate Object Model (IOM)

For maximum efficiency, all semantic and syntactical forms of multiple languages are mapped into a language-neutral modeling formalism, the IOM. The IOM is a language-neutral model into which all legacy source languages are transformed, and from which all modernized target languages are generated. The IOM is, in effect, a universal language-based, modeling and transformation system. Through the use of the IOM, TSRI simplifies the $O(S *T)$ language transformation problem to an $O(S + T + 1)$ language transformation problem, where S is the number of Source languages and T is the number of Target languages of practical interest. The IOM provides a set of generic language constructs that serve as a reusable language-neutral formalism for assessment, documentation, transformation, refactoring, and Web-enablement.

The conversion to an object-oriented design is driven by automated pattern-based transformation rules and semi-automated, human-directed refactoring plans. These are developed through iterative refinement to remove dead code, consolidate redundant code, and improve the resulting design and architecture of the modernized system. The rules that transform procedural or imperative languages into object-oriented languages are incorporated into the IOM to assure reusability across multiple languages.

## Level of Automation

In general, the level of automation achieved is 100% for all transformation and automated refactoring operations. This level of automation enables tasks that would otherwise take years if undertaken manually to be accomplished in a few hours as a model-based, rule-driven transformation process. By encoding complex tasks as rules, cycle times are reduced for iterative processes, permitting every modernization project to be undertaken as a series of iterative, incremental spiral development cycles. If errors are detected or enhancements are needed, the transformation rules are modified and the process is repeated.

## Documentation Products

The following products are generated for every functional or data unit of code and fully integrated in the documentation deliverable with hyperlinks provided between corresponding source and target (legacy and modernized) system application code, such that the line of the code is repositioned to the top of the display window as each node in the diagram, table, model, or graph is selected:

- As-Is Documentation: Functional analysis-level design model of the legacy system application code in its original state *prior* to modernization.

- To-Be Documentation: Functional analysis-level design model of the legacy system application code into its target state *after* modernization. The documentation provides a hyperlink between the legacy as-is source code and the modern target code, maintaining line-level correspondence between each line and every data element.

- Control Flow Graph (CFG): A graph of the control relationships between conditions, program branches, and called procedures in an application's paragraph or program. The CFG is depicted as a scalar vector graphic (SVG).

- Structure Chart (SC): A graph of the call relationships between paragraphs or programs and optionally the data inputs and outputs associated with the procedure call.

- State Machine Model (SMM): A graph of the states and state transitions of a procedure in which states are depicted as bubbles and state transitions are depicted as arcs between the states. The set of individual conditions in the preconditions associated with the set of state transitions out of a state are considered the control variables of the state. There is one action sequence associated with each state transition and one Boolean value assignment to the preconditions associated with each state transition. There is one or more state transitions (arcs out) potentially associated with each state and potentially zero or more state transitions coming into each state. There is a begin state and one (or more) end states associated with each state machine. A state machine is isomorphic with a state transition table.

- Cause-Effect Graph (CEG): A graph that depicts a sequence of rules that govern program behavior in terms of cause-and-effect nodes in a directed fashion. A cause in a CEG graph is an assertion of a Boolean value assignment to an observable condition or an assertion that an observable behavior (effect) has occurred. A CEG for a procedure or a program is a connected graph of cause-and-effect nodes for the procedure or program as a whole that operationally define a sequence of rules (precondition and associated action) that define the behavior of the program. A CEG is isomorphic with a state transition table.

- Data Flow Graph (DFD): A graph of the flow of data and of the transformations applied to data between the data stores of a program. Data stores (such as data records or classes) are the data structures used by the program for the storage of program data. Data flows are the fields or attributes used or assigned values by the data transforming statements of the program. The transformations are contiguous sequences of program statements that sequentially process input data to produce output data. The data transformations that update a data store as a whole or a substructure of a data store are called Methods. A paragraph data flow model is a formal description of the flows of data between data stores referenced within a paragraph. Nodes in a paragraph data flow model consist of data stores and data transformation processes. A data transformation process node can encapsulate several program statements that read and update several data stores.

- State Transition Table (STT): A table that provides a formal description of the state transitions of a state. A state table can be constructed for a state, a state transition, or an entire paragraph. An STT is a three-part table consisting of (1) preconditions and their Boolean value assignments, (2) the set of state transitions achieved by satisfying preconditions, and (3) the set of actions taken upon satisfaction of the transition preconditions. An STT is a formal description of the control conditions, actions, and state transitions of a particular procedure or of a state within a procedure. A state transition consists of a Boolean value assignment to the control conditions of the state (the precondition) and the sequence of actions (expressed as methods or block-level program slices) taken in the event the preconditions of the transition are satisfied. An STT for a procedure is isomorphic with a CEG and an SMM.

- Class Diagram (CD): Represents relationships among the classes. The black arrows represent the generalization or "is-a-kind-of" relationship, which depicts the subordination of a subclass to a superclass or base class. The diagram also displays the member variables and member methods associated with the class hyperlinked to the source code of the class. Clicking on a member variable or member method will realign the source code to that member. The source code in the text window is hypertext. The highlighted text in the source code is hyperlinked from usages of methods, classes, and fields to their definitions. Clicking on the hyperlinks in the hypertext source code refocuses the view to the definition of the selected method, class, or field reference.

- Data Element Table (DET): A tabular description of the location and usage of the definitions and references to data elements within an application's paragraph or program. DET defines relationships between procedures and data definitions and is used as the basis for data analysis. The table fields are Name, Type, and Refs. Clicking on a link in the Name section will re-center the hypertext code display on the definition of the Java code. Clicking on a link in the Refs section of the table will realign the hypertext code display to the usage location in the code where the item is referenced in the code. Data item usage is classified by its statement type in the Refs section of the table. The statement type appears to the right of the reference in an upper case font. Statement types are classified according to the statement classes in the OMG ASTM specification. The source code in the text window is hypertext. The highlighted text in the source code is hyperlinked from usages of methods, classes, and fields to their definitions. Clicking on the hyperlinks in the hypertext source code refocuses the view to the definition of the selected method, class, or field reference.

- Hypertext Code View: Selecting the method from the left pane will display the Java source code in the View Frame. This first view, known as Java-Source View, is the default view consisting of a hyperlinked source code page. Identifiers in the Java code link to their definitions.

- Source Code View: View of the source applications as hypertext code views.

- Target Code View: View of the target applications as hypertext code views.

- Both View: View of the source and target applications as conversely hyperlinked hypertext code views.

## Software Engineering Methodology Support

The transformation workbench's as-is and to-be documentation portal (aka Software Hypermodel Blueprint Portals) provides hyper-graphs, hypertext, hypermedia, hyper-search, and hyperlink for the depiction of the functional analysis design views of code of the applications modeled by the blueprints in adherence with the following leading software engineering modeling methodologies: Unified Modeling Language (UML), Model-Driven Architecture (MDA), Structure Analysis and Structure Design (SASD), Object-Oriented Analysis and Object-Oriented Design (OOA/OOD), and Business Rule Modeling (BRM).

The blueprints are presented in three major views: as-is, to-be, and side-by-side. The as-is view is a functional analysis-level design model of the legacy system application code in its original state prior to modernization. The to-be view is the functional analysis-level design model of the legacy system application code in its original state after modernization. The side-by-side view is a composite of the as-is view and the to-be view for a system that has been modernized.

The blueprints are presented in multiple composite views, which are the functional analysis-level design model as depicted by leading modeling methodologies: UML, MDA, SASD, OOA/OOD, BRM, and the SMM (State Machine Model). Each composite view presents a composition of the principle set of sub-views used in the methodology that are sufficient for depiction of the system from the functional analysis and design perspective adopted by that methodology.

The blueprint sub-views consist of graphical, textual, and index views that depict the detailed views of behavioral, structural, compositional, and conceptual properties of individual units of code in a system. Behavioral, structural, compositional, and conceptual sub-views are graphical depictions of the fundamental properties of software including control flow, data flow, caller, callee, part-of, kind-of, has-a, type-of, state, state transition, precondition, action, causality, composition, complexity, size, etc. Software engineering methodologies depict these properties using various kinds of graphical and textual models.

The hypertext as-is code view, to-be code view, and side-by-side code view depict the code as hypertext and have features for navigation via hyperlinks to refocus composite views and sub-views as well as to navigate between and view the correspondence between the source and the target code.

Many of the features of the graphical models are similar between the methodologies. In general we have chosen the more universal terms when selecting a terminology. The most common graphical blueprint sub-views consist of SCs, CFGs, (aka action diagrams), DFDs, state machine graphs (SMGs), STTs, CEGs, CDs, and DETs. The current set of metrics indices consists of a complexity index, fan-in index, fan-out index, and unreferenced variables index.

The current set of table of contents indices consists of a system package index and the system DET. In addition the blueprint provides a Google Search feature, which provides instantaneous search access to all identifier definitions and references in each system and a media-wiki page for every unit of code in the system. The media-wiki page can be edited by subscribers and authorized users.

- Business Rule Modeling System (BRMS): A software system used to define, deploy, execute, monitor, and maintain the variety and complexity of decision logic that is used by operational systems within an organization or enterprise. This logic — also referred to as business rules — includes policies, requirements, and conditional statements that are used to determine the tactical actions that take place in applications and systems. A BRM is a repository allowing decision logic to be externalized from core application code. This BRM model includes depiction of visualizations of the production rule representation (PRR) as STTs and CEGs. The PRR is a core OMG standard for the depiction of rules for production rule systems and they interchange with business rule engines that make up most BRM execution targets.

- Model Driven Architecture (MDA): Models are defined based on a multitude of standards and generally accepted open environments. These include the UML, the MOF, XML Metadata Interchange (XMI), Enterprise Distributed Object Computing (EDOC), the Software Process Engineering Metamodel (SPEM), and the Common Warehouse Metamodel (CWM). The focus of MDA is on forward engineering while the OMG's architecture-driven modernization (ADM) focuses on reverse engineering. The derivation of UML model from code to support forward engineering using model-driven approaches is a key objective of the OMG's ADM initiative, which seeks to derive models from existing software systems in a language-neutral way to enable the legacy systems to be maintained, modernized, and reengineered using MDA tools and technologies.

- OOA/OOD View: Selecting the OOA/OOD view displays a composite view of SCs, Java-Source Code, CDs, SMGs, DFDs, and STTs. These views all have hyperlink nodes to the source code displayed in the source sub-view of the OOA/OOD. Object-oriented analysis (OOA) applies object-modeling techniques to analyze the functional requirements for a system. Object-oriented design (OOD) elaborates the analysis models to produce implementation specifications. OOA focuses on *what* the system does; OOD on *how* the system does it. OOA looks at the problem domain with the aim of producing a conceptual model of the information that exists in the area analyzed. Analysis models do not consider any implementation constraints that might exist such as concurrency, distribution, persistence, or how the system is to be built. Implementation constraints are dealt with during OOD. Analysis is done before the design. OOD transforms the conceptual model produced in OOA to take into account the constraints imposed by the chosen architecture and any non-functional — technological or environmental — constraints such as transaction throughput, response time, runtime platform, development environment, or programming language. The concepts in the analysis model are mapped onto implementation classes and interfaces. The result is a model of the solution domain; a detailed description of how the system is to be built.

- SASD or SSADM Views: Selecting the view Structured Systems Analysis and Structured Design Method (SSASD) displays a composite view of SCs, Java-Source Code, CDs, DFDs, and CFGs. These views all have hyperlink nodes to the source code displayed in the source sub-view of the SSASD. SSADM is one particular implementation that builds on the work of different schools of structured analysis and development methods such as Peter Checkland's Soft Systems Methodology, Larry Constantine's Structured Design, Edward Yourdon's Yourdon Structured Method, Michael A. Jackson's Jackson Structured Programming, and Tom DeMarco's Structured Analysis. The three most important techniques that are used in SSADM are Logical Data Modeling, Data Flow Modeling, and Entity Behavior Modeling.

  - Logical Data Modeling: The process of identifying, modeling, and documenting the data requirements of the system being designed. These data are separated into entities (things about which a business needs to record information) and relationships (the associations between the entities).

  - Data Flow Modeling: The process of identifying, modeling, and documenting how data moves around an information system. Data Flow Modeling examines processes (activities that transform data from one form to another), data stores (the holding areas for data), external entities (what sends data into a system or receives data from a system), and data flows (routes by which data can flow).

- Entity Behavior Modeling: The process of identifying, modeling, and documenting the events that affect each entity and the sequence in which these events occur.

■ SMM (State Machine Model) View: Selecting the SMM view displays an aggregate view of the other views: STT, SMG, CEG, CFG, Source, and CEG. The SMG, CEG, and CFG all have hyperlink nodes to the source code displayed in the source sub-view of the SMM. The SMG, CFG, and CEG are all SVG graphs. The SMM represents the behavior of a system that is composed of a finite number of states. There are many forms of state diagrams that differ slightly and have different semantics. State diagrams can describe the possible states of an object as events occur.

Each diagram usually represents objects of a single class and tracks the different states of its objects through the system. The UML state diagram is essentially a Harel state chart with standardized notation that can describe many systems from computer programs to business processes. The SMM focuses principally on modeling states and events and their depiction as STTs, SMGs, and CEGs. The CFG depicts the refinement of an SMG into an imperative logic suitable for automated transformation into a programming language. The hypertext code view is a refinement of the SMM into the executable statements of Java, an imperative object-oriented programming language.

## POWERBUILDER AND 4GL GATEWAY DEVELOPMENT

At the commencement of this project, neither the 4GL COBOL generator nor the PowerBuilder Gateway existed as a part of an automated solution. Both language gateways were developed and customized to meet the company's specific needs during the pilot. In-house software architects defined the detailed conversion specifications for each language in the *4GL Conversion Specification* and the *PowerBuilder Conversion System Requirements Specification* documents.

Figure 6.6 depicts the generic architecture of any language translator within the JanusStudio™ transformation framework. This transformation framework facilitates the reuse of components between transformation projects including language grammar systems, target platform support libraries, intermediate object model, control flow analysis, data flow analysis, dependency analysis, metrics, the as-is and to-be HTML documentation generators, and intermediate object model-to-target language.

Addition of a gateway for a "new" source or target language entails new developmental tasks for its creation and development:

1. A language grammar system that involves writing the grammar rules, construction of a parser and printer, and development of a constrainer that determines the basic semantics for the language and annotates the abstract syntax tree with basic semantics that documents the data scope, data types, references, and definitions for the language.

2. The language-to-language transformation rules which, for a source language, entails writing rules that transform the source language into the IOM and writing special purpose intermediate-model-to-intermediate-model rules that address specifics of the particular source and target language model.

3. New target rules that transform from the IOM to the target language model must be written.

4. Writing rules that perform IOM2IOM refactoring rules to optimize the quality of the language transformation for the specific language pair.

5. Creation of target platform library functions for source platform utilities and services.

## The PowerBuilder Conversion

This section discusses an overview of the structure of a PowerBuilder application, the application conversion process, and related tooling requirements. It further discusses the conversion rules used and the conversion itself.

## Structure of a PowerBuilder Application

A PowerBuilder application consists of a *user interface* and *application processing logic*. The user interface is composed of windows, menus, and controls for a user to interact with and direct an application. The PowerBuilder IDE is used to visually compose the user interface of an application. The application processing logic is composed of event and function scripts (often called *handlers*) in which a developer codes control logic for mediating the interaction between the user and the backend 4GL generated COBOL services. PowerBuilder allows a developer to code application processing logic as part of the user interface or in separate modules (custom class user objects).

PowerBuilder applications are event driven. In a client application, users control what happens by the actions they take. For example, when a user clicks a button, chooses an item from a menu, or enters data into a textbox, one or more events are triggered. The developer writes scripts that specify the processing that should happen when events are triggered. Windows, controls, and other application components you create with PowerBuilder each have a set of predefined events. For example, each button has a *Clicked* event associated with it and each textbox has a *Modified* event. When the user clicks the mouse on a button, the script associated with the *Clicked* event gets executed. Most of the time, the predefined events are all you need. However, in some situations, you may want to define your own events.

PowerBuilder applications are written using the PowerScript language. Scripts consist of PowerScript commands, functions, and statements that perform processing in response to an event. For example, the script for a button's *Clicked* event might retrieve and display information from the database; the script for a textbox's *Modified* event might evaluate the data and perform processing based on the data. The execution of an event script can also cause other events to be triggered. For example, the script for a *Clicked* event in a button might open another window, triggering the *Open* event in that window.

Each menu or window you create with PowerBuilder is a self-contained module called an object. The basic building blocks of a PowerBuilder application are the objects you create. Each object contains the particular characteristics and behaviors (properties, events, and functions) that are appropriate to it. PowerScript supports basic object-oriented programming techniques such as encapsulation, inheritance, and polymorphism. PowerScript also seems to have some features of dynamic languages in which functions are treated as first class objects. However, this capability seems to only be used "behind the scenes" by the IDE and is not generally used in event handler scripts.

In PowerBuilder, you work with one or more *targets* in a workspace. You can add as many targets to the workspace as you want, open and edit objects in multiple targets, and build and deploy multiple targets at once. Within the context of this pilot project, the targets were "PowerScript" targets that may be executable applications or components of applications.

> **PBL Files and the Extracted Plain-Text Source Code:** PowerBuilder stores application code and resources in files with a .PBL extension. Each PBL (PowerBuilder Library) file can contain multiple PowerBuilder objects. The PowerBuilder IDE is designed to work with PBL files and the PBL files that comprise a given application are its "official" source code. However, various tools, including the PowerBuilder IDE, allow developers to extract objects into plain text. For the purpose of writing tools to operate on the source code of a PowerBuilder program, it is understandably more convenient to operate on this extracted plain text. However, there may be some risk in doing this if there is information contained in the PBL file that is not included when plain text is extracted.

**Table 6.1** Types of PowerBuilder Objects in General Use within the Environment

| Object | Use |
| --- | --- |
| Application | Entry point into an application |
| Window | Primary interface between the user and a PowerBuilder application |
| DataWindow | Retrieves and manipulates data from a relational database or other data source |
| Menu | List of commands or options that a user can select in the currently active window |
| Global function | Performs general purpose processing |
| Structure | Collection of one or more related variables grouped under a single name |
| User objects | Reusable processing module or set of controls, either visual or non-visual |

**PowerBuilder Objects.** The basic building blocks of PowerScript targets are PowerBuilder objects. These objects are summarized in Table 6.1 and discussed in more detail as follows.

**Application Objects**: The entry point into an application. It is a discrete object saved in a PBL file just like a window, menu, function, or DataWindow object. The application object defines application-level behavior, such as which fonts are used by default for text and what processing should occur when the application begins and ends. When a user runs the application, an *Open* event is triggered in the application object. The script you write for the *Open* event initiates the activity in the application. When the user ends the application, the *Close* event in the application object is triggered.

**Window Objects**: The primary interface between the user and a PowerBuilder application. Windows can display information, request information from a user, and respond to the user's mouse or keyboard actions. A window consists of:

■ Properties that define the window's appearance and behavior (i.e., a window might have a title bar and a Minimize box)

■ Events triggered by user actions

■ Controls placed in the window, including DataWindows and visual User Objects.

**Data Window Objects**: Retrieved and manipulated data from a relational database or other data source. DataWindows manipulate data that are accessed via calls to backed 4GL generated COBOL programs. DataWindow objects also handle the way data are presented to the user. The developer can choose from several presentation styles; for example, Tabular or Freeform. Tabular DataWindows use a spreadsheet, or grid, to interact with the user. Freeform DataWindows map individual controls such as textboxes and checkboxes to fields in the 4GL COBOL response.

**Menu Objects**: Lists of items that a user can select from a menu bar for the active window. The items on a menu usually constitute a logical grouping. They provide the user with commands (such as *Open* and *Save As* on an application's *File* menu) or alternate ways of performing a task. The user can select menu items with the mouse, the keyboard, or use accelerator (mnemonic access) keys defined for the items. The developer can define keyboard shortcuts for any PowerBuilder menu item.

**Global Function Objects**: PowerBuilder lets you define two types of global functions:

- Object-level functions are defined for a particular type of window, menu, or other object type and are encapsulated within the object for which they are defined. These are further divided into system functions (functions that are always available for objects of a certain object class) and user-defined functions.

- Global functions are not encapsulated within another object, but instead are stored as independent objects. Unlike object-level functions, global functions do not act on particular instances of an object. Instead, they perform general purpose processing such as mathematical calculations or string handling.

**Structure Objects**: A collection of one or more related variables of the same or different data types grouped under a single name. In some languages, such as Pascal and COBOL, structures are called records. Structures allow you to refer to related entities as a unit rather than individually; for example, the developer can define the user's ID, address, access level, and a picture (bitmap) of the employee as a structure called user_struct, and then refer to this collection of variables as user_struct. There are two kinds of structures:

- Object-level structures are associated with a particular type of object such as a window or menu. These structures can always be used in scripts for the object. The developer can also choose to make the structures accessible from other scripts.

- Global structures are not associated with any object or type of object in an application. The developer can declare an instance of the structure and reference it in any script in an application.

**User Objects**: Applications often have features in common; for example, several applications might have a *Close* button that performs a certain set of operations and then closes the window, or they might have DataWindow controls that perform the same type of error checking. Several applications might require a standard file viewer. If the same application feature is used repeatedly, a user object should be defined. The user object is defined once and used as many times as needed and can be visual or non-visual (class). They can be further divided into standard or custom user objects. Standard user objects, whether visual or non-visual, are system objects that are always available with PowerBuilder. You can also use controls for external visual objects that were created outside PowerBuilder. The main types of user objects are:

- Visual user objects are reusable controls or sets of controls that have a consistent behavior; for example, a visual user object could consist of several buttons that function as a unit. The buttons could have scripts associated with them that perform standard processing. Once the object is defined, you can use it as often as you need.

- Class user objects are reusable processing modules that have no visual component. You typically use class objects to define business rules and other processing that acts as a unit; for example, you might want to calculate commissions or perform statistical analysis in several applications. To do this, you could define a class user object. To use a class user object, you create an instance of the object in a script and call its functions. Custom class user objects, which define functions and variables, are the foundation of PowerBuilder multi-tier applications.

## PowerBuilder Conversion and Tooling Requirements

PowerBuilder is a Rapid Application Development (RAD) environment originally targeted for building two-tier client–server applications that interact with relational databases. PowerBuilder programs are written in a semi-object-oriented 4GL called PowerScript. PowerScript is an interpreted language and programs run on the PowerBuilder equivalent of a virtual machine. PowerScript supports object-oriented concepts/constructs like abstraction, encapsulation, inheritance, and polymorphism, but does not enforce their use.

PowerBuilder applications typically have a direct connection to a relational database, and PowerBuilder DataWindow objects are normally mapped directly to database tables or views. For this pilot project, DataWindows were mapped to backend 4GL COBOL services rather than SQL tables via SQLCA object running in PowerBuilder which calls a set of in-house developed DLLs that interact with 4GL generated COBOL programs via CICS.

The PowerBuilder Foundation Classes (PFC) define a library of classes that facilitate the rapid development of PowerBuilder applications. This library was designed to be extended, and in-house development teams took advantage of this feature by creating significant customizations of the PFC. The PFC was not translated because it would yield applications that were modernized in terms of syntax and language and would not look like other applications written using the target technologies (that were developed from a clean slate). To maximize the use of Java framework components that provided services similar to the PFC framework, code was established in the Java/JavaScript environment to stand in for the PFC code that will not be translated (see Figure 6.7).

The PowerScript-to-Java/JavaScript conversion tool was built with the assumption that the "framework" level components would be manually converted apart from the conversion tool and that the automatic conversion would generate code that references some of these externally-defined components (as shown in this chapter). The target environment, Java, JavaScript (J/JS), and JavaServer Pages (JSPs) will be referred to as the J/JS environment.

TSRI responsibility for the language conversion required development of a tool to migrate code from PowerBuilder/PowerScript language into J/JS and JSPs. This entailed developing: (1) a source-language-side PowerBuilder PowerScript gateway to parse, constrain, and model PowerScript; (2) a transformation

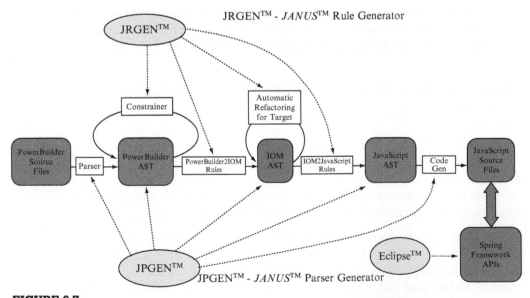

**FIGURE 6.7**

*The PowerBuilder-to-Java transformation process.*

mapping from PowerScript into the IOM; (3) a grammar system for the target-side JavaScript; (4) a mapping from the IOM into JavaScript; (5) a grammar system for modeling HTML, XML; and (6) transformation from the IOM to generate Java, JavaScript, HTML, and XML to construct JSP servlets.

The conversion tool can take one or more PowerBuilder source files as input and generate the corresponding Java, JavaScript, JSP, and XML configuration files as defined by an exacting specification defined by internal software architects. The target code can generate into the following components in the in-house Springboard Framework:

- JavaScript Framework: Modernized code runs in a Web browser and be generated in JavaScript and employs Web 2.0/RIA techniques.
- Dojo: To support this without creating extensive proprietary frameworks, the modernized code leverages the Dojo Toolkit.
- Web Container Frameworks: The modernized code running in the WebSphere environment is generated in Java.
- Springboard Framework: To support this in a manner consistent with other in-house applications, the generated code leverages the internal Springboard Framework.

## General PowerBuilder Conversion Rules

The following are high-level rules that the conversion tool had to accommodate.

- Coding Standards and Practices: In the PowerBuilder conversion, at least three different "languages" are targeted: Java, JavaScript, and JSP. The generated code should be compatible with the company's specifications given for each language.

- JavaScript: Unless otherwise specified in this chapter, the generated code adheres to Douglas Crockford's JavaScript Coding Standards.

- Java: Unless otherwise specified, the generated code adheres to in-house Java Coding Standards.

- JSPs: To the extent possible, JSP code should be structured in a human-readable format with indentation to highlight structure. Unless otherwise specified, the JSP code was to be consistent with the conventions outlined by Sun in the article, "Code Conventions for the JavaServer Pages Technology Version 1.x Language". An additional requirement was that JSP scripting elements (such as declarations, scriptlets, and expressions) be avoided. JSP tags (JSTL, Struts2) were used in situations where one might otherwise use scripting elements.

## THE 4GL CONVERSION

This section provides a detailed discussion of the issues and approaches required to plan and execute the 4GL conversion effort.

### 4GL Conversion Overview

The conversion effort required creation of 4GL-to-Java conversion tool as it relates to the 4GL application code (see Figure 6.8). The 4GL COBOL is supported in the legacy environment with COBOL framework code. The "framework" level components were manually converted externally from the conversion tool. The automatic conversion generates code that references some of these components as defined in the *4GL Conversion Specification* document developed by in-house software architects.

The goal of the conversion tool is to take one or more 4GL source files as input and generate the corresponding Java files as defined by the *4GL Conversion Specification*. Although round-trip engineering was not required, the tool needed facilities for handling overwriting existing files (e.g., an option to specify whether or not files were to be overwritten or an error reported). The conversion rule specifications in the *4GL Conversion Specification* were organized to correspond to the order in which the elements to which the rules pertained typically appeared within the 4GL programs to be converted.

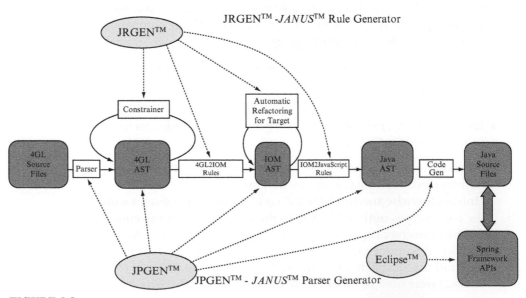

**FIGURE 6.8**

*The 4G- to-Java transformation process.*

### Supporting 4GL Frameworks

To simplify and standardize development practices, internally developed 4GL applications utilize INCLUDEs of numerous framework-level 4GL files. These INCLUDEs handle routine operations such as logging, tracing, security, error checking, etc. There were two main types of 4GL application programs:

- Business programs
- Data programs

The general rule is that business programs should not access the database directly and should instead make calls to programs that handle the database interaction. This roughly corresponds to the type of "Business Service" and "DAO" layering of many Java applications (and that is the approach taken for the generation of Java from the conversion tool).

## 4GL Program Types

There are two different types of 4GL programs used by the generated 4GL COBOL applications: business and data. The next two sections provide an overview of how these two types of programs were generated into Java code.

### 4GL Business Programs

Business programs have no data access code (if they do, they should be treated as data programs described in the next section). Basically, for each business 4GL file, three Java files are created. The three files are:

- xxxService.java: This is the interface definition for the service. It extends a configurable base interface.

- xxxServiceImpl.java: This is the implementation of the service and where the bulk of the conversion logic applies. It extends a configurable base class as well as implements the generated service interface.

- xxxServiceTest.java: This is a JUnit test scaffold that jump-starts developers who need to create application-specific unit tests. Note that the need for the Junit test scaffolds is based on the assumption that the logic is too data dependent for the conversion tool to automatically generate unit tests.

### 4GL Data Programs

Data programs should have no or minimal business logic and focus specifically on data access. The following section is an overview of the conversion approach for these types of programs:

For each data 4GL file there are five (or six) generated Java files (depending on whether both DAO implementations are requested or not):

- xxxService.java: This is the interface for the service. It extends a configurable base interface.

- xxxServiceImpl.java: This is the implementation for the service. It contains the majority of the converted code, except for the actual SQL, and it extends a configurable base class.

- xxxDao.java: This is the interface for the DAO used by this service. It represents separate methods for each specific SQL operation used by the data program, and it extends a configurable base interface.

- xxxDaoJDBCImpl.java: This is the JDBC implementation of the DAO interface, which is an implementation that uses Spring's RowMapper and DaoSupport to perform the actual SQL operations. It extends a configurable base class.

- xxxDaoHibernateImpl.java: This is the Hibernate implementation of the DAO interface, which uses Hibernate to perform the actual SQL operations. It extends a configurable base class.

- xxxServiceTest.java: This is a JUnit test scaffold to be used as a jump-start for developers to create application-specific unit tests (the need for test scaffold is based on the assumption that the logic will be too data dependent for automatic generation of actual unit tests). Note that the conversion tool has that a capability to generate unit tests in some circumstances, but this was not done for this project.

## ON-SITE PACKAGING, VALIDATION, AND ACCEPTANCE TESTING

This section discusses the roadmap approach applied to the on-site software packaging and testing cycle. The system segmentation and release plan relied on determining the optimal set of artifact combinations that maximize migration vendor productivity, testing, change control, production synchronization, and production turnover.

To support the change impact analysis the TSRI off-site team generated a Transformation Blueprint™ for the entire ~2.5 million lines of 4GL and PowerBuilder software. The Transformation Blueprint™ provided input to a roadmap for the entire conversion and follow-on modernization phases, which were still in the planning phase as of this writing.

### On-site Packaging and Project Phasing

Project phasing and staging were not very complex for the pilot as it had only a handful of work units, but the project team wanted to establish an approach that would work for subsequent, more complex project phases. The general approach is as follows.

- Complete baseline application analysis: Analysis of all interface points, data sharing, and application artifact sharing prior to completing this analysis.

- Develop first-level migration unit-of-work division: The first level of unit-of-work division is driven by application and subsystem delineations. There are certain units of work that are shipped for processing as a higher business priority than other application units of work. While the pilot project involved only a small handful of work units, future project work will be more complex.

- Refine migration unit-of-work division: Initial migration units-of-work is further refined to ensure that shared routines are converted first or with an initial unit of work. The next level of refinement is driven by regrouping units of work based on shared interfaces or shared database accesses. The application analysis results support this analysis.

- Identify migration sequencing plan: Once units of work are identified, the sequence of migration vendor shipments, testing cycle, and overall project estimates are put in place. Sequencing relies on business priorities, interface points, database usage, and other priorities driven by the stakeholders and project team.

- Identify sub-units of work for each migration unit of work: Sub-units of work are partial migration units of work that can be migrated independently and return to on-site teams for testing.

- Establish change control plan: The general change control approach reduces out-of-production time through smaller units of work. This in turn reduces the need to retrofit enhancements into a unit-of-work out of production. The alternative involves retrofitting changes into the baseline version of a unit-of-work and working out an approach with the migration vendor where a delta version can be shipped to the migration vendor to be re-migrated.

## Validation and Acceptance Testing

The project team followed a validation and user acceptance testing process that involved preliminary preparation as well as execution. The preparation phase followed the format below.

The validation preparation plan is invoked *before* a migration unit is returned to in-house teams and is applied to each migration unit-of-work shipped to the migration vendor and returned for validation testing.

Validation testing differs from traditional testing because validation testing seeks to prove that no functional changes have occurred within a migrated application subset. Traditional testing seeks to prove that a number of limited functional changes *did occur* and *were implemented properly*.

As a result, there are unique steps involved in validation testing that are addressed as they are identified in the following list. The first two steps are general setup steps while the remaining steps apply to each migration unit.

- Setup validation environment: This set establishes an isolated hardware and software environment that mimics the production hardware and software environment to the best degree possible. The migration validation environment may differ in terms of software and hardware, but the data and related test script inputs should remain constant.

- Establish testing goals: Validation testing goals should discuss coverage capability, acceptance criteria, degree of automation of test scripts, and other factors. Goals include:

  - The test environment for the baseline version and migrated version of the migration unit-of-work should be as identical as possible.
  - Validation data should have broadest coverage with least amount of volume to ensure a valid test while reducing execution time.
  - Rerunning data through the migrated code should be as automated as possible.
  - Change control should be handled in the most efficient manner as possible.

Note: The following steps apply to each migration unit undergoing validation. These steps may begin as soon as a migration unit is shipped to a vendor.

- Isolate validation units-of-work: The goal is to isolate the most granular set of programs undergoing migration testing as possible. This approach allows validation teams to isolate problems and resolve them quickly. Validation units-of-work may align with the sub-units in the migration sequencing plan or they may be even more granular. One approach for validation unit isolation is to set up a test for each 4GL generated COBOL entry point, which should correspond to a module within the PowerBuilder environment. The previous system's analysis result provides an entry point/call chain map as input to this process. This step is completed after identification of migration units-of-work.

- Setup test environment for validation test runs: An initial test environment is set up to determine the current level of execution coverage for the baseline (i.e., pre-migration) unit of work. The overall environment must be isolated for testing purposes, keeping in mind that the migrated unit-of-work will need to be tested in as similar an environment as possible. Changes in system software could cause mismatches in the results.

- Obtain test suite data for that environment: A set of test data must be identified and reproduced within the testing environment. This includes all files and databases that are to be used for the testing cycle including external interfacing files used as input to a given validation unit. Note that online systems are driven through, front end data entry while batch systems are driven by file and database inputs. Input data setup time for online systems is largely script driven while batch system setup involves input data streamlining.

- Obtain or build automated test scripts: Online systems require script setup to create inputs that can be replicated to validate migrated validation units. Automated test scripts help ensure that when the same data are run through the baseline and the migrated versions of the unit of work, the system outputs can be validated for apple-to-apple comparison purposes.

- Determine execution coverage of current test suite: This step involves running a test against the migration unit-of-work while using a coverage monitor to determine levels of execution coverage. Coverage requirements should be established in advance with few exceptions. Exceptions include situations where there are syntactically demonstrable occurrences of dead code or semantically dead code that cannot be executed.

- Refine execution coverage (online approach): This step examines current execution coverage levels to determine if the data that was run through the baseline version of the validation unit are adequate for testing. Program segments that were not executed should be addressed as follows.

  - If an entire program is not executed, determine how to trigger it to be executed by following the call chain for that unit of work.
  - Use the application analyzer to determine if it is syntactically dead.
  - Use the application analyzer and manual analysis to determine if that area of the code is semantically dead.
  - If the code should be executed, use the application analyzer to trace the logic back to the data input, or to the entry point in the call chain.
  - Identify the data that could trigger the code to be executed by mapping the PowerBuilder interface to the program logic that needs to be triggered.
  - Add the data to the input scripts and re-run the validation test.
  - Continue this process until the desired level of coverage is achieved.

- Refine execution coverage (batch approach): Batch programs undergo a similar process only using the input files or database as sources of data that are modified. A batch validation approach should be fully expanded should batch validation become an issue downstream.

- Synchronize sequencing plan with validation requirements: Analysts *revisit* the migration sequencing plan. This ensures that migration units or sub-units can be processed expeditiously as they are returned from the migration vendors.

- Repeat this process for subsequent migration units of work: Each migration unit-of-work undergoes steps above as they are shipped.

- The validation execution plan was invoked for each migration unit-of-work as portions of each migration unit or sub-unit are returned for validation testing.

- Perform production synchronization: The migration project work is synchronized with the ongoing maintenance and production releases performed by the application stakeholder teams. While the migration units of work are undergoing migration, the delta versions are made available for various sub-units as they were authorized by the application stakeholders.

- Deploy migrated code into the isolated validation environment: After establishing naming conventions to ensure that no baseline artifacts are be wiped out during the unload process, analysts deploy all migrated code into the validation environment.

- Compile or otherwise prepare the validation unit-of-work for execution: This prepares the software for validation testing.

- Execute the validation unit-of-work using automated test scripts: The test scripts (i.e., input data) run through the baseline version of the validation unit are the migrated version of the validation unit. This creates changes to the databases, file, and returned query scripts that can be compared to the baseline versions.

- Evaluate comparisons on the script results: This step compares the results between the original software and the converted software for the online portion of the systems.

- Run comparisons on the databases and data files: This final validation step ensures that the converted software works the same way as the original software.

## Stakeholder Acceptance

This last step involved turning the software over to the application team so that they could gain acceptance from the business users. The software at this stage had undergone thorough testing and the acceptance was a final signoff point. The acceptance criteria were that the new software functions identically to the old software with no errors or changes introduced, and with acceptably similar performance. This approach was *worked through* on the pilot stage and would be deployed more formally for subsequent project phases.

# SUMMARY

The pilot conversion of the 4GL code and PowerBuilder code was completed successfully for a small, self-contained application module and a subsequent follow-on expanded application undertaken in 2007 and 2008. During the pilots the TSRI off-site team extended its modernization framework by developing modeling, transformation, refactoring, Web-enablement, and transformation blueprints to support both the 4GL and PowerBuilder.

The pilots achieved 100% automation levels into Java and JavaScript that operated within internal Springboard Framework. Manual development of the replacements for the legacy services used by PowerBuilder and the 4GL proved to be technically challenging. PowerBuilder and the 4GL are both application development technologies that use highly complex services of highly optimized runtime environments. These underlying service layers had to be manually replicated because they encompass platform-specific functionality.

While acceptable performance was achieved with the Java equivalents for the 4GL code, at the completion of the two pilots the Java/JavaScript equivalent of the PowerBuilder GUI layer fell short of meeting performance objectives and requires additional manual tuning. Subsequent performance optimization was undertaken in 2009 concurrently with preparation of change impact analysis and roadmap for the full conversion. The likely conclusion is that some percentage of the generated GUI components will need to be manually refactored or even newly developed so as to ensure performance and to leverage UI design approaches found only in the Web 2.0 paradigm. This was not an unexpected result, and even being able to convert a percentage of the GUI is seen as a valuable achievement in converting this very large code base.

One key to the success of the project was a technology that maximized the utilization of the skills and technology of a multi-disciplinary architecture, management, and technical team through continuous iterative perfective metrics-driven adaptation of the tools and methods. The pilot project plan was to encompass the investigation, planning, and a proof of technology that would test efforts to move (or retire) applications from the technology stack using an iterative, phased approach that encompasses multiple methods of conversion. This goal was accomplished.

# CHAPTER 7

# Modernization Case Study: Italian Ministry of Instruction, University, and Research

Michael K. Smith, PhD, PE, and Tom Laszewski

## ABSTRACT

The Italian Ministry of Instruction, University, and Research (MIUR) desired to outsource its IT infrastructure, as well as modernize the IT systems supporting its most important administrative, financial, and HR processes.

This study describes the modernization component of the project, which was executed by Hewlett-Packard with support from several partners. The overall process included a variety of transformation strategies applied across characteristic sets of applications based on a business case and application analysis. The strategies included replacement with commercial off-the-shelf software (COTS), rehosting to less expensive platforms, refactoring user interface (UI) components as part of Web-enablement, and re-architecting and rewriting applications. The target platform was Oracle/UNIX running both Oracle applications and the migrated J2EE and batch COBOL applications.

The results so far have been impressive. The applications are now accessed through more efficient Web-based UIs (replacing green screens) and provide improved navigation with better overall system performance. End-user productivity has doubled in terms of daily operations for some business processes. The application portfolio has been greatly simplified—function point counts dropped by 33%.

From a financial perspective, the results are significant. Even with the organizational change management effort that was required, the program was completed on time and on budget, according to the original roadmap. After 24 months MIUR had more than 90% of the final functionality delivered to users. Hardware and software license and maintenance cost savings were €2 million in 2008 and are projected to be €3.4 million in 2009. This represents a savings of over 36%. New development costs have dropped 38%.

### CONTENTS

# THE MODERNIZATION PROBLEM

The Italian Ministry of Instruction, University, and Research (MIUR) is a large government organization with an overall budget of €55 billion. The modernization focus was on the Italian public education sector that serves 8 million students throughout 40,000 schools. Schools are grouped into about 10,500 major locations, with each one connected to information systems provided by MIUR. As a result, the Italian Ministry of Education is one of the largest employers in the world with over a million employees. Its systems manage both permanent and temporary employees (e.g., substitute teachers). The information systems support roughly 7,000 ministry users and 80,000 school employees.

The system that HP modernized was *Sistema Informativo Ministero della Pubblica Istruzione* (SIMPI), which had been built in the early 1980s on an IBM mainframe architecture. The new system, *Sistema Informativo Dell'Istruzione* (National Education Information System, SIDI), was targeted to a modern, open architecture.

## Business Issues

In the early 2000s a substantial organizational change occurred due to new legislation — the so-called "devolution" law. This required decentralization of processes to the school level and the movement of some administrative processes from the ministry level to the 20 different Italian regions.

This change implied completely different process workflows within SIDI, even as the system continued to work on essentially the same data. The existing process workflows were embedded in legacy code.

A number of point applications had been developed incrementally to fulfill some of these new organizational requirements and then were grafted onto the centralized legacy system. As a result, the system became completely unmanageable and inflexible. These aging legacy systems hampered the Ministry's strategy to devolve the management of education to each region.

In addition, costs were out of control. The single most important objective of the modernization initiative was to design and implement a new architecture that could reduce fixed costs and provide a more flexible infrastructure.

## Legacy Issues

The SIMPI components supporting HR and administrative processes were developed in the early 1980s in COBOL, CICS, and DB2 and had evolved over time with point solutions added to address new requirements. The system had grown to 19 million lines of code and required over 400 mainframe MIPS.

As a result, SIDI was experiencing

- High Costs: Needed to optimize licensing and maintenance costs and leverage existing investment in systems and people
- Inflexibility: A desire to improve speed and agility through a modern architecture with support for Web services
- Poor Manageability: Complexity caused high maintenance costs and difficulty managing the applications portfolio
- Long Time to Market: The system was slow to react to needed changes, which were costly due to reliance on outmoded development languages, methodologies, and inflexible interfaces

The Ministry realized the need for a large modernization program to move from a legacy platform to open systems to deal with the major organizational changes. They were determined to address both the cost issue and the need for new technology and architecture with a complete and radical transformation. The primary constraints on this project were twofold: the need to preserve a complex set of existing business rules and a limited time frame of 2 years for the overall project.

The highest level business rules were derived from legal requirements to have various tasks related to teacher and student allocations to schools, positions, and classes completed by specific months each year. For that to happen, various processes had to be initiated 10 months prior to completion. These rules were as follows.

- School quality and size for the next school year are to be set in December in cooperation with each regional government.
- Students wishing a specific school need to apply in January.
- By March, the number of classrooms provided by every school must be determined.
- Teacher and assistant positions are allocated for every school in March.
- Actual personnel available are mapped to these allocated positions during the July time frame.
- Temporary specialized substitute teacher lists, based on information on unavailable teachers and assistants, are determined in August.

The workflow had to be robust enough to perform these allocations in an environment where there were inevitable delays in completion of prerequisite steps.

One result of the combination of an extensive, legally mandated rule set, a relatively short timeline, and an enormous existing code base was that the orchestration of scheduled transformations, enhancements, and deployment of hardware and modernized software had to be done meticulously.

## The Client's Approach

Based on the business and legacy issues, the Ministry issued an RFP whose modernization components included:

- Migration to a new, rationalized infrastructure
- System transformation to support the new distributed administration model, per the devolution mandate

The application transformation was part of a large RFP that included both application outsourcing and information technology outsourcing. The systems integrators had significant latitude with respect to their proposed solution for the modernization component.

The full MIUR RFP included the elements in Figure 7.1. SIDI was just one of the 14 major contract items.

## HOW HP ADDRESSED THE OPPORTUNITY

The solution required a strong mix of business and technical knowledge.

- Strategy: HP proposed a multi-year series of projects to support the client's transformation.
- Assess: HP completed an application assessment to inventory and determine the maintainability of the current application portfolio.

| Total Contract Components |
|---|
| Mainframe management in Client Data Center |
| Web Hosting, including application and DB support |
| Management of 121 sites and over 8500 workstations in Italy |
| Service Desk |
| Software Development and Enhancement |
| Software Development Maintenance |
| Applications, Technology, and Business Process consulting |
| Training |
| Technical Training |
| Data and Business Process Management |
| Management of the MIUR Data and Training Centers |
| SIDI |
| Acceptance Testing of COTS Software |
| Procurement services |

**FIGURE 7.1**

*Total number of contract components.*

- Modernization Roadmap: HP designed a series of projects to be completed based on an overall understanding of the current state (applications and infrastructure) and the desired future state of operations.
- Enterprise Solution: HP designed a modern architecture with replicable, distributed components to support the business model.
- Technology Partners: HP leveraged a strong partnership model for key components of the solution — Oracle, Relativity (now a Micro Focus company), HTWC, Accenture, and Micro Focus.

The key factor to HP's success in winning the contract was the ability to develop a modernization roadmap aimed at maximizing the return on the investment (ROI) for each of the applications or groups of applications while minimizing the risks of transformation. Whereas other systems integrators proposed a uniform modernization solution for SIDI, either a full replace or a full redevelopment, HP was able to articulate a transformation strategy tailored to the specific SIDI subsystems.

## The SIDI Software Migration Journey

Figure 7.2 summarizes the overall software migration scale and timeline, from Assessment through User Acceptance Testing (UAT).

Of the original 19,000 programs, HP transformed about 11,100. The others were either replaced by Oracle HR Human Resources, Oracle HR Self-Service Human Resources, Oracle Financials, or they were eliminated because their functionality was no longer needed.

The technical assessment and the transformation pilot phases each required on the order of 7 HP staff members. At its peak in the course of the actual transformation, the project was supported by 47 HP staff members. Different strategies were developed for migrating the transaction processing and batch components of the applications. The next section describes these in detail. Figure 7.3 depicts project milestones.

| Technical Assessment | Transformation Pilot | Transformation and UAT |
|---|---|---|
| Jan 2006 to Mar 2006 | Apr 2006 to Jun 2006 | Jul 2006 to Sep 2007 |
| 16 Application Areas<br>20,000,000 Lines of Code<br>19,000 Programs<br>1,350 DB2 Tables<br>1,100 User Functions<br>2,200 Screens | 107 Programs<br>1 User Function<br>3 Screens | 3,599 Batch program rehosted<br>1,538 JCL to shell script<br>7,540 Online programs<br>2,200 Screens |
| Contract Effort: 4% | Effort: 5% | Effort: 90% |

**FIGURE 7.2**

*Overall software migration scale and timeline.*

| Project Milestones | |
|---|---|
| Jan 2006 – March 2006 | Assessment |
| April 2006 – June 2006 | Proof of Concept (POC) |
| July 2006 – Dec 2006 | User acceptance test passed for 3 subsystems |
| Jan 2007 – Sept 2007 | User acceptance test passed for all subsystems |
| Nov 2007 | New system goes live |

**FIGURE 7.3**

*Project milestones.*

## ASSESSMENT

HP developed a modernization roadmap that took into account organizational change management requirements and was based on the results of an Application Portfolio Assessment (APA). This is a standard HP engagement that analyzes a set of applications and associated data assets from multiple perspectives: financial, business, functional, and technical. The APA ensures that client business context and strategic drivers are understood before recommending a modernization strategy for a given application in the portfolio. A business case is developed for modernizing each application with an approach that is appropriate for the client situation.

This assessment resulted in the overall strategy for the application portfolio transformation described in the Transformation Strategy section. The Modernization Workbench, a Micro Focus software solution, was used during the technical assessment phase to collect technical data including cross-references, quality metrics, and sizing information.

This assessment resulted in the identification for four distinct subsystems, each with a distinct transformation approach.

### The Transformation Strategy

Figure 7.4 identifies the transformation strategy selected for each group of applications based on the business case.

**FIGURE 7.4**

*Five basic modernization strategies.*

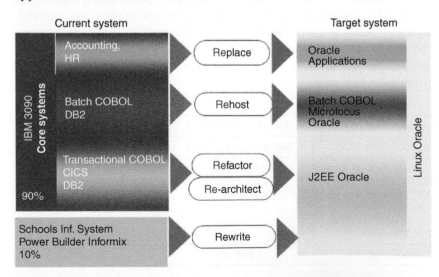

There were two primary platforms, with three core systems deployed in COBOL on the IBM 3090 system and the Schools Information System deployed on a PowerBuilder/Informix base.

Based on the customer business requirements and the characteristics of the applications and platforms, the main findings of the assessment were as follows.

- From a functional point of view, the logical database structure needed minor adjustments while the process workflows impacting online functions needed to be transformed.

- A pure *rehosting* strategy was viable for the batch COBOL programs, with the advantage of meeting cost reduction objectives while minimizing risk and effort. Micro Focus COBOL was selected as the target compiler. A decision was made to convert the batch JCL to shell scripts. To simplify this HP made use of a package that emulates certain mainframe operations including VSAM file management and IBM Sort.

- The online CICS COBOL programs needed to be reworked to fulfill functional gaps, fix old bugs, and introduce new functionality. It was decided to transform these to a Java/Oracle stack hosted on UNIX.

- The PowerBuilder-based Schools Information System required a complete rewrite.

The next sections elaborate on the four basic strategies that the project adopted.

### Replace Accounting and HR

Replacing the accounting system and the HR system for non-teacher employees was judged to be the best option given the low level of customization required and the relatively limited need for integration with the rest of the application portfolio. HP selected Oracle HR Human Resources, Oracle Self-Service Human Resources, and Oracle Financials as the packages to be implemented.

Twenty years ago when these custom accounting and HR systems were written in COBOL there were no alternative, suitable COTS applications available. With the existence of standard HR and financial accounting systems, it is often a logical modernization approach to replace aging legacy systems with packaged applications. COTS applications have the added benefits of being Web and services-oriented architecture (SOA) enabled, running on standard application integration platforms, with lower maintenance costs and built-in reporting and business intelligence. The vendor (in this case Oracle) now has ownership of significant application issues, leveraging broad industry knowledge and providing significantly enhanced reliability, availability, scalability, and performance. This portion of the project was performed by Accenture.

Replacing the rest of the system with packaged software was not practical, however, given the high level of customization required (more than 60% of the functions would have needed to be customized).

The Ministry needed to integrate and increase the efficiency of key processes in the management of non-teacher employees (10,500 school managers and 8,000 Central Administration employees). For this reason it was decided to replace the old system with elements of the Oracle HR Suite.

The HR System consists of several functional areas:

- Presence Detection System (RILP) including the infrastructure needed for collecting attendance and supporting controlled access
- Application management for employees of the Ministry (legal and economic processes)
- System Integration with other areas of SIDI

The project was divided into two phases: the first phase comprised setting up the core Oracle HRMS module, developing customizations, reports, and interfaces to SIDI, and re-engineering the associated business processes. In the second phase the RILP was integrated into the HR System.

The Presence Detection System RILP (produced by SELFIN-COMDATA) features the following:

- Time Clocks: These devices gather time information and interface directly with the Oracle HRMS. This included not only time clocks, but also badge readers, security access authorization components, and attendance recorders.

- Timesheets: Secure online routing of timesheets and approvals through workflow capabilities were designed to make the process of approving timesheets a real-time activity.

- Leave Tracking: This module tracks vacation, illness, disability, maternity, parental leave, and other employee absences. Trends and patterns can be identified and included in reports, some required by the government. Absence tracking maintains a running balance of various types of leave by employees including vacation, sick, personal holiday, unpaid leave, and others. HRM software also offers the ability to input online leave and vacation requests through a self-service module with automatic approval routing.

Oracle Workflow was also used to automate processes and provide alerts.

### Rewrite Schools Information System from Scratch

The Schools Information System (10% of the overall system) consisted of PowerBuilder and an Informix database. The technology was deemed technically obsolete with respect to the MIUR target architecture. The new target architecture consolidated the data and application in one location, eliminating costly database and application management at over 400 schools and securing fragmented data. More important, the use cases for this system had changed radically due to the increased autonomy of the educational institutions. The most practical strategy was a complete rewrite.

The client–server based application was moved to a new Java EE browser-based application with an Oracle database. Now school staff can access the application from any browser-enabled device including laptops, PCs, and smart phones. There is no need for IT staff to spend time and money upgrading and maintaining application software on hundreds of PCs. The benefits and value of moving from the legacy client–server IT application and infrastructure to a modern Web-based application and infrastructure are summarized in Figure 7.5.

The HP team researched and tested automated migration tools for both the application and database migrations. For the application migration, no tool in the market place was able to generate maintainable, three-tiered Java EE code that was considered acceptable. Automated database migration tools, like the Oracle Migration Workbench, were considered but dismissed for several reasons:

- There were only 960 tables to migrate.
- Each school had less than 1 GB of data to migrate.

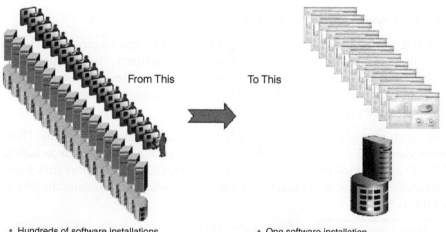

**FIGURE 7.5**

*Total number of contract components.*

- Hundreds of software installations
- Hundreds of databases
- Separate storage silos
- Multi places for things to go wrong or someone to break into
- Hardware proliferation
- No scalability or availability

- One software installation
- One database
- One storage device
- One place to manage, upgrade, tune, monitor, and secure
- Hardware consolidation
- On demand scalability and built-in availability

- There were no stored procedures or triggers in the database. Stored procedures and triggers are typically the most time-intensive activity in a database migration.
- An automated production database migration tool was required and no third-party database migration tools automated this process.

The database migration utilized a combination of the Informix UNLOAD command to export the data and Oracle SQL Loader to load the database.

For the production deployment, a database migration kit was distributed to the schools through the normal software distribution process. This kit unloaded the local Informix database and transferred the ASCII database files to the central server where they were loaded into the centralized database. Schools were then able to test the new application over the Web before moving off their PowerBuilder-based application.

This effort was carried out by an HP team based in Pozzuoli, composed of people experienced with the existing Schools Information System augmented with Java and Oracle administration and performance tuning resources.

### Rehost Batch COBOL

For the batch environment migration, HP collaborated with HTWC, using their services and their XEBE product, as well as the Micro Focus COBOL compiler for LINUX. XEBE is the batch component of HTWC's overall rehosting support solution, XFRAME. XEBE includes utilities to emulate mainframe-specific products and features: XVSAM to manage VSAM files, XSORT to replace the IBM sort, and many others.

The batch system consisted of the artifacts shown in Figure 7.6.

The JCL was migrated to C shell scripts with XEBE used to emulate selected mainframe batch operations on the new LINUX platform. The original application data was contained in DB2 tables and flat-files files. DB2 was replaced with an Oracle database and the VSAM files were managed using XVSAM, the VSAM emulator of XEBE.

The batch system components included SAS and assembler programs. These were converted to COBOL by HTWC to create a homogeneous solution. HTWC used a tool they have developed, ASM2COB, to support this transformation. For the SAS objects, a custom tool was built to migrate SAS to COBOL.

**FIGURE 7.6**

*Artifact type and count.*

| | |
|---|---|
| 3600 | COBOL programs (4.5 Million Lines of Code) |
| 2000 | JCL scripts |
| 80 | SAS programs |
| 4 | Assembler programs |

Additionally, HTWC migrated the job scheduling facility from Autosys on the mainframe to Autosys on LINUX, and then performed the system tests.

HP and the customer jointly executed final system tests and user acceptance tests.

The elapsed time for the project was 4 months, with the batch processes delivered incrementally. The rehosting effort was about 10–20% of the overall migration effort.

## Refactor and Re-Architect the Online COBOL

The online system consisted of 7,550 COBOL/CICS programs (13 million lines of code) supporting 2,230 screens using a DB2 database. This system was targeted to a Java/Oracle/LINUX platform.

Once a base strategy was identified for the online COBOL system components, a refined evaluation framework was created specifically for this system to further evaluate the programs in light of their requirements and business criticality. An analysis was also performed on program maintenance history and management costs.

Figure 7.7 describes the parameters that were used in this analysis and the sources for that information.

| Parameter | Meaning | Source |
|---|---|---|
| Change frequency (CF) | How many times has the program been changed during a fixed period? The higher this value the more the program is influenced by functional variations. | Amendment History from the Configuration Management System |
| Usage frequency (UF) | How many times is the program run during a fixed time period? | CICS logs |
| User criticality (UC) | The importance of the program for the customer business (e.g. is it used by the executives or does it execute critical financial calculations). | Interviews with responsible parties produced a subjective range of values from 1-5. |
| Conversion effort with halting barriers resolution (ES) | Estimation of effort needed to convert after halting barriers resolution. | Assessment documentation |
| Conversion effort with halting and maintainability barriers resolution (EC) | Estimation of effort needed to convert after halting and maintainable barriers resolution. | Assessment documentation |
| Rewriting Effort (ER) | Estimation of effort needed to rewrite the program. | Size in function points (via LOC calculation) plus productivity assumptions (rewrite and test) |

**FIGURE 7.7**

*Parameters used to analyze options.*

The Modernization Workbench identified *halting barriers* in the COBOL code that would have prevented automated transformation. This is just one of the capabilities provided by the Modernization Workbench for interactive analysis of large and complex applications.

Repairing halting barriers tended to require simple changes to the original COBOL and included modifications to some array features, certain kinds of conditions on numeric fields, particular PERFORM and EXIT combinations, and some SQL features. These programs were rarely run, so fixing the generated Java to be fully executable tended to be a onetime activity.

In addition to halting barriers, *maintainability barriers* were identified by the Modernization Workbench. To avoid generating incorrect code, the Workbench flags potential issues for SME assistance to ensure the correct generation of Java code.

Repairing maintainability barriers required more extensive modification to the source. HP modified the original COBOL code so that the Modernization Workbench could produce Java with identical execution semantics as the original code.

### Adopting a Common Infrastructure

Parallel with this SIDI modernization work a MIUR-wide Infrastructure renewal was taking place to target a common operating system platform for all servers. The new architecture was designed to support the newly mandated distribution of responsibility.

HP replaced the OS390 mainframe running the COBOL and DB2 with a distributed mid-range architecture base on Sun hardware with a LINUX OS, running J2EE, Micro Focus, and Oracle. Sun hardware was chosen because at that time Sun was an EDS Strategic Alliance Partner prior to the acquisition of EDS by HP.

This effort involved a refresh of 250 application servers and the deployment of 120 infrastructure servers. The target architecture is described in more detail in the following section.

## REFACTORING AND RE-ARCHITECTING PROCESS

All legacy programs are not created equal. Some are more mission critical than others, some are modified more frequently than others, and some just work and do not experience much in the way of maintenance or modification.

An early commitment had been made to adopt an online environment that was all J2EE. During the assessment phase it was recognized that many of the programs were in a *non-critical category*. They were not central to the core business processes, performed simple utility operations, and typically did not change. The question became: What was the most expeditious way to migrate the programs from COBOL to an executable state in the new environment?

Off-the-shelf automated programming language translation tools like the Modernization Workbench can generate code in the target language that can be compiled to produce semantically compatible executables. This automation substantially reduces the need for manual intervention at this stage, accelerating the transformation. Sometimes hand repairs are required to the generated code to complete the transformation.

There are drawbacks to transformation tools that are not subject to substantial application and project-specific configuration. Some tools support extensive modification to their rule bases and frameworks, usually based on a services contract with the tool vendor. However, shrink wrap tooling without this kind of customization typically produces code that can be difficult to maintain. The extent to which this is the case depends on the degree of semantic mismatch between the old and new programming languages. One aspect of automated COBOL translation that frequently causes issues is that the COBOL type system has a number of unique features. In addition, going from a procedural language like COBOL to an object-oriented language like Java can easily result in very procedural, non-standard Java.

With that said, it is important to be guided by business realities — if the code needs little or no maintenance, then odd-looking Java can be tolerated, with the expectation that over an extended maintenance lifetime such programs can be refactored into increasingly more natural Java.

The online COBOL programs were evaluated during the assessment phase based on their criticality and the frequency with which they were modified. These categories determined the strategy that was applied to their transformation.

Figure 7.8 shows how the programs broke down and strategies chosen to transform them.

| | Non-Critical Programs | Critical Programs |
|---|---|---|
| Frequently Modified | Clean up original source to permit fully automated transformation to compilable and executable Java (1%) | Rewrite (33%) |
| Rarely Modified | Clean up original source and modify the generated Java to be executable (66%) | |

**FIGURE 7.8**

*Program breakdown by criticality and volatility.*

Of the programs, 33% were deemed critical. They had high change frequency and/or user criticality. It was considered important that these be rewritten so that they could be maintained as pure Java.

Most of the non-critical programs were rarely modified and went through a onetime translation process. The rarely modified ones had hand-fixes applied to the generated Java to ensure their correct operation. This resulted in a significant time and cost saving that was important for the timely completion of the project on budget.

A small number of frequently changed but non-critical programs were modified so that they could be maintained in the original COBOL and generate executable Java. The expectation is that these will eventually migrate to pure Java. A lesson learned during testing (34% of the effort spent on testing and bug fixing) was that the option to simply use Micro Focus COBOL to compile the non-critical programs for LINUX would have been preferable.

## Proof of Concept

A proof of concept (POC) was run to finalize the migration process, refine the migration effort estimates, and to ensure platform suitability. In the course of the POC, the architecture demonstrated superior price/performance and had predicted lower maintenance cost versus the current system and other candidate platforms.

The Transformation Assistant was used to perform conversions on 107 selected programs.

During the POC it was recognized that automation could support substantial portions of the work. Skilled developers noticed regularities that could be taken advantage of to create Web pages from screen definitions, associate these pages with the respective online Java programs, and tie together the workflow sequences driven by the screens and programs. It was determined to develop in-house tools to take advantage of these regularities and expedite this process.

## The Software Transformation Approach in Detail

The COBOL/CICS to Java transformation followed the following steps:

- The business logic was completely separated from the UI and navigation logic to create components that would be suitable for further refinement into the model-view-controller design pattern. This consisted of eliminating all instructions related to UI processing from the COBOL programs; for example, "Exec CICS send map" as well as those instructions related to the program control of screen navigation like "Return trans-id."

- The Modernization Workbench was used to accomplish the following code refactoring changes:
  - Eliminate dead code and dead data
  - Eliminate halting barriers
  - Make the necessary changes to account for the differences between Oracle and DB2
- The database update logic was transformed from imbedded SQL to an abstraction defined in Java.

| Steps | |
|---|---|
| Separate business logic, controls, and user interface using the Modernization Workbench | |
| Business Logic | User Interface |
| 1. Refactor: Automatic modification of the COBOL using EDS developed scripts<br>2. Refactor: Manual modification of COBOL code<br>3. COBOL to Java automatic translation using the Transformation Workbench<br>4. Hand modification to the Java code | 1. Transform BMS maps to JSP using the EDS WIDE tool set<br>2. Modify the JSP |
| Integrate business logic and UI to create Java runtime environment | |
| Execute integration test | |

**FIGURE 7.9**
*Steps to address business logic and UIs.*

To implement the new UI and navigation and Control logic, an in-house tool was developed called the Web Interface Development Engine (WIDE).

WIDE was designed and developed to support J2EE applications using the Model-View-Controller pattern. WIDE was used to construct the UI (HTML, JSP) and UI screen flow (STRUTS) automatically, reading in CICS BMS maps and creating corresponding initial Web pages while providing a smooth integration with the business logic translated from the COBOL to Java by the Transformation Workbench.

The View components use the Struts and Tiles open source framework, with the usual JSP-Tag Library-Action-Form association. In addition, the struts-validation framework was used to enforce the same field validation checks as those used within the original COBOL programs.

The Control layer is split across Java objects (Action-Business, Delegate-Transfer) to bridge the View and the Business Model. The Model and the Business Logic are provided by means of Stateless EJBs — extended classes that mimic COBOL structures — and a Business Layer of Java programs, generated from the original COBOL using the Modernization Workbench tool. Figure 7.10 depicts the business logic and UI transformation.

The tool takes CICS BMS maps and a description of the navigation flows contained in an Excel spreadsheet as input and generates the corresponding JSP and necessary Java artifacts to implement the UI, navigation, and control:

1. Presentation Layer: JSP, tiles-defs.xml, validation.xml, ApplicationResources.properties, web.xml
2. Screen navigation and program control layer: Struts, Action Classes, Action Form Classes, and struts-config.xml

**FIGURE 7.10**

*Business logic and UI transformation.*

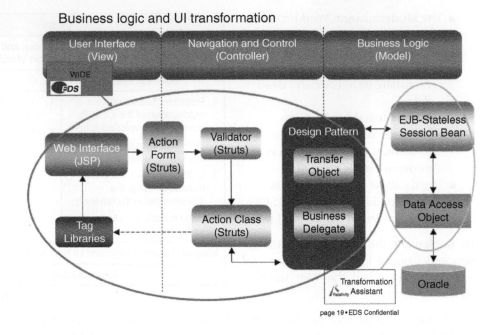

3. Business Layer: Enterprise Java Bean Classes, Extended Object Classes, ejb-jar.xml, orion-ejb-jar.xml

The Business Layer components are supported by classes generated using the Modernization Workbench.

WIDE provides a set of runtime libraries to support these generated components. These include

- BASE-BL: The Base Business Layer is a set of classes used to generalize common tasks executed by the original COBOL programs (e.g., the flow execution of COBOL programs is factored out in a BaseSession Bean so that other EJB beans do not have to repeatedly implement a common feature).

- BASE-Interface: The Base Interface Layer is a set of classes supporting the removal of interface code from the Business and Presentation Layer. It has interfaces for Business Delegates and Transfer Objects and certain generic Java objects to support COBOL behaviors. It also contains objects that mimic the COBOL Communication Area behavior.

- BASE-PL: The Base Presentation Layer is a set of classes used to inject needed properties in Action and Form objects; in addition, it contains some new Taglibs specific to COBOL emulation and some utility classes to dynamically automate the Action forwarding process.

The only human activity needed to complete this interface mapping was some refinement of the JSPs in the form of layout rework to make the pages more aesthetically pleasing and of course testing of the application.

## The Target Architecture

The target-distributed architecture was composed of a J2EE platform, Oracle business intelligence and data warehouse packages, LINUX OS, rack-based 64-bit Sun servers, and an Oracle RAC database.

The Java EE applications run on Oracle AS 10.1.3. The target OS was Sun Solaris for both Java EE and DB. The business intelligence platform similarly runs on Oracle AS 10.1.3 using Oracle Discoverer, and Oracle Warehouse Builder runs as a component in the Oracle RAC database.

We renewed the entire hardware platform using a common infrastructure based on up-to-date technology with improved environmental capabilities, which included a smaller form factor, lower power consumption, and lower heat dissipation.

This involved a refresh or introduction of departmental hardware at more than 400 sites and took advantage of horizontal scalability in the Oracle Real Application Clusters (RAC) database backend.

One of the key components of the architecture was the design of a modular enterprise application infrastructure, the Application Distributable Processing Unit (ADPU).

The ADPU is composed of a three-tier architecture where each of the three layers — Web, application, and database server — are hosted in a separate hardware server or cluster of servers connected in a dedicated gigabit LAN.

The clustering of the servers makes use of horizontal scalability for both application and database servers, creating a fault-resistant system. The Oracle Database RAC supports the transparent deployment of a single database across a cluster of servers, providing fault tolerance from hardware failures or planned outages.

The number of components (servers and storage unit elements) inside the ADPU can be varied and is dimensioned according to the number of users that access application services on the specific ADPU. An ADPU can be easily adapted to new workloads by dynamically adding or removing components without affecting normal operations. Figure 7.11 shows the workings of the ADPU.

## Project Team Organization

The migration project was split in 12 manageable subsystems. Initially there were several development teams, each in charge of the complete migration of an application subsystem. It was soon realized that a structure based on

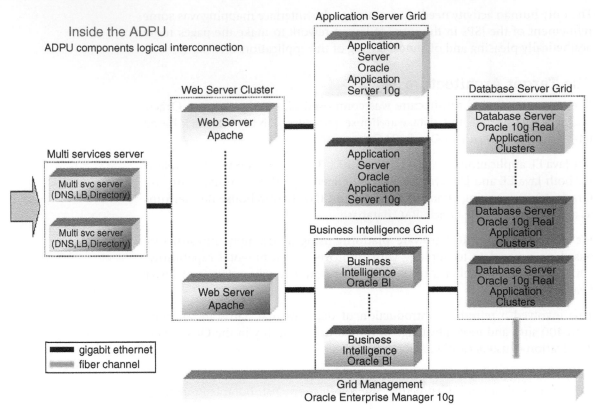

**FIGURE 7.11**

*Application Distributable Processing Unit ADPU.*

specific technology skills was more appropriate and the team reorganized according to "streams," complemented by functional skills in the assessment and testing phase.

### Technology Streams

- Manual screen conversion. Basic skills.
- COBOL rework. Moderate skills. This was 30% of the COBOL re-engineering effort, with the other 70% automated.
- Migration lab. Included 15 highly skilled staff with the most experience with the tools, languages, and architectures.
- Bug fixing. Required highly skilled staff.

The maximum HP team size working on the refactoring and re-architecting phase was 45–50 people, primarily COBOL and Java programmers. Functional specialists were used primarily in the testing phase.

The overall distribution of effort was recorded throughout the life of the project, post general assessment and post pilot. While these numbers are rough — because it can be difficult to always assign work to a single category — they are suggestive.

Testing and repair consumed a very high overhead. It is our expectation that as the automation tools improve, this ratio will drop. In addition, new models to track the relationship between old and new components would bear looking into, since *preparing* was such a large percent of the activity.

- 11% project management.
- 5% UI.
- 7% COBOL manual changes.
- 15% conversion support.
- 18% project and user documentation.
- 8% prepare. One issue that always needs to be addressed in projects like this is that the existing system must continue to run and be maintained. This phase compares the original source, the code that went through the transformation process, to the current source to make sure that any changes to the old system that occurred in the course of the project are incorporated into the new modules.
- 11% test.
- 34% error correction.

## PROJECT RESULTS

The program was completed on time, in compliance with customer requirements. The customer has been very satisfied with the results. Paolo De Santis, IT Executive for the Italian Ministry of Education, presented the project story jointly with HP at several technical conferences including Oracle OpenWorld 2009 in San Francisco.

The program was completed according to the initial roadmap that was developed. This roadmap includes a significant organizational change management effort to ensure the synchronization between infrastructure changes, training, database migration, and ultimate software deployment.

Users are experiencing an improved UI and navigation together with an overall improvement in system response time. While we do not have rigorous data to validate this, we have observed business processes for which user productivity doubled. Figure 7.12 provides a side-by-side comparison between a sample of an old UI and a newly modernized UI.

**FIGURE 7.12**

*Comparison of old vs. new UI results.*

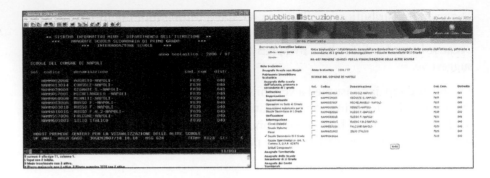

There were major hardware and software license (including maintenance) cost savings:

- In 2007 hardware and software costs were €7.4 million. In 2008, the year the project completed, the cost had been reduced by €2 million. In 2009 it is expected that the cost will be further reduced by €3.4 million.

- The application portfolio was significantly reduced, down 33%, from 218K function points to 145K function points.

- The new software architecture reduced the function point development cost by 38% as compared to the old COBOL environment. This alone accounts for a €3.7 million yearly savings.

A critical success factor was the high level of automation achieved during the project. Not only did this save costs but it also ensured consistency in the generated software and reduced the number of simple programmer errors.

## SUMMARY

Flexibility and innovation need to be part of the team's mind-set so that new solutions can be quickly shared and new opportunities for improvement detected and acted upon.

The POC was crucial. Analyzing a small subset of the programs turned up problems specific to this code base and permitted their resolution prior to taking on the entire system. The regularities in interface development that were observed permitted the investment in the WIDE toolset, which more than paid for itself in effort and time saved. Selective investment in process automation and support tools can provide high ROI. Fairly simple, home-grown tools that target the specific issues of a particular project can make a large difference. This has clear implications for the makeup of the migration team. You need people who can recognize and capitalize on these opportunities.

Migrating the non-critical online COBOL/CICS directly to run on Micro Focus/ LINUX (rather than Java) would have saved time, particularly in the test phase. Practitioners needed to closely monitor the automated conversion of statements containing arrays or GOTOs. We estimate that the savings for a COBOL-to-COBOL conversion migration would have been roughly one-third of the testing phase.

Eighty percent of the migrated code is very stable code, infrequently modified, and 20% continues to be extensively modified and will be gradually rewritten.

The HP MIUR team could have benefited from more extensive training on the Oracle Business Intelligence and Oracle Application Server products. The Oracle Application Server performance met all service level requirements, but it was felt that additional knowledge of Oracle Application Server would have helped with tuning the Java-based application for higher transaction levels.

The attention to continuous improvement in processes and tools meant that by the end of the project our best practices had evolved significantly. Not only did we have new and reusable project-developed tools (WIDE and scripts to scan programs for key features and perform modifications), but the team had developed a much more precise estimating model, refined the transformation processes significantly, and evolved into a highly effective modernization team.

# CHAPTER 8

# Modernization of Reliability and Maintainability Information System (REMIS) into the Global Combat Support System-Air Force (GCSS-AF) Framework*

Philip H. Newcomb, Joyce McPeek, Mark Purtill, and Luong Nguyen

## ABSTRACT

Northrop Grumman Corporation (Northrop Grumman) teamed with The Software Revolution, Inc. (TSRI) to convert COBOL85 server programs running in a Hewlett-Packard (HP) Himalaya environment interfacing with a non-stop SQL database into object-oriented C++ and Java/J2EE programs interfacing with an Oracle 9i database in support of the AF/A4M directive that REMIS be migrated to the GCSS-AF IF. The screen presentation layer was re-engineered by Northrop Grumman into Java J2EEusing WebSphere Application Server 4.0 (WAS 4.0). This project was a technically successful application of architecture-driven modernization (ADM) techniques to a large-scale systems engineering, development, integration, and operational process that supported modernization of a major component of the United States Air Force (USAF) Integrated Depot Management System (IDMS). This project was undertaken in support of the Air Force Materiel Command (AFMC), Electronic Systems Center (ESC), 554th Electronic Systems Wing (554 ELSW), 754th Electronic Systems Group (754 ELSG), REMIS Program Management Office (PMO) (754 ELSG/LRX).

## CONTENTS

## INTRODUCTION

REMIS is a key component of the Air Force Depot Maintenance System. It consists of 3.1 million lines of source code written in COBOL85, Tandem Application Language (TAL), and C. The system runs on a Tandem Symmetric Multiprocessor with non-Stop SQL/MP DDL and a Tandem database. Northrop Grumman maintains REMIS at Wright-Patterson AFB for the Air Force Materiel System Group (MSG).

The Air Force strategy for modernizing legacy applications (such as REMIS) that run on stand-alone hardware such as the Tandem is migration into the GCSS-AF Integration Framework (GCSS-IF), an open service-oriented technical architecture that provides a common Web-gateway integration framework for application software of the Air Force enterprise.

Migration of REMIS into GCSS-AF is expected to result in cost savings by sharing the expense for the hardware platforms and eliminating the expense of supporting individual hardware for each application. By modernizing the legacy applications software to run within the GCSS-AF Integration Framework (IF), the migrated applications will use common software technologies that allow better interoperability with each other and improved accessibility by Joint and Air Force users. The modernized applications are then positioned to integrate more easily with other migrated legacy applications. Once the legacy systems are modernized and migrated, they are established within a common integrated framework supportive of subsequent consolidation to eliminate redundant processing and reduce the footprint of software maintained by the Air Force.

The migration of REMIS was undertaken in support of the AF/A4M directive of the AFMC, ESC, 554 ELSW, 754 ELSG, REMIS PMO 754 ELSG/LRX. the Northrop Grumman acted as prime contractor and integrator and developed a strategy to undertake the migration of REMIS in six increments into the GCSS-AF IF. Northrop Grumman undertook Increment-1 and Increment-2 in 2002, and Increment-3 in 2005–2006, respectively, with TSRI serving as a subcontractor providing automated information system transformation services. During Increment-1 Northrop Grumman re-engineered the screen presentation layer into Java running in the WebSphere Application Server 4.0 (WAS 4.0) implementation of J2EE while TSRI transformed the IF Resident TAL COBOL85 REMIS applications into C++. During Increment-2, Northrop Grumman converted REMIS standard reports using the Cognos ReportNet software, a Web-based software product for creating and managing ad hoc and custom-made reports. During Increment-3, undertaken after a hiatus of 3 years, Northrop Grumman contracted with TSRI to convert additional subsystems of REMIS from TAL COBOL85 into Java.

The purpose of the REMIS migration was both to demonstrate the feasibility and assess and realize benefits (economic, schedule, and qualitative) of using automated transformation to create a GCSS-AF Resident version of the REMIS Application. This project was a technically successful application of ADM techniques to large-scale systems engineering, development, integration, and operational processes of a major component of the USAF IDMS.

The focus of this case study is Increment-1 and Increment-3, which were technically successful demonstrations of ADM techniques applied to a large-scale systems engineering, development, integration, and operational processes for a major component of the USAF IDMS.

# REMIS INCREMENT-1

## REMIS COBOL to C++ and Oracle 9i Modernization

To achieve compliance with GCSS-IF the IF Resident REMIS Application was converted into a Web-enabled user interface developed in J2EE Java technology interfacing with refactored C++ components. Northrop Grumman manually converted the existing REMIS presentation layer source code into Web-enabled pages. TSRI used its automated *e*Volution 2000™ Toolset to convert the existing REMIS database access layer source code into object-oriented C++. A new Graphical User Interface (GUI), written as Java components, was separately developed by Northrop Grumman to interface with C++ components via a Java/C++ Application Program Interface (API) developed jointly by TSRI and Northrop Grumman. The language transformation was provided by TSRI and was accomplished using a four-phase code conversion process consisting of automated assessment, automated transformation, automated refactoring, and semi-automated refactoring.

### Assessment Summary

During the assessment phase roughly 300,000 lines of COBOL85 were parsed and analyzed by the TSRIs *e*Volution 2000™ Toolset to produce a model from which the "as-is" documentation consisting of structure charts, control flow graphs, state machine models, data flow diagrams, and data element tables hyperlinked to the code were automatically generated to meet GCSS documentation standards. This documentation was delivered as a large Web document consisting of several million Web pages. Combining high-fidelity scalar vector graphics views hyperlinked to the COBOL code with navigable indices and software metrics, the TSRI Software Hypermodel Blueprint™ provided a comprehensive software engineering design model of the as-built REMIS Increment-1 source code accessible by any number of Northrop Grumman or Air Force personnel via Web interface.

### Transformation Summary

During the transformation phase the roughly 300,000 lines of COBOL85 were converted by TSRI's *e*Volution 2000™ toolset into object-oriented C++, and the Tandem RDBMS was updated into an Oracle 9i database. The COBOL to C++ conversion process included transforming embedded TAL SQL into Oracle SQL for Pro*C and automated formation of C++ classes and methods from COBOL records, programs, and paragraphs.

The target system required a five-tier Web architecture, which was achieved by the automatic creation of distinct classes separating the business code from the data access code and by introducing database and system support API layers integrated through a thread-spooler to spawn programs as needed. The business logic and database logic interleaved but were easily distinguishable because of C++ method invocations defined for operations specific to each of these layers. The transformation of REMIS COBOL85 and TAL into C++ and SQL was accomplished with 100% automation.

A common requirement of many ADM projects is the need to undertake innovative performance optimizations to the application architecture to assure performance goals are met when the application is transformed from the original into the new language and platform. A crucial performance optimization, undertaken during the REMIS migration to assure the transformed applications met performance goals, was a custom "pooling" system, designed by TSRI, that provided multiple pre-initialized instances of each derived C++ program. The pooling system allowed the transformed REMIS system to be scaled for any number of users to support Web-enablement of REMIS without degrading performance. All TAL COBOL programs were turned into C++ objects and made "thread safe." Large programs in the business logic layer required pre-initialization to reduce load times. Prior to the *pre-initialization optimization*, the performance of the transformed REMIS programs did not meet mandatory performance goals. The *pooling mechanism* component improved performance by minimizing load times during program instantiation by caching many copies of pre-initialized programs in advance for instant availability and by re-setting program data elements to their original state before returning used programs to the pool.

Another innovative optimization was the use of *Boost* multi-threading libraries to achieve cross-platform compatibility in the transformed REMIS system architecture. This was necessary because REMIS application layers were distributed onto separate processes and distributed geographically on different machines to allow the transformed REMIS to scale to support any number of users.

### Refactoring Summary

During the refactoring phase of REMIS Increment-1 several forms of refactoring operations were used to optimize the target C++ code. Fully automated refactoring was employed in the consolidation of "identical" C++ code derived from COBOL copybooks and in the detection and elimination of dead code. The classes initially derived by transformation from copybooks or introduced for other program structures contained redundancies for which an additional form of automated refactoring was applied to automatically derive common base classes from classes containing similar member methods and data member so as to superimpose a hierarchical class structure upon the nested classes. The data classes derived from COBOL records that were "similar," but not identical, were good candidates for semi-automated consolidation through a semi-automated refactoring technique that requires a human to choose a standard similar data member. Cluster indices were generated to support semi-automated refactoring operations used by Northrop Grumman subject matter experts to consolidate similar classes. Northrop Grumman engineers participated in defining refactoring specifications semi-automatically for "similar" data structure consolidation through a remote interface into TSRI's operation center. With VNC allowing remote access to TSRI refactoring tools across the Web, Northrop Grumman personnel were presented with clusters of C++ structures that TSRI tools had determined were sufficiently "similar" for consolidation. Northrop Grumman engineers selected candidates for consolidation and specified the names to be used in unifying these similar data structure elements (aliases). The refactoring specification was generated from this interaction and applied during a refactoring phase to the transformed REMIS system, automatically consolidating the C++ classes. This data class consolidation refactoring operation reduced the line count in the refactored code by 30% and demonstrated the ease and effectiveness of semi-automated refactoring.

## Transformation Testing

TSRI internal testing of transformed REMIS programs was accomplished by testing increments (or units) as they were transformed. Instead of testing at a very small level such as a routine-at-a-time as is the accepted practice during new development projects, REMIS testing was done on larger aggregate units. Each individual routine *was* validated for basic compilation/assembly, *but* larger groups of routines were tested as single aggregate test units in an approach that was more appropriate since the purpose of the testing was to verify the correctness of transformation and the logic flow for units whose functionality should not have changed whatsoever from the original. Testing in this manner allowed TSRI and Northrop Grumman to utilize regression test scripts previously developed for testing of REMIS incremental releases for testing the functional equivalence of the migrated system to the original. Since the inputs and outputs of the legacy system testing could be compared against the inputs and outputs of the transformed system for correctness and accuracy, TSRI and Northrop Grumman could safely reuse the preexisting test suites relying on "BLACKBOX TESTING METHODS" alone.

For the testing process, Northrop Grumman provided TSRI with the data loads, test scripts, and test scenarios deemed appropriate to test the REMIS transformation at a time defined by the project schedule. These test scripts and scenarios represented the criteria for successful completion of the transformation phase of this project. Northrop Grumman attested that the test scripts and scenarios given to TSRI successfully and properly executed against the legacy system. Northrop Grumman gave TSRI the outputs from the tests so TSRI could verify the results of the tests of the transformed REMIS code and data against the tests of the legacy REMIS code and data. TSRI and Northrop Grumman established a release schedule during the testing phase of the project to incorporate corrections to errors found during the testing of the transformed REMIS subsystem. TSRI and Northrop Grumman also established a Web-based database for reporting and tracking errors. TSRI and Northrop Grumman project management held telephone conference calls at least once a week to discuss any issues regarding testing or other issues pertinent to the project and to determine the priority and disposition of errors.

### Northrop Grumman and TSRI Remote Interaction and Cooperation

To reduce the effort associated with testing and to facilitate integration with the Java front-end under development by Northrop Grumman, a "Matterhorn" User-Interface Emulator running on the Apache Web server interfaced with the original GUI still running on the TANDEM mainframe. This interim user interface mechanism allowed presentation tier components developed by Northrop Grumman to be integrated and tested with the business logic and database access layer generated by TSRI's automated modernization processes, even though these components were running at sites 2,500 miles apart on different schedules. The automated modernization of the business logic layer of REMIS Increment-1 was completed months before the Java GUI manual re-development was completed. Use of the Matterhorn User-Interface Emulator allowed the TANDEM mainframe GUI to interface with the transformed C++ business logic and database while development of the replacement Java GUI was completed.

## Details of Approach

This section delineates the tasks addressed by TSRI and the approach taken to accomplish those tasks. It is interesting to note that TSRI employed different versions of its modernization tool suites during the first and second phases of the REMIS migration in 2002 and 2005, respectively. During the REMIS Increment-1 and -2 migration from COBOL85 to C++ TSRI used a tool suite based on *e*Volution 2000™, an early generation modernization technology that the company based on Refine*COBOL™ from Reasoning, Inc. TSRI replaced *e*Volution 2000™ with *Janus*Studio™ in 2003 (a TSRI proprietary model-based, rule-driven, multi-source, and multi-target transformation framework), and used *Janus*Studio™ for the REMIS Increment-3 transformation of COBOL into Java in 2005.

### Assessment Technical Approach

Assessment captures the legacy system's as-is state by extracting properties of the existing system's design and simultaneously generating detailed documentation of the system. The Increment-1 code was parsed to build an in-memory abstract syntax tree (AST) model of the entire COBOL system. An inventory was developed, using an iterative process, against the AST to (1) determine if any components of the application system were missing, (2) detect multiple versions of code, and (3) identify linkage problems. Deviation of the TANDEM COBOL85 dialect from the COBOL language standard made it necessary to modify the parser to address non-standard constructs of the application code.

After development of the AST code model, a preliminary transformation of the source code into the target to-be model was performed to assess and compare the "as-is" and "to-be" system models and determine modifications to the transformation process to achieve a highly automated transformation into the target language.

This "dry run" of the transformation process created an Intermediate Object-Oriented Model (IOM) from which transformation metrics were derived, including: (1) identification of the percentage of redundant and reusable code, and (2) potential code and data size reductions possible in the refactoring process. Additionally, the IOM formalism allowed detailed analysis and assessment of the properties of the target system. Of key significance in this process was (1) extraction, parameterization, and merging of derived methods associated with derived classes; and (2) measurement of the amount of decoupling, and the degree of cohesion and coherence that could be obtained in the resultant system.

The *e*Volution 2000™ toolset generated graphical documentation to support legacy code assessment. The *e*Volution 2000™ toolset provided structure charts, data element tables, state machine models, state transition tables, data flow models, control flow models, cause–effect graphs, redundancy analysis, and architecture analysis as an HTML format documentation for every program, function, and data element of the REMIS system.

### Transformation Technical Approach

TSRI used the assessment as the basis for a transformation of each specified module of code into platform-independent C++ code coupled to an Oracle 9i database. TSRI performed unit testing to assess the partial equivalence of the original code to the transformed code. Unit testing was performed with the generated C++ code. The transformation phase included compilation using the provided Forte C++ 6.0 compiler on a Solaris 2.8 O/S with Oracle 9i and implementation of the platform-specific infrastructure code for any source code not converted by automation. TSRI developed infrastructure code according to mutually agreed upon technical specifications with Northrop Grumman. TSRI delivered a technical report at the conclusion of the transformation phase included testing results, build scripts, and operating instructions for executing the delivered software; transformed C++ code (both source and object); and a system demonstration using the provided REMIS POBJ via the Matterhorn/Mattweb commercial-off-the-shelf (COTS) software invoking the generated C++ objects. The system demonstration included updates to the generated Oracle 9i database.

Northrop Grumman provided Oracle 9i DDL for SQL tables required to support converted programs. When technically possible, the Oracle SQL tables perfectly mirrored the existing REMIS tables. Northrop Grumman provided test data to populate Oracle SQL tables. Northrop Grumman performed a complete system test of the Transformed C++ code at the Northrop Grumman facility in Beavercreek, Ohio. The system test was performed using existing REMIS POBJ via the Matterhorn/Mattweb COTS software which invoked the generated C++ objects and accessed and updated the generated Oracle 9i database running on a Solaris 2.8 O/S. When generating Transformed C++ code, existing IPM linkages in REMIS source code were maintained in like form to support system-testing generated C++ objects using the REMIS Legacy POBJ via Matterhorn/ Mattweb software. This provided a consistent interface to generated C++ code for testing purposes.

The transformation modernization process begins with the automatic identification of candidate classes and objects for representation in the IOM. The IOM is a relatively complete transformation of the input source code consistent with the structure of object-oriented C++. This transformation into the IOM formalism locates redundant, duplicate, and similar data and processes and abstracts them into classes. The classes, relationships, attributes, and operations of the derived IOM model conform approximately to Universal Modeling Language (UML) standards, except the IOM model and the documentation produced from it is much more precise and detailed than UML documentation that is produced manually.

The IOM is a hybrid between object-oriented modeling languages, imperative languages, and event-driven programming languages containing a union of language elements from all of these language families. The mapping from procedural code into object-oriented code creates an intermediate *abstraction* of the software system expressed in the modeling elements of the IOM that are functionally faithful to the original procedural system, but expressed using syntactic modeling elements found in object-oriented languages like C++ and Java. The IOM bridges the conceptual gap between the legacy imperative languages and the target object-oriented language and is also used to generate *bridge documentation* that exhibits the relationships between the source and the target code, and the source and target design and architecture. Used by TSRI computer scientists and the Northrop Grumman REMIS engineers, architects, and subject matter experts, the bridge documentation was used to examine and compare the original system to the derived system and develop strategies to improve the modernization process. Improvements to the modernization process were implemented by tuning and adjusting the transformation and refactoring rules that carried out the transformation rather than manually changing the code.

Figure 8.1 illustrates the process for legacy system modernization by means of TSRI's model-based transformation process. This process is fully automated, but it can be tuned to introduce human-guided optimizations. Although not

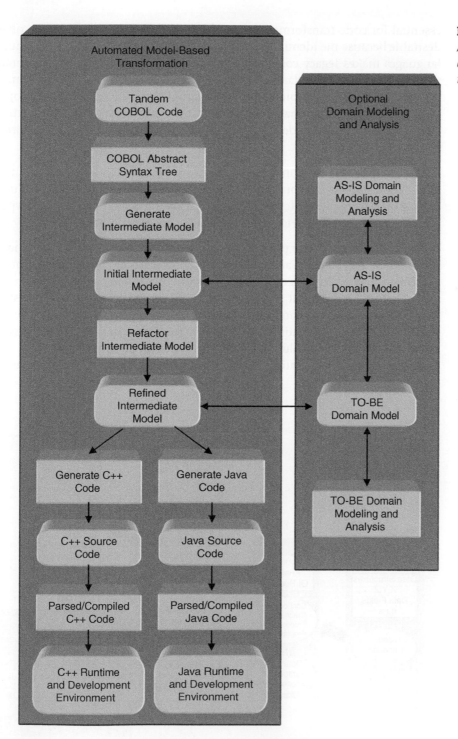

**FIGURE 8-1**

*Automated modernization of COBOL source into C++ target.*

essential for code transformation, standardization of variable names is often desirable because the identifier name length limitations of older programming languages makes legacy code cryptic. With the exception of trivial reformatting, variable name standardization cannot be accomplished without human expertise, and is a common example of a simple kind of human-guided optimizations, or semi-automated refactoring, that is undertaken in conjunction with fully automated code transformation and fully automated refactoring operations.

The overall process for transforming from a procedural to an object-oriented application starts with input of application programs and ultimately produces as output a completely integrated system consisting of C++ classes, data types, methods, and functions. Figure 8.2 illustrates this overall process.

Table 8.1 summarizes the principal processes of scope analysis, set-use analysis, program unit analysis, alias analysis, and physical data modeling previously illustrated. The evaluation of the structure and relationships between the data and processes in the input system provides the starting point for the transformation from the source language into the IOM. The generation of the IOM is preparatory to transformation into C++. The following analyses are performed automatically by the *e*Volution 2000™ toolset and captured within the AST model as auxiliary semantic models to support analysis and transformation operations.

**FIGURE 8.2**

*Procedural to object-oriented transformation.*

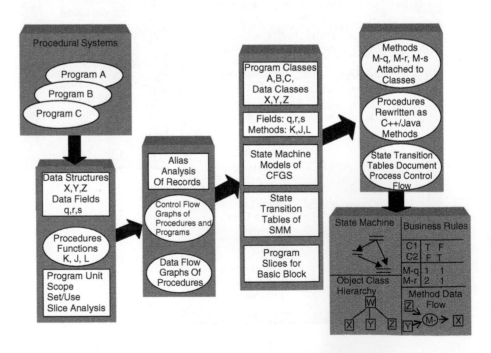

**Table 8.1** Data and Unit Analysis

| | |
|---|---|
| Scope analysis | Relates the occurrence of a variable to its declaration. |
| Set-use analysis | Identifies the definitions and usages of variables in a program with respect to usage semantics for each class of constructs occurring in the programming language. |
| Program unit analysis | Describes the local properties of each designated program unit in the programming language. It describes a data unit's type and location of its declarations, definitions, and references. Program unit analysis describes the signatures of functions: the number, order, type of all procedural objects, declarations, and occurrences. |
| Physical data modeling | Consists of analyzing each data item and data structure for its size, the byte offsets of every field, field length, and the types of each field. The physical data model is used in alias analysis to compare the properties of data structures. |
| Alias analysis | Analyzes every record and field for its occurrence in other programs and the identification of the aliases for data structures that may occur in a disguised or modified form in different programs. |

**Table 8.2** Control Flow Data Flow and Slice Analysis

| | |
|---|---|
| Control flow graph | Describes the points of entry and point of exit of each procedure and intermediate control conditions. |
| Data flow graph | Describes the definition of each data node and its usages. A usage-definition (UD) link connects a usage of a variable to a definition (assignment) of a variable. |
| Program slice | Transitive closure of one or more UD arcs (usage to definition) with respect to a variable for a scope determined by the slicing criteria. |

Table 8.2 is a summary of the principal control, data flow, and program slice analyses that are used to guide the transformation from the source language into C++. The following analyses are performed by the *e*Volution 2000™ toolset[1] and made available within the IOM as auxiliary semantic models that support analysis and transformation operations.

Table 8.3 is a summary of the principal as-is and to-be design artifacts that are the by-products of the transformation from the source language into C++. These design artifacts are hyperlinked to parallel mouse-sensitive window views of the source language and target C++. The following documentation is generated automatically by the *e*Volution 2000™ toolset and available to support analysis, documentation, and transformation operations.

---

[1] *e*Volution 2000™ was based on Refine™ from Reasoning. It was replaced by *Janus*Studio™ in 2002–2003.

**Table 8.3** Derived Design Artifacts

| | |
|---|---|
| Object model outline browser | A structured outline browser for navigating derived objects, classes, methods, and procedures. Pop-up and pull-down menus provide commands for displaying integrated graphical and textual views of source and target code and derived design and allow operators to perform operations upon the evolving software configuration. |
| Process data flow | Its behavior is depicted by process data flow graphs that depict the flow of data through the procedure as data flow graphs whose begin and end points are data sources and sinks (i.e., parameters and designated classes and their fields) and whose processes are methods. |
| State transition table | Consists of a table depicting one or more states and the conditions and actions involved in transitions between the states depicted as a limited entry decision table. |
| State transition graph | Consists of a start state, an end state, and a set of intermediate states joined by state transitions. |

**Table 8.4** Object-Oriented Model Entities

| | |
|---|---|
| Object-oriented data class | Top-level object-oriented data class member elements are formed from large-grained or top-level data structures from the legacy application, and methods are derived from functionally cohesive slices of code associated with the class's member elements. |
| Object-oriented process class | Object-oriented process classes whose instances are transformations of procedures into object-oriented processes, which refer to the elements of classes. Calls to methods formed from statement can be invoked from object-oriented processes. |
| Object-oriented methods | There are several classes of methods. Data transforming methods are formed from block-level slices between designated classes. Side effecting methods are formed from sequences of statements that invoke procedures or use data, but do not directly transform data. |

Table 8.4 is a summary of the principal object-oriented model components that are partial products of the transformation from a source language into intermediate C++. The following object model components are generated automatically by the *e*Volution 2000™ toolset and made available within the IOM to support analysis, documentation, and transformation operations.

At the conclusion of the transformation process, TSRI had taken the Northrop Grumman REMIS components and transformed them into compiling and linking C++. Matterhorn/Mattweb was used to execute the compiled and linked C++ components while the Java GUI front-ends were redeveloped by Northrop Grumman. This provided a vehicle for testing with an unchanged front-end (SCOBOL programs) to test the converted C++ components.

## Refactoring Technical Approach

Refactoring is the process of changing a software system so the software's structure and performance are improved without altering the functional behavior of the code. Refactoring is used to improve system maintainability and extend its usable life span. Refactoring operations are used to restructure design, eliminate, replace, or rewrite code to improve its efficiency and understandability, or to transform applications to use modern infrastructure support functions.

Larger grained refactoring transformations are accomplished by applying multiple sequential refactoring operations to accomplish the overall larger restructuring objective. These refactoring operations can be broadly scoped to preserve functionality while improving code quality.

Examples of refactoring include:

- Decoupling a slice of code from its original context and making it into a reusable method by encapsulation into a method body, derivation of actual and formal parameters, and giving the method a name descriptive of its purpose.
- Merging and consolidating similar or identical methods.
- Reducing the set of methods associated with a class to the minimal set of well-understood operations associated with the class.
- Moving methods between classes to improve the coupling, cohesion, and comprehensibility of the overall application.
- Consolidating redundant methods to reduce overall code duplication and code redundancy in the application.
- Combining classes or extract common data elements of several classes into a common parent class to improve the structure of the application data model by reducing data duplication.

The eVolution 2000™ toolset combines refactoring with large-grained transformation to achieve a high-quality object-oriented design. The toolset applies an initial large-grained transformation upon the entire application to generate an initial IOM representation. Subsequent refactoring operations under domain expert guidance are performed to refine the IOM representation thus improving the application's structure before going on with the transformation process.

Target code generation can be performed at any point once the IOM model is available. Some individual classes or groups of classes not dependent on infrastructure components are unit tested at a very early stage in the process. Because the system is required to conform to a specified set of infrastructure support utilities, testing of the generated code cannot be started until the infrastructure interface has been adapted to use equivalent utilities in the target platform. Once the system is generated, compiled, load modules are created, and mappings to replacement utilities of the target framework are completed, unit testing and system testing can begin.

A complex transformation and refactoring process should proceed in small increments with testing scheduled upon completion of the initial transformation and at frequent intervals between refactoring operations. This tightly iterative development process results in reduced errors and higher-quality code. The additional effort of more frequent testing is offset by reduced error correction time because the set of changes to each successive increment is relatively small, and with fewer changes, problems can be quickly isolated.

Legacy applications invariably have many dependencies on the legacy software infrastructure. Consequently, legacy code is usually not directly portable to another software environment. Modernization of applications generally requires isolating the mission-specific application code from the code associated with various environment-specific utility/support functions, known as *infrastructure code*.

After isolating the infrastructure code from the application software, the application software is analyzed and refactored without risk that the functional essence of the mission-critical software application is obfuscated by legacy infrastructure code. One common objective in refactoring the mission-critical software application is to minimize and isolate the target system's unique features by partitioning the software application code by means of design-level refactoring into functional-area generic and mission-specific classes. In a green-field development process this partitioning would occur during the design phase before commencing coding. During an architecture-driven modernization project design-level refactoring operations are used for a similar purpose. The domain model, specifically dependency models, constructed during the assessment guides this partitioning. Although some forms of repartitioning can be accomplished automatically, human insight is usually required to determine how components of the target system can best be re-partitioned. When the reorganization of components can be expressed as a formal refactoring plan, the eVolution 2000™ toolset can execute these refactoring operations automatically.

Often the legacy infrastructure functionality does not exist in the new environment or exists in a different form. Thus, this layer of software services must be discontinued, redeveloped, or suitably replaced. The definition or introduction of an appropriate interface to the facilities/services layer into the newly derived application, and the testing of both the interface and the services layers accessed through the facilities/services layer interface, is an iterative process. Subtle changes in the way the application interfaces with its database or environment is a common source of errors in a transformation project. Separation of the infrastructure layer from the application layer by means of an application program interface (API) isolates the adaptations that are required, and expedites recognition and resolution of flaws that originate in differences between services and utilities of the legacy and new operational environment.

Decoupling the infrastructure code from the application code by encapsulating calls to external services and utilities into a separate layer of code that is accessible through an API is a common form of architecture-oriented refactoring operation. The API hides the complexities of the infrastructure code from the application logic and allows the infrastructure layer code to be maintained without modification of the application code layer. This approach has the twin benefits of (1) separating the intricacies of the infrastructure code layer from the application logic layer so that the infrastructure code can be easily developed or adapted to different needs without necessitating changes to the application logic, and (2) making the application logic easier to maintain by separating it from the intricacies of the infrastructure layer implementation.

After the legacy infrastructure facing code is refactored or transformed to operate within the target environment, testing can commence. The infrastructure code should be tested, prior to application unit-testing, and system testing should be completed and a stable baseline established before commencing other forms of code-level, design-level, and architecture-level refactoring.

Code size reduction through code consolidating refactoring is one of the most tangible benefits that conversion to an object-oriented form can bring. Table 8.5 summarize metrics that are available in automated toolset that are used to measure the benefits of refactoring and other forms of code optimization.

Optimization to improve the structure or architecture of programs or data can sometime introduce additional runtime overhead. For instance, call-overhead can be increased by code consolidation operations. This overhead is nearly always easily offset by improvements in system performance brought about by refactoring to optimize the utilization of multiple processors, by speedups from a broader array of hardware choices, by tuning the way the database is utilized within the target environment, by exploiting larger memory spaces that are available with modern hardware, and, where such support is available, by rewriting the software application to take advantage of parallel programming constructs. Modern computing languages and architectures afford many opportunities for performance optimization. Systems Architects are usually able to identify and develop mitigation strategies for most performance problems before they

**Table 8.5** Transformation Metrics

| | |
|---|---|
| Method instance table (MIT) | Describes the number of instances created per class. This provides an indication of the amount of code reduction associated with the description of data structures for the target language. It is a partial measure of data redundancy eliminated through object class and instance formation. The C++ application may dynamically create the data structures rather than statically pre-allocate the data. This dynamic allocation is taken into account. The MIT also indicates the number of methods eliminated through method merging. This measure, combined with the amount of code per method, provides a reasonably accurate measure of the amount of code reduction achieved by the transformation and refactoring processes. |
| Model statistics report | Provides a measure of the amount of functional and structural compression achieved through method-merging reductions and object-instance abstraction. |
| State transition table parallelism | An indication of the potential amount of block-level parallelism is indicated by sequence numbers associated with the method invocations in a state transition table. (Methods are independent if they are not dependent upon one another by a Set-use-chain relationship and hence could be invoked simultaneously rather than sequentially.) Invocations of a transition's action are independent of one another if their invocation sequence numbers are identical. |

arise. A well-structured modernization project should have a planning phase to identify problems and issues and develop strategies for their resolution as early as possible in the project life cycle.

## REMIS-Specific Refactoring

Northrop Grumman provided REMIS functional expertise where necessary to support the fine- and large-grained refactoring operations. These experts worked with TSRI engineers to define specifications for refactoring operations that TSRI implemented. Completed refactoring deliverables included (1) a technical report detailing the refactoring operations that were performed, (2) testing results, (3) build scripts, (4) operating instructions for executing the refactored software, (5) refactored C++ code (both source and object), and (6) a system demonstration using the provided REMIS POBJ via the Matterhorn/Mattweb COTS software invoking the generated C++ objects.

The system demonstration included updates to the generated Oracle 9i database. Updated technical reports in the form of a set of structure charts, data element tables, state machine models, state transition tables, data flow models, control flow graphs, cause–effect graphs, redundancy analysis, and architecture analysis were also delivered.

Northrop Grumman performed a complete system test of the refactored C++ code at the Northrop Grumman facility in Beavercreek, Ohio. The system test was performed using existing REMIS POBJ via the Matterhorn/Mattweb COTS software invoking the generated C++ objects and updating the generated Oracle 9i database running on a Solaris 2.8 O/S. When generating refactored C++ code, existing IPM linkages in REMIS source code were maintained in like form to support system-testing generated C++ objects using the REMIS Legacy POBJ via Matterhorn/Mattweb software. This provided a consistent interface to generated C++ code for testing purposes.

### Java/C++ API Components
TSRI created Java/C++ API components that were used to invoke the C++ modules from the J2EE Java components created by Northrop Grumman. Northrop Grumman developed the presentation layer of the IF Resident REMIS Application using JSP, Servlet, and Java Bean components. The agreed upon technical solution for the Java/C++ API was developed by TSRI.

TSRI delivered a technical report including testing results, build scripts, and operating instructions for executing software; unit tested Java/C++ API components (both source and object); and a system demonstration using the Java/C++ API. The Java/C++ API deliverables were delivered along with the refactored C++ code. The Java/C++ API was system tested by Northrop Grumman when corresponding J2EE Java components were system tested.

### Java/C++ API Components Approach
TSRI and Northrop Grumman jointly designed and developed an application interface specification based on the technical requirements of the J2EE/Java runtime environment developed by Northrop Grumman and the TSRI transformed REMIS application. TSRI and Northrop Grumman used the current data input and output requirements of the REMIS legacy system as a basis for the design of this application interface. Using a standard object interface protocol, TSRI and Northrop Grumman developed a design that satisfies the input and output requirements of the transformed REMIS system. TSRI, with the assistance of Northrop Grumman, then developed, tested, and integrated this newly developed REMIS Java/C++ API into the REMIS application that was transformed to C++. Northrop Grumman tested and integrated the REMIS Java/C++ API with the J2EE/Java servlet environment.

## Project Reporting
TSRI provided weekly status reports in a mutually agreeable format indicating actual versus planned progress (i.e., number of units converted vs. total planned over time inception to date, problem report statistics of number created vs. number resolved, etc.), issues, scope considerations, and risks.

## Project Deliverables

### Assessment Deliverables

The Assessment Deliverables consisted of as-is blueprints in the form of structure charts, data element tables, state machine models, state transition tables, data flow models, control flow graphs, cause–effect graphs, redundancy analysis, and architecture analysis, and including possible problem conversion areas and percent of overall attainable conversion. Acceptance criteria was completion of the Northrop Grumman review of as-is documentation within 10 business days from date of delivery.

### Transformation Deliverables

The transformation deliverables consisted of testing results, build scripts, and operating instructions for executing software, transformed C++ code (both source and object), a system demonstration using the provided REMIS POBJ via the Matterhorn/Mattweb COTS software invoking the generated C++ objects, and updating the Oracle 9i database created using Northrop Grumman-provided Oracle 9i DDL. Acceptance criteria were the resolution of all identified problems and completion of the NG IT system test for transformed C++ components.

### Refactoring Deliverables

The refactoring deliverables consisted of testing results, build scripts, and operating instructions for executing software, the refactored C++ code (both source and object), a system demonstration using the provided REMIS POBJ via the Matterhorn/Mattweb COTS software invoking the generated C++ objects, and updating the Oracle 9i database created using Oracle 9i DDL provided by Northrop Grumman, updated *as-is* and *to-be* system documentation in the form of a set of structure charts, data element tables, state machine models, state transition tables, data flow models, control flow graphs, cause–effect graphs, redundancy analysis, architecture analysis, technical reports of Java/C++ API testing results, build scripts, and operating instructions for executing software, Java/C++ API components (both source and object), and a system demonstration using the Java/C++ API. The acceptance criteria was the resolution of all identified problems and completion of Northrop Grumman system test for refactored C++ components and Java/C++ API components.

### Project Assumptions and Obligations

TSRI undertook a final code/DDL count on the REMIS components provided by Northrop Grumman upon final delivery of the project code/DDL. At that time, TSRI provided an amended fixed price project bid making adjustments for the kind of quantity of code, by a Letter of Amendment, to the initial Subcontract.

Northrop Grumman provided:

- The full suite of applications code at the current configuration level for all Computer Program Configuration Items (CPCIs) and data associated with the REMIS system at no cost to TSRI.
- A fully functional demonstration of REMIS CPCI provided to TSRI at the Northrop Grumman facility in Beavercreek, Ohio.
- An Oracle 9i Database Manager Developer with documentation and with 1 server database license and 15 concurrent client licenses for the duration of the project. All licenses and documentation were returned to Northrop Grumman at the conclusion of the project.
- Required Matterhorn/Mattweb software, Forte C++ compiler developer IDE.
- Documentation for the following items: Matterhorn/Mattweb, TAL, Embedded SQL, and TAL system commands.
- REMIS domain expertise at TSRI's request provided functional testing and technical guidance to ensure that all task deliverables met task requirements.
- Test scenarios and scripts acceptable for TSRI to execute at each phase of the testing process.
- REMIS data and system interfaces required for executing the selected test scenarios.
- Sample data loads in a mutually agreed upon format prior to the commencement of the testing.

TSRI provided:

- eVolution 2000™ toolset for use during the project.
- Solaris computer running Solaris 2.8 O/S to support Northrop Grumman-FE provided Forte C++ Compiler and Oracle 9i database.
- NT Server 2000 with IIS Web server to support Matterhorn/Mattweb COTS software for validating system test problem reports.
- Virtual networking software to provide remote Northrop Grumman expertise to TSRI and reduce travel required for project.

Caveats and limitations:

- Northrop Grumman mandated the choice of operating system, hardware, compiler, and database. As Northrop Grumman-developed software could impose constraints upon final system performance optimization that were beyond the control of TSRI, and as these factors were outside of the control of TSRI, TSRI made no specific claims, warrantees, guarantees, nor representations with respect to any possible, predicted, or estimated performance improvements that might result from any single, or any combination of, architecture, design, and performance-oriented refactoring optimizations to the transformed information system.

## Project Set-Up Tasks

The assessment and transformation *setup* tasks associated with the project are identified in Table 8.6. Set-up tasks are analysis tasks performed early in the project to research, analyze, or adapt TSRI processes to the client's specific needs.

## Lessons Learned (Increment-1): Northrop Grumman's Perspective

Northrop Grumman provided TSRI the unexpanded source code for all of the REMIS COBOL programs to be converted. This included all called modules and all copy code along with all of the data definition language (DDL) for the existing database and export files to load necessary data into Oracle database tables for testing purposes. Northrop Grumman also provided TSRI with Himalaya systems manuals for the TAL operating system, non-stop SQL, TAL, and TACL, so TSRI engineers could develop an understanding of the O/S-specific components with which the REMIS programs interfaced. From these inputs TSRI modified and adapted their toolset and then applied it to

**Table 8.6** Set-Up Tasks

| Assessment Set-Up Task Descriptions |
| --- |
| Research TAL Operating System functions |
| Research Java/C++ API layer requirements |
| Research Oracle 9i API layer interface requirements |
| Research preservation of IPM linkages to support testing |
| Research test driver adaptations to support using REMIS POBJ with Matterhorn/Mattweb |
| Extend Document Generator for TANDEM COBOL to support generation structure charts, data element tables, state machine models, state transition tables, data flow models, control flow graphs, and cause–effect graphs for REMIS COBOL only |
| Extend TSRI SQL parser for TAL and Oracle SQL |
| Research TSRI test bed adaptations for REMIS |
| Research any other infrastructure code set-up requirements |
| Extend TSRI COBOL Parser for TANDEM COBOL |
| **Transformation Set-Up Task Descriptions** |
| Extend TSRI Operation System Layer API for TAL Operating System functions |
| Extend TSRI Java/C++ API layer for REMIS requirements |
| Extend TSRI API layer for Oracle 9i using embedded SQL |
| Adapt transformation process and interfaces to provide IPM linkage support for testing |
| Extend TSRI test drivers APIs to support using REMIS POBJ with Matterhorn/Mattweb |
| Extend TSRI translator for TAL to Oracle SQL |
| Extend TSRI test bed for REMIS |
| Extend TSRI COBOL to C++ Translator for TANDEM COBOL |

**Table 8.7** Code Metrics

| Code Type | Original Code Count | Revised Code Count | Transformation Rate Structure | Refactoring Rate Structure | Refactoring Rate Structure |
|---|---|---|---|---|---|
| COBOL85 | 152,082 | 149,395 | FFP | FFR | FFR |
| Embedded SQL | 25,244 | 24,861 | | | |
| Comments | 80,461 | 85,213 | | | |
| DDL | 11,315 | 11,053 | | | |
| Total | 269,102 | 270,522 | | | |

the REMIS code. TSRI provided Northrop Grumman with a firm fixed price (FFP) quotation based on the code count in a contract ROM as shown in Table 8.7.

It should be noted that due to efficiencies and advances in its new JanusStudio™ technology TSRI pricing structure changed since this project was undertaken, hence pricing in Table 8.7 is omitted because the old pricing information is no longer applicable.

TSRI priced the Increment-1 and Increment-3 projects as FFP contracts. Northrop Grumman negotiated a final code count that would occur by some identified period of time, because by the time Northrop Grumman went on contract and delivered the final version of code to be converted, some of the code would have changed due to ongoing maintenance tasks. TSRI had the right to adjust the price dependent on the actual code count based from the final code count to reduce the price for less code, or increase the price for more code in the final count.

TSRI took the Northrop Grumman code through three phases of its modernization process: Assessment, Transformation, and Refactoring. Northrop Grumman performed the system testing at the Transformation and Refactoring stages. The output from the assessment phase was the HTML documentation that depicted the existing design for the *as-built* COBOL and DDL as modeled by the IOM.

During Assessment, TSRI identified the level of effort required to create system functionality in the C++ and estimated the re-engineering required to interface with the GCSS platform. Northrop Grumman employed a C++ architect who worked on the Northrop Grumman team to consult with TSRI on the architecture decisions associated with re-engineering decisions. The transformation phase created converted C++ code that was testable working in the Windows environment. Commercial off the shelf (COTS) client software was used to interpret the original screen presentation layer and interface with the C++ code. The refactoring phase consolidated reusable components and adapted the code to run in the UNIX environment.

Northrop Grumman created the glue C++ layer that provided for the Java front-end built by Northrop Grumman to interface with the C++ servers created by TSRI. This was engineered by the Northrop Grumman C++ architect and was a part of the project requiring intricate re-engineering. Northrop Grumman experimented with several approaches providing specifications for each approach to TSRI to implement, and TSRI created rules to implement each of the requested approaches.

After refactoring was completed, TSRI provided metrics for the *before-and-after* SLOC counts as follows:

Before refactoring:

> Header: 112,687 SLOC
> Source: 141,003 SLOC
> Total: 253,690 SLOC

After refactoring:

> Header: 38,809 SLOC
> Source: 117,149 SLOC
> Total: 155,958 SLOC

As a result of code consolidation and reuse, the declaration code was reduced to 34% of its original size. The total line count was reduced to 61% of its original size.

Key to the success of the project was a good working relationship between Northrop Grumman and TSRI that was due to a good understanding of the roles and responsibilities of the two companies, a precise statement of work specification, mutual respect for each team's respective technical competencies, and excellent team synergy. TSRI stayed very close to schedule throughout the project and accommodated all requests. Several instances occurred where small code changes were required due to problems uncovered when the COBOL code was converted. On each of these occasions TSRI implemented the changes, re-transformed, and re-delivered the system under Northrop Grumman direction without raising issues.

TSRI successfully performed the assessment, transformation, and refactoring of the 300,000 line COBOL subsystem in Increment-1. Northrop Grumman was particularly pleased by the smooth delivery of both the transformed and the refactored versions of the REMIS C++ code. As a result of these efforts TSRI was selected for Northrop Grumman's "2002 Small Business of the Year Award" citing the low level of defects in TSRI deliverables, TSRI's disciplined approach to problem identification and resolution, and its expedient resolution of issues and problems as justifications for the award and the strong improvements in performance and maintainability that were achieved by refactoring and performance optimization. Significantly, the number of defects found during system testing after transformation was 7 problem reports across the 44 converted programs. The number of defects found during system testing after refactoring was 15 problem reports. TSRI provided a Web-based tool named Bugzilla for use in reporting defects to TSRI as they were found. Bugzilla was effective and helped REMIS to track the status of the fixes. TSRI was cited as expedient in fixing the problems as they were reported. Northrop Grumman was also pleased with the strong improvements in performance and maintainability that resulted from the refactoring process.

TSRI was on contract with Northrop Grumman from the end of May 2002 to the end of January 2003 to accomplish the code conversion. Following TSRI completion of its work on this project, Northrop Grumman modified several of the C++ programs for ongoing maintenance and found just a couple of subsequent issues that Northrop Grumman discussed with TSRI, and TSRI provided proper fixes. Northrop Grumman project management issued a published report stating it was very pleased with the TSRI effort on the REMIS project and would not hesitate to use TSRI again if the chance arises.

The following is a list of items provided by both teams that made the project successful:

Northrop Grumman provided the following items:

1. REMIS unexpanded source code and called modules
2. Legacy System Documents for O/S, SQL, TACL
3. Oracle Database DDL and export file of data to be loaded for testing
4. Unit test plans to be executed by TSRI during unit test
5. Matterhorn software — COTS tool used to execute C++ servers with existing SCOBOL screen programs
6. Oracle 9i license
7. C++ Coding Style Guide
8. POC — Project Leader and technical POC (with strong SQL skills)
9. Glue layer C++ code for interfacing Java with C++ servers

TSRI provided the following items:

1. Access to a server to FTP large files
2. Project Manager and Technical POC
3. Weekly status reports as directed by Northrop Grumman
4. HTML documentation after assessment and refactoring
5. SLOC statistics after refactoring
6. Bugzilla tracking tool for tracking and reporting defects

The following items are recommended to assure a successful project when working with TSRI:

1. Document roles and responsibilities of both parties
2. Assign a single POC for project management and technical issues on both parties
3. Hold weekly status meetings to review status report
4. Establish connectivity to TSRI server for transferring large files
5. Provide Coding Style Guide for target code
6. If transforming to C++, eliminate type casting to multiple levels for embedded SQL code

## Project Outcome

TSRI successfully performed the assessment, transformation, and refactoring on the 300,000 line COBOL subsystem of Increment-1. TSRI delivered the code in two increments. Northrop Grumman was particularly pleased by the smooth delivery of both the transformed and the refactored versions of the REMIS C++ code. They were also pleased with the unexpectedly strong improvements in performance and maintainability that resulted from the refactoring process. After a month of acceptance testing only 1 flaw was detected in the 300,000 lines of transformed code. No flaws were found in the 200,000 lines of refactored code. TSRI was selected for Northrop Grumman's "2002 Small Business of the Year Award" as a result of these efforts.

# REMIS INCREMENT-3

## REMIS COBOL to J2EE and Oracle 9i Modernization

REMIS Increment-3 source code was comprised of 91,382 lines of COBOL source code and 54,853 comments supported by a database that uses SQL and flat file, running on an HP non-stop with a G06.25 O/S using an HP non-stop RDBMS. The user interface is a 6530 terminal emulation that is Web accessible. The application used external calls to the operating system: FTP, TAL, and e-mail. The external data interfaces consist of outbound flat files that were sent by FTP to external systems and inbound flat files that were sent by FTP to REMIS.

The desired target for the modernized REMIS Increment-3 application was J2EE Java version 1.4.2 utilizing an Oracle 9i (currently 9.2.0.6) database and running on a Sun K15 platform with Solaris 8 O/S.

TSRI provided the complete set of its services at TSRI's "deployment ready" level to convert the remaining legacy REMIS Increment-3 code and make it fit within the existing Web application infrastructure that Northrop Grumman has already developed. Some parts of the desired target services needed to be "integrator ready" where manual integration to existing infrastructure was required. TSRI worked with Northrop Grumman to obtain the desired final state by employing both automatic and semi-automatic refactoring. TSRI worked with Northrop Grumman during the engineering support phase to ensure successful testing and integration of the migrated system. Northrop Grumman was responsible for the final implementation and fielding.

## Technical Approach Summary for the COBOL to Java Conversion for Increment-3

Steps involved in the TSRI code conversion include set-up, transformation, refactoring (automatic and semi-automatic), and engineering support as defined below:

- Set-Up: Modification of the TSRI JANUS™ toolset to be able to ingest and parse the REMIS legacy code.

- Transformation: TSRI's process using the JANUS™ toolset whereby the legacy REMIS code is automatically rewritten into compiling and linking Java version 1.4.2 with embedded SQL rewritten into data access object (DAO) and all external calls "stubbed out." All external system calls (TAL) were stubbed out to access equivalent Java components that replaced the Legacy system calls. TSRI integrated J2EE Java classes/methods encompassing legacy TAL functionality provided by Northrop Grumman as replacements for "stubbed out" calls to TAL external system services.

- Automatic Refactoring: Identification and removal of dead and redundant code by TSRI to improve system maintainability without changing the functionality of the REMIS application.

- Semi-Automatic Refactoring: TSRI working with Northrop Grumman identified additional opportunities for code consolidation for analysis by Northrop Grumman domain experts and then used the JANUS™ toolset to make those consolidations in a uniform and traceable manner.

- Engineering Support: TSRI supported the REMIS post-modernization system transformation issue resolution, integration, implementation, and unit testing in coordination with, and at the level of, support requested by Northrop Grumman.

## Customization During Transformation and Refactoring

### SSO Task Handlers

The Legacy COBOL SSO programs were translated into Java by TSRI using the JANUS™ toolset. The Java Task Handlers will comply with the REMIS S2S/Batch application architecture. These Java Task Handlers extracted the data from the appropriate database via JDBC. These data were then formatted for each record mnemonic as flat file output data or placed into a temporary SQL table. The output format supported up to two format versions as currently used in legacy REMIS with versioning configuration.

### REMIS JUnit Test Classes

Each translated Java class was tested via a JUnit test class. The JUnit test class was generated by Northrop Grumman and delivered to TSRI for their use in verifying the accuracy of the translation. In addition to the test software, Northrop Grumman provided an Oracle test database and a sample of the Legacy output generated for each record mnemonic to compare against.

### REMIS Data Access Layer

REMIS uses a data access layer consisting of data access objects (DAO), query access objects (QAO), and value objects (VO). The DAO and QAO classes extend from an open-source project from Apache named Commons DB Utils. More information on this package can be found at http://jakarta.apache.org/commons/dbutils/index.html.

The DAO class contained all of the SQL statements, but very little, if any, JDBC code. The DB Utils classes encapsulated all of the JDBC code reducing the amount of repetitive coding required. A DAO only accesses a single database table, so it contains rather simple SELECT, INSERT, DELETE, and UPDATE statements.

The mechanism for passing data to and from a DAO is the VO. The VO is a simple Java Bean with a field corresponding to every field in the database table that the DAO represents. One might think of a VO returned from a DAO as representing one row in a table.

The INSERT, UPDATE, and DELETE methods in a DAO always return an integer that represents the number of rows modified in the database table. The input argument would typically be a VO that identifies the precise criteria to use in the SQL statement. On occasion, it was more convenient to just pass a list of arguments rather than a single VO. If a SELECT statement would return at most one row, than a single VO was the return argument. If a SELECT statement could return multiple rows, then a list of VOs is returned.

The QAO class is where multi-table joins are coded. Since DAOs refer to a single database table, a consistent place was needed to put multi-table joins. The QAO did not have any INSERT, UPDATE, or DELETE statements, but otherwise were identical to DAOs. If a method returned a single row, a VO was returned, and if the method returned multiple rows, a list of VOs was returned. The VO that was used by a QAO is a bit different than the VO used with a DAO. The difference is that a VO used with a DAO represents a single table, but the VO used with a QAO represents the data that may be collected from multiple tables.

## DAO Data Query Object Specification

The following sections outline rules that should be adhered to when generating QAOs for REMIS. QAOs are very similar to DAOs, but instead of a one-table, one-object paradigm, QAOs access multiple tables in the form of a join or a union in SQL or implement a parent/child relationship.

## Task Handler Architecture

The COBOL servers migrated during Increment-3-generated outbound files that were transmitted to REMIS customers. Many of the COBOL servers that TSRI was tasked to translate contain the business logic behind the generation of the output. Within the REMIS J2EE application architecture, this most closely resembles the "TaskHandler" components.

In the REMIS J2EE application architecture, "Task Dispatchers" were scheduled Java Threads (TimerTask) that periodically wake up and look for work. If work was found, a "Task" was created that describes the piece of work. The Task was then provided to a TaskHandler, which starts the business process that "handles" the task.

The Task classes were usually quite small, but contained enough information for the TaskHandler to find the work it is supposed to process. Often the Task contained the values for a Primary Key to a table that the TaskHandler would query. Sometimes the Task would contain parameters needed by the TaskHandler. Regardless of how much information it contained, the Task was a JavaBean with a well-defined set of fields. The Task classes needed for Increment-3 were provided to TSRI by Northrop Grumman.

## REMIS Java Coding Standards Compliance

The REMIS Java Coding Standards Guide defined the standards that TRSI was required to follow when developing Java source code on the REMIS migration project. The guidelines were much more comprehensive than those presented here. Those presented in the next sections illustrate the coding standards requirements the code TSRI emitted was required to meet when generating Java, JSP, and JavaScript.

### If, If-Else, If Else-If Else Statements

The following example demonstrates the preferred way of writing if-else-type statements. Be sure and use braces, regardless of whether there is more than one line or not.

```
if (condition) {
statements;
}
else if (condition2) {
statements;
}
else {
statements;
}
```

### REMIS Java Naming Conventions

Table 8.8 summarizes the recommendations on naming conventions.

### REMIS Java Programming Practices

Listed in the following sections are some encouraged programming practices.

**Providing Access to Instance and Class Variables**: Do not make any instance or class variable public. Provide accessor and mutator methods (getField() and setField()) instead. Use a default of private on instance class variables unless you know that this class may be inherited. In that case, use protected instead so that subclasses may have access to the variables without calling the accessor methods.

**Referring to Class Variables and Methods**: Avoid using an object to access a class (static) variable or method. Use the class name instead. For example:

```
Cat.getMaxLives () // Good
morris.getMaxLives () // confusing as the class has
                                  info, not object.
```

**Coding Standards References**: Legacy COBOL SSO programs were translated into Java classes through services by TSRI using the TSRI Janus™ toolset. The Java Task Handlers complied with the REMIS S2S/Batch application architecture. These Java Task Handlers extracted these data from the appropriate database via JDBC. These data were then formatted for each record mnemonic as flat file output data or placed into a temporary SQL table. The output format supported up to two format versions as currently used in legacy REMIS with versioning configuration.

**Table 8.8** Element Naming Conventions

| Element Type | Convention | Examples |
|---|---|---|
| Package | All lowercase letters. | com.Northrop Grumman.remis.common.support |
| Class | Capitalize first letter and all sub-words. In general this is a noun. | ActionServlet, Rees1440lpmOut2, BillTheCat |
| Action class | Same as class, except add Action to end of name. This should inherit from RemisScreenAction instead of Action. | Efm1440Action |
| Exception class | Same as class, except add Exception as suffix. | InsufficientFundsException |
| Interface | Same as class. | httpServletRequest, httpServletResponse |
| Method | First letter is lowercase and capitalize all sub-words. In general this is a verb. | doPost (), doGet (), kickCat() |

- Sun's Code conventions for the Java programming language — http://java.sun.com/docs/codeconv/
- InfoSpheres Java Coding Standard — http://www.infospheres.caltech.edu/resources/code_standards/java_standard.html
- Java Programming style guide — http://www.javaranch.com/style.jsp

# CONCLUSION

## REMIS Modernization Summary

REMIS was designed to enhance the front-end design of new weapon systems and to increase the readiness and sustainability of existing USAF weapon systems by improving the availability, accuracy, and flow of essential equipment information. REMIS provides the capability to collect, edit, validate, process, store, and report reliability and maintainability data on aerospace vehicles, trainers, automated test equipment, selected support equipment, and communications-electronics in the following functional areas: equipment maintenance, time compliance technical order (TCTO), time change inspection (TCI), configuration, debriefing, inventory, status, and utilization.

Northrop Grumman teamed with TSRI to convert REMIS, which was originally implemented in COBOL85 server programs running in an HP Himalaya environment interfacing with a non-stop SQL database, in two separate contractual increments in the 2002–2005 time frame into object-oriented C++ and Java/J2EE programs interfacing with an Oracle 9i database in support of AF/A4M directive that REMIS be migrated to the GCSS-AF IF. The screen presentation layer was re-engineered by Northrop Grumman in J2EE Java using WAS 4.0.

## REMIS Modernization History

On 27 Nov 2001, the government briefed the customer, AF/A4M (Mr. Grover Dunn), on the overall strategy for migrating to the GCSS-AF IF. The customer approved the overall plan and granted approval to proceed with Increment-1, -2, and -3. Increment-1was placed on contract 1 May 2002. On 18 Mar 2004, the government briefed AF/A4M (General Gillett) on the REMIS migration status. AF/A4M verified that REMIS should continue with the migration effort as planned. Increment-2 (Spirals 1–2) was placed on contract 27 Sep 2004 and Increment-2 (Spirals 3–5) was placed on contract 11 Apr 2005. Increment-3 migrated all outbound interfaces to the GCSS-AF. Outbound interfaces designated "operational" used the REMIS real-time operational database as the data source. Interfaces designated "analytical" used the GCSS-AF Data Services (formerly Air Force Knowledge Services; AFKS) database as the data source. The GCSS-AF IF Enterprise Service Bus (ESB) was used, where possible, as the interface transport mechanism. Increment-3 permitted the development and implementation of user-directed Information Technology/National Security

Systems Requirements Documents (ITSRDs) during the period of performance. From both a technical and cost perspective, the contractor leveraged all learned knowledge and actual project artifacts generated during the government's previous attempt to migrate the REMIS outbound analytical interfaces to GCSS-AF Data Services. This attempt was made in the 2004–2005 time frame under the auspices of the GCSS-AF Data Services program office (EISS/EIDA). The contractor participated extensively in that effort and is well positioned to evaluate the practicality of using any previously generated artifacts.

## REMIS Modernization Benefits from Business and Technical Perspectives

REMIS capabilities and functionality will ultimately be absorbed into an Air Force enterprise-level product under the Expeditionary Combat Support System (ECSS) program. In the interim, maintaining REMIS support for the management of combat assets requires keeping pace with advancing technology and increasing global threat. Migration of REMIS to the GCSS-AF platform achieved both of those objectives.

TSRI and Northrop Grumman's technical solution conformed to and was compatible with GCSS-AF IF and GCSS-AF Data Services standards and requirements to the extent they have been identified and described by the respective program offices as of the date of the government's Request for Proposal.

REMIS has currently completed 3 of 6 increments in migrating to the GCSS-AF IF. Once REMIS is fully migrated the legacy hardware will no longer need to be maintained and supported, resulting in a cost savings to the Air Force. Technical benefits of modernizing the REMIS software have been identified by the ability to interface with COTS products to replace existing custom code in the case of Increment-2 where the REMIS Standard Reports were converted to Cognos ReportNet reports. Services offered by the GCSS-AF IF have replaced equivalent services that were hosted on the REMIS stand-alone hardware and used only by the REMIS application. The migration effort has allowed the REMIS data to be published using the GCSS ESB, which provides REMIS data to other systems with less level of effort in development for each interfacing system.

This project was a technically successful application of ADM techniques to large-scale systems engineering, development, integration, and operational processes of a major component of the USAF IDMS.

# CHAPTER 9

# Federal Agency Case Study: Role of Modernization in a Greenfield Replacement/ COTS Project*

Ed Seidewitz and William Ulrich

## ABSTRACT

Richard Nixon was in the White House, Watergate had yet to hit the headlines, and the war in Vietnam was still a reality when a group of university graduates set out to build a financial system for an agency of the U.S. Federal Government ("Agency"). That system became the financial system of record for the Agency and continues to run to this day, performing many of its original financial accounting functions just as it has been for the better part of four decades.

This system ("Core System"), along with numerous other systems, people, and business processes, accounts for the transfer of billions of dollars in transactions on a year-to-year basis. Key functions include billing, asset accounting, and accounts receivable functionality for the Agency. The longevity and robustness of the Core System is a testament to the durability of old software systems and a living example of how enterprise systems reflect business complexities and realities while tying an enterprise to decades-old business practices.

In the mid-to-late 1990s, the Agency embarked on a project to replace the Core System. The first phase of this project, completed in the early part of the decade, transitioned certain financial accounting functions from the Core System to a commercial-off-the-shelf (COTS) software package ("Software Package"). The Software Package became the new system of record for accounting transactions as performed across the Agency. However, the Core System still runs in parallel to and interfaces with the Software Package.

## CONTENTS

*This case study is an ongoing story that has not had the final chapter written. We felt that it was important to share the experiences because many enterprises are in a very similar situation when it comes to managing the transition from older to newer enterprise systems. Also note that publication of this case study required that it be published without specific reference to the government agency, individuals, or systems involved. In addition, certain information was omitted or sanitized to accommodate the need for confidentiality.

The functions shifted over to the Software Package constituted a small portion of the overall functionality originally supported by the original Core System. As a result, the Core System feeds transactions into the Software Package and, in some cases, receives transactions back from the Software Package. Subsequent phases of the replacement initiative began to tackle the more customized and challenging aspects of the Core System replacement effort. These subsequent phases of the ongoing replacement and Core System deactivation effort are the basis for this case study.

## THE PLAN

The planning portion of this initiative involved establishing and justifying a roadmap for the first project phase. Much of this was done prior to the beginning of the initial enterprise assessment and incorporated work related to the creation of the high-level financial architecture. The business case and roadmap for phasing out of the 35-year-old Core System are as follows.

### The Business Case

The business case was reasonably straightforward and was established in the late 1990s. The processes and rules deployed within and around the Core System were aligned with non-standard accounting practices and, therefore, had to be replaced. This dictated both the need and, to a great degree, the approach. While cost was a factor, there was no choice but to attempt to move forward with a phased systems replacement and deactivation of the old Core System.

Prior to acquisition of the Software Package, certain in-house personnel submitted a plan for incrementally improving and migrating the existing systems to accommodate the changes in accounting practices. Management, however, wanted a fresh start. Subsequent analysis, as explained later in this case study, found that incremental improvement through refactoring and other modernization techniques may have been possible, but would have been extremely difficult given the complexity and cryptic nature of the existing application and data architecture. In addition, because business logic, data structures, and processes were woven around non-standard accounting functions, the reuse of the business logic extracted from the Core System would not be of high value. In other words, the die was cast in terms of the approach.

This analysis would have been useful as a prerequisite to management deciding to go with a third-party software package, but it was a reasonable decision at the time — assuming that the package could support the needs of the agency. The decision, therefore, was to move forward with a combination of a Software Package solution, coupled with custom development of services-oriented architecture (SOA) interfaces and overarching architecture.

Management did have enough insight, however, to realize the importance of understanding the architecture they planned to dismantle and largely replace. There was a general sense that knowledge of the existing business data and logic could provide insights into the evolution of the replacement architecture. In addition, the data flowing into and out of various business units and other agencies had to remain intact. This dictated that the team expose and document all data interfaces into and out of the Core System as well as analyze the prime data being used by the Core System.

Therefore, one aspect of the project was to incorporate architecture-driven modernization (ADM) analysis principles and techniques into various stages of this effort. The resulting plan envisioned a multi-phased roadmap that incrementally moved the Agency toward its goal of replacing the Core System through a series of incremental deployment steps.

## The Roadmap

Certain preliminary work had been performed leading up to the first phase of analysis on the Core System and surrounding business and technical environment. One important step was the creation of the high-level, target architecture for financial management, which was established in 2004. The financial management enterprise architecture ("financial architecture") created the boundaries and blueprint that would guide subsequent implementation efforts.

Figure 9.1 depicts a high-level snapshot of the roadmap plan for the eventual phasing out of the Core System and deployment of the Software Package.

Note that Phase 0 was a preliminary step that is highly recommended when attempting to perform major architectural "surgery" within a complex systems environment. Having a vision provided the agency with a way to set priorities, build business support, and provide a target for phased deployment.

The financial architecture could be considered a Greenfield architectural analysis as it depicted the ideal financial environment that the Agency envisioned. In a perfect world, this is the way in which a project like this should be pursued because it created a visionary target for all follow-on work.

The work discussed in this case study involved follow-on initiatives that leveraged the high-level financial architecture. Phase one of the financial architecture project involved a three-pronged approach and ran approximately 1 year. The three major aspects of this project are summarized as follows.

**FIGURE 9.1**

*Phased roadmap snapshot.*

- Phase 0:
  - Creation of high-level financial architecture from business perspective
- Phase 1:
  - Development of detailed architectural view for subset of accounting capabilities
  - Mapping of current environment to:
    - Facilitate and augment top-down functional and data architecture
    - Assist with crafting migration strategy
- Phase 2:
  - Derive additional current systems analysis details to support migration
  - Phased design & deployments to target architecture
- Note: Top-down architecture required to align, augment 3rd package functionality

## Financial Architecture Project Phase One Summary

1. Detailed expansion of selected financial architecture functionality to provide more depth in a subset of topical areas
2. Business process mapping across various business units
3. Initial assessment of as-is IT architecture including:
   - Enterprise assessment
   - Detailed assessment

The bulk of phase one of the case study addressed task three in the previous list, but the importance of each of the other tasks and how they relate to the initial assessment will also be discussed. The second major project phase, which started up roughly 1.5 years after the end of phase one, is called phase two and is summarized as follows.

## Financial Architecture Project Phase Two Summary

1. Detailed design and development of selected functional components
2. Detailed assessment of selected segments of the as-is application and data architecture
3. Transition planning
4. Implementation testing and deployment

The intent of phase two was to deploy a small set of functionality and deactivate the corresponding functionality within the Core System. This phase would determine the viability of the replacement/transition strategy and establish a pattern for future implementations that would ultimately replace and deactivate the Core System altogether.

# PROJECT PHASE ONE — INITIAL ASSESSMENT: ENTERPRISE ASSESSMENT

Management allotted a 45-day window to perform the enterprise assessment phase of the project. We initially had a team of one assigned to this effort but this was expanded during the 45-day window. The steps involved in the enterprise assessment included:

- Organizational analysis
- Capability analysis
- Application/capability mapping
- Agency-wide application architecture analysis
- Core System application analysis tool selection

As we repeatedly reminded management, an assessment of a complex enterprise environment is very much like peeling an onion. You never know what the next layer will yield until you get there. This was certainly the case for the Agency enterprise assessment. The project was bid, as is true with most government projects, as an architecture creation effort coupled with business process analysis and an analysis of the existing Core System environment. As a result, we had to structure an approach that allowed us to visualize the whole prior to dissecting the parts and this led to the enterprise assessment.

## Getting Started

We had no information about the organization as it related to systems or business capabilities so we were starting from square one. As with any project of this nature, we immediately went to the unofficial historians within the Agency, and this took us to the person that managed the consolidation and upgrade of the Core System during the mid-1980s. We were quickly educated on the platform and environment. The Core System ran on a small IBM mainframe and was essentially a batch COBOL environment. Data was fed into the Core System from many sources that management called feeder or interface systems.

To the central office executive sponsor (project sponsor), the interface systems were little systems on the other side of the wall that collected and loaded data into the Core System. As we sleuthed our way through the history of the systems and the systems' relationship to the business, we were pointed to a retired employee who had a clear message for us. If you really want to know how all of the pieces fit together, you need to visit the world on the other side of that wall. This meant traveling to the regions and business units that owned the interface systems.

After some nominal pushback ("why do you need to talk to those people?") we packed our bags and took a tour of the regions. Much of the information we gathered was incorporated into later stages of the analysis, but the trip also opened our eyes to how the entire systems and business ecosystem fit together. This trip was quite valuable in terms of structuring our organizational and systems analyses.

## Organizational Analysis

Understanding the Agency organizational structure was an important step in understanding the systems as there were cross-functional dependencies. After all, how can one determine who does what and who uses which systems if the "who" is unknown. The central office project sponsor commissioned the financial architecture project, but there were unique business units outside of the central financial group that were affected. In addition, the Agency had a number of regional business units that were highly autonomous. These business units and regions had developed a number of software systems to support their business requirements. Many of these systems were quite sophisticated in terms of the functionality they contained and supported.

Understanding the organizational structure was the foundation of our analysis. As we examined each business unit or region, we determined which business units had certain business capabilities. In addition, we mapped these business capabilities to the corresponding systems upon which they relied. Collectively, this provided us with a high-level, cross-functional mapping of business units, business capabilities, and application architecture.

The analysis process included initial interviews, documentation reviews, and a series of increasingly detailed management and analyst discussions. The organizational units and capabilities (functions) were loaded into a simple metamodel for later cross-reference purposes. The Access version of this metamodel is shown in Figure 9.2.

Note that the metadata view in Figure 9.2 may seem more complicated than it is due to the connecting tables where there are many relationships involved. In addition, the concept of multiple applications per system (which is a reversal in commonly found terminology) was somewhat unique to this environment, as was the Agency's unique concept of a module. Also note that the detailed artifacts related to program, business process, and business rule were never populated due to time constraints. However, we did export the business information from this database into our analysis tool repository as discussed later in phase one of the case study.

Variations on the Figure 9.2 structure have been used over the years on other projects to keep track of analyst-captured metadata during enterprise assessments of business and IT architectures. In later portions of the enterprise assessment, systems and subsystems (applications) were added to this data tracking facility.

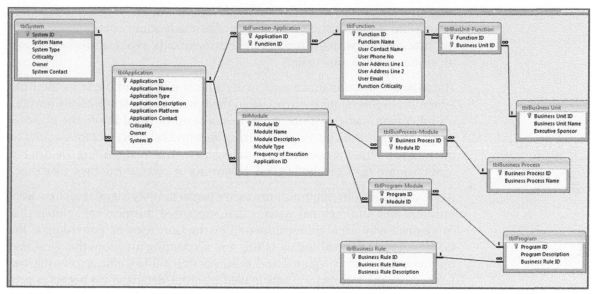

**FIGURE 9.2**
*Data model used for tracking enterprise metadata findings.*

Our analysis focused on all major accounting functions. What we discovered as part of our analysis was that the project sponsor, the business units, and key regions had billing and other accounting capabilities. This was reflected in our analysis gathering process. Upon completion of the first cut of the organizational analysis, we moved on to examine the systems supporting these business units and capabilities.

## Application Architecture Analysis and Capability Mapping

The application analysis required obtaining whatever baseline documentation was available and interviewing appropriate individuals to determine the correctness and completeness of these application views. Note that at this point in the assessment, tool utilization would have been inappropriate. Our analysis was still at a very high level and spanned both the business utilization as well as the systems. In addition, the tool-based analysis would be limited to the system targeted for replacement — the Core System. Assessing the entire Agency architecture at any degree of depth would have prolonged our assessment efforts by months and was not a requirement for this project.

The business units and certain regional units each had their own systems, processes, and data. Our main goal involved identifying all interface systems that sent data to or received data from the Core System. The project sponsor clearly stated that interfaces to and from these regional and business unit systems were to be maintained as the new architecture was deployed and the Core System was deactivated. On the surface, this made some sense and we began our investigation with the regions and business units. What we discovered was more than we had anticipated.

The interface systems functioned in an almost parallel universe to the Core System from several perspectives. First, there were major applications running on other mainframes within certain business units. In addition, the business units and regions had been customizing systems and processes for decades to maintain an efficient operation for the Agency while maintaining the need to feed data into the Core System and, beginning in 2002, the Software Package.

As we continued our mapping process, we began to understand that there were business unit and regional systems that supported business capabilities that overlapped with capabilities supported by the Core System. For example, the Core System performed certain billing and accounting functions that were also implemented within regional and business unit billing and accounting systems. Once the information was loaded into our database, we began to produce mapping reports by business unit, capability, and system. We found, in just one example, that there were more than a dozen billing systems or subsystems that supported similar Core System billing capabilities. This pattern was repeated for other systems and business capabilities.

Understanding the underlying functionality and future of these interfacing systems was essential to transition planning because each interfacing system required its own mini-strategy. We had to understand a key element of the future of the interface. Would the interface system be retained intact or would the Core System replacement subsume the old interface system? In many cases, regional analysts assumed that the new environment would eliminate the interface system and we communicated this back to the project sponsor and the target architecture design team.

We felt that the best way to communicate how the pieces fit together was to create a high-level diagram depicting system interfaces to and from the Core System. Figure 9.3 depicts a sanitized version of this diagram (system and business unit names were removed along with other modifications). Figure 9.3 shows the Core System and interface systems that reside in various business units, regional units, and other agencies or private sector external entities.

The box in the center of Figure 9.3, identified as "core processing systems," represents the Core System and the Software Package environment. To the left, we have depicted regional and business unit systems and feeds into and out of the Core System and the Software Package. The Software Package interfaces were highly customized and had to be documented because of their intersection with and relationship to the Core System.

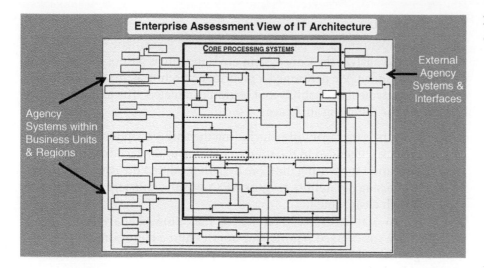

**FIGURE 9.3**
*System interface diagram.*

The diagram in Figure 9.3, coupled with the application/capability/organizational unit mapping, served as the baseline for more detailed interface and system decomposition and mapping to be performed in the phase one, detailed assessment.

## Enterprise Assessment: Snapshot of Findings

The enterprise assessment ran only 45 days and used a minimal amount of resources, yet the information uncovered during this phase of the project provided essential information that assisted with the planning and deployment of subsequent assessment and implementation efforts. A summary of the findings include

- Discovery of a high degree of redundant business capabilities and related systems
- Redundant processes across business units using redundant shadow systems
- Over 100 interfaces into and out of Core Systems, few of which were well-defined or understood
- The need to either subsume or replace certain interface systems as part of the Core Systems replacement
- Requirements to align redundant processes and eliminate related shadow systems to ensure smooth transition to the replacement architecture
- Business units had little appetite for coordinating work with other business units or regions, including a reluctance to coordinate with the sponsors of the Core Systems replacement project

The gravity of this last point became painfully clear as we moved into the next stage of the assessment.

## Tool Selection

The last task performed as part of the enterprise assessment was to select a tool that could analyze the Core System environment as part of the phase one, detailed assessment. We performed a preliminary technical analysis during the enterprise assessment to establish tool section parameters. The tool we required had to have the following attributes:

- COBOL parsing capabilities, including the ability to ignore customized constructs embedded in the source code due to the fact that the organization supporting the Core System modified the compiler.
- REXX parsing capabilities because REXX was the language controlling the batch environment.
- An open, standards-based repository that allowed analysts to produce customized reports and queries and a commitment to align with Object Management Group (OMG) ADM modernization standards.
- Ability to produce customized data definition cross-reference analysis beyond out-of-the-box reporting provided by the vendor.
- The tool had to run on a non-mainframe network because the team did not have mainframe access.
- In addition to basic analysis capabilities, the tool had to provide business logic extraction capabilities.
- A vendor-supplied support team that could ease the process of analyzing the system, populating the tool repository and producing customized reports.

Given that we had very specific requirements, we narrowed the list to three vendors. We held three vendor product walkthroughs and, because only one vendor met the above criteria, we quickly moved on to a decision. We should note that REXX analysis is not very common and having this capability gave one vendor the edge. We selected the ASG Becubic product for our needs.

## Enterprise Assessment Deliverables

We delivered a presentation to the project sponsor at the end of the 45-day enterprise assessment window to provide them a progress report and our preliminary findings. This included

- Populated repository (database) of organizational units, business capabilities, applications, (sub)systems, and the relationship among each of these business and IT artifacts
- Cross-reference reports summarizing the relationships among business units and regions, business capabilities, and systems and applications

- Diagrammatic overview of the relationships among and across the Core System, the Software Package, and related interface systems
- Concise identification of scope for subsequent assessment and implementation projects
- Identification of all relevant parties and identification of the roles of those individuals within subsequent assessment and implementation efforts
- Summary of findings to date
- Recommendations for acquisition of a vendor tool that could perform detailed analysis of the Core System
- Plan for detailed assessment

We confirmed that our detailed analysis would narrow specifically to the Core System environment and direct interfaces. We additionally agreed to summarize our findings by interface system for the analysis work that was performed across the regions and business units.

## PROJECT PHASE ONE — INITIAL ASSESSMENT: DETAILED ASSESSMENT

The detailed assessment involved a logical expansion of the enterprise assessment with the enterprise analysis building a foundation for the next set of tasks. We had roughly allotted 60–70 days of time to the detailed assessment task. Steps involved in this assessment included

- Technical architecture assessment
- Data architecture and interface assessment
- Application architecture assessment
- Business logic analysis
- Target financial architecture mapping

Note that the team performing the analysis on the existing systems environment had been expanded at this point to two analysts working at roughly 90% capacity. In addition, we added two tool support analysts to the project for the remainder of the phase one assessment.

### Technical Architecture Assessment

An analysis of the technical architecture was important to understand the foundation of where the systems were running, the relative size and scope of the systems, and the relationship between the Core System and other systems. The focus, however, was limited to understanding the essentials necessary to assess the application and data architecture and develop a transition strategy to the target architecture.

We ran the analysis tool against the Core System and obtained a software inventory, certain artifact related information, and basic cross-reference reports. This portion of the assessment was quite extensive in terms of the depth required to truly understand the overall environment. With a modified compiler, custom-built REXX batch jobs, and modified data access facility, the analysis required some tool customizations. We also had to assess which modules and jobs remained active versus which portions of the system were turned off over the years.

The approach may be summarized as follows.

1. Obtain all the Core System software artifacts from the Agency, which required providing the software to the analysis team so that it could be loaded onto a workstation for analysis.
2. Obtain a list of active Core System modules from analysts.
3. Use available documentation to create a first-cut mapping between the Core System modules and the REXX routines running the batch job environment.
4. Fine-tune the list of active REXX routines based on an analysis of naming conventions and supporting documentation.
5. Run analysis tool against the artifact library to obtain a list of active COBOL source code and Copy routines.
6. Refine the active artifact list based on additional Agency reviews, documentation reviews, and tool results.
7. Repeat this process until the list was as accurate as possible.

We should note that there were actually jobs that were still running in production but the programs being executed had been gutted of any functionality. In addition, there were reporting routines still running that did not actually produce any reports. As a result, determining what software was still active involved more than analysis of the execution environment.

In summary, the analysis team analyzed and cross-referenced 750,000 lines of COBOL and 100,000 lines of REXX source code. We found close to 4,000 data files, over 300 reports (many of which were not in use), and 100 separate applications and modules. Note that a module and an application were interchangeable terms that just reflected the age of a given subsystem component. This analysis provided us with a baseline for subsequent interface, application, and data architecture analysis.

## Data Architecture and Interface Assessment

The data architecture analysis focused on identifying "prime" data candidates within the Core System that would need to be carried forward within the target architecture. The target architecture team used the as-is data analysis results as input to validate the target data architecture. Data interface analysis additionally provided the information needed to keep the business units and regions functioning while ensuring that the systems of record had access to essential business data as the replacement architecture was being deployed. The approach used to assess the Core System data architecture is as follows.

1. The team scoured documentation to determine major data flows into and out of the Core System. The results were incorporated into our interface analysis.
2. Interviews were conducted with Core System stakeholders and regional and service area personnel to determine where and how data was flowing into, out of, and across the Core System.
3. We extracted specific outputs from our analysis tool based on the following tool-derived extract reports:
   - Record Grouping Summary Report
   - Data File Inventory and Program Mapping
   - Literal Analysis Report
4. Analysis tool outputs, interviews, and documentation reviews were used to create the Core System Data Interface analysis summary.
5. The Interface Map and other reports were used to create the data record inventory and produce data layouts of "prime" record groups. Prime record groups represent essential data that should be incorporated into the replacement data architecture to ensure the continuity of key business capabilities in that new architecture.
6. Prime record layouts were forwarded to the financial architecture team.

A snapshot of the data-related statistics for the Core System is provided in Figure 9.4.

Figure 9.4 shows the type of statistics (modified for confidentiality purposes) collected by the analysis team through automated tool analysis and subsequent examination and aggregation of that data. The number of files (approximately 3,800) is extremely large when one considers the size and functionality of the Core System. Even more troubling is the number of record layouts (approximately 17,000) defined within the software itself. When compared to the number of actual data files, the implication was that there is a high degree of redundancy of the data definitions within the source code as compared to the actual number of files used by the system.

| Data Related Statistics | Artifact Counts |
| --- | --- |
| Total Number of 01 Record Definitions | Approx. 17,000 |
| Number of 01 Records in Working Storage Section | Over 13,000 |
| Number of 01 Records in File Definitions (FD) | Over 2,700 |
| Number of 01 Level Copy Books | 700 |
| Total number sequential files | Over 3,000 |
| Total number of indexed files | Approx. 900 |
| Total number of Data files | 3,800 |
| Report Total | Over 300 |
| Note: Exact totals adjusted to address confidentiality issues. | |

**FIGURE 9.4**

*Summary data statistics for core system.*

Data complexity was extreme and these statistics drove further investigation into exactly what was going on behind the scenes. The situation was not good. Findings include

- Batch files manually sent via File Transfer Protocol (FTP) into the batch COBOL system reader

- Multiple definitions of a single file that used conflicting and virtually incoherent data names

- Numerous temporary files that were used between program execution for no business purpose

- No concept of databases or data architecture

- Prime data (the data necessary to support or re-create the functionality supported by this system) element total was well under 300 data elements, which led to the conclusion that data definition redundancy within the software and within the file structures was extreme

- Customized data access and file structures (homegrown indexing scheme) and related functional complexity required the data to be re-architected

- In short, the data definitions merely reflected the archaic nature of the Core Systems environments. The incoherence of the data definitions and the proliferation of these data definitions across the subsystem modules within the Core System made two points very clear. The source code itself could not be salvaged without unreasonable efforts to rationalize data usage and make major adjustments to the functionality of the system. In addition, business logic extraction was going to have to be done very judicially and only after additional analysis of the extracted data definitions.

Determination of the actual prime data within the Core System was important, however, for the top-down architecture design team and to support business logic extraction. To accomplish this, analysts whittled down prime record layouts from 17,000 record layouts identified in Figure 9.4 to just 100 data record layouts. The process used to extract prime data from a mountain of data definitions involved focusing on interface data layouts, master file layouts, and transaction record definitions.

The analysis team used the Becubic tool very strategically to create a Record Group Summary Report that listed data record layouts by name, in order of size, and other specified criteria. If a prime group contained multiple layouts, we selected the more complete view of the data. Each prime record identified included a layout, description, and identification as to whether it was internal or external. If it was an external interface file, it was included in our interface analysis. Note that the tool did not come with this feature but had to be adjusted on-site to accommodate this level of data definition analysis.

The literal analysis provided another insight into the functionality of specific source code. There were many tens of thousands of embedded literals or constants within the source code. Many of these literals provided clues to the business functionality within the software. The Becubic tool's analysis capability was customized to collect and sort all literals and provide a cross-reference as to where these literals were used in the Core System. Consider the following literal definition and related interpretations.

| "PAID BILLING STATEMENT" | This portion of the Core System appears to calculate or create the Paid Billing Statement. |
|---|---|

The literal extracted from the software (shown on the left) provided analysts within the interpreted insights into the function performed (shown on the right). This was largely used as input to the business logic extraction discussed in the section Business Logic Analysis.

There were approximately 100 interfaces sending data to and from the various modules and applications that comprised the Core System. These interfaces took various forms and included data entry formats from the regions. Analyzing these data interfaces was essential to developing a transition strategy and a plan to maintain or modify interfaces to the entities within and outside the agency. This particular analysis could not be automated effectively because the interface references were modified dynamically by the customized data access facility in use by the Core System. In other words, the tool could not track this information.

Therefore, we created a spreadsheet (time constraints prevented us from loading this information into our database) that identified the sending/receiving application name, the sending/receiving Core System module, a description of the data transferred, and a note indicating if the Software Package was a recipient of outbound Core System data.

One additional point involved the identification of selected desktop, business unit–developed spreadsheets and similar desktop tools that were being used to manipulate and send data to the Core System or were built around data being received from the Core System. These user-based environments were not formal interfaces but were still relevant in terms of transition planning. We called these "secondary interface systems" and raised the issue to management that more research into these shadow systems should be incorporated into later project phases. (Note that management ignored this recommendation as being out of scope and out of budget.)

## Application Architecture Assessment

The application architecture assessment expanded on the enterprise assessment work in several ways. We provided a narrative description for each Core System module or application and grouped that module by major functional category. We provided a summary of the module or application as well as a description of the functionality supported by that module or application.

We additionally provided a separate data and execution flow for the main capabilities supported by the Core System. These capabilities included cost allocation, asset management, billing, and accounts receivable. Our analysis of module functionality was based on prior documentation that we discovered, system flows and verification of the correctness through subject matter expert reviews, and the integrity of the information we had collected.

We included an analysis of the functional redundancy across the Core System and the other systems we analyzed. In addition, we highlighted where functional redundancy and fragmentation existed within the Core System. Finally, we created summary level descriptions for all interfacing systems and systems that were directly related to these interfacing systems. The intent was to provide a guide to implementation teams on both sides of the interface regarding the impact on systems that directly or indirectly interfaced with the Core System.

## Business Logic Analysis

The assessment approach ended up being highly customized for this project. While customization is not uncommon in an assessment, certain steps were moved up into this assessment phase that would normally have occurred later. For example, as a general rule, the business logic analysis step would have been delayed to Phase 2, as depicted in Figure 9.1.

In this situation, however, the financial architecture architects required early validation of selected business logic, along with insights into the existing data architecture and business data. Therefore, business logic analysis was moved into this stage of the assessment. The process used to extract the business logic from the Core System was as follows.

1. Determine a common format for business logic extraction that would be provided to the top-down financial architecture design team.
2. Use the Functional (Capability) Decomposition created during the application architecture assessment as a guide to identifying where major functions and sub-functions are defined across the Core System.
3. Use the prime record definitions extracted during the data architecture assessment to identify data elements of interest that could help identify related business logic.

4. Additionally use the literal analysis extracted during the data architecture assessment to specify rule selection criteria.

5. Narrow the scope of the logic extraction process to modules and programs related to accounts receivable and billing.

6. Use the Core System Module to Source Program Cross-Reference report to identify the Module to Program relationships.

7. Ensure that operational logic is filtered from business logic. This involved applying a predetermined set of criteria for identifying operational logic to be excluded.

8. Agree on a delimiting factor that would extract a block of logic that had a defined start and stop point; for example, extracted logic related to an "IF" statement identifies that the extracted block of logic would end at a period or ENDIF.

9. Feed data elements of interest into the business logic analyzer one item or category at a time.

10. Run the Becubic business rule extraction facility to identify candidate business logic to be packaged into business rules.

11. Review each rule for validity, i.e., does it represent a useful piece of logic from a business rule perspective in accordance with the aforementioned criteria.

12. Capture and store the logic along with the module, program, paragraph, and search criteria.

We should make it very clear that the work done up until this point in the assessment project was absolutely critical to quickly pinpointing and extracting the select set of business logic required by the financial architecture team. Business logic was stored and cross-referenced in the Becubic analysis tool repository and also within an Excel file for ease of access and reference. Figure 9.5 depicts an enhanced form of a captured set of logic.

| Title | XXXB-1. | REPORT DUPLICATE & ERROR BILLING RECORDS |
|---|---|---|
| Precondition | | FD-XXXB input file (Billing Records File) not empty |
| Trigger | | FD-XXXB record contains non-zero Error-Code(s) |
| Post Condition | | Record removed from data stream and "printed" |
| | | |
| Title | YYYB-2. | OUTPUT VALID BILLING RECORDS |
| Precondition | | FD-YYYB input file (Billing Records File) not empty |
| Trigger | | FD-YYYB record contains all zero Error-Code(s) |
| Post Condition | | Record written to FD-ZZZC Valid Billing Records File |

**FIGURE 9.5**
*Business logic transformation.*

For the most part, raw business logic was captured and provided to the design architects for areas where they requested specific information related to a given business capability. The enhanced format of the rule extraction process, where logic is repackaged into a rule such as that shown in Figure 9.5, was not extended to most of the extracted business logic in this project because there was no automation support to transform the logic into a rules-based format.

## Target Financial Architecture Mapping

The financial architecture team used all of the information gathered throughout this assessment phase to inform their work on the target architecture. In addition, they reviewed the results of the business process analysis effort. To leverage the existing systems analysis results within the larger financial architecture project, captured information had to be made available to the top-down design team. This was done in a variety of ways including:

- Provision of recaptured system documentation, including functional decomposition of applications and modules, to the top-down design team via our cross-reference database (as shown in Figure 9.2)
- Use of an open repository containing detailed, electronically captured metadata from the Core System programs, execution routines, and data structures
- Delivery of the Core System input/output (I/O) and other prime data structures to top-down, data designers
- The capture, filtering, and sharing of extracted business logic from the Core System programs with top-down designers
- Review and input from the ADM team on the proposed transition from the current Core System architecture to the replacement architecture

Unfortunately, the business process analysis results were not connected to the analysis of the as-is IT architecture and never mapped to the organizational unit, capability, and systems mapping. We will discuss this further in the section Lessons Learned. The financial architecture work continued for 4–6 months after completion of the current systems architecture assessment. This set the stage for the phase two work that began roughly 1.5 years later.

Of note is that an initial transition plan was established for subsequent phases of the project but that the actual transition effort required the next level of analysis. In summary, however, the transition strategy was to migrate off of the Core System one business capability at a time. The first capability targeted by Agency management, primarily because it represented a narrow slice of Core System functionality, was asset accounting.

# PROJECT PHASE TWO — DETAILED ASSESSMENT

This project phase was an implementation effort that focused on a detailed examination of a small cross-section of the Core System, as dictated by the portion of the Core System to be replaced by the Software Package and SOA-based interfaces developed by the financial architecture project team. Much of the detailed analysis that would typically be completed during this stage was actually completed during the phase one assessment.

As a result, the analysis at this stage was very focused on documenting the exact nature and specifics of the data interchange between selected portions of the Core System and external systems as well as the flow of the Core System modules and related interface systems. The project was focused on delivering a functioning set of software to support asset accounting and to deactivate corresponding functionality within the Core System.

This selected business capability, asset accounting, crossed two main business lines within the Agency and impacted multiple regions and business units. In addition, the same routines within one major business line that performed asset accounting also supported certain billing and receivable capabilities. Therefore, the analysis and deactivation process had to be very precise. We began our analysis where we left off, at the end of phase one.

Figure 9.6 depicts the same Core System/Software Package/Interface Systems overview as shown during our discussion of the phase one assessment. The circles highlight the modules within the Core System and within the interface systems environment that supported asset accounting capabilities. Note that the picture to the right looks nothing like the pictures to the left. This was a direct result of peeling that next layer of the onion, as we discussed early in this case study.

The diagrams to the left and bottom of this diagram were derived through another series of documentation reviews and interviews with subject matter experts. The two pictures on the left of Figure 9.6 represent one line of business processing for daily, weekly, monthly, and year-end cycles. The diagram at the bottom right of Figure 9.6 represents an entirely different line of business. These diagrams represent detailed, cross-functional views of the systems and data used for all interfacing systems as well as the modules and applications within the Core System.

These snapshots have been sanitized and reduced for purposes of this case study, but they fully represented the asset accounting functionality for the Core System and surrounding environments. These diagrammatic views provided the baseline for a detailed analysis of the data interfaces and the modules on either side of those interfaces. There were numerous data structures used that were either split along functional lines or overlapped across functions. These data structures would need to be phased out over time along with the applications as data were consolidated in the Software Package.

**FIGURE 9.6**

*System interface diagram decomposition for selected applications.*

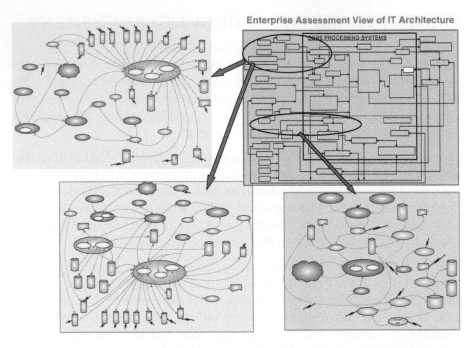

The process of documenting each module within Figure 9.6 involved building a precise and in-depth profile of each module involved in the flows shown within those diagrams. Figure 9.7 depicts the form analysts used to gather and publish information for each module. This information could have been added to our original database but timing did not allow for an updating of the data structures we used in the first project phase.

The team of two analysts for this project, working at 80–85% of capacity, completed the interface diagrams in Figure 9.6 as well as a series of completed forms (shown in Figure 9.7) within a 45-day window for each asset accounting module involved. These documents provided a description of the data involved, the understanding of which was essential to ensuring business continuity under the new architecture. We relied heavily on analysis performed during the prior phase of the project. The form in Figure 9.7 allowed the team to:

- Collect relevant interface system and file structure information on interfacing modules that ran on a variety of platforms using a variety of technologies
- Cross-map business unit information between Core System modules and interface systems modules
- Cross-check interface analysis to ensure the accuracy of information collected from various parties
- Document selected shadow systems to show criticality of those shadow systems to business processes and business continuity under the target architecture

| MODULE DESCRIPTION QUESTIONNAIRE | | | |
|---|---|---|---|
| **Module Name:** | Module Name | **Module Contact:** | |
| **Contact Phone:** | | **Contact Email:** | |
| **Description:** | | | |
| | | | |
| **Run Cycle Name (If Applicable):** | Not Applicable | | |
| **Run Frequency:** | Daily | | |
| **Manual Execution Process Description:** | | | |
| **Input Parameters (If Applicable):** | | | |
| | | | |
| **Other Manual Interventions:** | | | |
| **Special Processing Requirements:** | | | |
| | | | |
| **Number of Input Data Sources:** | | | |
| **Number of Output Data Sources:** | | | |
| **Number of Source Programs in Module:** | | | |
| | | | |
| **Functional Changes Planned for 2007:** | | | |
| **Percentage of Asset Accounting Functionality:** | | | |
| | | | |
| **Reports Produced by Module – Report #/Report Name/Report User(s):** | | | |
| | | | |
| | | | |
| | | | |
| **Additional Comments:** | | | |
| | | | |

**FIGURE 9.7**

*Module description form.*

One situation emerged that should have been found during the process analysis work performed during phase one. There were parallel processes running within regions and business units that used very similar, yet distinct, interface system environments to support these processes. As a result of not identifying these in phase one and because the business units and regions did not collaborate across business lines, there was no effort to streamline and align those common processes. In addition, there was no effort to identify and eliminate shadow systems connected to these business processes and no work to assist the regions and business units to create common input systems to the Core System.

This was a missed opportunity that can be attributed directly back to the fact that the process modeling work was completed in isolation from the rest of the project and was never synchronized using common approaches found within the business architecture discipline discussed in earlier chapters. Having an entirely business process-focused mind-set, as opposed to considering the business architecture as a whole, leads to these problems within projects. More about this issue is covered in the section Lessons Learned.

The assessment effort in this phase lasted roughly 60–70 days. The information gathered was provided to the financial architecture design and development team. The work of this team continued beyond the assessment work involved within this phase for another 6 months.

## PROJECT PHASE TWO — TRANSITION PLAN AND DEPLOYMENT

Transition planning had to be completed with two goals in mind. First, we could not disrupt any existing functionality but still had to deactivate that same functionality from the Core System. This was relatively straightforward for one line of business but very complex for a second line of business. In addition, we could not disrupt the work or the systems running in the regions and business units.

An approach was created that addressed this through a data switching service provided to the interface system owners. Certain data would be fed into the Core System, when not related to asset accounting, while asset accounting data would be fed into the new services and ultimately the Software Package. This, in effect, would "starve" the Core System asset accounting modules of data and the Core System would stop outputting asset accounting transactions to the Software Package. The final, delivered solution incorporated the following software components.

- Portions of COTS package deployed to replace asset accounting functionality formerly running in Core System

- SOA-based interfaces from interfacing systems into the Core System and COTS environment, which replaced aging file transfer protocols
- Intelligent transaction routing facility to rout asset accounting functions to COTS services and rout all other transactions back into the Core System

The results of the overall solution worked as designed, yet were rejected by the owners of the Core System environment. Reasons for this include a change in executive management and sponsorship during the course of the project and a lack of comfort with the degree of sophistication of the solution.

## LESSONS LEARNED

Several lessons can be taken from this project. The positive lessons can be summarized as follows:

- Creating an overarching architecture as a front-end strategy to drive a collective vision for all parties is highly recommended. The financial architecture created during this project will continue to guide future initiatives at the Agency.
- Performing a current systems assessment to identify interfaces and provide a replacement roadmap provided the Agency with insights into how it can pursue future projects of this nature.
- Functionally decomposing segments of the as-is application architecture facilitates the creation of a transition strategy that allows for the phased deactivation of the current system.
- Exposing as-is data views and business logic provides insights into the creation of replacement functionality.
- The results of the ADM-related assessment work will serve as a baseline for all future projects that need to understand the Core System environment as the transition process unfolds.

On the other hand, this case study also provided us with the ability to look back and consider what should and could have been done differently. Consider the following lessons on issues that should have been addressed in alternative ways.

- Analyzing the business processes to be replaced is a worthwhile effort, but not if the work begins and ends with the creation of process diagrams that are disconnected from the rest of the project. Business processes should have been incorporated into the analysis database so they could be used to identify redundant processes and related desktop systems that should have been targeted for streamlining, consolidation, and automation. The process analysis portion of the project was performed by the prime contractor in phase one of the project and was out of the hands of the rest of the team.

- More time was required during the phase two portion of the project to map business processes to organizational units and capabilities, business processes to interfaces, and interfaces to modules and applications. In addition, more time was required to provide the business and IT people in the regions and business units with a way to adapt to the changes in the Core System architecture. The concurrent alignment, streamlining and automation of business processes, and elimination of shadow systems, discussed in chapter one of this book, could have been deployed with a good chance of success if the timing had been considered.

- The business units and regions should have been engaged as partners, not advisories at the onset of the project. At one point, one of our analysts was told not to contact or speak to any individuals in a particular business unit, leaving a gaping hole in the phase one analysis.

- Given the autonomous nature of enterprise organizational units, the sponsoring executives should have established a partnership with the executives within the business units and regions. This would have opened up a much more collaborative relationship structure for the mapping and alignment of the systems, processes, and shadow systems woven around the Core System.

## SUMMARY

One final lesson that can be taken away from this project involves the folly of attempting to drive an IT solution out to the business while not engaging the business units and regions as partners. Significant change in IT must support appropriate improvements in business processes, which can only happen through a partnership between the consumers and providers of IT-enabled business services.

The target financial architecture developed during phase one of the project envisioned some significant improvements in the business processes between the central office financial organization and the business units and regions. The technical solution implemented in phase two was required to follow this target business architecture. But, not only had the new business processes *not* been adopted by the central organization, the possibility of such changes had never even been communicated to the client business units.

As a result, the asset accounting implementation in phase two was sometimes put in the difficult situation of interfacing financial feeder systems and a COTS package, all of which presumed the old business processes, via an integration architecture that presumed the new processes. This led to technical and management confusion that eventually resulted in the abandonment of the ambitious business-architecture-based SOA implementation and the loss of the opportunity to effect important business process improvements. Instead, the organization is now focused on implementing a technical SOA integration solution directly to the COTS financial package to achieve the basic goal of migrating asset accounting off the old Core System.

On a positive note, however, is the fact that the fundamental architecture work and as-is IT architecture assessment are still critically important to the re-scoped implementation effort and should stand the test of time. Future projects aimed at replacing all or portions of the Core System environment can rely on the deliverables from these portions of the project to build a new approach and deploy alternative solutions. This is an important lesson for any project of this nature. The assessment and documentation of complex IT architectures can continue to provide a foundation for numerous projects involving those architectures well into the future.

# CHAPTER 10

# Legacy System Modernization of the Engineering Operational Sequencing System (EOSS)*

Mark Kramer and Philip H. Newcomb

## ABSTRACT

Functional Area Managers (FAMs) and Central Design Agencies (CDAs), responsible for modernizing aging applications to function within the Navy Marine Core Intranet (NMCI), face a large and expensive task to modernize aged applications so that they meet stringent NMCI security requirements. Applications that fail to meet NMCI security requirements are subject to quarantine. This case study describes a pilot project sponsored by the Department of the Navy (DON) to develop alternative methods for modernizing software application in the NMCI workplace desktop environment. The pilot focused on modernizing aged applications that no longer meet NMCI security requirements by demonstrating development and application of a Legacy Systems Modernization (LSM) transformation process that was applied to the Navy Engineering Operational Sequencing System (EOSS). This pilot project was undertaken to produce, demonstrate, and evaluate modernization methods, technology, and processes applicable for employment by the Office of the Chief of Naval Operations (OPNAV) Logistics and Readiness (N40) and Naval Network Warfare Command (NETWARCOM) to reduce the risk and cost for modernizing software applications. The pilot leveraged an existing commercial practice and technology developed by The Software Revolution, Inc. (TSRI), a commercial provider of automated legacy system modernization services and products, to take an existing system, EOSS and transform it into a modernized software application with little human involvement.

## INTRODUCTION

The transition to a single secure enterprise network is forcing the DON to quickly modernize many legacy systems. FAMs and CDAs face a large and expensive task to modernize aged applications so that they will function within NMCI. Furthermore, applications that cannot run within NMCI are subject to quarantine restrictions which severely limit their usefulness in the Navy's desktops work environment.

This case study examines the results of an LSM pilot project executed by OPNAV Logistics and Readiness (N40) and NETWARCOM and sponsored by the DON Business Innovation Team (BIT) for the purpose of creating and proving a process for migrating quarantined aged legacy applications into the NMCI-approved environment by automating legacy system transformation into modern languages, modern databases, and N-tiered architectures rather than through manual conversion.

The pilot focused on modernizing aged applications that no longer met NMCI security requirements, and successfully demonstrated a more cost-effective automated transformation process alternative for FAMs and CDAs to use for modernizing workplace desktop applications than the conventional manual process. Specifically, the Naval Surface Warfare Center Carderock Division (NSWCCD) Surface Ship Engineering Site (SSES) was experiencing an NMCI system quarantine firsthand with the EOSS system. The EOSS system is the authoritative hull configuration management data system for all ships in both the active and inactive Fleets. Like many other Department of Defense (DoD) applications, EOSS is a unique high-value application for which no viable commercial alternative exists.

The EOSS application, in addition to being written in legacy Virtual Address eXtension (VAX) BASIC, did not meet a key NMCI security standard for inclusion in the operating enclave due to the Telnet sessions it required for system access. To meet NMCI basic security requirements, NSWCCD was faced with the decision to either replace or upgrade the EOSS system. Conventional replacement or upgrade would entail a risky manual redevelopment or re-engineering of the EOSS software which lead the Navy to explore alternatives.

Not wishing to risk the long timelines and possible operational disruption of either of the conventional choices and seeking an alternative, the Navy decided upon a strategy that would convert the replacement and upgrade challenge of the EOSS system into an opportunity to achieve the upgrade objective as well as to identify an alternative business process for migrating applications into the NMCI.

The pilot described in this case study combined the replacement and upgrade of the existing legacy EOSS into a modern NMCI compliant system with the development of a repeatable architecture-driven LSM process leveraging existing commercial technologies to demonstrate repeatable process for transforming NMCI applications with little human involvement into the desired modernized NMCI compliant applications.

## Findings

The Navy eBusiness office produced an independent evaluation report of the pilot to identify and measure the return on investment (ROI) and validate the LSM process for future use and scalability. This opportunity analysis findings report,

*Opportunity Analysis For Legacy Systems Modernization,* prepared by DON Business Innovation Team, OPNAV Logistics and Readiness (N4), and NETWARCOM, dated 10 Dec 2004, provided guidance for modernizing the workplace desktop environment, and is the source of claims attributed to the Navy in this chapter. The Navy opportunity analysis reported on lessons learned during the user interface modernization, preservation of legacy design/methodology, preservation of legacy database design, and identified the characteristics of NMCI applications suitable as future LSM opportunities.

TSRI completed the modernization of the EOSS system and the development of the LSM process in a 6-month period from January 2004 to June 2004 under a sole-source firm-fixed price contract, #4400083940. Under this contract TSRI ported the functionality of the existing VAX hosted EOSS accountability system to a new N-tiered Web-enabled application, and modernized EOSS into J2EE using Microsoft IIS running on an Intel-based server as the front-end with J2EE/Oracle running on a Sun SparcServer as the backend. This effort included the one-time development of the LSM process and adaptation of TSRI technology to handle VMS VAX BASIC as a legacy input language and the extension of TSRI Java target language capability to target the NMCI framework.

This case study draws upon materials in the Navy opportunity analysis with citation, and shares insights the TSRI project team gained during the execution of the project. The Navy methods of analysis and findings from the pilot as well as the LSM process developed by the pilot are the subject of this case study.

## Business Problem Satisfied by the Pilot

The NSWCCD SSES experienced NMCI system quarantine firsthand. The EOSS application, written in legacy VAX BASIC, did not meet NMCI security standards for inclusion in the operating enclave. Telnet sessions, vital to the passing of data in EOSS, are not permitted to cross NMCI boundaries. Additionally, the VAX BASIC-based application was costly and difficult to maintain. To meet NMCI basic security requirements, NSWCCD was faced with the decision to either replace or upgrade EOSS. This created the opportunity to investigate a legacy system transformation method and produce a business case analysis for future use by Navy organizations faced with the same challenges imposed by NMCI compliance.

## CURRENT SYSTEM AND PROCESS

The EOSS system is used to access and maintain revisions and provide versioning control for hull configuration documentation. As such, it is the authoritative hull configuration management data system for all ships in the current and inactive fleets. EOSS was developed to provide sailors with technically correct, logically sequenced written procedures, charts, and diagrams tailored to each ship's specific configuration. It dictates the procedures to be followed to complete major propulsion plant status changes. Use of EOSS ensures proper operation and minimizes damage to equipment or injury to personnel.

EOSS was originally written in VAX BASIC, and remote users accessed the system via a VAX VT100 Telnet session. The EOSS database for documents is a separate software system that serves as a storage and production area for EOSS documents. These documents are stored as a VAX flat file database accessible via a customizable, commercial-off-the-shelf (COTS) content management system. These lists of procedures are laminated and bound in procedure books stored on the ship for reference. At NSWCCD, the EOSS procedure books are updated and stored electronically. This EOSS information system is divided into two main parts, the EOSS-Accountability Configuration Management (ACM) system and the EOSS Document Database (EOSS-DD) repository. The EOSS-ACM system is used to access and maintain revisions and provide versioning control for hull configuration documentation. The EOSS-ACM version-control capabilities provide a cross-reference for EOSS procedure books and Watch Stations. The EOSS-DD serves as a storage and production area for EOSS documents. This storage and production area provides controlled access for Subject Matter Experts (SME) to perform Life Cycle Maintenance of EOSS documentation. Both of these legacy systems resided on the NAVSEA Philadelphia Local Area Network (LAN) which was to be converted over to NMCI. Local users access the systems via the NSWCCD-SSES LAN, while remote users connect via an Internet Service Provider (ISP) by using Virtual Private Network (VPN) software with a Telnet interface. The user interface displays a text-based menu that incorporates user authentication and data entry while providing limited query capabilities and standard reports. The rollout of NMCI to the NAVSEA Philadelphia network would not support the remote user log-on to the network due to the NMCI Security Enclave Compliance Policy that prohibits the use of Telnet interfaces. Data access to the legacy EOSS systems was controlled by a combination of system interfaces, either by Telnet or FTP. Those interfaces are not NMCI supported, and had caused EOSS-ACM to be placed into NMCI system quarantine.

## EOSS Technical Architecture Upgrade

The EOSS business process depicted in Figure 10.1 did not meet the NMCI security requirements in its original legacy architecture. Specifically, the Telnet sessions, the dotted circle on Figure 10.1, were not permitted to cross NMCI boundaries. For the system to function within the NMCI environment it needed to either be replaced or upgraded to satisfy this requirement. Additionally, programming support for maintenance and upgrades to the VAX BASIC system

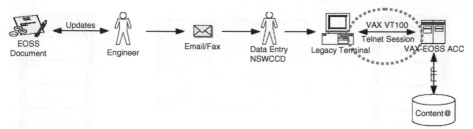

**FIGURE 10.1**
*Current EOSS-ACM business process.*

was costly and increasingly difficult to obtain. The existing EOSS engine and interface(s) had been written 18 years earlier in VAX BASIC. In today's programming world, programmers for VAX BASIC are difficult to find and are costly for providing basic database maintenance and/or application upgrades. These two factors combined to make the EOSS system a good candidate for the automated transformation pilot.

The modernized EOSS-ACM, depicted in Figure 10.2, eliminates the Telnet and FTP interfaces allowing the ship engineers to make changes to EOSS documents through a secured NMCI connection over the Internet. Data Entry personnel are no longer needed to key in changes sent to them by the engineers. The engineer now logs directly into the EOSS-ACM application server, retrieves and changes the EOSS data, and finally logs out without the mediation of a Data Entry specialist.

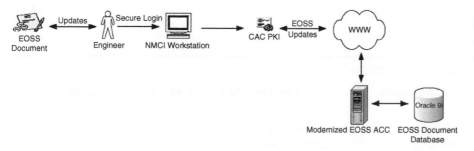

**FIGURE 10.2**
*Modernized EOSS-ACM data flow.*

# DESCRIPTION OF MODERNIZATION TECHNOLOGY AND PROCESS

TSRI *Janus*Studio™, illustrated in Figure 10.3, is a multi-source, multi-target, model-based automated architecture technology framework that was adapted to support the Navy Legacy System Modernization (LSM) process that is described in this case study and applied to modernize the EOSS system.

**FIGURE 10.3**

*TSRI* Janus*Studio™*
*architecture-driven*
*modernization framework.*

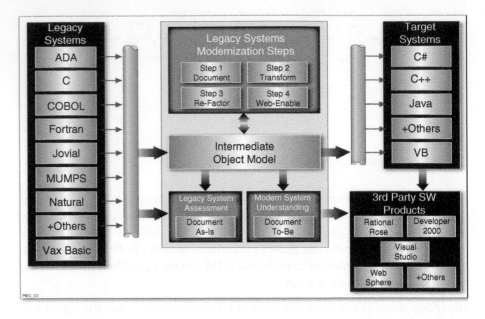

*Janus*Studio™ supports automated modernization of many source languages into and target languages using a uniform, repeatable, and consistent process that is easily adapted to new requirements and usage scenario. As of this publication date, *Janus*Studio™ has been used on several hundred information systems comprising more than a hundred million lines of code. *Janus*Studio™ handles nearly 30 legacy and modern languages in multiple dialects enumerated in Table 10.1 and has been used for transformation between more than 40 pairs of languages.

**Table 10.1** LSM Language Capabilities

| Application Blueprints Languages | | Transformation Blueprints Source to Target | |
|---|---|---|---|
| Ada | PL/1 | Ada to C++/ C# | JCL to C++ |
| C | PowerBuilder | Ada to Java | MagnaX to Java |
| C# | VAX BASIC | C to C#/C++ | MUMPS to Java |
| COBOL | VB.6 | COBOL to C/C#/C++ | Natural to C#/Java |
| FORTRAN | VB.NET | COBOL to Java | PL/1 to Java |
| Java | JCL | COBOL to VB | PowerBuilder to Java |
| JavaScript | DCL | DCL to Java | COBOL to JavaScript |
| Jovial | SQL | FORTRAN to C#/C++ | JTGEN/JPGEN/JRGEN to |
| MagnaX | XML | FORTRAN to Java | C++ |
| MUMPS | PROC | Java to C#/C++ | Vax BASIC to Java/C# |
| Natural | Refine | Java to Java (*refactoring*) | VB6 to C# |
| | | | VB6 to Java |

The adaptation of *Janus*Studio™ to support the Navy LSM process as it was applied to modernize EOSS is described in the next section and depicted in Figure 10.4.

## LSM Technology

JPGEN™ is TSRI's technology for generating parsers that process code to generate abstract syntax tree (AST) models and printers that generate code from AST models from a grammar specification for a computer language. JRGEN™ is TSRI's technology for automatically recognizing AST patterns and transforming AST models. TSRI employs JPGEN™ and JRGEN™ in a highly disciplined process that transforms the entire legacy application into an Intermediate Object Model (IOM) upon which a sequence of transformation and refactoring operations are applied before target code is generated from the AST models.

Parsing into the Legacy AST model is carried out by a parser generated by JPGEN™ and basic semantics generated by a constrainer generated by JRGEN™. The transformation between the Legacy VAX BASIC AST model and the IOM AST model is carried out by VAXBASIC2IOM transformation rules generated by JRGEN™. The transformation between the IOM and the target Java AST is carried out by the IOM2Java transformation rules generated by JRGEN™.

## LSM Scenarios

Multiple modernization scenarios were combined to accomplish the EOS LSM pilot. Just as software patterns are used for programming, scenarios are patterns for guiding the application of methods and techniques in a complex engineering undertaking. The Architecture-Driven Modernization (ADM) Task Force of the Object Management Group (OMG) identified 13 common recurring ADM scenarios in modernization projects, which are described in Chapter 4.

**FIGURE 10.4**

*TSRI's JanusStudio™ LSM for EOSS.*

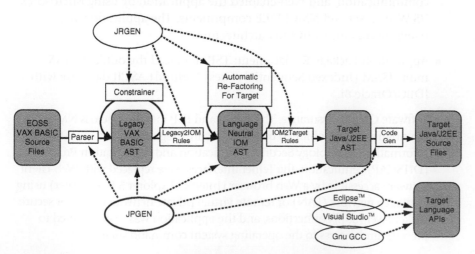

**FIGURE 10.5**

*ADM scenarios used in the LSM Pilot.*

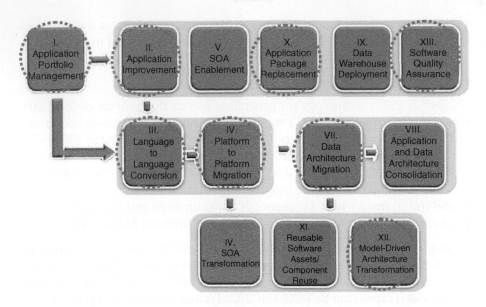

Frequently, combinations of these ADM scenarios are used on modernization projects. These scenarios have loose dependency relationships as indicated by the arrows between these scenarios depicted in Figure 10.5. The following ADM scenarios, circled in the figure, were employed during the EOSS pilot project.

- Application Portfolio Management: TSRI documented the "as-is" and "to-be" EOSS source and target code and design and metrics describing their properties as Application Blueprints™ and Transformation Blueprints™.

- Application Improvement: TSRI modernized the language and platform of the EOSS application, upgraded its database and inter-process communication, and Web-enabled the application by using Microsoft's IIS Web server and NMCI J2EE components. The application was re-engineered into a five-tier architecture.

- Application Package Replacement: TSRI replaced the outdated VAX multi-ISAM (Indexed Sequential Access Method) ASCII database with JDBC/Oracle 8i.

- Software Quality Assurance: The Telnet and FTP interfaces across NMCI boundaries were prohibited by NMCI security regulations. To meet DoD Information Technology Security Certification and Accreditation Process (DITSCAP) certification, the Telnet interfaces were replaced with Web-client software accessible by a Web browser (Internet Explorer 5.5 or greater) using local area network (LAN) or remote virtual private network (VPN) or secure socket layer (SSL) connections, and the application was re-engineered to prevent direct access to the operating system command shell.

- Language to Language Conversion: The outdated VMS VAX BASIC was replaced with Java. The user interface was replaced with JavaScript and HTML and the Microsoft IIS Web server. Database access calls were replaced with a Java Data Base Connectivity (JDBC) interface layer and SQL calls to the DB.

- Platform to Platform Conversion: The VMS VAX BASIC platform was replaced with Java 2 Enterprise Edition (J2EE), and the application was recompiled on Sun Server and re-engineered into a multi-tier Web architecture.

- Data Architecture Migration: Direct access to the legacy VAX ISAM ASCII database was replaced with Oracle 8i and the VAX ISAM ASCII database structures and data were converted into schema and data tables in Oracle 8i.

- Model-Driven Architecture (MDA) Transformation: UML models were derived for both the "as-is" and "to-be" design.

To accomplish these modernization scenarios, TSRI performed a set of services employing the *Janus*Studio™ Technical Framework depicted in Figure 10.3 using a combination of automated modeling, analysis, transformation, mapping, refactoring, and documentation generation technologies within the scope of the LSM system engineering process described in Figure 10.6.

## LSM Systems Re-Engineering Process

The scenarios, methods, and practices employed by TSRI for the EOSS project took place within the systems re-engineering process shown in Figure 10.6. Systems re-engineering projects are typically large, multi-year endeavors requiring the successful execution of a wide variety of administrative, technical, and operational tasks. When viewing the total project opportunity from a broad perspective, it is good practice to separate the project into a series of distinct major and minor tasks, with some of these tasks performed by the customer and/or integrator and others by the automated services provider distributed according to the proficiencies of each party.

In a LSM systems re-engineering project, the role of automation is amplified and the identification and definition tasks that can be automated become a primary driver on the identification of the roles of the project participants. Automation reduces many tasks to routine, uniformly repeatable automated processes with little or no human component, but the risk of automation is that the process can be inflexible. Henry Ford's adage that his customers could have any color Model T they wanted "as long as it was black" is sometimes applicable to automated software processes. The power of automated processes is that they are dependable, repeatable, and uniform, it is essential that they also be *customizable* to

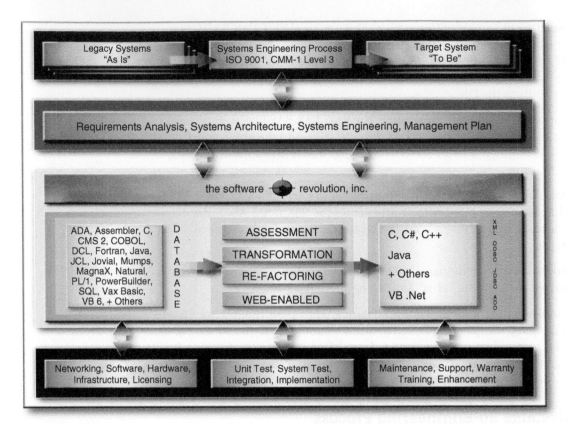

**FIGURE 10.6**
*LSM roles and responsibilities.*

meet the specific requirements and end goals of the modernization project without the need for manual reworking to achieve the final product.

In the LSM process the actual transformations of the code, design, and application architecture become automated processes; the definition and customization of the automated analysis, documentation, transformation, and refactoring operations to tune these automated processes toward end goals and objectives was the focus of many of the tasks performed by software engineers and architects on the LSM project.

On the EOSS pilot the principal roles of the Navy and Integrator were management and architectural at the outset of the project, oversight as it was conducted, acceptance and validation of deliverables, follow-on deployment, and maintenance, and the capture of project performance data to support preparation of the opportunity analysis upon conclusion of the project. Within the EOSS project, the roles and responsibilities of the Task Force Navy personnel encompassed the following set of tasks:

- System/Program Office identification and interface
- Requirements definition
- Project execution plan development
- Analysis of Alternatives (AOA)
- Functional Baseline study (if required)
- Project oversight
- System testing and implementation
- Future system enhancements
- System life cycle support

On the EOSS pilot the principal role of TSRI personnel was to extend and customize the *Janus*Studio™ to support the specific requirements of the EOSS pilot, and apply the *Janus*Studio™ to convert the EOSS legacy code into the code, design, and architecture specified by members of the Navy architecture team. Another key TSRI role dictated by TSRI's proficiency in its technology framework was advisory and consultative. In this capacity TSRI recommended strategies for achieving automation customization goals, and participated in a guiding capacity in defining strategies for customizing the automation toward the end goals articulated by the NMCI architects and EOSS application subject matter experts. Within the EOSS project, the roles and responsibilities of TSRI encompassed the following set of tasks:

- System/Program office interface (as required)
- Requirements definition (support to Task Force Navy personnel as requested)
- Engineering support to determine minimal set of code needing to be transformed
- Project execution plan development (support to Task Force Navy personnel as requested)
- Analysis of Alternatives (AOA) (support to Task Force Navy personnel as requested)
- Functional Baseline study (support to Task Force Navy personnel as requested)
- Dependency analysis to support the Navy in decisions regarding refactoring
- Code transformation
- Automatic and semi-automatic refactoring to tune the transformation, to tailor and optimize the transformation scheme and refactoring patterns for many language constructs and programming idioms to meet Navy specifications
- Stub and API implementation
- System integration and test support
- "as-is" system documentation
- Evaluation and analysis

- Data transformation
- "to-be" system optimization and consolidation
- Definition and performance of steps in the LSM process

Thus, the TSRI role, as the ADM provider in the LSM modernization process was in performing tasks associated with fully understanding and documenting the legacy or "as-is" system structure and functionality, transforming the legacy system applications software and data into a modern, platform-independent computer language, and optimizing and consolidating the new or "to-be" system to maximize the EOSS system future operation.

### Step 1: Document the Application Portfolio

The first step in the LSM process is the analysis of the application to document it, and capture it in an application portfolio management (APM) repository. For the EOSS project TSRI automatically generated both an Application Blueprint™ and a Transformation Blueprint™ as APM repositories for the existing source code and derived target code, design, and architecture documentation. It is best practice to produce an Application Blueprint™ to model the "as-is" and "to-be" Transformation Blueprint™ at the outset (Step 1) of the LSM process.

**Application Blueprint™:** This is an exquisitely detailed model of the existing system permitting accurate inspection of the design and architecture of the existing system as-built to assure requirements as implemented are not lost, and all details and aspects of the system to be modernized are fully understood. The Application Blueprint™ is a high-fidelity, graphical model that depicts the structure of data, modular composition of application procedures, and flow of logic and data in the procedures of the entire system presented in the form of a Web-based Unified Modeling Language (UML) design document.

Hosted on a Web server, the Application Blueprint™ permits the entire design and architecture of the application to be accessed by any number of software engineers simultaneously. To ensure rapid access the entire blueprint is batch generated at the outset of the project as a single cohesive Web document. For large systems the Application Blueprint™ can comprise hundreds of thousands, possibly millions of separate HTML and XML files. The graphical models of the blueprint are accompanied by navigable metrics indices, each produced by an analytical method that measures properties of the application. The metrics indices are presented as outline browsers with hyperlinks to the parts of the application that exhibit the code and design properties the metrics measure. Predefined metrics indices measure properties such as logical complexity; inter-component dependency and coupling; intra-component cohesion, similarity, and redundancy; and duplication of data and statements. Custom analytics are used to locate parts of the application that exhibit a particular property of interest and measure the frequency of occurrence of that property within the application.

**Transformation Blueprint™:** This allows system architects to look into the crystal ball and see the baseline iteration of the source and target code, design, and architecture at the outset of the project presented as side-by-side views, and subsequently as the customization of the LSM process is undertaken. A Transformation Blueprint™ captures both the source "as-is" and target "to-be" code, design, and architecture models as side-by-side views that permit inspection of the before-and-after states of the legacy and the modernized application code, design, and architecture deliverables. At the outset of the project LSM teams use Transformation Blueprints™ to define requirements and strategies to guide customization of the automated transformation, refactoring, and Web-enablement processes of the LSM technology framework to the specific needs of the project.

During the project the Transformation Blueprint™ is used to support inspection of interim deliverables, troubleshoot errors in deliveries, and pinpoint opportunities for optimizations. Similarly to the Application Blueprint™, the Transformation Blueprint™ is batch generated as a complete and cohesive document for rapid access by the LSM project team, but distinctively the Transformation Blueprint™ is regenerated repeatedly throughout the project to capture the state of the target application as iterative customization is performed during the LSM process to achieve the target final state. Transformation Blueprints™ play an essential part in a disciplined LSM process by permitting the application portfolio to become a living document that perfectly reflects the state of the target code, design, and architecture as the outcome of an iterative model-driven, rule-based, repeatable, perfective automated process.

Blueprints support the functional analysis-level design models of leading software engineering modeling methodologies with composite views presenting the principle set of sub-views used. The perspective of each methodology is viewed as graphics, text, and indices that capture the detailed behavioral, structural, compositional, and conceptual properties of individual units of system code and design as summarized in Table 10.2.

## Step 2: Transform the Application

The second step (Step 2) in the architecture-driven LSM process is the transformation step, which combines language-to-language conversion with platform-to-platform migration. In the language-to-language conversion, legacy code is transformed by a model-based, rule-driven transformational process into a modern language compatible with the target platform. In the past code translations were often of very poor quality, but with decades of continuous improvement in the state-of-the-art modeling and model-base transformation technology, high-fidelity code transformation can be accomplished with 100% automation between many legacy languages and modern languages with time-to-delivery, levels of quality and consistency that are unattainable by any comparable manual process.

In performing this process, post-transformation manual modification is sometimes admissible, but is to be avoided whenever possible. Patches require special

**Table 10.2** LSM Blueprint Capabilities

| Blueprints Support Multiple Software Engineering Methodologies |
| --- |
| MDA (UML) View — Model-Driven Architecture (Unified Modeling Language) |
| SASDM View — Structured Analysis System Design Methodology |
| OOA/OOD View — Object-Oriented Analysis/Object-Oriented Design |
| BRM View — Business Rule Modeling Methodology |
| SMM View — State Machine Modeling |

| Behavioral, Structural and Compositional, and Conceptual Properties, Models, and Indices | | |
| --- | --- | --- |
| **Relationships** | **Metric Indices** | **Diagram Types** |
| Control flow | Cyclomatic Complexity | Structure Charts |
| Data flow | Call Fan-In | Control Flow Graphs |
| Caller | Fan-Out | Action Diagrams |
| Callee | Class Subclass | Data Flow Diagrams |
| Part-of | Superclasses | State Machine Graphs |
| Kind-of | States | State Transition Tables |
| Has-a | Rules | Cause–Effect Graphs |
| Type-of | Statement Complexity | Class Diagrams |
| State | Dead Code | Data Element Tables |
| State Transition | Redundant and Duplicate | |
| Precondition | Code | **Hypertext Code** |
| Action | Unreferenced Variables | "As-is" Source Code |
| Causality | System Package Deployment | "To-be" Target Code |
| Composition | System Data Element Tables | "Both" Side-by-Side |
| Complexity | | |
| Code Size | | |

handling of the target code configuration to assure they can be seamlessly applied to the code deliverable. The major disadvantage of hand patches is that they break the automation paradigm and are ad hoc unmanaged, non-uniform processes. The presence of patches is a fidelity issue that reflects the degree to which known correctable flaws in the final deliverable have not yet been eliminated by improvements to the transformation rules that carry out that process. In practice, flaws that are patched are ultimately replaced with process corrections expressed as rules. Manual modifications, if unavoidable, can be seamlessly integrated with the automated transformation through the application of source control merging techniques following each code regeneration cycle. Eventually all "hand-fixes" are retrofitted into the rule-driven process.

Nearly all applications depend upon external service calls to services available on the platform on which they reside. During the platform-to-platform migration process automated dependency analysis is performed to identify external services, and services external to the application are mapped onto equivalent or alternative services of the target platform. Calls to operating system services and calls to database, math, or graphical user interface libraries and packages are common examples of external services. The TSRI transformation process provides compiling and linking target code with calls to external services stubbed out as functional prototypes. A major part of the effort of *one-off* modernization projects is the manual efforts associated with aspects of platform-to-platform migration that require manually writing code to implement functions that map legacy platform services to the replacement target platform services. This effort can be amortized on future projects to the same target language and platform services.

The terms "external stub resolution" and "application programmer interface development" are euphemisms for "this part of the process is manual." In an automated LSM process the legacy code serves as the detailed specification for functions the target system is to replicate. Calls to the O/S and external services, or anything else that is not defined in the legacy code, define the ultimate limits of what can be automatically transformed and define the boundaries of APIs and the stubs that must be resolved to achieve a running system. The skills and expertise required for developing APIs and external stubs include a detailed understanding and knowledge of the legacy and target platform services as well as the target architecture, target languages, and target component frameworks. These skills are often possessed by the customer, the integrator, and TSRI. Skill set and resource utilization considerations are key drivers guiding the determination of roles and responsibility distribution between the customer, integrator, and TSRI.

Senior analysts and highly skilled architects define the target application architecture, identify and construct the target component and target runtime framework, define the functional, architectural, and performance requirements of the modernization target, perform requirements gap analysis and participate in the specification and definition of transformation and refactoring strategies, and define the specification for the standards and metric yardsticks pertaining to measuring the LSM products, process, methods, and techniques as well as the development of models and rules used to carry out the automated transformation.

## Step 3: Refactor the Application

Refactoring is the process of changing a software system in such a way that it does not alter the function of the code yet improves its internal structure. When carried out manually, refactoring is applied directly to the source code and is generally a labor-intensive, ad hoc, and potentially error-prone process. In contrast to conventional manual refactoring, TSRI has achieved a highly automated refactoring process characterized by the application of pattern-based transformations to a model of the software rather than to the source code. This approach allows refactoring to be applied reliably and safely on a massive scale as a rigorous, disciplined, multi-level process.

Automated and semi-automated refactoring is accomplished by transformation rules generated by JRGEN™ that are applied to the IOM AST model to improve its structure before transformation into the target Java AST model. Refactoring operations vary greatly in their granularity and scope. Some refactoring operations are atomic and limited in scope, while others are more complex, composed by applying many more finely grained refactoring operations to accomplish a larger grained restructuring objective. The order in which a refactoring operation is performed is crucial to assuring its proper application. Some refactoring operations must be done prior to others to establish the appropriate state of the software model for subsequent refactoring operations. Many refactoring operations are application domain-neutral and are applied whenever transforming between any procedural and any object-oriented language. Others are language-pair specific, and are applied only when transforming between a particular source and target language. Table 10.3 and Table 10.4 categorize and summarize refactoring operations that are common to LSM projects.

### Step 4: – Web-Enable the Application

Finally, the software is Web-enabled using J2EE, Microsoft .NET, or CORBA components as defined by the DON or client. The derived components are refactored to segregate client-side Web browser and user interface code from the server-side data manipulation and access code. This creates flexible components that are better suited for future development.

### LSM Database Conversion

An architecture pattern common to many modern applications is the segregation of application code into separate tiers that isolate the user interface logic from business logic and the business logic from the data access logic. Modern applications with multi-tier architectures consisting of compact components running on low-cost, ubiquitous processors are inherently more scalable than the monolithic mainframe-bound legacy applications they replace. The EOSS LSM process derived the N-tier Java/J2EE target architecture by combining the transformation of the VAX BASIC code into Java with refactoring of the legacy application logic into separate horizontal tiers: data access layer, user interface layer, and application logic layer components.

During this conversion the data access layer's VAX BASIC file descriptors were refactored into data layer classes, VAX record layouts were mapped into member data of these classes, and I/O statements associated with accessing VAX files were converted into methods of data layer classes. The design pattern for instantiating this separation is the data access object (DAO) pattern. The DAO pattern encapsulates underlying details of DB manipulation from the business

**Table 10.3**  LSM Refactoring Capabilities

| Code-Level Refactoring | Functional Refactoring | Architecture-Level Refactoring |
|---|---|---|
| Dead and unused code elimination, commenting, and marking operations — user-guided and automated | Function-level refactoring merge and consolidate redundant and duplicate code, classes, methods and code blocks | Generate new class hierarchy, re-componertize classes and packages to improve coupling and cohesion, and segregate business from technical logic: |
| Rename all references to identifier across entire program: | Consolidate similar statements, classes, types, methods, and data members | • Extract subclasses from superclass |
| • Class, method, field, variables, and import | Merge similar code blocks, code statement slices into methods | • Consolidate superclass from similar subclasses |
| • Automated based on entry points and call-tree | • Extract dissimilarities (literals and variables) to parameters of methods | • Move classes between packages |
| • Any user-specified package, class, method, variable, or formal parameter | Create methods from heuristically specified code slices: | • Move members (method or field) between classes |
| Reduce number of formal parameters to method: | • Generate new classes as directed by heuristic functions or refactoring plan | Refactor derived components to segregate: |
| • Package multiple formal parameters into a class (pass as parameter) | • Extract-related statements detected by code pattern analysis | • Client-side Web browser and UI code |
| • Detect default-value instances for classes and merge into class constructors | Evolve code, function, and architecture via iterative refactoring: | • Server-side data manipulation and access ccde |
| • Convert global variables into class data members | • Carry out third-party refactoring plans and specifications | • Generate multi-tier application architecture separating high-level business ogic from client-side presentat on and low-level DB definition and manipulation |
| Create accessor methods for data members: | | • Component-oriented refactoring |
| • Referenced as member data or pass as function arguments | | • SOA and Web-enablement refactoring |
| • Replace direct data references with data accessor methods | | Create flexible and extensible components to support: |
| • Replace user-defined types with native built-in types | | • Future erhancements |
| Minimize class member visibility: | | • Code reuse |
| • Make method/field private instead of public | | • Component-oriented refactoring |
| | | • SOA anc Web-enablement refactoring |
| | | • Re-archifect and redesign |

*(Continued)*

**Table 10.3** LSM Refactoring Capabilities—Cont'd

| Architecture Refactoring (Extract Horizontal Services) | Architectural Refactoring to Web Services and Service-Oriented Architectures | Architecture Refactoring to Use Target Framework Components |
|---|---|---|
| Data Access Layers:<br>• File descriptors converted into data layer classes<br>• IO statements (SQL or I/O) converted into method of data layer classes<br><br>User Interface Layers:<br>• Screens converted into display layer classes<br>• Screen statements converted into methods of display layer classes | • SOAP, WSDL, UDDI, XML–RPC, UBR, XHTML, JavaScript<br>• Microsoft IIS/.NET/UDDI Services, Ajax, IBM WebSphere, Sun JES | • Map to J2EE Components (JDBC, JSP, JavaScript, HTML)<br>• Map to Microsoft Net Components (ADO, ASP)<br>• Map GCSS Framework<br>• Map to NMCI Component Framework<br>• Map to Spring Framework |

logic layer. The DAO is a fully object-oriented logical data interface that encapsulates all the details of maintaining the state of the data access, and operations upon data members and methods of data classes that become the sole method of access to the underlying database. The graphic in Table 10.4 depicts the data architecture conversion undertaken in the EOSS LSM pilot. The EOSS data architecture conversion is underlined.

Benefits of the DAO pattern refactoring include separation of the data tier logic from business tier logic in order to isolate changes in one from the other thereby achieving separation of concerns for future maintenance operations, the introduction of the JDBC interface layer to achieve an RDBMS-neutral data tier with inherently better scalability than legacy data access methods.

# EOSS ARCHITECTURE CONVERSION OVERVIEW

The purpose of this section is to describe the modernized system's architecture and how the modernization effort preserved the interfaces between the modernized EOSS-ACM system and the external systems with which it interfaces. The section Maintaining System Interfaces describes the method by which

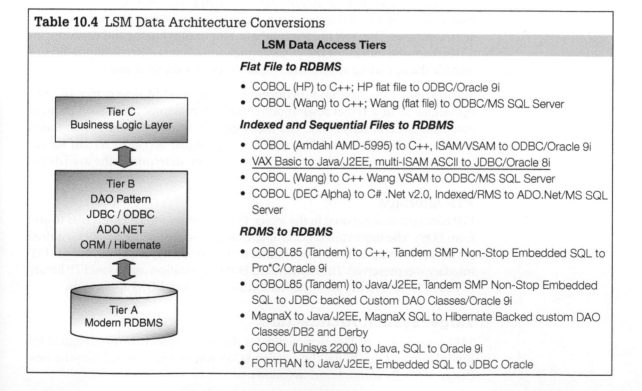

**Table 10.4** LSM Data Architecture Conversions

| LSM Data Access Tiers |
|---|
| ***Flat File to RDBMS*** |
| • COBOL (HP) to C++; HP flat file to ODBC/Oracle 9i |
| • COBOL (Wang) to C++; Wang (flat file) to ODBC/MS SQL Server |
| ***Indexed and Sequential Files to RDBMS*** |
| • COBOL (Amdahl AMD-5995) to C++, ISAM/VSAM to ODBC/Oracle 9i |
| • VAX Basic to Java/J2EE, multi-ISAM ASCII to JDBC/Oracle 8i |
| • COBOL (Wang) to C++ Wang VSAM to ODBC/MS SQL Server |
| • COBOL (DEC Alpha) to C# .Net v2.0, Indexed/RMS to ADO.Net/MS SQL Server |
| ***RDMS to RDBMS*** |
| • COBOL85 (Tandem) to C++, Tandem SMP Non-Stop Embedded SQL to Pro*C/Oracle 9i |
| • COBOL85 (Tandem) to Java/J2EE, Tandem SMP Non-Stop Embedded SQL to JDBC backed Custom DAO Classes/Oracle 9i |
| • MagnaX to Java/J2EE, MagnaX SQL to Hibernate Backed custom DAO Classes/DB2 and Derby |
| • COBOL (Unisys 2200) to Java, SQL to Oracle 9i |
| • FORTRAN to Java/J2EE, Embedded SQL to JDBC Oracle |

Tier C
Business Logic Layer

Tier B
DAO Pattern
JDBC / ODBC
ADO.NET
ORM / Hibernate

Tier A
Modern RDBMS

interfaces were preserved, thus allowing interoperability of the modernized EOSS-ACM system and any external systems. The section Target System Architecture describes the modernized system's architecture. This architecture provides significant scalability benefits. Although the system resulting from the pilot effort was deployed on only two machines, the architecture supports further distribution to additional machines if required to meet future requirements. To reduce the technical risk associated with this architecture, TSRI completed a mock-up of the architecture in-house to validate the approach.

## Maintaining System Interfaces

There were two types of system interfaces to replace or preserve from the existing EOSS-ACM system so as to achieve DITSCAP certification of the modernized EOSS. The first was the user interface, which was provided by user Telnet sessions via remote terminals. The second type was FTP, transferring to and from various external systems.

### The User Interface

User terminal interfaces were replaced by Web browser connections. These browser connections can be made within a LAN, through a VPN, from external Internet sites using SSL, or combinations of these modes. Application behavior remains the same regardless of the chosen network security scheme. HTML forms presented by Web server scripts provide screen I/O similar to the original Telnet sessions. The new interface did not aim to provide the full capability of a Telnet session outside of the EOSS application context. Specifically, it did not provide the operating system shell capabilities of a Telnet session.

This precluded the user from performing, create, modify, delete, run, or print operations as in a Telnet session. All EOSS system components such as main executables, COM scripts, and text files were presented in a new master menu to the user's Web browser. This menu also provided access to certain system text files. User access level, based upon the log-on, determined the availability of different system components.

### FTP Interface

FTP connections were used in the legacy EOSS system to transfer text files to and from EOSS. The modernized EOSS application produces and reads files required for the FTP interfaces in the same format as the current application. Thus the FTP interface was preserved. The modernized EOSS application uses a Java FTP library to push FTP files to the same destination as the current EOSS application.

## Target System Architecture

TSRI proposed an N-Tier architecture for the new system that was designed for modularity and flexibility. The existing EOSS system transformed into the new design is briefly summarized as follows:

- Original VAX BASIC EOSS code was transformed into JAVA/J2EE while preserving exact code functionality.
- User Telnet sessions and terminal I/O were replaced by SSL Web connections and HTML pages.
- The VAX flat file database system was replaced by an Oracle relational database accessed through a JDBC-based API.
- Scheduled automated processes on the VAX system were replaced by UNIX system "cron" scheduled processes.
- FTP sessions to and from external sessions work the same way as before by using a Java FTP library.

Components residing in tiers A through D run on a Sun Solaris server, and those in tier E run on a Windows IIS server. Though this is the fielded arrangement, the nature of such an N-Tier system allows for different components to run on different computing platforms, and at different physical locations. For example, each of tiers A through D can exist on different computers. Application processes in tier C can also be distributed across multiple platforms. Such flexibility allows for future growth and reorganization without major modification to the system.

## Data Tier (Tier A)

This tier was implemented in the form of a single Oracle 8i (or Oracle 9i) database running on a Solaris-based server. The database contains only EOSS-ACM system data. No business logic in the form of stored procedures, triggers, or any other Oracle programmatic interfaces was encoded in this database. The database was implemented using standard data types and table formats so that it can be rehosted to other database servers such as Oracle 9i or Microsoft SQL Server.

## Data Access Tier (Tier B)

This tier is the interface layer between the EOSS Business Logic Tier (C) and the Data Tier (A). It is written in Sun J2SE Java using JDBC. Its function is to perform I/O operations on the database in place of the original VAX flat file operations. Such layering isolates the business logic code from implementation details of data storage.

## Business Logic Tier (Tier C)

This tier contains all EOSS Java code translated from VAX BASIC and any scripts designed to replace other functionalities such as "cron" batch scripts and FTP scripts. Formerly separated processes were grouped into a single Java application with logic to be invoked separately via a menu or command line option. These processes are invoked and managed by a master "broker," enabling multiple simultaneous, multi-threaded execution instances. This tier interfaces with the Data Access Tier (A) and the Presentation Tier (D) through API's isolating the business logic from screen I/O and database implementation details.

### Presentation Tier (Tier D)

This tier encompasses all functionality related to generating the user interface. To accomplish this, it has a "Screen API" written in Java to set up and manipulate screen I/O data. Screen I/O and process synchronization data are stored in another database in this tier. This database is different from the one in tier A, but resides on the same physical machine as the Oracle server, although it could reside on a different Oracle server to meet future scalability requirements. This database provides inter-process communication and synchronization between this tier and the Web Tier (E). Communication messages are stored as rows in a table with columns representing data fields such as process ID, session ID, message type, message status, date/time, and message data. Both tiers (D and E) maintain synchronization and data display continuity through this mechanism.

### Web Tier (Tier E)

This tier is an IIS Web server running VB Scripts and providing SSL communication with end-user browser sessions. It communicates with the Presentation Tier (D) using ADO. The user authentication process runs on the Web server in this tier, but it can be adapted to use the standard Navy portal for user authentication in the future.

## Target System Processes and Components

### *Log-In and Business Logic Thread Instantiation Process*

Initially with all components of the system up and running, the main application "broker" in tier C waits for a user to begin a new session. The user begins a new session by opening a URL to the Web server (tier E) and logging on successfully. After successful authentication, the Web server tells the application broker that a new session has begun by entering a record into the message database in tier D. The application broker detects this new record and instantiates a new EOSS business logic thread based on the log-on authentication level. This thread and the corresponding user browser session are correlated by unique session and process identification numbers, which are recorded in the message database record along with other state information. After the business thread is started, the application broker continues to scan for other new session requests. It cleans up the EOSS business logic thread when there is information in the message buffer saying it has been terminated.

### *Log-Out Process*

An application session can end in several ways. The first occurs when the business logic comes to an end and returns. The second occurs when the user terminates the browser session by either clicking a "log-out" button or simply closing the Web browser. The third occurs when the browser session has been idling for too long and the Web server automatically terminates it. In any case, the appropriate client synchronization record in the presentation database is modified with a "TERMINATED" status. In the first case, the business logic and the application broker make the modification, whereas the Web server makes the modification in the second and third cases. The Web browser and the application broker scan for this termination status and clean up the appropriate browser session and the business logic thread as required.

## Application Database Access

The VAX flat file database implementation is replaced by a modern relational database system. The transformed EOSS business logic accesses this database through a Data Access API which uses JDBC and SQL to interface with the database. During normal operation, the application logic might open an indexed file using a certain channel and perform I/O operations on it.

To open a new file, it calls an open_File() API function with the channel number, file name, file access mode, associated record buffer, etc. The data access API takes this information and creates a "File" object and associates it with a database table with the same name. Depending on the specified open mode and the existence of the database table, it can be created, appended, or truncated at this point. Other file behaviors are also replicated by the file object. Upon a successful "open," the API uses a Java map language construct to associate the channel number to the file object so it can be referred to later by the channel number.

To write a record to a file, the application prepares the record buffer and invokes the file object .put() method to transfer data from the record buffer to a row in the database table. The opposite occurs when reading from a file using the .get() method. Other file operations such as delete and insert are handled similarly by other API methods using JDBC and SQL. Both sequential and indexed data files are stored in the database and treated in a similar manner with the exception that all operations are not valid for all file types. Figure 10.7 diagrams the application database access.

## Screen (Terminal) Input and Output

The user interacts with the application using a secure Web browser. Beside the initial log-in screen, EOSS application screens are presented as a succession of HTML forms that display text information and a maximum of one input field in an area 80 columns by 25 rows. Around this text area are other HTML graphics and buttons such as the EOSS logo, the log-out button, and the "help" button. The help button may be used to provide usage and contact information. There is also a list of links to text files generated by the current user. For each user, these print files persist from one session to another until specifically deleted by the user. The user can download these files to a local machine for viewing or printing. This functionality replaces the user's ability to view, modify, and print files on the original VAX system.

During an interactive process, the application logic displays something on the screen by invoking the `.io_Put()` method of a screen API object; passing to it the text to be displayed and position information. The screen API collects these display messages and builds up a screen buffer. Once the application issues a "flush" command or requests a user input with the `.io_get()` method, the screen API completes the screen image in buffer and generates a corresponding HTML form. It then sends this output request to the Web server by inserting an entry into the presentation database with the HTML form as a data field. The Web server (tier E) detects and reads this entry and sends the form data to the user Web browser. It also deletes the output database entry after reading it.

If the previous screen ended with a request for input, once the user enters a value into the input field and submits the form the Web server sends the input data back to the application by adding a record to the presentation database with the input value in the data field. The screen API, which has been waiting for a user input, reads this database entry and copies the input value into the application variable associated with the original `.io_Get()` method. This cycle repeats until the application thread ends.

It should be noted that the mechanisms for inter-process communication and session management that were created for EOSS LSM in 2004 predate technologies that may now exist in J2EE.

Figure 10.7 diagrams the application database access.

**FIGURE 10.7**

*Application database access.*

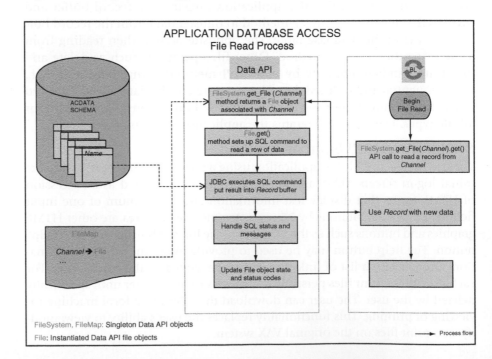

# OPPORTUNITY OBJECTIVES AND ANALYSIS OF PILOT RESULTS

The LSM project had two objectives. First, the EOSS-ACM modernization effort needed to be measured to identify possible ROI. Second, the LSM process needed to be validated for future use and scalability. This section describes the metrics and goals, developed by the Navy pilot during the initial planning sessions in developing the Project Charter, to assess the effectiveness of the LSM process.

## Cost Avoidance of Re-Engineering EOSS-ACM

The cost to manually analyze, re-engineer, and certify the EOSS system was compared to the piloted modernization process. Baseline statistics were gathered to measure the traditional method for system re-engineering. The Gartner Group study "Forecasting the Worldwide IT Services Industry: 1999" provided a cost for manual code conversion ranging from $6–26 per Line of Code (LOC) used for the manual vs. automated cost comparison.

The LSM pilot project transformed approximately 61,000 LOC averaging $5.68 per LOC. This cost included one-time costs that would be not be incurred on future similar projects. For example, excluding the one-time *setup fee* of $97,474 to create a translation engine for VAX code, the price per LOC is lowered to $4.08, significantly below the 1999 cost estimates for a manual rewrite. Using the figures from the Gartner Group study, the cost for manually rewriting the EOSS-ACM code would have been between $366,000 and $1,586,000. Using the average of these figures ($976,000), the cost avoidance LSM provides is approximately $855,646.

## Time Avoidance of Re-Engineering EOSS-ACM

The time required to manually re-engineer a legacy system was used as a baseline for comparison of the pilot modernization process. Because of the tasks previously mentioned, the cycle time to re-engineer EOSS-ACM using traditional methods was estimated to take 76 weeks (1.5 man-years). The expected result was a 75% reduction of hours spent re-engineering the EOSS-ACM system.

The pilot used artificial intelligence methods to re-engineer the VAX BASIC code into a modern J2EE architecture. The transformed code and data portion of the deliverables was delivered 60 business days after the target architecture was complete, much faster than a manual process could have been delivered. The pilot team estimated that the project shaved at least 64 weeks off the manual schedule, cutting project cycle time by approximately 85% compared to a manual process.

## Reduction of Maintenance Costs

The original EOSS-ACM configuration required three full-time contractors to enter engineering changes to EOSS documentation. Other associated hardware maintenance costs averaged $46,000 annually. The labor costs for Full-Time Equivalents (FTEs) personnel under contract to support the legacy EOSS-ACM system were eliminated. In addition to the reduction of personnel, the pilot reduced maintenance costs of a VAX-based system and replaced legacy hardware. The annual cost for a staff of three contractors was $180,000. The pilot process eliminated the costs of maintaining the VAX system. The data entry staff was no longer needed because the system was accessible without using Telnet interfaces or FTP uploads. These operational cost reductions are shown in Table 10.5.

## Completely Successful Modernization of VAX BASIC to J2EE

The legacy EOSS-ACM system was written in the VAX BASIC language with multiple ISAM files that stored data as ASCII text. EOSS-ACM was to be transformed to a J2EE application code with an N-tiered architecture utilizing an Oracle 9i database management system. The transformed EOSS-ACM CM system retained 100% of its original functionality. The modernization pilot achieved 100% success in porting the EOSS-ACM system. Using automated tools, the code for the business logic was transformed from VAX BASIC into J2EE while preserving the original functionality. As a part of this process the "as-is" and "to-be" system architecture was mapped. This showed a reduction in redundant and dead code. SMEs at NSWCCD tested the modernized EOSS-ACM system extensively and found it to retain all critical functionality of the mission-critical system. The modernized version is now in use.

## Improved Application Security

The legacy EOSS-ACM was not NMCI approved due to its Telnet session interface. To obtain compliance with approved security practices the modernized N-tier EOSS system underwent full DITSCAP certification. To comply with NMCI policy, the Telnet interfaces were replaced with Web-client software

**Table 10.5** Comparison of Annual Costs

| Legacy | | | Modernized | | |
|---|---|---|---|---|---|
| Description | Quantity | Cost ($) | Description | Quantity | Cost ($) |
| Data entry clerks | 3 | 180,000 | Data entry clerks | 0 | 0 |
| Hosting | N/A | 46,000 | Hosting | N/A | 52,000 |
| Total | | 226,000 | Total | | 52,000 |

accessible by a Web browser (Internet Explorer 5.5 or greater) using local LAN or remote VPN or SSL connections. The goal of 100% compliance and NMCI Approval was met.

## Elimination of Legacy Systems

The pilot project objective was to replace the existing VAX legacy application registered in the DON Application and Database Management System (DADMS). EOSS-ACM was successfully ported to a modern N-tiered J2EE architecture and the modernized system was registered in DADMS. The LSM pilot effectively ended the life cycle of the VAX-based EOSS-ACM and its dependent legacy components.

## Qualitative Analysis and Intangible Benefits

In addition to the previously mentioned quantifiable metrics, the modernized system was accessible by any NMCI desktop providing a level of convenience for engineers evaluating ship operational sequencing procedures at any location worldwide.

## Alignment of Pilot and Enterprise Goals

The LSM process was evaluated by the Navy FAM Council to determine how it could be used in the future transformation of other legacy systems. Table 10.6 is a goal alignment table developed by the FAM council that demonstrated how the enhanced legacy system modernization capabilities offered by the LSM pilot directly contribute to the satisfaction of enterprise goals and objectives.

**Table 10.6** Goal Alignment Table

| Enterprise Goals and Objectives (Critical Success Factors) | Pilot-Enabled Capability | Key Performance Indicators (Metrics) |
|---|---|---|
| Increase application security | Removal of Telnet interfaces | NMCI approval of transformed EOSS-ACM |
| Reduction of a Legacy System | Create a modernized J2EE system | Elimination of VAX-based EOSS ACM from DADMS as approved application |
| Document process attributes to ensure interoperability for other FAM legacy systems | FAM modernization process for mapping "as-is" and "to-be" system states | Identify other common systems that are candidates for system rationalization and modernization |

## Cost-Benefit Analysis and ROI

The LSM pilot costs were mostly made up of software analysis, testing, and documentation costs for contract work. The modernized EOSS-ACM system resides on existing hardware that leverages multiple applications. Two major costs to the pilot were the setup of the AI translation engine to handle a VAX code base for modernization and the extension of TSRI Java target language capability to target the NMCI framework. These costs are rolled into the Total Annual System Costs statistic (shown in Table 10.7) as the costs for the pilot in the year in which the system was transformed.

Second, the EOSS-ACM modernization effort was measured to identify possible ROI. The LSM process was validated for future use and scalability. Table 10.8 shows the estimated ROI for the LSM pilot based on the cost avoidance of developing and applying the LSM process instead of manually re-engineering the EOSS-ACM system.

Table 10.8 compares the *estimated* cost of a manual process conversion to the actual costs of the development and application of a repeatable and scalable LSM process as well as the cost of the conversion using the LSM. It should be noted that if the one-time costs of creating the LSM technology and process and the extension of TSRI Java target language capability to target the NMCI framework were subtracted the ROI would be much higher than the 2.47 to 1 ROI in Table 10.8.

Since the LSM pilot focused on the modernization of a single legacy application, the cost-benefit analysis shows the savings and cost-avoidances based on replacing EOSS-ACM in FY04. The project baseline statistics used for comparison is the Gartner Study. Table 10.9 shows the breakdown of Legacy EOSS-ACM costs versus the Modernized EOSS-ACM costs.

**Table 10.7** Summary of Legacy Systems Modernization Development and Life Cycle Support Costs

| Description | FYOR |
| --- | --- |
| Cost of pilot system | |
| Hardware | 0 |
| Labor | 0 |
| Documentation and test plans | $47,973 |
| System testing | $79,277 |
| Government (civilian and military) | $ 0 |
| Subtotal labor | $127,250 |
| Software | $219,284 |
| Recurring System life cycle maintenance, operations, and support (projected) | $ 0 |
| Total annual pilot system costs | $346,534 |
| Cumulative system costs | $346,534 |

**Table 10.8** Five-Year Cost/Benefit Summary

| Description | FYOR |
|---|---|
| Annual gross productivity savings using LSM | $ 953,120 |
| Cumulative gross productivity savings using LSM | $ 953,120 |
| Cumulative system costs | $ 97,474 |
| Cumulative total net cash flow | $855,646 |
| ROI | 2.47:1 |

**Table 10.9** Five-Year Legacy Systems Modernization Cost-Benefit Analysis

| Description | FYOR |
|---|---|
| **Business Operations Costs for EOSS-ACM Modernization** | |
| *EOSS-ACM Operating Cost and Manual Re-Engineering Costs* | |
| EOSS-ACM LOC | 61,000 |
| Average Cost LOC | $ 16 |
| Avg. cost to re-engineer EOSS-ACM | $ 976,000 |
| Annual maintenance cost for EOSS-ACM | $ 46,000 |
| Data entry personnel | $ 180,000 |
| **Total Re-engineering Cost** | **$ 1,202,000** |
| *Transformed EOSS-ACM Costs* | |
| EOSS-ACM LOC | 61,000 |
| Average Cost per LOC using transformation software | $ 4.08 |
| Cost to re-engineer EOSS-ACM | $ 248,880 |
| One-time translation engine setup | $ 97,474 |
| Data entry personnel | $ 0 |
| Annual maintenance costs | |
| **Total Annual Cost** | **$ 346,354** |
| *Benefits/Savings* | |
| Annual gross productivity savings using LSM process | $ 953,120 |
| Cumulative gross productivity savings using LSM process | $ 953,120 |
| Cumulative system costs | $ 97,474 |
| **Cumulative Total Net Savings** | **$ 855,646** |

## PILOT LESSONS LEARNED

The following section discusses topics for consideration for future modernization projects. These are lessons learned by the project team during their performance of the LSM pilot project.

### User Interface Modernization

One area in which the project might not be considered fully successful is the assumed goal of presenting a modernized interface to the end users of the system. It was assumed that, in the course of moving the system from a Telnet-based interface to a Web-based one, HTML forms would be used in building the modernized system interface. In a standard redevelopment effort, this sort of improvement would likely have been included naturally as a part of the new design. Replicating the legacy interface would actually have been a more difficult task. When viewed from the point of view of a transformation methodology, however, moving to a forms-based interface would have required a more major modification of the core application code, which was outside the scope of the software transformation as it was defined. In the future, this should be stated as a requirement in the statement of work when sourcing a modernization project.

### Preservation of Legacy Design/Methodology

The transformation of EOSS-ACM also preserved the programming methodology contained in the legacy system. Systems designed more than 5 or 10 years ago tend to be procedural programming systems, often called silos, which are difficult to integrate with other software systems. Today's approach to software development tends to emphasize modularity, layering, and encapsulating specific functional sections of the system to promote interoperability with other systems and future implementation of new interfaces. In preserving the legacy software's design, the LSM porting method did not obtain this side benefit of traditional modernization, leaving the system still in need of re-coding to support future system enhancements. More radical refactoring should have been undertaken but was not within the scope of the LSM project as it was defined.

### Preservation of Legacy Database Design

When modernizing a system using a porting methodology, the underlying design of the database continued to reflect the limitations of the legacy system. There is an additional analysis and design required to utilize a relational database when porting from an ASCII text legacy repository. In the case of EOSS-ACM, referential integrity and other such tasks that could be taken care of by the database engine are still handled by the modernized code rather than by the database engine.

# FUTURE OPPORTUNITIES AND NEXT STEPS

## Future Opportunities for the Pilot Program

The LSM pilot project was an opportunity to show how the industry is using transformation tools to modernize legacy systems. The pilot's findings were promoted by the FAM Council as an alternative process for modernizing legacy applications that are currently quarantined.

In addition to the process for legacy system modernization, an opportunity to identify aged systems with similar functionalities was identified. The identification, modernization, and rollup of like systems into a Web-centric portal were a defined goal of the FAM. During the selection process for FY05 Business Innovation funding, OPNAV N40 submitted a proposal for a pilot to rationalize aviation maintenance systems into a portal architecture by using the LSM process to harmonize data, application platforms, and business practices.

## Migration Strategy/Action Plan

The LSM process was determined by the Navy pilot evaluation team to be a valid option for remediation of applications that have been quarantined due to failure of the certification process for any of the rule set failures cited below. The LSM process is not always the preferred option, and the characteristics for which LSM is applicable should be clearly understood. Applications that are especially suited to the LSM process are those that have one or more of the following characteristics:

**Applications that overlap in functionality with other approved applications (especially if they are owned/used by a single FAM)**: These applications are considered especially good candidates because the LSM process will result in a new architecture that is conducive to merging with the other overlapping applications. Combining the various overlapping applications into a single application (or integrated suite of applications) reusing applicable code and data objects reduces the number of applications and associated data stores that must be maintained with the potential for significant savings. If the other overlapping application must also go through the remediation process the case is even stronger.

**Applications where significant functional or business logic changes are desired or anticipated which will require an extensive re-engineering effort**: The LSM process is well suited to this type of effort. The deliverable code is in a format that lends itself to future modifications derived from changing functional requirements (i.e., modern language, Web-enabled, documented, etc.).

Applications written in old/obsolete languages on legacy hardware systems where maintenance and programming support is expensive and may be difficult to obtain: Also, they may be poorly documented and there may little (if any) corporate knowledge as to the design and inner workings of these applications. These applications will continue to become more and more expensive to support in the future, and the initial investment in the code transformation will result in significant future cost savings in maintenance cost avoidance.

Applications that violate NMCI Boundary (B1/B2) Policies and will not obtain a waiver or boundary policy change: These applications must have at least some portion of their code rewritten to comply with the NMCI policy. The Web-enablement associated with the LSM process automatically addresses many of these situations. These applications will be more able to be integrated into future NMCI architectures without extensive rework to comply with the DON goal of Web-enabling as many applications as possible.

8/16-Bit Applications: Although it was previously stated that this is not a sufficient criterion in and of itself to justify the LSM process, the practicality of the situation is that if these applications just needed to be recompiled into the 32-bit architecture this would have already occurred. There is almost certainly some overriding constraint that has prevented them from being updated, whether it is legacy hardware requirements, lack of documentation, obsolete programming language, etc. These applications should still be evaluated in the context of the other available options, but they should be considered good candidates for the LSM process.

## Five Failure Conditions for the LSM Process

There are five rule set failures that are potential candidates for the LSM process. All five failures have potential security issues associated with them (see Table 10.10):

**Table 10.10** Rule Sets Applicable to LSM Pilot Process

| Rule Number/Name | Security Issue |
|---|---|
| 1/Windows 2000 compatible | Applications that are not compatible with the Windows 2000 operating system may introduce vulnerabilities due to interference with the normal functionality of the operating system. |
| 2/NMCI Group Policy Object (GPO) compatible | Incompatibility with NMCI GPO requirements may allow users access to system resources beyond what they are supposed to have according to NMCI policy. |

**Table 10.10** Rule Sets Applicable to LSM Pilot Process—Cont'd

| Rule Number/Name | Security Issue |
|---|---|
| 4/Comply with DON/NMCI Boundary 1 and 2 Policies | Applications that violate the NMCI Boundary Policies expose the NMCI to vulnerabilities associated with prohibited protocols and services. |
| 11/Gold Disk compatible | Applications that are not compatible with the NMCI Gold Disk suite of applications may introduce vulnerabilities due to interference with the normal functionality of those applications. |
| 14/8- and 16-bit applications | An application process running in the Win16 emulation environment shares information with processes running on other computers in the same way, with the same reduced protection that an application running on a Windows 3.1-based computer shares information. Applications in emulation environments are potential weak points in system security if they are allowed to share critical resources over the network. For this reason, emulation must not be run on computers that store sensitive information. |

## CONCLUSION

According to Navy eBusiness evaluation, the LSM pilot reduced the cost and time to convert the EOSS system, increased its security to meet NMCI security requirements, achieved annual application operational cost reductions of $226,000, and achieved an N-tiered NMCI-compliant Java/J2EE architecture with a modernization project ROI estimated to be at least 2.47 times better than the manual alternative. The EOSS pilot pioneered a highly effective automated transformation LSM process alternative for FAMs and CDAs to use for modernizing aged applications to function within NMCI. The FAMs determined LSM to be a valid option for remediation of NMCI applications that have been quarantined for NMCI rule set failures and articulated the characteristics of the systems which made them appropriate for the LSM process.

# CHAPTER 11

# Model-Driven Reverse Engineering of COBOL-Based Applications

**Franck Barbier, Sylvain Eveillard, Kamal Youbi, Olivier Guitton, Arnaud Perrier, and Eric Cariou**

## ABSTRACT

Model-Driven Development (MDD)[1] is a proven paradigm for constructing cost-effective applications. The MDD design cycle satisfies time-to-market constraints. Inspired by object-orientation (OO programming languages, OO databases, OO analysis and design methods), MDD promotes software quality, reusability, and maintainability. Models,[2] which are first-class components in the development process, also facilitate portability. More precisely, Platform-Independent Models (PIMs) are free from technical concerns, while Platform-Specific Models (PSMs), derived from PIMs by means of model-based transformations, are annotated with platform-oriented configuration information to generate end-user applications.

Tools like BLU AGE® have proven the efficiency of the model-driven approach. Applications built on top of these concepts are now spreading to enterprises. However, this expansion will soon be limited by legacy systems. The question is: How can MDD be applied to legacy applications that have not been derived from models? With a controlled *generation* process in place, the answer is obvious. Model-driven reverse engineering allows MDD to be applied to legacy systems. If a model from a legacy application is obtained, then, thanks to consecutive model transformations, this application is generated to another platform.

To that extent, this chapter discusses a method and a tool that provides an integrated, reverse engineering framework. To illustrate this method, we present a pilot project called SCAFRUITS. The goal of this project was to demonstrate the technical and economic viability of reverse engineering based on MDD. The legacy application involved in this project comes from the real world and is used every day by the Groupement des Mousquetaires, one of the main European companies in the retail sector with around 4,000 outlets and 112,000 employees. This project was achieved in business conditions with clearly defined objectives and deadlines.

## CONTENTS

The tool used to achieve this project is named BLU AGE®,[3] which has the ability to generate applications from models without writing a single line of code. In BLU AGE®, PIMs are constructed by software analysts while technical cartridges (Platform Description Models; PDMs) are designed by software architects. BLU AGE® is able to transform PIMs into PSMs and to link these PSMs to PDMs. This chapter explores how PIMs can be, as much as possible, automatically generated from legacy systems with a focus on COBOL applications.

## GOALS

The key goals of this project discussed within this case study are as follows.

■ Non-OO Code Issues: We discuss the reverse engineering of common[4] COBOL in a specific context. Precisely, this code is written in COBOL, but conforms to the IBM VisualAge PACBASE (VAP) tool. The code structuring thus respects particular rules and formats. Concretely, VAP programs are written by means of a superset (a dialect) of the COBOL language. Programs are also equipped with helpful VAP-based configuration data linked to legacy technology (e.g., character screens). However, one must remember that this tool comes from programs created in the 1980s, so code complies with the standards and the structured programming spirit of that time. That is why there is a high degree of code and functional redundancy. The difficulty in converting such legacy information systems — particularly where there is such a high degree of redundancy — into models remains high, especially OO models. This chapter will not explain all of the technical elements of the transformations involved in the reverse engineering process, but it will expose a method used to divide this tedious problem into easier, more manageable pieces.

■ Semantic Issues: Simply having a graphical view of old COBOL is not enough. So models are not only partial or complete viewpoints of legacy systems, but also include a re-formalization of the business rules engraved in COBOL programs. As a result, models obtained from reverse engineering are intended to become the inputs of the generation processes, which are used to rebuild applications based on today's platforms. This is mainly Java EE and .NET, but also includes their associated components: Struts, JavaServer Faces (JSF), Hibernate, Java Persistence API (JPA), and Windows Presentation Foundation (WPF). Regarding semantic issues, this case study also sketches the alignment of the proposed reverse engineering process using the Knowledge Discovery Metamodel (KDM), an Object Management Group (OMG) standard for representing existing software systems.[5]

- Systematic and Automated Reverse Engineering Issues: The most important goal of this project was to produce a reverse engineered application in a totally automated way. Although human intervention is inevitable, a tool is required to support most of the tedious tasks caused by sizeable volumes. To that extent, we utilized and will discuss the REVERSE component of BLU AGE®, an Eclipse/EMF-based Computer-Aided Software Engineering (CASE) tool that enables the elaboration of PIMs that are endowed with context-specific annotations (aka. stereotypes in UML). These PIMs result from the extraction of legacy code. The case study described in this paper is the first COBOL benchmark of the REVERSE module of BLU AGE®. Until now, the perfecting of this module has occurred by means of Java only. The results exposed in this paper show the need for a more open and sophisticated reverse engineering process and tool due to, essentially, the non-OO nature of COBOL and VAP. The discussion of lessons learned will comment on the large-scale factors of this project and its economical facets.

## MODERNIZATION CONTEXT

VAP is an application generator. Billions of lines of COBOL software, generated through this application generator, are in production in enterprises all over the world. Despite its recognized qualities, the VAP-integrated development environment raises critical problems:

- The environment, and thus its resulting applications, will be maintained by IBM only up to 2015
- VAP does not support any kind of interoperability with modern non-proprietary platforms
- Expert users exist,[6] but advances in computer and software technologies create difficulties and even risks, when relying on a dwindling number of skilled experts
- Applications based on this environment contain an important amount of business knowledge; the need for extracting this knowledge in a readable and usable way is a crucial and perennial investment issue
- Maintenance costs cannot be cut down and are high due to the significant dependency upon external assistance and support

For historical reasons, such applications require specific execution contexts; namely old terminals (non-graphical window-based screens), mainframes, and Customer Information Control System (CICS). Regarding CICS, VAP legacy systems mix business logic and CICS commands. So, an important challenge is to first separate both aspects to converge with the "PIMs versus PSMs" philosophy. The next challenge is to substitute CICS for another execution platform such as a Java EE server.

# MODERNIZATION APPROACH

Given that legacy applications are based on various old software technologies, the overall goal of modernization is a priori to replace this application by another equivalent one (in terms of functions offered to users). One of the benefits of having a renewed application, based on Java EE in this case, is the gain in technical agility provided by Java EE. These include Web integration abilities, load balancing, ease and transparency of service access and distribution, compliance with standards, and Java EE product server independence (see Figure 11.1).

Using MDD for reverse engineering provides the opportunity to change and/or to extend the set of functions to achieve corresponding user requirements. Models (PIMs) formally express these requirements. PSMs linked to Java EE, for example, may thus be derived from these PIMs, which are outputs of the reverse engineering process (see Figure 11.2).

The reverse engineering approach taken for this project required three phases:

1. Reverse Engineering Process: Implementation principles and details of the REVERSE component of BLU AGE® involved the generation of text based on a semi-natural language. This language shares a common metamodel (i.e., "it is an instance of") with a prefabricated metamodel, which is dedicated to the way people may use VAP (Figure 11.1). Programs are described in a COBOL-like language that is associated with screen layout/control information. These results are recorded as an instance of a metamodel. In this respect, reverse operations intensively use model transformation technologies. More precisely, the Atlas Transformation Language (ATL)[7] instruments these reverse actions.

2. Validation Phase: Models were used to generate the new application. This means that all functions and business rules in legacy code must be properly captured. This phase is called validation. Once the PIMs

**FIGURE 11.1**

*VAP organization.*

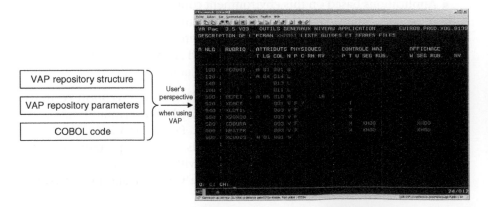

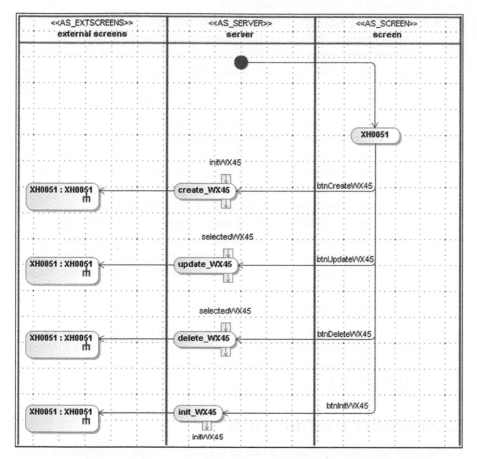

**FIGURE 11.2**

UML *dynamic model generated from reverse engineering process.*

are viewable as outputs of the reverse process, model-based testing determines that the results are trustworthy representations of the existing system. Test data and scenarios established from the existing system can be replayed for the renewed application. By means of another component (named BUILD), the testing of models is carried out within Eclipse. This is done with the help of the new generated code, which is graphically synchronized to models. In this respect, Figure 11.2 shows a UML model that represents screen linking and data processing. On the right-hand side, there is a UML activity, which describes a given screen. Several scenarios exist to move from this screen to others (on the left-hand side) through an intermediate column (called "swimlane" in UML jargon). In this column, activities represent data processing in servers (queries, for example). Testing facilities allow one to assign breakpoints to activities. One can carry out debugging step by step to complete the validation phase, provided that user test data is sufficiently comprehensive.

3. **Measurement Activity:** The reverse modeling process has to be proven economically relevant. However, demonstrating that PIMs are trustworthy and provide a complete representation of current functionality can be time-consuming. While elementary operations are treated automatically, complex operations are progressively controlled and scored.[8] These operations are annotated, at first manually, with technical and/or functional markers. The reverse process captures the available knowledge to avoid subsequent manual intervention. In this scope, the pilot project (see the section Case Study Description) attempted to anticipate the scalability of the proposed modernization process; particularly if it can be generalized. In this case study project, we did not focus on the re-generation of the existing application to target modern platforms. If the targeted application's PIMs are consistent and complete, rebuilding a new system with BLU AGE® is quite simple compared to computing these PIMs by means of reverse engineering (phases 1 and 2). Moreover, phase 3 can be done in a cost-effective way. Projected man-month charges were established for the pilot project as a basis for determining forward-looking costs.

4. **Scope of Result:** At this time, the feasibility and the applicability of this reverse engineering process have been demonstrated on a medium scale and in a cost-effective way. Future work is required to assess the scalability of such an effort.

## CASE STUDY DESCRIPTION

Groupement des Mousquetaires is one of the main European companies in the retail sector. STIME is its information system division. The SCAFRUITS application is concerned with the provisioning of fruits and vegetables from referenced suppliers, as well as the sale and distribution of these items to franchised outlets all over Europe. Shops interact by means of the SCAFRUITS application to have the best products at the best prices under the best conditions. This includes reduced short-time delivery, sanitary quality assurance, and synchronization with volatile demand.

The business scope of SCAFRUITS is broad and includes order management, shipping, supplier and product qualification and referencing, timely price management, and product activation/inhibition. The application is composed of numerous programs and sub-programs, which collectively provide common functionalities needed for business-oriented primary use cases.

The application's design and initial utilization date back to 1994 and the system has continuously evolved since that time. From a business perspective, the application is composed of 85 Transactional Processing (TP) functions and

23 batch job streams. A TP is a typical interactive use case where a user carries out the referencing of a fruit supplier through an old-fashion screen and is then notified about the success (or possible failure) of its operation. Additionally, transversal facility subprograms are used for checking the conformity of products to EU sanitary standards.

Concerning its technical facets, the size of the application is estimated to be equal to 3 million LOC, 600 programs, 400 screens, 200 batch programs, 300 potential users, and 48,000 product references with only 2,000 active references at a time. There are 350,000 transactions per day and 100,000 created order lines per day. The savings, if the full application can be moved from VAP to a modern platform like Java EE, are estimated at around €1.5 million per year.

The pilot project, called VisualAge PACBASE to BLU AGE® (VAP2BA), was limited in scope from a functional perspective. In addition, the scope was limited to product referencing and ordering, including all Create, Read, Update, and Delete (CRUD) operations. The pilot project is limited to 15 TP and 15 batch processes. Use case examples that were a part of the pilot project included:

- Supplier order creation
- Supplier order reception

Test scenarios and data rely on these use cases. Building test cases was equivalent to collecting data. However, legacy data had to be restructured into objects to accommodate the new OO system architecture. More precisely, these objects and their links are instances of the classes and associations found in the PIMs, which are outputs of the reverse engineering process. Once established, testing occurs through scenarios; for example, screen linking is required for running the "supplier order reception" use case.

## REVERSE ENGINEERING METHOD[9]

The technical approach is based on the PACBASE Access Facility (PAF) component of VAP. VAP developers use the VAP user interface (Figure 11.1) to build their applications by means of a COBOL-like language, while adhering to VAP design guidelines. This amounts to taking into account numerous flat files with a complex specific organization (redundancy, implicit dependency among files based on implicit string matching, etc.). Practically speaking, PAF offers a SQL-like language that can access data in the form of VAP repository entities.

The proposed method intensively relies on predefined metamodels (Figure 11.3). It starts from an Ecore-like DSML.[10] Ecore, as shown in Figure 11.4, is the Eclipse meta-language for coping with any kind of model. The structure of the PAF tables is thus represented by means of the Ecore-like meta-language.

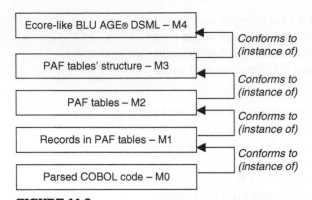

**FIGURE 11.3**

*Metamodel layering.*

The result is that the complex organization of VAP is captured once and for all.[11] The logic of VAF relies on meta-types, which are members of this metamodel (M3 level): Role, Table,[12] Column, Library (of code), Session, and User. It also relies on associations between these meta-types: a role is composed of zero or *n* tables; a table is composed of at least one and at most *n* columns. For example, the Table meta-type conforms by definition to a BLU AGE® meta-type specifically designed for reverse engineering.

Another metamodel (M2 level shown in Figure 11.3) is application dependent. A SCAFRUITS table structure is an instance of the Table meta-type at the M3 level. For instance, the EC02 table structure in SCAFRUITS has five columns, each having a given size, format, and label. Copies of the EC02 table are thus located at the M1 level as instances of the EC02 table structure.

PAF is used to populate records at the M1 level. Data samples extracted by means of PAF are described in Figure 11.5. This figure shows rough XML resulting directly from PAF queries.

Since extractions are composed of several XML files, removing useless (parasite) data and redundancies is a primary issue; for example, a TP may use the SE01 segment, while a batch process uses the same segment. This segment must appear once and for all in an appropriate model.

The PAF extraction model is intentionally used to first eliminate redundancy. Next, several ATL transformations are run in sequence to explicitly re-create the dependencies between VAP entities. These are shown in Figure 11.6.

The PAF persistence model shown in Figure 11.6 is computed by means of an ATL transformation from the PAF extraction model. The same applies to the

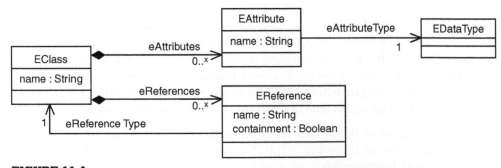

**FIGURE 11.4**

*Ecore core meta-types in Eclipse.*

PAF associations, which add meaningful inverse references to the VAP entities that come from the PAF persistence model. The PAF persistence model recreates references (instances of EReference in Figure 11.4) from flat files. The PAF associations are composed of inferred inverse references from the PAF persistence model.

As an illustration, each VAP entity (a batch process, for example) has a main screen (PG01, for example) and some possible screens. Each COBOL statement is registered in a VAP entity, say PG08. One must then recompose the link between PG01 and PG08 in the models. In VAP however, string matching and cross-references between files are the only way to determine dependencies.

Following this logic, an instance of the PAF associations model is shown on the right-hand side of Figure 11.7. The CGPM batch process, also called a VAP entity, supports navigation to all of its linked PG01 objects and to all of its PG08 objects. In short, the PAF associations model complements the PAF persistence model by supplying reverse navigability.

```
<PG01>
<CPGM    valeur="FLLF99
<LPGM    valeur="SS-PGM ACCES LIEU FONCTION
<CPGMC   valeur="FLLF99
<TLANP   valeur="X
<OPGMCO  valeur="
<CCAVP   valeur="E
<CCAPP   valeur="E
<EPGM    valeur="FLLF99D
<OPGMPR  valeur="P
<TPGMNA  valeur="B
<TPGM    valeur="D
<OPGMCP  valeur="
<OSQL    valeur="
<DENTME  valeur="
</PG01>
```

**FIGURE 11.5**

*Rough XML data resulting from PAF queries.*

**FIGURE 11.6**

*VAP information processing.*

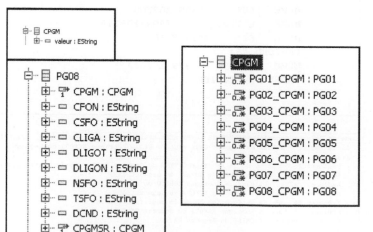

**FIGURE 11.7**

*PAF persistence and PAF association samples.*

The reverse engineering method is divided into three phases:

- The extraction phase is fully generic (i.e., independent of the SCAFRUITS application) and fully automated. This phase is built onto the metamodels in Figure 11.3. It contributes to having a nice and rich graphical view of a VAP application within Eclipse. This phase is based on the above-described transformation processes.

- The interpretation phase is semi-automated in the sense that it depends upon the deep natures of the legacy technology and business application. The COBOL-like code shown in Figure 11.8 is parsed and transformed into a semi-natural language[13] as shown in Figure 11.9. This code conforms to a predefined metamodel. One key advantage of the proposed method is that the semi-natural language in Figure 11.9 conforms to a metamodel, which is an ATL-based transformation of the semi-natural language.

- To more or less automatically generate business rules in a neutral formalism, reverse engineers provide on-the-fly information on (1) what are the means, constraints, and rules of the legacy technology to manage business rules and (2) what are and where are the true business rules of the reversed application. As a result, the semi-natural language sentences are a great help for readability and comprehensibility for both the application and its support technology. Outputs allow the direct generation of BLU AGE® material. This holds true for even Object Constraint Language (OCL) constraints, which are in charge of representing business rules in BLU AGE®.

**FIGURE 11.8**

*VAP-oriented COBOL.*

```
SousFonction 'FERMETURE DU FICHIER RFTZ93WL' F2OSFPA {
    IF(Z499-XCF06A = SPACES AN Z499-XCF07A = SPACES) {
        MOVE    5-PA00-CPTENR    Z499-X09929
        MOVE    'LUS'    Z499-X07X00
        MOVE    'RFTZ93WL'    Z499-X08X18
        MOVE    'FI'    Z499-XCF02A
        PERFORM F8A
        MOVE    SPACES    Z499-XCF02A
        CLOSE PA-FICHIER
    }
}
```

**FIGURE 11.9**

*Semi-natural language (in French) generated from VAP-oriented COBOL.*

```
Code de la sous-fonction "FERMETURE DU FICHIER RFTZ93WL" , nom technique :  F2OSFPA {
  Si la Rubrique XCF06A du Segment Z499 vaut "" et la Rubrique XCF07A du Segment Z499 vaut ""
faire
    Déplacer le compteur de la Rubrique CPTENR du Segment PA00 dans la Rubrique X09929 du Segment Z499
    Déplacer "LUS" dans la Rubrique X07X00 du Segment Z499
    Déplacer "RFTZ93WL" dans la Rubrique X08X18 du Segment Z499
    Déplacer "FI" dans la Rubrique XCF02A du Segment Z499
    Exécuter le code de la fonction ou de la sous-fonction F8A
    Déplacer "" dans la Rubrique XCF02A du Segment Z499
    CLOSE la Rubrique FICHIER du Segment PA
  finfaire
}
```

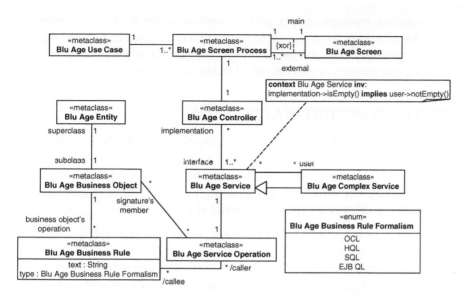

**FIGURE 11.10**
*BLU AGE® meta-types.*

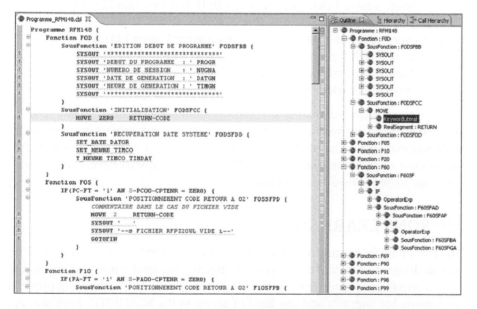

**FIGURE 11.11**
*COBOL code management within Eclipse (right-hand side).*

- The publication phase leads to the ability to view, transform, and refactor the material coming from the interpretation into BLU AGE® meta-types as shown in Figure 11.10. However, all of the COBOL can be easily and straightforwardly managed within Eclipse, shown on the right side of Figure 11.11. At this time, there is a Java-like language, which is offered to users to translate COBOL-oriented models into this language (i.e., on the right-hand side of Figure 11.11). The mapping of entities, business objects, and controllers (in the BLU AGE® jargon) is, for efficiency reasons, carried out with a certain strategy. As an ongoing implementation, the inclusion of a representation phase in the reverse engineering process is described in the next section.

## METHOD INDUSTRIALIZATION

The SCAFRUITS project was a great opportunity to establish an industrialization process for reverse engineering. To follow up project progress and ensure functional conformity, an integration suite, based on Hudson (https://hudson .dev.java.net/), has been built on top of the BLU AGE® REVERSE module. This integration process is composed of several stages:

- The knowledge base is first launched and populated with the legacy technology knowledge
- Extraction files are processed to build the PAF extraction model
- Reverse engineering workflows are launched consecutively to finally produce a model that conforms to a BLU AGE® metamodel and an XHTML mock-up
- An application is generated from this material using BLU AGE®
- Tests and Web tests are then carried out and reports are established
- The knowledge base is enhanced to enlarge its scope with new contextual knowledge

Launching such an automated integration chain several times a day allows the project team to measure project advancement and project conformance to functional requirements. Existence of such a tool is a crucial point in the perspective of industrialization, allowing project teams to have better views and comprehensions of project progress.

## LESSONS LEARNED

The first phase (the extraction phase) required 4 man-months (2 persons). This was to design and perfect the reverse engineering method while making slight implementation amendments in the CASE tool possible. To obtain appropriate knowledge, support, and any kind of access to the SCAFRUITS application, a half man-month support was provided by STIME. Minor modifications of the REVERSE component of BLU AGE® occurred during this first stage. The unique result of this phase was a beta "industrial" version of this component. The application-independent nature of the process leads to success, even though a functional subset of SCAFRUITS was used for the experimentation.

The second phase is an ongoing phase (3 months). This phase covers the interpretation and publication phases. This last phase includes BLU AGE®

training and the construction of BLU AGE® models within Eclipse to be reverse engineered and implemented in Java or .NET for the product referencing and product ordering use cases. Each TP requires 2 man-days of support and each batch process requires 1 man-day of support from each side (BLU AGE® expert group and STIME).

Even though the manual building of models within BLU AGE® is strongly inspired by the success of the commented output of the reverse engineering process, a significant gap in research and development remains. The goal is to obtain maximum automation.

# PERSPECTIVES: GENERALIZING THE APPROACH

The reverse engineering process previously described is strongly coupled with VAP. Another modernization context associated with a different legacy development tool or language requires other metamodels and other transformation chains. In short, the ultimate intention of the BLU AGE® REVERSE module is to become free from a legacy technology. To avoid the redefinition of such metamodels and transformation chains, a more generic framework is expected (Figure 11.12).

---

Transformation chains: The complexity of certain model transformations needed in the reverse engineering process led to unintelligible transformation programs. The need for segmentation of these complex transformations amounts to creating transformation chains. Transformation chains involve a special kind of model: weaving models.

Instead of having sizeable metamodels that capture an entire domain, relationships and correspondences between models can be described by specialized weaving models. Weaving models in essence depend upon the source and the target models of a transformation.

Dependencies are expressed using model elements from the source, from the target, and from markers in profiles.

---

In the transformation workflow from Figure 11.12, VAP may be viewed as a technical ontology: a set of technical concepts, terms (Table, Column ... see prior sections), and their semantic relationships. These concepts are currently (manually) implemented by means of an Ecore metamodel. As a result, any project involving a different legacy technology would require construction of a new metamodel.

To eliminate the creation of a new metamodel for each newly encountered legacy technology, to the degree possible, a meta-metamodel is required. This meta-metamodel would instantiate a technology as a metamodel that conforms to this meta-metamodel. In addition, creating interoperability within BLU AGE® and with other reverse engineering tools requires such a normative meta-metamodel. In our analysis, the KDM can adequately serve this purpose.

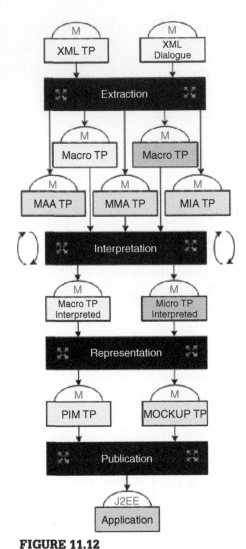

**FIGURE 11.12**

*Transformation chain with its required input and output models.*

The primary purpose of an enhanced reverse engineering process is, therefore, the discovery of the various attributes of a given technology to interactively populate the metamodel that can describe this technology. Under this approach, a knowledge base of the legacy technology can then be produced as a referent. This environment would also require an interactive aspect to support the need for future manual interventions that may be necessary to classify all concepts of the targeted technology.

KDM is used to support this feature and the resulting transformation workflow is shown in Figure 11.12. The macro/micro dichotomy is indeed a key notion in KDM and is linked to the Micro KDM domain.[5] This package includes the model elements that allow the characterization of elementary actions in the target legacy technology. For instance, a MOVE statement in COBOL which is also present in the VAP dialect maps to an instance of ASSIGN in KDM, a micro action.

The transformation chain in Figure 11.12 shows up as outputs of the Extraction phase's[14] five models.[15] The Micro TP model records all the concepts of the VAP programming language to manage a TP within the reverse engineering process. In the same logic, the Macro TP addresses small-scale architectural issues such as function keys in old character terminals that are used for screen linking.

The Micro TP and Macro TP models are thus two sets of VAP markers. Ideally, according to the KDM philosophy, these markers come from the extraction process. In our case study project they have been constructed from scratch. In any case, they are independent of the application being reversed.

In contrast, the MAcro Annotated (MMA) TP model and the MIcro Annotated (MIA) TP model refer to all of the data capturing the nature and the status of a given TP. These two types of models are business oriented; for example, one may use an MAA TP model to determine how display screens are linked, more precisely, which function key of the TP of interest leads to another TP. In an MIA TP, one may find, in a structured way, all the material found when parsing the code relating to a TP. By definition, the MMA TP and MIA TP models are annotated with markers coming from the Micro TP and Macro TP models, but annotations are physically present in the weaving model. This is the Merged Model with Annotations TP model.

Another key research focus is the systematic discovering of the legacy technology. The described project (as a perspective) is to concomitantly create knowledge about the reversed application and its support technology. A transformation framework is under specification and development to achieve this goal.

# REFERENCES

1. France R, Ghosh S, Dinh-Trong T, Solberg A. Model-Driven Development Using UML 2.0: Promises and Pitfalls. *IEEE Computer.* 2006;39(2):59–66.
2. We consider Unified Modeling Language (UML) models.
3. www.bluage.com.
4. The proposed approach is not dedicated to object-oriented COBOL but to ordinary COBOL.
5. *Architecture-Driven Modernization (ADM)/Knowledge Discovery MetaModel (KDM).*, *version 1.1.* 2009.
6. www.napug.com.
7. www.eclipse.org/m2m/atl/.
8. The number of elementary statements like GOTO, performed modules (PERFORM command), called subprograms are computed at this time.
9. Eveillard S, Henry A. *Transforming VAP metamodels into UML, talk at the industrial track of MODELS. 2008.* France: Toulouse; 2008.
10. Domain-Specific Modeling Language.
11. Section Lessons Learned discusses why this solution is not satisfactory in forthcoming developments of BLU AGE®.
12. In the VAP logic, a table is a unit of organization; for example, a table may describe a batch process.
13. For example, the French word *Déplacer* means to move in English. Generally speaking, people are more confident when reading text close to their native language.
14. The XML TP and XML Dialogue input models as just results of filter application (e.g., control character cleaning) on VAP rough files.
15. An M mark on the top of a rectangle means that it is a "model."
16. For example, specific database accesses that have no counterpart in the modern application, or international date formatting which is already available within the Java core library.

# CHAPTER 12

# Veterans Health Administration's VistA MUMPS Modernization Pilot*

## Philip H. Newcomb and Robert Couch

## ABSTRACT

This case study documents technologies, processes, and methods of a 100% automated conversion of the Veterans Health Administration (VHA) Veterans Information System Technical Architecture (VistA) system, written in 2.1 million lines of MUMPS, into Java compatible with the J2EE framework. VistA is the core Electronic Healthcare Recordkeeping (EHR) system for the VHA hospital system, which provides EHR record keeping for more than 4.5 million veterans. A pilot project, conducted in 2005 under VHA auspices as a sole source contract, converted: (1) the Voluntary Timekeeping System (VTS), a module of VistA into Java; (2) FileMan, the VistA file management system into Java Database Connectivity (JDBC) interfacing with an Oracle 9i Relational Database; and (3) the VistA user interface into a Java Server Pages (JSP) browser user interface using the Microsoft IIS Web server. The pilot conclusively demonstrated the feasibility of a fully automated conversion of MUMPS into Java, achieving a transformation that encompassed nearly all of MUMPS language features. The technical strategy achieved a clear separation between application logic business rules, data handling presentation elements, and Web-enabled front-end/user screens. The project was prematurely ended in 2006 due to funding restrictions associated with the Iraq war after the successful completion of a small pilot for the VHA. In 2009 all 2.1 MLOC of MUMPS in OpenVistA, the open source variation of VistA, was converted into Java as a scalability demonstration. The conversion of OpenVistA is available on the Web (at URL: http://www.softwarerevolution.com/open-vista/) as a Transformation Blueprint™, where it serves the open source community as a roadmap toward a future open source EHR system.

## CONTENTS

## INTRODUCTION TO MUMPS

### What is MUMPS?

MUMPS, or "M", is the Massachusetts General Hospital Utility Multi-Programming System. It is a procedural, interpreted general-purpose programming language oriented toward database applications.

MUMPS is an important programming language and database system heavily used in medical applications such as patient records and billing. It was developed in the 1960s at Massachusetts General Hospital, a teaching hospital associated with Harvard University in Boston, as a specialized language for medical use that ultimately achieved widespread adoption by the healthcare and financial industries as the MUMPS language during the 1970s and early 1980s. The principal language characteristics that led to its widespread adoption are its flexible data manipulation and interpretive features that allowed non-programmers to code in MUMPS with little to no formal computer science training.

## The Problem with MUMPS

"When I look back on my Fortran code from school I am a little embarrassed, but I understand it. When I look back on my MUMPS I can't even read it without slow token-by-token translation. It's amazing to me how fluent I was when I wrote it and how fluent I'm not when I read it."

**Steve J. Morris**

It's possible to write completely obfuscated MUMPS code, and too many MUMPS programmers do it. Some even brag about nobody else being able to read their code. Fortunately for those of us in the VA who have to maintain that code, they are becoming a minority.

**John E. Kemker, III**

A typical MUMPS application consists of thousands of files that contain MUMPS code along with a MUMPS database. It is a common practice when programming in MUMPS for a programmer to leave dead code within the files that contain the MUMPS application. In fact, any number of files are typically present that contain nothing but dead code. MUMPS supports this practice by allowing a function to be called by referencing the name of a function within a named file.

Similarly, a MUMPS database is also typically full of dead and irrelevant data. It is a networked collection of strings organized solely by data manipulation functions within the MUMPS application.

MUMPS was designed to be interpreted. A MUMPS application can be extended interpretively by loading code from a MUMPS database that is then executed. It is common practice to build MUMPS code on the fly by assembling parts of the MUMPS source code dynamically.

MUMPS code has a very large expansion ratio when translated into any other language. A typical single line of MUMPS may contain the equivalent of five to seven separate executable statements in any other language. MUMPS is highly cryptic, with terse acronyms that obscure the meaning of the code. MUMPS programmers happily follow this style by naming variables and callable functions cryptically. MUMPS programmers often brag that they can program rings around other languages because of MUMPS' brevity. But the obscurity of the MUMPS code that is produced makes sustainment and maintenance of MUMPS applications an ongoing challenge.

There is a limited supply of MUMPS programmers and a small community of adherents and followers with a shared interest compared with many of the more modern languages such as C, C++, Java, and C#. Programmers trained in modern languages find MUMPS antiquated, peculiar, and very difficult to read and understand.

There are serious sustainment concerns associated with MUMPS. Open-M (MUMPS) software maintenance and ownership costs are steep. The cost of adding on MUMPS package applications is very high. The choice of hardware platforms applications is restricted compared to modern languages. Outdated feature sets and obscure runtime architecture increases support costs.

## What are the Principle Features of MUMPS?[1]

Modern languages depend heavily upon reusable component frameworks and open source communities to boost programmer productivity through the reuse of components and sharable software. Modern programming practice depends heavily upon languages following established, sound principles of computer science. MUMPS fails to satisfy these principles in virtually every category. The principle characteristic features and their variance with modern practice are briefly summarized in the following list:

- Untyped variables that can be converted automatically between numeric and string — *violates principles of data typing.*
- Multi-dimensional associative arrays that can be mapped directly into the MUMPS hierarchical database, which is implicitly open to every application — *violates principles of data and business logic decoupling.*
- Global variables ("globals") that are mapped to the persistent database maintain value until the application ends and are visible to other running applications — *violates principles of data visibility and information hiding.*
- All variables, whether global or local, support dynamic definition of nested hierarchical data structure that are persisted as sparse arrays giving applications good document handling characteristics — *obfuscates the definition of data by coupling the definition of data with application logic.*

---

[1]M Technology and MUMPS Language FAQ, Part 1/2, Dan Baer, 2007, Version: 1.6, Web posting.

- MUMPS has string handling capabilities, although there are no true regular expressions on strings — *outdated and non-standard string manipulation.*
- MUMPS "indirection" allows strings to be computed at runtime that become part of the executable M program, hence MUMPS is an interpretive language — *an application's runtime characteristics cannot be determined by static analysis.*
- Multi-user/multi-tasking support is built in to the language — *an architectural limitation that restricts scalability compared to modern N-tier architectures.*
- *Real* compilation of an M program into a machine program for the target machine is not feasible *in general* due to MUMPS indirection, which allows substitution of runtime string values as executed source code.
- The XECUTE verb allows execution of a runtime string value as an M program — *thus requiring a complete M interpreter be present at runtime.*
- The $TEXT function allows access to the MUMPS program source text at runtime (to permit its modification) — *violates principles of software assurance and safety.*
- Thus, in principle the whole source must be kept together with the compiled program.

In practice, most M interpreters pre-compile programs into an intermediate, binary form that is more compact to store and more efficient to execute. The requirement of keeping the source text around is relaxed by *conventions* limiting the use of $TEXT to comment lines, or to comments starting with two semi-colons, and M interpreters often offer the option of keeping just these parts of the source (which of course breaks programs not respecting the convention).

## What is FileMan?

FileMan is a set of utilities written by George Timson in the late 1970s and early 1980s using MUMPS to provide a metadata function for MUMPS applications in the form or a persistent repository and active data dictionary. The sparse hierarchical array structure provided by MUMPS permits EHR data records to be defined as arrays that can be indexed by strings to an arbitrary number of levels, which is a natural fit for EHR data. FileMan was first used as the database management system for the development of medical applications for the VA VistA system. FileMan data records survive the termination of the programs by being transparently stored on a permanent storage medium. FileMan uses an active data dictionary to invoke the full interpretive power of the MUMPS language. FileMan utilities support the definition of data structures, menus, security, reports, and forms, allowing someone without tremendous experience in the MUMPS programming language to set up applications quickly.

While a relational database can represent this EHR data, for many years relational database technology did so only with great complexity or inefficiency compared to FileMan. This contributed to a reluctance to abandon FileMan as a data record management system. Today's advanced database technology provides many technical advantages over FileMan. While a properly designed and configured modern RDBMS system can match or exceed FileMan performance, the current impediment to FileMan replacement is the inertia associated with its entrenchment within MUMPS applications, particularly VistA. Whereas most modern languages and RDBMS distinguish between persistent and temporary data, MUMPS applications, built upon FileMan, preserve all data whether it needs to or not. One of the principal technical deficiencies of MUMPS applications using FileMan is the overutilization of persistent data storage. The common failure of MUMPS applications to distinguish between variables that really need to persist from those that should be local is a major technical challenge in any conversion of MUMPS applications.

Because it is work created by the U.S. Federal Government, a copyright cannot be placed on FileMan source code, making it part of the public domain. As the DBMS for VistA, as VistA became widely adopted by the VHA hospital system, FileMan became the de facto DBMS for MUMPS applications, and its use spread across a number of organizations, including commercial products. In 2004 The VHA released FileMan as an open source software system.

## What is VistA?

VistA is an enterprise-wide health information system built around an EHR system used throughout the United States Department of Veteran Affairs, now the Veterans Health Adminstration (VHA). VistA evolved from the Decentralized Hospital Computer Program (DHCP), a program launched in 1978 with the deployment of the initial modules in twenty VA Medical Centers. VistA today is a collection of about 120 integrated software modules written in approximately 2.1 million lines of MUMPS code.

The name VistA was adopted by the VA in 1994. Variations of VistA have been deployed by the Indian Health Services, where it is known as the Resource and Patient Management System (RPMS); and the U.S. Department of Defense (DoD), where it is known as the Composite Healthcare System (CHCS). In the 1980s it was adopted by major hospitals in Finland where it became known as MUSTI and Multilab, which were adopted by medical institutions in Germany, Egypt, Nigeria, and other nations.

By 2001, VistA was the largest single medical system in the United States, providing care to 4 million veterans, employing 180,000 medical personnel, and operating 163 hospitals, over 800 clinics, and 135 nursing homes. By providing EHR capability, VistA is one of the most widely-used EHR systems (EHRS) in the world. A quarter of the nation's population is potentially eligible for VA benefits and services because they are veterans, family members, or survivors of veterans. Nearly half of all American hospitals that have a full implementation of an EHR are VA hospitals using VistA. Because of its award-winning success as a healthcare delivery system, there have been many advocates of VistA to become the basis for the EHR of a universal healthcare plan.

## VistA Modernization Challenges

Given the extraordinary success of VistA, why contemplate modernizing it? VistA's business logic/rules are obscured by MUMPS syntax and architecture; consequently, its ongoing maintenance costs are very steep. VistA is under continuous pressure to evolve to meet new demands, and its existing language, design, and architecture are costly obstacles compromising these objectives. Manual restructuring of MUMPS into a modern language and architecture has proven to be very labor-intensive and extremely high risk. Every attempt to replace VistA has failed. When the numerous deficiencies of MUMPS as a programming language are considered coupled with the obscurity of the language, obsolescence of its GUIs and DBs, lack of modern component framework, and inadequate support for programmers, programmer productivity in MUMPS is much less than modern component-oriented object-oriented languages. These limitations shape the basis of many of the arguments given for VistA's wholesale replacement or redevelopment.

Like most organically grown, highly successful business applications, the business services VistA delivers are vital to the healthcare organizations it supports, but its technical infrastructure (the language, database and platform, user interface) in which it is implemented is highly outdated. If VistA *could* be modernized into a contemporary language, database, and platform, and the business rules and business logic of its core modules could be preserved in a modern object-oriented language, VistA could continue to evolve organically throughout the 21st century, as a cost-effective foundation for the agencies that already use it, and perhaps as the basis of a viable universal EHR system far into the future.

Development of a viable automated approach for VistA modernization is technically challenging. There can be no loss of functionality and no loss of compatibility with interfacing systems during the conversion of the system that manages more than 4.5 million patient records. The EHR database VistA manages is critical and cannot suffer information loss. There can be no possibility of human corruption of VistA application logic, and the database conversion must be perfect. Compared to modern languages, MUMPS is very difficult to analyze using formal language modeling techniques, making the construction of grammar systems, parsers, constrainers, and translators for VistA a major challenge. The VistA database conversion is very complex because MUMPS uses a multi-dimensional/post-relational database, effectively making it a completely free-form database. Despite these challenges, if it can be achieved, the least risk approach to VistA modernization is automated architecture-driven modernization (ADM). This case study documents steps taken toward this objective.

# VISTA MODERNIZATION PROGRESS OVERVIEW

In February 2005 the VHA awarded contract number 4400109256 to the Science Applications International Corporation (SAIC) and The Software Revolution, Inc. (TSRI), of which TSRI received a $451,600 subcontract to develop a demonstrated pilot to prove the feasibility of fully automated conversion of the VistA legacy MUMPS application language into J2EE Java coupled to an Oracle 9i database.

Phase I of the pilot project focused on VTS, a small, simple application with a relatively independent and self-contained "roll-and-scroll" user interface device handler that interfaced with the FileMan database using the ^DIC and ^DIE APIs. In the performance period from November 2004 through November 2005, TSRI developed the MUMPS to Java translator, and ultimately demonstrated 100% automated transformation of FileMan and the VTS module from the VistA system comprising several hundred thousand instructions of MUMPS into functionally equivalent Java/J2EE N-Tier Web application interfacing with the Oracle 9i database exposing VTS GUI as a Web service.

Prior to this contract award, TSRI's prior experience with MUMPS had included conducting a Y2K Independent Verification and Validation (IV&V) of over a million lines of MUMPS code for the Boeing Employees Credit Union (BECU), and the development of a MUMPS to Java translator under contract with SAIC from November 2004 through January 2005 to jump-start the anticipated VHA pilot. TSRI's experience prior to the contract award, as a provider of automated modernization services, was extensive, including more than 30 modernization projects of mission-critical information systems, a success record that expanded to over 60 successful modernization projects by the end of 2009.

In a subsequent technology demonstration undertaken in 2009, TSRI: (1) modernized 2.1 million lines of code of OpenVistA, the open source version of VistA and FileMan, into Java with better than 99.995% automation; (2) generated a Transformation Blueprint™ to document and compare the source MUMPS and target Java/J2EE VistA and FileMan with side-by-side views of the code and UML design and architecture; (3) provided a conclusive demonstration of the technical feasibility of fully automated conversion of VistA; (4) established a comprehensive initial baseline of the modernized VistA system; and (5) provided an extensible open source visual roadmap for planning the eventual modernization of the VistA core system and all of its many variations.

The Transformation Blueprint™ for VistA and FileMan can be found at TSRI's open source Application Blueprint™ and Transformation Blueprint™ portal Web site. Screenshots from the Transformation Blueprint™ are in Figures 12.2 and 12.3.

The 2005 TSRI/SAIC/VHA VTS Pilot and TSRI's subsequent 2009 conversion of the entire OpenVistA and FileMan MUMPS code were steps toward development of an overall ADM process for VistA that were directed toward the following long-term modernization goals:

1. Achieve the use of lower cost platforms (J2EE, .NET) through the modernization of VistA and FileMan into Java or C#
2. Replace MUMPS internals and services with target platform standardized components
3. Map the VistA FileMan database definition into target Schema of a modern relational DB
4. Assure VistA integrity/operational capability during the conversion is uncompromised through the use of a fully-automated transformation process that permits no possibility of human-introduced errors
5. Reduce cost of VistA modernization by conclusively demonstrating the feasibility of its automated conversion
6. Consolidate Core Components of VistA into a set of modernized component libraries in Java (or C#) to improve reusability and eliminate redundancy
7. Incorporate into shared component libraries the diverse VA Hospital unique extensions that exist in 160+ variations at the VA hospital systems that have created site-specific variations of VistA
8. Consolidate redundant functionality in MUMPS modules in the Core Components and hospital Variations into a common baseline
9. Reduce future long-term maintenance costs and total cost of hardware and software ownership by enabling VistA to be maintained in the superior software development environments available in Java/J2EE or C#/.NET

The activities to date have made significant progress toward objectives 1, 4, 5, and 9 from this list. The Future Directions section outlines activities to advance toward the remaining objectives. The upcoming sections discuss progress made to date and the technology, processes, and methods used to achieve it.

## MODERNIZATION TECHNOLOGY AND PROCESS

TSRI's approach to legacy system modernization permits gradual integrated steps within a model-driven modernization methodology. Each step adds to a comprehensive model-based repository of knowledge about the corporate application portfolio and guides subsequent steps in the enterprise application portfolio process. Human hands rarely or never touch the code being modernized. Automation is used whenever practical. Human decision-making is introduced only as necessary to guide automated processes. Modernization is carried out by applying rules to generate Platform-Independent Models (PIM) from legacy application source code. Source code for the modernized applications is derived from Platform-Specific Models (PSM) derived from the PIMs. Any change to the model-driven modernization process is accomplished by modifying rules or models. UML documentation can be generated that supports multiple views of all transformation products. Code models and UML design can be interchanged using XML Metadata Interchange (XMI) with other vendors' tools. JanusStudio™ traces all rules to every modeling object ever touched or created during the transformation process.

At the kernel of the JanusStudio™ are three high-level specification languages: JPGEN™ for defining grammar system and language models, JTGEN™ for defining transformations between these models, and JRGEN™ (a fifth generation artificial intelligence language) for model manipulation and analysis that supports first-order logic and predicate calculus as well as 3GL and 4GL language constructs. For efficiency and portability, JPGEN™, JTGEN™, and JRGEN™ compile into platform-neutral C++ and allow the use of 64-bit multiprocessor LINUX platforms to analyze massive software models using parallel processing. JPGEN™, JTGEN™, and JRGEN™ are compact highly expressive domain-specific languages ideally suited for their roles within the transformation framework.

- JPGEN™ defines compact and efficient grammar systems for mapping application source code into model bases.
- JTGEN™ defines the complex rewrite rules that map between these model bases to ensure that the semantics within a source language are accurately re-expressed within the semantics of a target language.
- JRGEN™ communicates between model bases and alternative representations including design, documentation, software metrics, and visual presentations.

JPGEN™ is TSRI's technology for generating parsers that process code to generate abstract syntax tree (AST) models and printers that generate code from AST models from a grammar specification for a computer language. JTGEN™ is TSRI's technology for automatically recognizing patterns in and transforming AST models. TSRI employs JPGEN™ and JTGEN™ in a disciplined process that transforms the entire legacy application into an Intermediate Object Model (IOM) upon which a sequence of transformation and/or refactoring operations are applied before target code is generated from the model.

**FIGURE 12.1**

*TSRI's JanusStudio™ technology modernization process.*

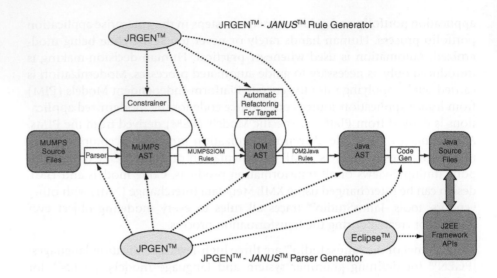

In Figure 12.1 the AST is a memory tree base representation of the system. The Constrainer adds symbol linkage and expression types to AST nodes. The IOM is a TSRI-developed intermediate language into which all source languages are mapped and from which all target languages are generated. The transformation into the Legacy AST model was carried out by a parser generated by JPGEN™ and a constrainer generated by JTGEN™. The transformation between the Legacy MUMPS AST model and the IOM AST model is carried out by MUMPS2IOM transformation rules generated by JTGEN™. The transformation from the IOM to Java is carried out by IOM2Java transformation rules generated by JTGEN™. Refactoring for Java is carried out by language-neutral IOM2IOM refactoring rules and language-pair specific MUMPS2Java rules.

TSRI solved the O (S × T) language transformation combinatorics problem by means of the TSRI IOM Language. The IOM is a language-neutral model into which all legacy source languages are transformed, and from which modern object-oriented target languages are generated. The IOM consists of a set of language constructs common to all languages and serves as a comprehensive foundation for application transformation that supports a unified rather than a fragmented process. Using the IOM as an intermediary, the inherently O (S × T) language transformation problem is reduced to an O (S + T + 1) problem, (where S is the number of source languages, T is the number of target languages, 1 is the IOM) and processes for assessment, documentation, and refactoring are reduced to O (1) problems that are consistently and uniformly solved within the IOM.

The VistA Modernization Process is carried out in four steps:

## Step 1: Assessment and Documentation

TSRI captures and documents the legacy system's "as-is" mode, or Application Blueprint™, providing a detailed evaluation of the existing system's design and architecture. This step creates a language-neutral PIM of the application in the IOM augmented with semantic analysis including control flow, data flow, state model, cause–effect and class model, code complexity metrics, and code redundancy clusters from which an "as-is" UML is generated (via look-back at the MUMPS AST) in various presentation and exchange formats, including Rational Rose compatible XMI. The baseline model, metrics, and documentation support the transformation business case and guide subsequent modernization steps.

## Step 2: Transformation

TSRI automatically rewrites the legacy application from the PIM into object-oriented platform-specific code models (PSM, C++, Java, C#, etc.) and couples it to relational or object-oriented databases. This step transforms and flexibly generates object-oriented code into multiple modern implementation languages, accurately converting all internal and external interfaces. A Transformation Blueprint™ which models the "as-is" and "to-be" code and UML for side-by-side presentation is generated following transformation (see Figures 12.2 and 12.3).

## Step 3: Refactoring

TSRI re-engineers the resulting target language and components to improve the modernized system's design and architecture and enhance performance and maintainability. All semi-automated and automated refactoring operations are carried out against the IOM to generate redesigned code modules and re-architected application tiers. "TO BE" UML is generated and quality metrics are measured continuously for any module within the evolving Transformation Blueprint™.

Automatic refactoring removes dead and redundant code without changing a system's functionality and converts unstructured code into well-structured code and procedural code into object-oriented code.

Semi-automatic refactoring identifies situations within the code or design where customer-provided domain experts can opt to improve design parameters or code structure to improve the object-oriented design.

Custom refactoring operations are tailored and applied efficiently across the entire model-based repository to uniformly upgrade applications in the corporate application portfolio to improve their modular composition, clarify business entities and business rules, and improve access to the business services of enterprise application architectures to better support enterprise business processes.

**FIGURE 12.2**

*OpenVista and FileMan Transformation Blueprints™.*

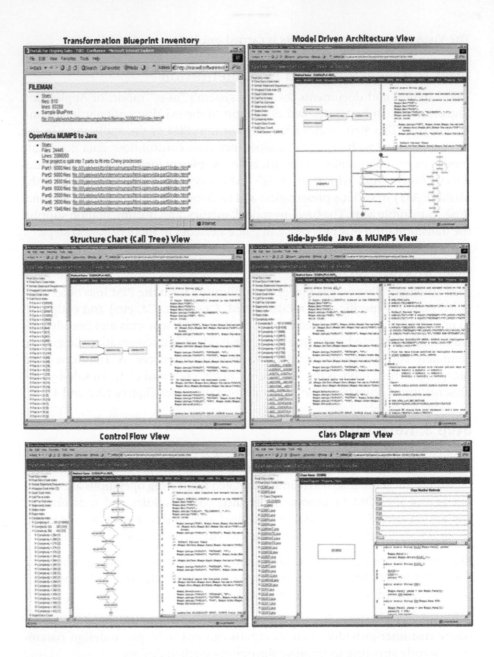

## Step 4: Web-Enablement and Services-Oriented Architectures

TSRI generates applications into Web-enabled and service-oriented architectures (SOA) within multi-tier architectures with componentization for modular reuse, and adaptations and extensions to run as multi-processor

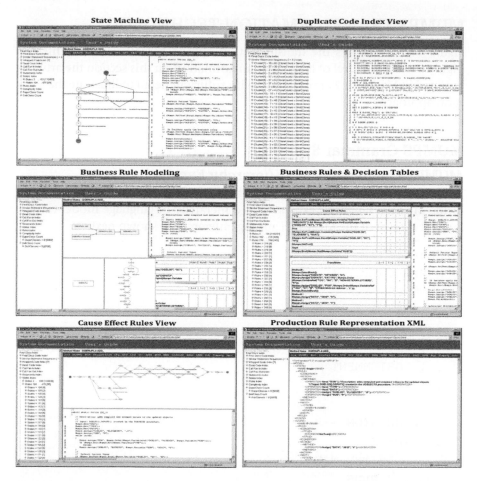

**FIGURE 12.3**

*OpenVista and FileMan Transformation Blueprints™.*

distributed applications using the client's preferred Message-Oriented Middleware (MOM) for inter-process communication and integration with Enterprise Service tiers. Java is generated to run in J2EE, C#, Managed C++, or VB.NET generated to run in .NET. Components of an SOA are derived automatically or semi-automatically. Derived components are segregated into layered, distributed architectures consisting of tiers in the modernized application.

TSRI's JanusStudio™ modernization technology minimizes the testing and implementation costs associated with the redeployment of a modernized information system by minimizing human contact with the code. Changes to code are made by transformation rules. Errors attributable to manual editing and human mistakes are eliminated.

# MUMPS TRANSFORMATION TECHNOLOGY

Figure 12.1 illustrates the transformation approach TSRI uses to achieve a highly automated level of language transformation. In this section the artifacts outlined in Figure 12.2 are described with sufficient detail to illustrate the technical approach.

## MUMPS Grammar System

### MUMPS Language Model Hierarchy Excerpt

The MUMPS Language Model hierarchy consists of more than 110 features of the MUMPS language, expressed as a hierarchy of language model classes. A small excerpt of the MUMPS Language hierarchy is shown next.

```
Hierarchy
MUMPS-OBJECT (
. MUMPS-FILE
. LINE
. COMMAND (
. . SET
. . ASSIGNMENT
. . IF
. . ELSE
. EXPRESSION (
. . INFIX (
. . . ARITHMETIC (
. . . . PLUS
. . . . MODULO )
. . . RELATIONAL (
. . . LOGICAL (
. . . . AND
. . . . OR ) )
```

### MUMPS Extended BNF Grammar Excerpt

The MUMPS Grammar System consists of several hundred extended BNF (EBNF) rules and directives to a parser generator that are used to generate a parser and printer. A very small excerpt of EBNF specification rules for the MUMPS grammar is shown next to illustrate the approach taken to modeling the MUMPS language. The EBNF rules describe the syntax of the SET, PLUS, and AND language constructs.

```
Command

  -> [ Command-Spaces: Spaces ? ("S" | "SET" )
       Command-Postcondition: Postcondition ? " "
       Set-Assignments: Assignment + ","
       ] => SET
Expression
  -> [ Op: Expression "+" Op2: Primary ] => PLUS
  -> [ Op: Expression "&" Op2: Primary ] => AND
```

## Java Grammar System

The Java Grammar System consists of Java Language Model hierarchy and grammar specification. These specifications are used to generate highly efficient C++ parsers and printers for modeling applications transformed from MUMPS via the IOM into the Java language.

### *Java Language Model Hierarchy Excerpt*

The Java Language Model Hierarchy consists of more than 200 features of the Java language, expressed as a hierarchy of language model classes. A very small excerpt of the Java Language Hierarchy is shown:

```
Hierarchy

JAVA-OBJECT (

. COMPILATION-UNIT

. QUALIFIED-IDENTIFIER

. IDENTIFIER

. STATEMENT (

. . IF-STATEMENT

. EXPRESSION (

. . ASSIGNMENT (

. . . SIMPLE-ASSIGNMENT (

. . . ADD ) ) )
```

### *Java Language Model Grammar Excerpt*

The Java Grammar consists of several hundred EBNF rules and directives to a parser generator, which are used to generate a parser and printer. A very small excerpt of EBNF specification rules for the Java grammar illustrates the approach taken to model the Java language:

```
Expression
  -> [ Op1:Expression10 "+" Op2:Expression11 ] =>
ADD
  -> [ Op1:Expression10 "-" Op2:Expression11 ] =>
SUBTRACT

IfStatement ->
  [ "if" IfCondition:ParenthesizedExpression
    ThenStatement:Statement
    [ "else" ElseStatement:Statement ]?
  ] => IF-STATEMENT ;
```

## MUMPS to IOM Transformation

Transformation mapping consists of rewrite rules that are applied to the AST constructs that result from the application of a parser to the sentences of a language. A collection of transformation mapping rules is written that define a set of model-to-model mapping from the original legacy language into the target language. The rule below handles the mapping of the MUMPS PLUS statement from the Mumps AST construct into the IOM AST construct. Much more complex rules than the one shown next are required for transforming more complex language features.

### *Transformation Mappings from MUMPS into the IOM Excerpt*

```
//. . . PLUS
Xform-Mumps-Expression
  ( < mumps::PLUS
      Omitted - TSRI Proprietary > )
    ==>
    < IOM::ADD-EXPRESSION
      Omitted - TSRI Proprietary > ;
```

## IOM to Java Transformation

Transformation mapping consists of rewrite rules that are applied to the AST constructs that result from the application of a parser to the sentences of a language. A collection of transformation mapping rules is written that define a set of model-to-model mapping from the original legacy language into the target language. The rule below handles the mapping from the IOM into Java. Much more complex rules than the one shown next are required for transforming more complex language features.

```
// IO::ADD-EXPRESSION to java::ADD Transformation
Mapping
Jform ( < IOM::ADD-EXPRESSION
          Omitted: TSRI proprietary > )
  ==>
  < java::ADD
    Omitted: TSRI proprietary > ;
```

## MUMPS to Java Code Translation Examples

The transformation between the IOM and the target Java AST is carried out by
the IOM2MUMPS transformation rules generated by JRGEN™. The following
three sections illustrate this process.
This is an example of MUMPS code

```
LEAP(%) ;Check if a Leap year
S:%<1700 %=%+1700
Q (%#4=0)&'(%#100=0)!(%#400=0)
```

### IOM Code

It is translated into this IOM code:

```
LEAP (%)
   ;
  if (% < 1700) then
    % <- (% + 1700);
  endif
  return ((((% % 4) == 0) & (!((% % 100) == 0))) |
  ((% % 400) == 0));
```

### Java Code

The IOM code is translated into this Java code:

```
public static String LEAP_()//Check if a Leap year
  {
    if (M.Bool(M.Less(M.Variable("%"), "1700")))
      M.Assign("%", M.Add(M.Variable("%"), "1700"));
    return M.Or(M.And(M.Equal(M.Modulo(M.Variable("%"),
    "4"), "0"),
    M.Not(M.Equal(M.Modulo(M.Variable("%"),
    "100"),"0"))),
    M.Equal(M.Modulo(M.Variable("%"), "400"), "0"));
  }
```

# MUMPS REFACTORING TECHNOLOGY

Refactoring is the process of changing a software system in such a way that it does not alter the function of the code yet improves its internal structure. When carried out manually, refactoring is applied directly to the source code and is generally a labor-intensive, ad hoc, and potentially error-prone process. In contrast to conventional manual refactoring, TSRI has achieved a highly automated refactoring process characterized by the application of pattern-based transformations to a model of the software rather than to the source code. This approach allows refactoring to be applied reliably and safely on a massive scale as a rigorous disciplined multi-level automated and machine-mediated process.

Automated and semi-automated refactoring is accomplished by transformation rules generated by JRGEN™ that are applied to the IOM AST model to improve its structure before transformation into the target Java AST model. Refactoring operations vary greatly in their granularity and scope. Some refactoring operations are atomic and limited in scope, while others are more complex and composed by applying many more finely-grained refactoring operations to accomplish a larger-grained restructuring objective.

The order of refactoring operations is crucial to assuring their proper application. Some refactoring operations must be done prior to others to establish the appropriate state of the software model for subsequent refactoring operations. Many refactoring operations are application domain neutral and are applied whenever transforming between any procedural and any object-oriented language. Others are language-pair specific and are applied only when transforming between a particular source and target language.

## MUMPS Refactoring Challenges

The MUMPS programming language contains several features that represent technical challenges to automatic transformation:

- Dynamically maintained local variable environment
- Indirection of variable names and various arguments to commands
- Persistent and shared global variable environment
- Indirection of targets of routine calls and control-flow branches
- Control-flow branches that cross routine boundaries
- Execution of dynamically created MUMPS source code

Some of these language "challenges" can be completely solved while others can only be partially solved, with certain extreme uses of the particular feature that need to be handled with less automatic techniques. The solutions to each of the previous translation challenges are outlined in the following section. We follow this with a brief overview of the parts of the MUMPS programming language that are more easily handled by our automated transformation capabilities along with artifacts from our grammar specification systems for MUMPS and Java and transformation specification systems that are used to define the automated software transformation process.

## Dynamically Maintained Local Variable Environment

What are referred to as "local variables" in MUMPS are actually visible to all code in a given MUMPS process, and as such are more similar to global variables in most 3GLs. What makes them different from variables in typical programming languages is that they are created and destroyed dynamically as opposed to being static entities. Additionally, new versions of variables can be created "on top of" previous versions, then later the new versions can be retracted at which time the old versions are restored.

The solution to handling these semantics in a typical programming language such as Java is to develop a data structure capable of representing the names and values of all local variables, including the ability to introduce new versions and later retract them. The primary component of such a data structure would be a map from strings to "values," where the string represents the name of a given variable and the value is either a string or another such map. Add to this a stacking mechanism to allow a new map to be pushed on top of existing maps and later popped off to reveal the previous map, and you have sufficient representational power to accommodate the semantics of MUMPS local variables.

In Java this data structure would be represented with a class, and MUMPS code that sets and retrieves the values of local variables would be translated into calls to methods of this class that manage a data structure as previously described. MUMPS code that creates and destroys local variables is similarly translated into calls to methods that perform the appropriate pushing and popping as described.

## Indirection of Variable Names and Various Arguments to Commands

Part of the design considerations for the solution to handling MUMPS' local variables was the fact that names of variables manipulated by MUMPS code are not always known at compile (or translation) time. The solution to translating assignments and uses of variables with names known only at runtime is addressed by the use of strings to represent the names of local variables in the data structure designed to represent them. This allows the methods written to perform the actual assignments and retrievals to operate on dynamically created strings as the names of the variables referenced. Statically known uses of variables simply translate into passing a literal string for the variable name as opposed to passing the value of some variable or even an expression, which would be the more general situation. What look like subscripts in MUMPS variable references can be considered as "nested" variables used to look up values in the lower level maps that are suggested by the hierarchical nature of MUMPS local variables. So a complete variable reference can be described with a list of string values, the first for the name of the "root" variable, and each subsequent string specifies a subscript value that is used to descend the hierarchy of values rooted at the specified root variable. The resulting value may be a simple string, or a map from strings to values, which can be further subscripted or used in its entirety; for example, by passing it to another routine or a function.

In a few places in the MUMPS language definition, more than just the name of a variable can be indirected, such as an assignment that can have the entire assignment taken from the value of a dynamically constructed string. In these more general uses of indirection, the need for some level of "interpretation" of MUMPS commands and their parts is called for. This aspect of the problem is addressed more fully in the section Execution of Dynamically Created MUMPS Source Code.

### Persistent and Shared Global Variable Environment

Values stored in MUMPS global variables persist beyond the execution of the applications that read and write those values and can be shared across applications and users' systems. Concurrently running applications can communicate and share information by reading and writing MUMPS global variables. Also, "soft" locking can be performed at any level of the global variable hierarchy. Other than that, MUMPS global variables have the same structure as MUMPS local variables; a variable represents a map from strings to values where each value is either a string or another such map.

There is an additional constraint that involves a selected portion of the currently in place global variables, which are managed by the FileMan subsystem. Even though MUMPS global variables can be introduced and removed in a similar fashion to that of MUMPS local variables, there is a set of "by convention" global variables and values that are always present in the current system. This subset has been extracted and retargeted to be available for use via an off-the-shelf DBMS (Caché). This imposes an additional constraint on any solution designed to handle the more general semantics of MUMPS global variables so that a solution must interoperate with the architecture-imposed off-the-shelf DBMS.

The solution to handling MUMPS global variables must be aware of the fixed set of root variables that have been ported to the off-the-shelf DBMS, and the implementation must direct references to those variables to the DBMS through the schema that was extracted as a result of the porting process. References to root variables not within the ported set can be handled with a more general, non-domain-specific mechanism that mirrors the mapping semantics of MUMPS variables without having to know the actual names of the variables and subscripts involved. Additionally, the locking mechanism is modeled by additional relations that can be queried to determine the locked state of any "node" in the global variable hierarchy (outside of the ported set).

## Indirection of Targets of Routine Calls and Control-Flow Branches

Indirection of targets of routine calls and control-flow branches is by far the toughest challenge to automatic translation of MUMPS code to traditional programming languages. The partial solution to this problem is to statically analyze any such "label indirection" in an effort to determine what the set of possible values of the label might be. To the extent that such static analysis succeeds, code to handle the use of the indirect label is generated that performs case analysis over the set of possible label values determined by the static analysis. Additionally, some of the uses of label indirection fall into categories of "clichés" that can be detected by the translator and replaced with structured control-flow constructs in the target language.

Any label indirection situations left over after both the static analysis and the cliché recognition have handled all that they can, are resolved by some amount of manual re-engineering of the affected portions of the original MUMPS code. An additional and related problem caused by dynamically computed labels is labels with offsets that are variable. Such situations can also be handled to some extent by the static analysis and cliché recognition.

## Control-Flow Branches that Cross Routine Boundaries

MUMPS allows "GOTOs" that leave one routine and enter another, which cannot be done in typical programming languages that include Java. The solution to this problem involves either duplicating portions of code that can be determined to be shared by multiple routines, or equivalently, to factor the shared portions of code into separately-callable program units (member functions in the case of Java). Although the duplicating solution is somewhat simpler, it creates additional code that may be undesirable if extensive. Based on the actual quantity of code that is identified by the translator as needing duplication, the factoring solution, while slightly more involved, is necessary to maintain reasonable target code size.

## Execution of Dynamically Created MUMPS Source Code

MUMPS allows execution of dynamically created strings that contain source code for up to one line of MUMPS. To handle this, an interpreter capable of scanning a string containing a MUMPS line of source code was built. This was not difficult, with the exception that any GOTOs in the line being interpreted could not be handled. Since we will already have functions for handling such things as setting and getting the values of local and global variables or creating and destroying new versions of local variables, the interpreter — when it sees MUMPS code that performs these operations — simply makes the appropriate calls with the arguments involved. Expression evaluation is also implemented within the interpreter. Control-flow constructs are recognized and handled by the interpreter implemented in Java with appropriate control-flow constructs.

One exception to this strategy involves MUMPS source code embedded in the subset of the "global variable" database served by the FileMan subsystem. These strings of MUMPS source code are typically used to validate user input from various prompts as the user traverses the menu hierarchy. The approach taken was the one-time translation of these strings into Java program units (member functions) that were then referred to from the database using a dispatch mechanism. MUMPS code that was used to dynamically execute these strings was translated into calls to one-time-translated Java code.

## Brief Overview of Less Difficult-to-Translate MUMPS Language Features

Various MUMPS commands allow file manipulation. These are translated into calls to a functional interface with underlying functionality that was developed to model the semantics of MUMPS file manipulation commands.

Most of the expression operators provided by MUMPS are translated into calls to a library of Java functions built to provide the functionality represented by MUMPS operators. Any MUMPS operators whose semantics Java provides directly with a Java operator are translated into uses of that Java operator.

MUMPS is fairly rich in built-in functions and routines. Uses of these are translated into calls to a library of Java functions built to provide the analogous functionality in Java.

A good example of this kind of feature is MUMPS' structured control-flow constructs, such as the IF and FOR commands. Straightforward translations of this class of construct is performed. The argumentless DO command (with its indented nested substatements) also falls into this category.

Over the course of the project, the more notable challenges were in the Java implementation of the MUMPS language indirection and the Xecute command (X). In a MUMPS program, the Xecute command allows execution of a runtime string value as an M program; indirection allows for the substitution of either the name of a variable or the string argument to a MUMPS command with the runtime string value found in that variable or string argument.

The use of indirection in the VistA/FileMan MUMPS environment is common. Indirection is a powerful language construct that allows programmers to dynamically store string values in variables and arguments and then perform operations on those values in generic manners. This capability is not found in Java. To successfully transform MUMPS programs that contained instances of indirection, the following approach was developed.

Indirection in DO and GOTO commands was handled with a dispatch function taking the string name of the target function. Indirection in variable references was handled by using the string names of variables to access their contents:

- D @X → funDispatch(V("X"))
- G @X → survey and strategize (40 in Voluntary Timekeeping)
- X "LiteralStmt" → LiteralStmt
- X ^DD(2,1) → execVar("^DD(2,1)")
- X expr → exec(expr)
  - Embedded Quit → flag
  - Embedded Do → funDispatch
  - Embedded Goto → static survey, run time detection
- S X = "A" → S("X", "A")
- S @X = Y → S(V("X"), V("Y"))
- S @X = @Y → S(V("X"), V(V("Y")))

## Overview of the More Difficult-to-Translate MUMPS Language Features

### Interpretation

The successful transformation of the Xecute verb required development of a mini-MUMPS interpreter written for Java. This interpreter was invoked with whatever string expression (usually dynamically created) was originally passed to the MUMPS Xecute command.

Utilizing this solution, TSRI develop a 100% automated MUMPS to Java conversion. The approaches described for both indirection and Xecute are available for all future MUMPS transformations as these (and many other) language-specific transformation rules are part of the TSRI core toolset:

- For-loop constructs
- MUMPS indirection
- Use of DO and GOTO with indirection arguments
- G @X, D @X
- Indirection assignment of variables
- S @X=@Y
- Xecute command
- Embedded GOTO statements in execute string
- FileMan APIs

### Handling Indirection, Qualified and Unqualified Locations

A MUMPS system consists of a collection of routines, each in a source file. The name of the routine is taken from the first line of the source file for the routine, which must have a label consisting of the name of the routine.

Within each routine are "local" labels, which may be either called or gone to by either code in the same routine or code in other routines. Such use of a local label from the same routine need not be qualified, but if the label is from another routine the use must be qualified with the name of the containing routine.

Unqualified locations (references to labels) in MUMPS are identifiers having the same name as the label referred to. Qualified locations are suffixed by the name of the qualifying routine and separated from the name of the label with an up-arrow character. References to the top label of a routine may also be made, in which case the label name is dropped and just the up-arrow is followed by the routine name.

It is also possible to have a call or goto with a target that is an indirection and therefore is not statically known by the translator. These may refer to either locations within the routine containing the reference or to locations in other routines. These indirect references take the form of a string value whose contents abide by the description of references in the previous section.

A final context in which references to locations may occur is that of $TEXT calls. The result of such a call is the line of MUMPS code at the referred location. An additional complexity is that these references may contain offsets, which are integer values that cause the reference to refer to nearby lines of MUMPS source code: an offset of 1 refers to the line after the one indicated by the location, an offset of 2 refers to the line 2 lines after the indicated line, etc.

### Use of Dispatch Functions

Each MUMPS routine becomes a Java class in the TSRI global package. There is one additional class, MUMPS Application, which contains boilerplate methods such as main and some dispatching functions to be described later in this chapter.

Within each Java class that represents a MUMPS routine, there is a method for each entry point (label) contained in the MUMPS routine. Each method takes no arguments and returns a string. The MUMPS code present in the routine between the label for the entry point and the next label (or end of routine) is represented in this function. Additionally, there is a second method for each entry point that may take a list of Parms (how Java passes parameters in the current architecture) that handles the semantics of when the entry point is called (as opposed to gone to).

This callable entry point does the appropriate Enter call (as is currently done), handles the parameters, then calls the "inner" entry point method described earlier to perform the code for the entry point; whatever value that returns is then returned from the callable method as well and funneled through the MUMPS API Return method (as is done now) to undo the Enter call. There are also overloaded versions of the callable method that take varying numbers of single Parm arguments from none up to the number of declared parameters for the entry point (if any).

This allows us not to have to copy code that is gone to from one routine to another, as is done now. Instead, any goto to an entry point is translated into a return of the value returned from a call to the "inner" method for that entry point. This gets inside of the Enter/Return behavior since the entry point was gone to rather than called. When the called inner entry point (eventually) returns, that value is the value that the original MUMPS code would have returned, despite any number of GOTOs to labels either local or in another routine. The one downside to this approach is that one level of stack depth is used for each of these gotos, so if there is a loop formed by these GOTOs that executes many times, there could possibly be problems with running out of call stack depth.

With this architecture, there are no GOTOs at all to eliminate, with one minor exception: When a so-called DO block of code that is not contained in a loop does a QUIT, the result is a goto to the end of the block, and this kind of goto could be eliminated at translation time in favor of an if-then-elsewhere if the skipped code is in the else block.

### *Additional Methods per Routine Class*

These are the methods in the Java class for a given MUMPS routine:

- Call Dispatcher: Takes a string naming an entry point local to the routine and a list of Parms, and returns the string that results from calling the named entry point's "callable" method with those arguments.

- Goto Dispatcher: Takes a string naming an entry point local to the routine and returns the string that results from calling the named entry point's "inner" method (not the callable method).

- Text Dispatcher: Takes a string naming an entry point local to the routine and a string specifying an integer offset, and returns the MUMPS source code present at the specified location.

The "inner" methods are given names distinguished from the callable methods by a trailing underscore character. Additional "Javifying" of the MUMPS names consists of turning percent characters into "pc_", and prefixing any name starting with a digit with an underscore character.

The translation would need to know only the following information of a system-wide nature:

- Which entry points are defined within each routine and the routine names.
- Which labels have their text asked for (possibly with offsets) via $TEXT.

There is no need for a goto information file for handling indirect GOTOs. Similar information is still required to be able to anticipate which labels are involved in $TEXT queries, but the analysis required to determine this information proved to be far simpler than that required by the indirect GOTOs.

An initial pass is made over the set of MUMPS routines to be translated with a special purpose MUMPS analyzer that only needs to determine the previous two sets of information, which need to only go through the Constrainer. The resulting files can be used in a main translation phase that can operate on each MUMPS routine in isolation if necessary. This greatly alleviates the time and (mainly) space requirements for translating large collections of MUMPS routines. The information extracted by the preliminary pass is also fairly static in the sense that the preliminary passes do not generally need to be run every time the main translation pass occurs.

## Main Class

As previously mentioned, there is one main class that is generated from just a small part of the information gathered about the set of MUMPS routines in the preliminary pass recently described. In fact, all the final translation pass knows is the names of the routines for which it is to generate the various dispatching functions. This boilerplate MUMPS Application class contains the following methods:

- Main: Takes the command line arguments and uses the Call Dispatcher to execute the routine (or entry point within a routine) specified by the first command line argument, passing the subsequent arguments as parameters.

- Call Dispatcher: Takes a string naming a qualified location, and a list of Parms, determines the individual routine and entry point names, and returns the value resulting from calling the Call Dispatcher in the class for the indicated routine, with the name of the entry point as a string, and the passed Parms.

- Goto Dispatcher: Takes a string naming a qualified location, determines the individual routine and entry point names, and returns the value resulting from calling the Goto Dispatcher in the class for the indicated routine, with the name of the entry point as a string.

- Text Dispatcher: Takes a string naming a qualified location, and a string specifying an integer offset, determines the individual routine and entry point names, and returns the value resulting from calling the Text Dispatcher in the class for the indicated routine, with the name of the entry point as a string, and the passed offset.

The three Dispatcher functions also each have an overloaded version which takes an additional argument that specifies the name of the calling routine. This is used to qualify any indirect entry point names that are not already qualified.

## Additional Automated Refactoring Details

When application code contains a call of a static location that is contained in the set of routines translated (which is known from the information created in the preliminary pass), a call to the "callable" version of the method for that entry point is made. For a call to an indirect location, the main Call Dispatcher is called with the value of the indirection as a string along with the name of the calling routine as a string (and any parameters) in case the indirect location is local and needs to be qualified before it can be dispatched.

For a static goto, a return of a call to the "inner" version of the method for the entry point occurs. For an indirect goto, a return of a call to the GotoDispatcher with the value of the indirection occurs (also passed is the name of the "calling" routine for use in any needed qualification).

Sometimes an indirection is only partial where the routine name is static and only the entry point is dynamic. In that case the main Dispatcher function is skipped, and the call is made directly to the routine-specific Dispatcher function (Call or Goto), assuming the routine in question is among the set of routines translated.

Finally, when a $TEXT query involves a static label that is local to the calling routine, or the same but with a static offset (integer literal), the text can be substituted directly (as is done now). $TEXT queries of such static labels in other routines are handled by that routine's Text Dispatcher function to maintain the ability to translate a single MUMPS routine in isolation. Giving up on this requirement allows such $TEXT queries to be handled the same as with local labels. But in either translation scenario, static labels with dynamic offsets and dynamic labels (indirections) with or without offsets are handled via the main Text Dispatcher function.

For all of the previously mentioned situations, if the reference is to an undefined entry point, it is handled via the Dispatcher functions (local or main), since this allows the resulting code to compile and link successfully. Since all of the Dispatcher functions cause failure messages when they are unable to dispatch successfully, the missing entry point is detected at runtime. The translator indicates a warning for each instance of this type of situation.

# VTS PILOT SYSTEM ARCHITECTURE AND INTERFACE

This section describes TSRI's modernization effort of the VTS modernized system's architecture and how TSRI preserved interfaces between the modernized VTS and the external systems with which it interfaces.

The next section describes the method by which interfaces were preserved, thus allowing interoperability of the modernized system and any external systems. Following that, the section System Architecture describes the modernized system's architecture. This architecture provides significant scalability benefits. Although the system resulting from this effort was deployed on only two machines, the architecture supports further distribution to additional machines if required to meet future requirements.

## Replacement of User Terminal Interfaces with Web Browser Connections

User terminal interfaces are to be replaced by Web browser connections. These browser connections are made within a LAN, through a virtual private network (VPN), from external Internet sites using SSL, or combinations of these modes. Application behavior remained the same regardless of the chosen network security scheme. HTML forms presented by Web server scripts provided screen I/O similar to the original Telnet sessions.

The new interface did not aim to provide the full capability of a Telnet session outside of the VTS application context, i.e., it did not provide the operating system shell capabilities of a Telnet session. The user can not create, modify, delete, run, or print arbitrary applications or files as in a Telnet session. Required system entry points are presented in a new master menu to the user's Web browser. This menu also provides access to certain system administration capabilities. User access level, based upon the user id, determines the availability of different system components.

## System Architecture

The architecture for the new system is an N-Tier system designed for modularity and flexibility. Figure 12.4 shows the major system components. Briefly, the existing system is transformed to the new design as follows:

- Original MUMPS code is transformed into Java while preserving exact code functionality.
- User Telnet sessions and terminal I/O are replaced by Web connections and html pages.
- Persistent MUMPS global data items are stored in a relational database accessed through a JDBC-based API.

The nature of such an N-Tier system allows for different components to run on different computing platforms and at different physical locations. For example, each of the tiers (A through D) can exist on different computers. Application processes in tier C can also be distributed across multiple platforms. Such flexibility allows for future growth and reorganization without major modification to the system.

### *Data Tier A*

This tier is implemented in the form of a relational database server. The server is required to support JDBC. The database contains only application data. No business logic in the form of stored procedures, triggers, or any other programmatic interfaces is encoded in this database. The database is implemented using standard data types and table formats so that it can be easily ported to different database servers.

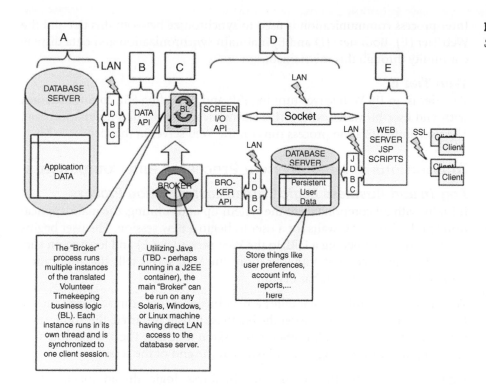

**FIGURE 12.4**
*System architecture.*

### Data Access Tier B

This tier is the interface layer between the business logic code and the Data Tier (A). It is written in Java using JDBC. Its function is to perform I/O and persistence operations of the original application. Such layering isolates the business logic code from implementation details of the data storage.

### Business Logic Tier C

This tier contains all Java code translated from MUMPS. Formerly separated processes are grouped into a single Java application with logic to be invoked separately via a menu. These processes are invoked and managed by a master "broker," enabling multiple simultaneous, multi-threaded execution instances. This tier interfaces with Data Access Tier (A) and the Presentation Tier (D) through API isolating the business logic from screen I/O and database implementation details. All of this is written in Java.

### Presentation Tier D

This tier encompasses all functionality related to generating the user interface. To accomplish this, it has a "Screen API" written in Java to set up and manipulate screen I/O data. There is also a database that stores persistent information about a user, such as their account profile, preferences, generated reports, etc.

Inter-process communication is used to synchronize between this tier and the Web Tier (E). Both tiers (D and E) maintain synchronization and data display continuity through this mechanism.

### Web Tier E

This tier is an IIS Web server running JSP and providing SSL communication with end-user browser sessions. It communicates with the Presentation Tier. The user authentication process runs on the Web server in this tier.

## Illustrations of Major System Processes and Components

### Log-in and Business Logic Thread Instantiation Process

Initially with all components of the system up and running, the main application "broker" in tier C waits for a user to begin a new session. The user begins a new session by opening a URL to the Web server (tier E) and logging on successfully. After successful authentication, the Web server tells the application broker that a new session has begun.

The application broker instantiates a new business logic thread based on the log-on authentication level. After the business thread is started, the application broker continues to scan for other new session requests. There is a reaper that cleans up the business logic thread when at the end of the session.

Figure 12.5 depicts the log-in and business logic thread instantiation process.

**FIGURE 12.5**

*Log-in process.*

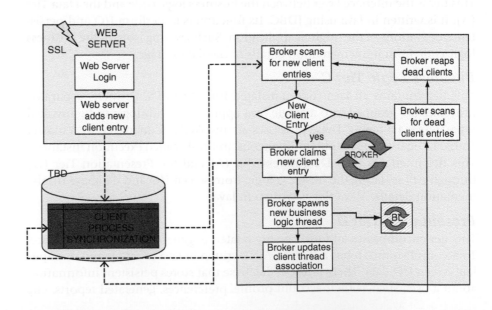

## Log-Out Process

An application session can end in several ways. The first occurs when the business logic comes to an end and returns. The second occurs when the user terminates the browser session by either clicking a "log-out" button or simply closing the Web browser. The third occurs when the browser session has been idling for too long and the Web server automatically terminates it.

Figure 12.6 shows an overview of the log-out process.

## Application Database Access

Figure 12.4 depicts the system and database access logic. The database access tier sits between the business logic code and the database. It is written in Java using JDBC and performs I/O and related persistence operations of the original application.

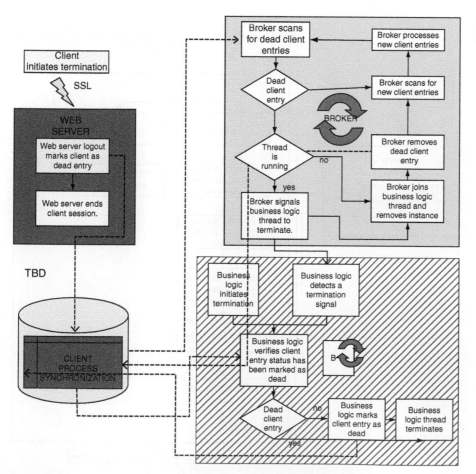

**FIGURE 12.6**

*Log-out process.*

### Screen (terminal)I/O

The user interacts with the application using a secure Web browser. Besides the initial log-in screen, the application screens are presented as a succession of HTML forms that display text information. Around this text area are other HTML graphics and buttons such as the VistA logo or whatever the user wants, the log-out button, and the "help" button. The help button may be used to provide usage and contact information. There is also a list of links to reports generated by the current user. For each user, these reports persist from one session to another until explicitly deleted by the user. The user can download these files to his local machine for viewing or printing. Figure 12.7 depicts the screen I/O process.

During an interactive process, the application logic displays something on the screen by invoking the `.io_Put ()` method of a screen API object, passing to it the text to be displayed and position information. The screen API collects these

**FIGURE 12.7**

*Screen I/O.*

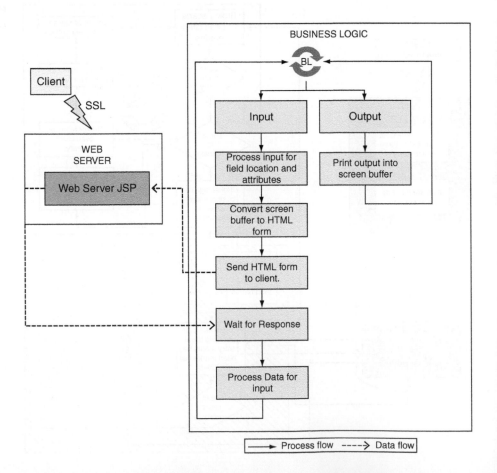

display messages and builds up a screen buffer. Once the application issues a "flush" command or requests a user input with the `.io_get()` method, the screen API completes the screen image in a buffer and generates a corresponding HTML form. It then sends this output request to the Web server. The Web server (tier E) sends the form data to the user Web browser.

If the previous screen ended with a request for input, once the user enters a value into the input field and submits the form, the Web server sends the input data back to the application. The screen API, which has been waiting for a user input, copies the input value into the application variable associated with the original `.io_Get()` method.

## VTS PILOT CONCLUSION, LESSONS LEARNED, AND RECOMMENDATIONS

On August 16, 2005, the SAIC and TSRI project team demonstrated conversion of the VTS MUMPS module of the VistA system to senior VA IT leaders[2] in San Diego. This demonstration included the live transformation of several hundred thousand instructions of MUMPS code constituting the VTS and the FILEMAN DB systems into an N-tier Java/J2EE architecture, directly followed by execution of the transformed code as a Web application in the Web server application framework described in the previous section. Discussions ensued wherein SAIC and TSRI were requested by the senior VA IT management present to prepare a "lessons learned" section outlining project findings and enumerate a set of recommendations for a Phase II pilot and possible broader program preliminary to full-scale conversion.

> Events overtook these plans when congressional cuts to the VHA budget at the beginning of the 2006 budget year to support Iraq war funding precluded the possibility of continuing the planned Phase II of the MUMPS Conversion Pilot and possible follow-on conversion.

---

[2]VA Attendees included Robert N. McFarland, Assistant Secretary for Information and Technology; Craig B. Luigart, Associate Deputy Assistant Secretary for Policy, Portfolio Oversight, and Execution, Office of Information and Technology; Robert M. Kolodner, M.D., Acting Deputy Chief Information Officer for Health and Acting VHA Chief Health Informatics Officer; Scott Cragg, Associate Deputy Assistant Secretary for Enterprise Architecture; Pedro Cadenas, Associate Deputy Assistant Secretary for Cyber and Information Security; Jim Demetriades, Chief Health Information Architect of the Veterans Health Administration's Office of Information, Jeff Shyshka, Regional Chief Information Officer, Veterans Health Administration's Department of Veterans Affairs, San Francisco, CA; Ray Sullivan, Chief Information Officer, VA Northwest Health Network; Dave Eaton, Assistant Director for Program Management (282), Vocational Rehabilitation, and Employment Service; Ross Smith, Director, Enterprise Architecture Technology Staff; William "Bill" L. Miller, Director, Hines Information Center.

Upon completion of Phase I of the pilot, the TSRI and SAIC team had successfully transformed, with an automated code conversion percentage of 100%, the vast majority of the MUMPS language syntax and programming constructs/complexities, as well as significant portions of VistA FileMan APIs.

The Phase II conversion of the Time and Attendance application would require the team to convert to ScreenMan. However, as envisioned, Phase II of the pilot would not have addressed all of the elements/challenges required to convert the entire VistA application suite. This section presents the "lessons learned" by the conversion team during Phase I of the MUMPS Conversion Pilot, and enumerates tasks ordered by priority of an extended Phase II pilot that would address the broader set of technical challenges associated with the automated conversion necessary to undertake the entire VistA application suite. For each task a brief technical discussion is presented with benefits and rationale for consideration. While the list is comprehensive, it may not be exhaustive, and additional issues would likely have been discovered during a follow-on pilot that were not previously envisioned by the team:

1. Database performance enhancement
2. Semi-automated use case capture and automated "use case modeling" documentation
3. Relational data model enhancement
4. Service-oriented architecture (SOA) enhancement
5. Healthevet SOA interoperability
6. Relational FileMan
7. Automated business rule extraction
8. Clinical application modernization and RPC Broker with HL/7
9. Integration of applications manually-converted to Java

## Database Performance Enhancement

The database utilization design pattern of the MUMPS VistA application introduces a severe performance penalty when used in modern Java relational database re-implementation. To correct these performance problems the process for deriving the Java code from the VistA MUMPS code should be modified by a refactoring to reduce the excessive use of the RDBMS server for accessing data elements that were previously FileMan DB globals in the MUMPS application. The existing conversion process should be modified to automatically refactor designated "globals" into persistent Java types. Refactoring to eliminate inappropriate use of the MUMPS database utilization design pattern would reduce the load on the RDBMS server and would improve overall performance.

The primary strategy to improve the performance of this interface is to find ways to minimize round-trips to the RDBMS and to minimize the data flowing across this interface. To accomplish this, the team identified several areas of investigation:

- It may be that there are MUMPS global variables that are read only, or at least are only written by a system administrator–type user to configure the system. These could be moved out of the RDBMS into a configuration file that is read by the application at startup time. Subsequent accesses to these variables would use the values from the configuration file rather than retrieving it from the RDBMS.

- A particularly expensive operation in the transformed system is the $ORDER intrinsic. The design of the RDBMS schema was made to provide better performance of inserts at the expense of $ORDER. It may be that an overall performance increase can be achieved by revising the schema to include linked list information that significantly reduces the cost of $ORDER with a slight penalty for inserts.

- There may be instances of temporary data associated with a particular user's session being stored in MUMPS globals. Since these data have only the life span of the current session, it could be moved off of the database and stored within the application.

- Currently JDBC is used to access the RDBMS to provide RDBMS vendor independence. All of the JDBC interface code is isolated into a single module. It may be possible to provide implementations of this module that are RDBMS-vendor unique and use proprietary, but higher performance, interfaces to the vendor's RDBMS. Since the affected code is isolated to one module, switching vendors simply entails using a different version of this module.

- There may be a way to reduce the round-trips to the RDBMS by adjusting the buffering between the application and RDBMS to bring more records across in a single trip in anticipation of their future need, under certain circumstances.

Benefits:

- Improved performance and system response for end users and batch processing.

Refactoring Strategies

- Setup for Performance Optimization: Engineering support during alpha release of JanusStudio™ MUMPS Performance Optimization task.
- Move Configuration Globals into Config File: Detect which global variables are essentially of a read-only nature and move these into a configuration file.
- Optimize Performance of $ORDER Intrinsics: Revise the RDBMS schema to improve $ORDER performance.
- Make Temporary Globals into Application Globals: Detect global variables serving as locals and convert them into locals.

- Replace JDBC Interface with Native RDBMS I/O: Implement native RDBMS interface for Oracle.
- Buffer Data between RDBMS and Application: Experiment with adjusting buffering between the RDBMS and the application to improve performance.
- Other Optimizations: Investigate and implement other potential optimizations.

## Semi-Automated Use Case Capture Automated "Use Case Modeling" Documentation

"Use Case" Models were produced manually for Phase I. The VA expressed a desire to have Use Cases produced automatically. After considerable investigation, the project team concluded that it was not possible to produce Use Case documentation through a fully automated process. Some degree of manual intervention would always be required. Several approaches seem viable:

Option 1: **Dynamic Trace Capture Approach**: Each Use Case Scenario is executed by a VA functional analyst(s) and trace output is captured. The captured trace outputs will then serve as input to a system to be developed by TSRI that applies the traces to the MUMPS code base, determines the Prompt Locations traversed by the execution represented in the trace output, and generates as output a Use Case Analysis Report for each Use Case Scenario traced.

Benefits:

- Use Case Scenarios are specified more explicitly via a single path through the portion of the system of interest, resulting in just the paths of interest, compared to Option 2, which can only generate all possible paths within the specified segment of the system.

Option 2: **Behavior Model Analysis Approach**: A behavior trace output is captured during actual use of a subject system or subsystem. The behavior trace is automatically correlated with a behavioral model of the application code. An analyst working with the behavior trace completes a Use Case Analysis Report by supplying descriptions of each distinct step in the behavior step that are combined with user inputs and the system outputs captured in the behavior trace. A model of all execution traces steps, user inputs, system outputs, and analyst descriptions is managed to prevent duplication and facilitate creation of partitioned and hierarchical Use Cases.

Benefits:

- The manual effort associated with capture of each Use Case scenario is minimized because, except for descriptions of step names provided by the analyst, Use Case scenarios are captured as a by-product of an expert user exercising the system through its behavior sequences. The resulting reports will contain indications of the input by the user that caused the next part of the path to be taken (to the extent that the user's input is echoed by the system) as opposed to Option 2, which is a static analysis of the code alone and cannot determine the user input that should be associated with each branch following a decision point. The resulting reports will (optionally) contain indications of the output by the system between Prompt Locations.

**Option 3: Static Path Analysis Approach**: Collections of Use Case Scenarios are specified by the Conversion Team or a VA functional analyst(s) via Entry/Exit Points, along with optional Prune Points (parts of the system to exclude from the analysis), and these Entry/Exit/Prune Point specifications serve as input to a system, to be developed by TSRI, that determines the statically determinable set of paths through the MUMPS code base for each set of Entry/Exit/Prune Points and the Prompt Locations present along those paths, and then generates as output a set of Use Case Analysis Reports, one for each possible path.

Benefits:

- The manual effort of driving the system through each Use Case Scenario can be eliminated from the overall effort of generating the Use Case Analyses. However, considerable, if not more, manual effort will still be expended to determine the Entry/Exit/Prune Points and the Prompt Locations.

**Option 4: Static Analysis Approach**: The set of statically-determinable paths is derived through automated analysis of a static behavioral model of the system. An analyst inspects and documents each discrete statement Sequence, Entry, Exit, and Prune Points to create notations required in a Use Case Analysis Report. A set of Use Case Analysis Reports will be produced, one for each possible path.

Benefits:

- The manual effort of driving the system through each Use Case Scenario is eliminated; but manual effort is expended to describe the Steps, Entry, Exit, and Prune Points and the Prompt Locations and effort is expended to prune paths that are infeasible. If less than 100% automated Use Case generation is still of interest, it is more important to capture the normative Use Cases rather than to consider the vastly larger set of all possible Use Cases.

- Will produce Use Cases that more closely resemble those produced by a human.

- Captures Use Cases as a side effect of user exercising the system while actual runtime behavior is unobtrusively monitored, recorded, and later documented as a Use Case.

- Allows the Use Case Analyst to spend time documenting only the realistic Use Cases of the system's actual behavior whereas under Option 2 the Use Case Analyst must spend a lot of time pruning from the set of many Use Cases considered, which would never actually occur in practice.

## Relational Data Model Enhancement

The VistA FileMan database will be analyzed to identify those characteristics of the FileMan hierarchical database management system that can be incorporated into the VistA relational database model. Those characteristics will include such attributes of FileMan as indices, cross-references, and data types. Other features of FileMan will be studied and designed into the relational VistA database model where appropriate and compatible with the relational model. For those features of FileMan that are critical to the preservation of the embedded application logic contained in FileMan data dictionaries, but are incompatible with a normalized database schema (such as FileMan MUMPS input transforms), design work will be performed to ensure that the application logic is transformed into appropriate Java classes that will be invoked as methods as part of the transformation process.

The design of the VistA relational database model will ensure compatibility with the VistA FileMan data structures, as well as with the transformed VistA Java code with no loss of application logic or business rules. For the VistA relational database design, FileMan files will map to equivalent relational tables. Within the FileMan files, the fields will map as columns in the corresponding relational tables. The FileMan field data types will be modeled as comparable relational data types. FileMan file entries will be mapped as rows into the appropriate relational tables. FileMan indices and other technical attributes will be analyzed and incorporated into the relational database design as appropriate and warranted for performance considerations.

Benefits:

- The relational form will greatly simplify database and application maintenance by allowing employment of general and accepted RDBMS practices.

- RDBMS vendor independence: Allows the VA to implement the VistA relational database on any commercial-off-the-shelf (COTS) RDBMS system. The database model will be implemented to not include vendor proprietary code or syntax.

- Development: Provide the basis for future development of applications using standard RDBMS development technologies.

- Maintenance: Allow for general and DBA maintenance activities using COTS and industry-standard RDBMS practices.

Strategy:

- The application and database conversion process will be enhanced to replace the multi-dimensional relational model with a true relational database model using a combination of automated refactoring and semi-automated refactoring operations applied to the code and database.

- The MUMPS multi-dimensional database design pattern persists in the current Java conversion. This task will investigate and develop a set of refactoring methods that can be applied synchronously to the application logic and the database structure and data.

- The Java application code database access and manipulation methods and the Oracle database structure and contents will be redesigned and replaced using a combination of automated and semi-automated refactoring operations.

## SOA Enhancement

The automated conversion process will enhance the exposure of interfaces to an SOA for top-level classes and methods and integrate these produced services within the VA's soon-to-be-published SOA. A suitable MUMPS application will be transformed to generate SOA objects and services for the derived Java code. The SOA services will be integrated and made interoperable within the VA's target SOA.

Benefits:

- Leverages existing VistA applications to achieve interoperation with existing SOA service layers in a consistent, efficient, and maintainable process thus exposing modern Java applications derived from the VistA legacy data and application logic to the HealtheVet architecture.

- Preserves investment the VA has made in its legacy business process by exposing it and making it interoperable with the service layers of the VA HealtheVet SOA.

Strategy:

- Extend JanusStudio™ support SOA Interface Generation.

## HealtheVet SOA Interoperability

Analysis and design will be performed to identify object model architecture that interoperates with the HealtheVet SOA. The objective will be for the transformation of the MUMPS VistA code to generate objects and services that will interoperate with the target SOA. Joint analysis of the existing HealtheVet SOA services will be performed with VA system architects for identification of those services that can be utilized into the design of the transformed system object model. Potential services will also be identified as part of the design effort to expose the HealtheVet architecture as a by-product of the VistA transformation. An example of a possible service layer that could be candidate for design and development as part of the transformation is the database services. This will require focused interaction with the VA architects.

Benefits:

- Leverage existing VA HealtheVet SOA services: Interoperation with existing SOA service layers will provide a consistent, efficient, and maintainable architecture.

- Exposure of the VistA legacy data and application logic to HealtheVet architecture: The investment the VA has made in its legacy business rules and logical data layouts will be preserved, exposed, and interoperable with the service layers of HealtheVet.

## Relational FileMan

For the transformed VistA Java code to accommodate the VistA relational database model, a relational version of FileMan must be developed. The relational version of FileMan will provide data services that interact with the VistA relational database. Software engineering will be performed to make the transformed Java version of FileMan compatible with the new relational data structures. This new version of Relational FileMan will be designed and re-engineered so that the FileMan APIs are all compatible with SQL and operations, as well as with the normalized VistA relational database model. This re-engineering of FileMan will include automatic transformation of all FileMan APIs to analogous Java APIs.

The design and development of Relational FileMan through automated processes will require the systematic study and analysis of the existing FileMan APIs. This analysis will involve the identification, through automated processes, of all references to MUMPS global syntax in the FileMan DI* routines. Refactoring design work will be performed for replacing all MUMPS global operations with analogous relational operations within the FileMan API routine set. This will involve replacing the intrinsic MUMPS functions ($Order,

$Next, $Query, $P, etc.) that operate on the VistA globals with analogous relational capabilities as part of the transformation.

Strategy:

- MUMPS global Sets, Reads, Kills, etc., will be replaced with their equivalent SQL Insert, Select, Delete, statements and so forth.

- Also included will be the design work for automatically transforming the application logic in the FileMan data dictionaries into Java methods that are invoked when operating on the appropriate relational data structures.

- Additionally, patterns on the use of the FileMan APIs within the VistA application code will be analyzed for identifying the appropriate analogous relational operations when invoking the Java version of the FileMan APIs.

- This design and development engineering for the relational form of the FileMan code that operates against the normalized VistA relational database will be incorporated into the automated transformation process as part of the refactoring process.

Benefits:

The benefits of implementing a relational version of FileMan are

- No loss of VistA application logic: Business rules and application logic embedded in the FileMan data dictionaries will be preserved by moving that logic out of the database and into methods contained within Java classes.

- Eliminates MUMPS code: MUMPS code embedded in the database will be eliminated. More generic programmer skill sets will be utilized for development and maintenance of the code set.

- Java development and maintenance: FileMan Java APIs can be used for development and maintenance by Java programmers.

## Automated Business Rule Extraction

With the awareness that the VHA's ultimate goal is a distributed service-oriented business-rule system, the Conversion Team proposed to develop a capability to extract business rule and business process from the existing MUMPS applications for export into a standards-based distributed-services-oriented vendor-neutral architecture backplane. The extraction of business rules from existing applications entails separating the code, data, and logic that is associated with "technical" implementation details from the code, data, and logic associated with "business" decisions, business entities and business processes. Both the technical as well as the business code of the legacy system must be re-engineered to create a functionally-equivalent replacement.

The code associated with business decisions has to be re-engineered into well-structured business rule sets that can be exported into a suitable business-rule engine, whereas code associated with embedded business processes must be re-engineered into business-process descriptions suitable for export to a business-process engine. Finally, the code associated with the legacy system technical implementation has to be re-engineered or replaced with replacement services of a target language and platform.

Benefits:

The key goals/benefits of this proposed new tasking are to

- Demonstrate the technical feasibility of highly automated extraction of business rules, business processes, and technical service modules that conform to industry-based standards

- Demonstrate their export into a vendor-neutral distributed SOA services backplane

- Achieve an SOA services backplane for business rule, business process, and technical service invocation that is fully standards based and independent of any specific business-rule engine or business-process engine

Strategy:

Building upon the code transformation and modeling accomplished in Phase I, the following semi-automated process for business rule and process extraction will be established:

- Employ semi-automated domain analysis (with a domain expert in the loop) to separate technical domain from business domain

- Code instrumentation (with a programmer in the loop) to separate code associated with business decision points from code associated with business process flow and code associated with technical support services

- Re-engineering to transform code associated with business decision points into business rule sets suitable for export into business rule engines

- Re-engineering to transform code associated with business processes into business process models suitable for export to a business process engine

- Re-engineering to transform technical services code into target technical services modules

- An XML generator to export business processes, business rules, and SOA service modules in an XML format consistent with Object Management Group (OMG) standards

- An XML reader to import business process, business rule, and technical services modules into an SOA services backplane

- A distributed SOA services backplane with interfaces that simulate invocation of business-rule engine, business-process engine, and technical services modules

Invocation of business rule sets, business processes, and technical service modules will be simulated to decouple BRE and BPE product selection and integration from this task.

## Clinical Application Modernization and RPC Broker with the HL/7 Server

The VA may wish to augment the currently identified Phase II application (Employee Timekeeping and Attendance) with a VistA clinical application that interacts with VistA Order Entry, as well as utilizes external interfaces, such as HL7 and RPC Broker. The transformation of clinical application modules that exercise more of the capabilities and interfaces (those that exercise cross-cutting functionality) within VistA will advance the automated transformation and modernization processes of the VA's legacy system forward enough to assess readiness for production deployment. Critical interfaces to the VistA legacy system, such as HL/7 messaging and RPC Broker communication with CPRS, will require integration with Health*e*Vet SOA that will be transparent to the end users. This will accelerate production-level integration with the SOA and modernization of legacy VistA through automated methods.

Benefits:

- Able to assess any next steps for production-level automated modernization
- Allows for further automated transformation of any VistA legacy module
- Addresses any patient safety issues with automated transformation processes

## Integration of Applications Manually Converted to Java

TSRI will build a Java front end for its JanusStudio™ toolset. This will allow JanusStudio™ to consume Java, map it into the toolset's IOM, document the Java, perform refactoring operations on that Java, and re-emit the Java in a more maintainable form.

Benefits:

- Documentation can be created for the Java-to-Java output similar to the documentation created for the MUMPS-to-Java process.

- Refactoring operations could be applied to the manually-created Java to make it compatible with the automatically-created Java and/or to map it into some prescribed architecture. This enables JanusStudio™ tool suite to be applied across the entire functionality of the VistA environment to facilitate VistA integration with future Health℮Vet SOA services.

Strategy:

- None needed. TSRI implemented this capability in 2007.

## AFTERMATH

The VHA VTS Modernization pilot conclusively demonstrated the feasibility of architecture-driven modernization of MUMPS into Java/J2EE N-Tier Web architecture. It achieved a fully automated transformation that encompassed nearly all of MUMPS language features with an application architecture that achieved a clear separation between application logic business rules, data handling presentation elements, and web-enabled front end/user screens application interfacing with an Oracle 9i database and GUI which exposed the VTS module as a Web service. At the conclusion of the Phase 1 pilot the project team proposed a follow-on Phase II pilot to focus on resolution of remaining technical objectives as preparation for a possible full-scale conversion.

**FIGURE 12.8**

*ADM applied to VistA in this case study.*

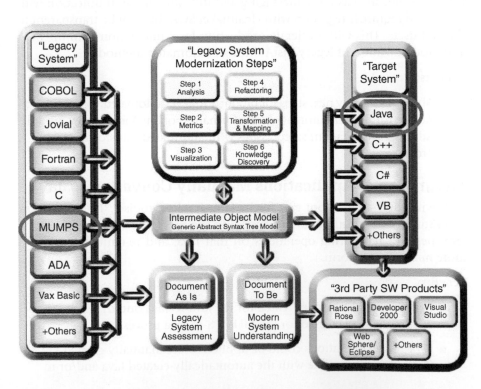

Unfortunately, events overtook these plans when the VHA suffered budget cuts that preclude continuation of the pilot program, and the follow-on conversion of VistA.

In February 2009, as a scalability and feasibility demonstration, TSRI applied the technology developed during the pilot to 2.2 million lines of MUMPS code in OpenVistA and Open FileMan demonstrating 99.995% automated transformation into Java and documented the complete design and architecture of the modernized OpenVistA as a UML Transformation Blueprint™ in compliance with OMG's architecture-driven modernization/model-driven architecture (ADM/MDA) approach to model-driven modernization.[3]

Accessible on the Web at http://www.softwarerevolution.com/open-vista/), the OpenVistA Transformation Blueprint™ serves the open source community as a roadmap toward a future universal open source EHR system based on the VHA's MUMPS VistA. Figure 12.8 illustrates the core ingredients of OMG's ADM/MDA approach to information system modernization that are realized in the OpenVistA Transformation Blueprint™.

---

[3]Architecture-Driven Modernization is the name of the initiative OMG applies to extending the modeling approach to existing software systems. The acronym for architecture-driven modernization, ADM, looks like MDA in reverse (MDA is the acronym for OMG's Model-Driven Architecture), or using modeling to deliver new software.

# CHAPTER 13

# Delta Lloyd Deutschland Data Migration Case Study

Bernhard Düchting and Tom Laszewski

## ABSTRACT

Delta Lloyd Deutschland AG is fully owned by Delta Lloyd NV, Amsterdam, and is a member of the UK-based Aviva Group, one of the top five financial services companies worldwide. Delta Lloyd Deutschland AG is a holding group with private banking, life insurance, mortgage services, and corporate pension funds.

This study highlights the steps and deliverables of the Ablösung Host (ABLH) project, which involved modernizing a number of core applications from an outsourced IBM mainframe to an internal open systems data center. The modernization effort included database management systems, application systems, and batch operations as well as development tools. The project started in September 2005; it was signed off to production in October 2008.

The focus of our discussion is on the database and application migration to the new target platform. We will exam in detail the mapping of the legacy data model to a relational Oracle data model and the migration of production data to an Oracle database with maximum flexibility. On the application side, we will illustrate the re-platforming from IBM mainframe to open systems, and explain the steps for porting these applications to access an Oracle database. The project was completed 2 months ahead of the agreed timeline, and on budget.

The benefits are significant, both in terms of technology advances and cost savings. Delta Lloyd Deutschland AG is now able to manage and operate their core applications on an internal infrastructure with higher efficiency, better manageability, and in full compliance of governmental financial transactions regulations. The ROI is expected to be 2 years.

## THE MODERNIZATION PROBLEM

Delta Lloyd Deutschland AG (DLD) was faced with rising costs for hosting the IBM mainframe platform. At the same time, a corporate initiative was put in place to integrate new business partners into their IT portfolio. This situation was putting company-projected growth plans at risk.

## CONTENTS

Compounding these business issues was an initiative led by the IT organization to achieve the following objectives:

- Online services for all products in a 24/7 environment
- A services-oriented architecture (SOA) with Web-based access and agile business processes
- Higher security standards for access to products

## Business Issues

DLD was implementing company-wide efficiency, innovation, and growth initiatives while a reorganization effort was underway as part of the Aviva group in 2001. Increasing legacy application complexity became apparent when DLD was dealing with the Y2K and EURO conversion. In addition, the rollup of a commercial-off-the-shelf (COTS) application on distributed systems and Java EE replacing an equivalent legacy application on the mainframe was taking place.

## Legacy Issues

With the continued growth of the application portfolio came new challenges for the IT organization to manage, test, and monitor these applications on top of the existing legacy infrastructure. The risk to the business was that IT could not deliver new functionality or provide a stable, high-performance system.

The COTS replacement previously described was solving some of the legacy issues; in particular there was no need to use CICS-based transaction management. The user interaction was moved to client-server, thus eliminating the need for 3270 emulation.

## The Client's Approach

DLD wanted to find answers to their business and technical requirements and contacted Oracle in July 2005. An initial meeting with DLD was held at the Oracle Potsdam office in June 2005. The meeting objectives were to understand the Oracle offering around mainframe modernization, the suitable options, and available success stories.

DLD had also engaged an independent management consulting firm to conduct a study of their existing host environment, application portfolio, and business processes. As a result of this study, DLD decided to look at in-sourcing the entire operation of the core applications that were hosted on an IBM mainframe. The main motivation was to regain full control over their IT assets, deploy them on an open systems infrastructure, and reduce overall operating costs. The production rollout of a new COTS Java EE-based application also influenced the decision to modernize their existing mainframe infrastructure and to complete the move to an open systems platform.

After the study, Oracle was invited back by DLD to derive Oracle target architecture recommendations. Other Oracle modernization partners were involved at various stages of the project, such as UC4 for job scheduling and FreeSoft for the database migration.

# HOW DID ORACLE ADDRESS THE OPPORTUNITY?

The Oracle account manager reached out to the Oracle Modernization Sales team to request assistance. The Oracle Modernization Sales team understands legacy environments, modernization approaches, and can architect open systems based solutions. As part of the engagement process, the Oracle Modernization Solutions team was brought in to advise the project on suitable modernization partners. Oracle Consulting Germany was brought in as well to discuss their involvement in the database modernization effort.

## The Software Migration Journey

The first step was to conduct a Modernization Discovery Workshop at the DLD premises. The objective of this workshop was to establish a comprehensive snapshot view of all of the relevant IT assets at DLD, regardless of platform. The resulting assessment report was the starting point for determining the next steps on the road to modernization.

The Oracle Modernization Discovery Workshop was aligned with the overall Oracle Modernization roadmap approach as depicted in Figure 13.1.

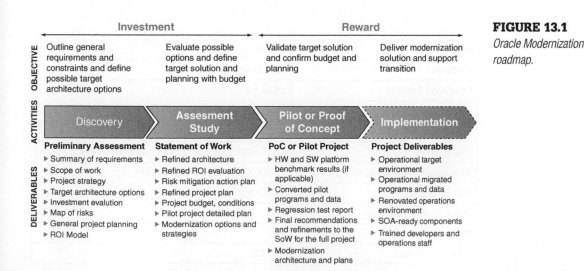

**FIGURE 13.1**

*Oracle Modernization roadmap.*

## ASSESSMENT

Every assessment starts with establishing a comprehensive snapshot view of the IT infrastructure. Figure 13.2 depicts a high-level overview of the host environment at DLD.

Further details were obtained during the Modernization Discovery Workshop. The focus was on the application metrics and DB2 database configuration.

### The Transformation Strategy

Following the study done by CSC and the Oracle Modernization Discovery Workshop, a roadmap was adopted by DLD with the following transformation strategy for each of the six host applications:

- Application rehost: One application was ported to the target platform, no change to functionality.
- COTS replacement: Four applications were replaced by one standard application package.
- Application rewrite: One application was replaced by a newly developed Java EE application.
- Database modernization: The operational database was migrated from mainframe DB2 to Oracle on open systems.

Oracle Consulting was chartered with the migration of the DB2 databases to an Oracle database, including the required database management infrastructure.

The Oracle Modernization partner UC4 was responsible for mapping the job scheduling from IBM mainframe (under OPC) to the target architecture, including converting the jobs scripts (JCL).

**FIGURE 13.2**

*Overview of host environment.*

| Component | Model |
|---|---|
| Platform | IBM System z |
| Operating System | z/OS 1.4 |
| Database | DB2 v7.1 on z/OS |
| Transaction Monitor | CICS v2.3 (was re-architected and replaced) |
| Dialog System | CSP, 3270 Emulation (was replaced by client-server) |
| Programming Language(s) | REXX, COBOL, ASSEMBLER |
| Job Scheduler | TWS/OPC |
| Number of applications | Six |
| Number of Users | 400 |
| Total DB2 Data | 500 GB |

# THE DATABASE MIGRATION WORK STREAM

This section describes the activities that were necessary to build a new target architecture based on an Oracle Database 10g Grid infrastructure. It also illustrates how each of the components in the host operating environment were mapped to the target operating environment, resulting in higher flexibility and reduced total operating cost.

## The Target Architecture

The new target architecture consists of an open systems infrastructure based on 2 × IBM pSeries servers and the RedHat LINUX operating system. A Storage Area Network (SAN) is connected to both servers.

The DB2 databases on the IBM mainframe were replaced by a single operational Oracle database consisting of

- Oracle 10g Enterprise Server Database
- Oracle 10g Data Guard
- Oracle 10g Partitioning
- Oracle 10g Management, Diagnostic, and Tuning Packs
- Oracle 10g Enterprise Manager
- Oracle Internet Developer Suite with Pre-Compilers for C/C++, and COBOL.

The Oracle Database Gateway for DRDA was licensed for 1 year to support repeated data loading during the migration project. Figure 13.3 depicts the target architecture for the project.

Oracle Maximum Availability Architecture (MAA) is Oracle's best practices blueprint based on proven high-availability technologies and recommendations.[1] The goal of MAA is to remove the complexity in designing the optimal high-availability architecture. In addition, the MAA will handle most outages, so they have little to no impact on availability and limiting catastrophic outages from causing more than 30 minutes of downtime.

Oracle MAA provides a simple, redundant, and robust architecture that prevents different types of outages. The best practices embedded in Oracle's MAA leverage years of experience-building and managing high-available systems to your own configuration.

### Proof of Concept

A total of three prototypes were built to validate the best approach:

1. Integration between DB2 on z/OS and Oracle through Oracle Streams
2. Tool-based conversion of JCL scripts with ESQL to UNIX shell scripts with the UC4 solution

**FIGURE 13.3**

*Target Oracle architecture.*

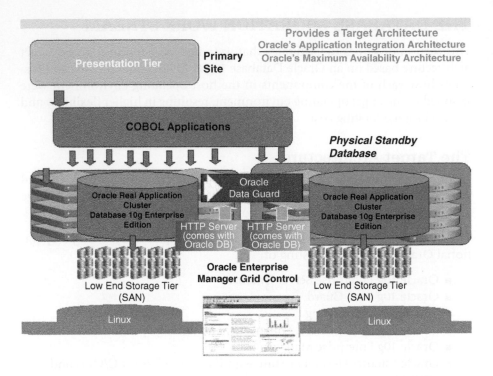

**3.** Tool-based conversion of DB2 ESQL to Oracle ESQL with the FreeSoft solution.[2] All of the previously listed prototypes were small in scope, requiring few implementation resources. After careful evaluation DLD decided to perform the required application porting in-house, with contributions from FreeSoft and coaching from Oracle Consulting.

## THE DETAILED SOFTWARE TRANSFORMATION APPROACH

This section discusses the detailed transformation approach and includes team organization, platform sizing, data type mapping, and the actual migration.

### Project Team Organization

The overall project management was in the hands of Delta Lloyd Deutschland GmbH, specifically in the hands of the Chief Information Officer. Based on an overall project plan, specific deliverables were contracted out to external partners; in particular, Oracle Consulting was responsible for the following project deliverables:

- Scope of the migration project: Included services, required software, and hardware components
- Detailed assessment of DB2 database and database model

- Requirements specification: Mapping of DB2 data types, data load provisions, user access, and roles
- Project management: Tasks and milestones, test strategy, sign-off criteria

Oracle Consulting provided project management support and coaching throughout the entire implementation of the project.

## Hardware Platform Sizing

The target open systems platform sizing was done by selected hardware vendors based on information obtained during the Modernization Discovery Workshop. As a result of our discussions with DLD we could narrow down the target architecture to these configurations:

1. 1 × SMP Server for Production and Dev/Test each in one LPAR
2. 2 × Separate Servers for Production and Dev/Test
3. 1 × SMP Server for Production, 1 × SMP Server for Dev/Test Server with Oracle 10g Data Guard
4. 2 × Blade Servers for Production with Oracle 10g RAC, 2 × Blade Servers for Dev/Test with Oracle 10g RAC

DLD selected an IBM pSeries platform with configuration 3 from the previous list, that is two separate LINUX servers with Oracle 10g EE Database, and Oracle 10g Data Guard as the stand-by server.

## Database Migration Approach

The migration of the DB2 database on z/OS to an Oracle database involved the following steps:

- Create a detailed description of migration process for DLD
- Develop a specification of agreed mappings from DB2 to Oracle, e.g., DB data types, user privileges
- Unload DB2 database objects
- Migrate DB2 database objects to equivalent Oracle database objects
- Install Oracle database infrastructure on target platform
- Establish database users
- Create target Oracle database schema based on DDL scripts
- Load DB2 data into Oracle database using agreed mappings
- Perform sign-off test on migrated Oracle database
- Modify DDL scripts as applicable to reproduce loading process
- Finalize the QA check

Figure 13.4 shows the metrics of the IBM DB2 database objects that were established as part of the assessment.

**FIGURE 13.4**

*Database metric summary.*

| Database Objects | Production Database | DWH Database | Total |
|---|---|---|---|
| DB2 Databases | 59 | 19 | 78 |
| DB2 Tables | 899 | 482 | 1381 |

## Mapping of DB2 Data Types

When loading data from a DB2 database (on any platform) to an Oracle database (on any platform), we examined the data type compatibility. Oracle has published guidelines with recommended mapping for each DB2 data type. The guidelines for DB2 on the mainframes can be found on the Oracle Web site.[3] The final data type mapping required customer review and authorization, based on their specific requirements. The mapping shown in Figure 13.5 was agreed to with DLD.

### Specified Data Type Mappings

The following mappings were specified for DLD:

- Data type CHAR: All occurrences of IBM DB2 CHAR columns with Length >1, were mapped to ORACLE VARCHAR2 column.
- Data type TIME: All occurrences of IBM DB2 TIME columns with Length >1, were mapped to ORACLE DATE column.
- Data type DATE: All occurrences of IBM DB2 DATE columns with Length >1, were mapped to ORACLE DATE column.
- Empty String: There was a significant difference when dealing with strings of Length = 0 in an IBM DB2 database. IBM DB2 has the capability of storing an empty string. On the other hand, Oracle treats this column as NOT NULL, which forces the column to be Length >0 by definition. The agreed mapping therefore is a string containing one blank character.

The table shown in Figure 13.6 summarizes the mapping of DB2 Empty String to Oracle.

The application (i.e., ESQL command) needed to be aware of this change. The new commands therefore required minimal changes to the source program, which is one of the documented guidelines followed by the team.

## Oracle Schema

The following IBM DB2 database objects were migrated to an equivalent Oracle database object:

- Table
- Primary Key
- Foreign Key

| DB2 Data Type | Oracle Data Type | Comments |
|---|---|---|
| CHAR(N) | CHAR(N) VARCHAR2 | Max. Size 2000 |
| VARCHAR(N) | VARCHAR2(N) CLOB | N<= 4000 N>4000 |
| LONG VARCHAR | | N<= 4000 N>4000 |
| CHAR(N) FOR BIT DATA | RAW(N) BLOB | |
| VARCHAR(N) FOR BIT DATA | RAW(N) BLOB | N<=2000 N>2000 |
| LONG VARCHAR FOR BIT DATA | RAW(N) BLOB | N<= 2000 N>2000 |
| DATE | DATE | Including Time |
| TIME | CHAR(8) DATE | Including Time |
| Timestamp | TIMESTAMP(06) | Max. Digits Milliseconds = 9 Length 06 is Default |
| CLOB | CLOB | |
| DECIMAL(P,S) | NUMBER(P,S) | Floating Point |
| INTEGER | NUMBER(10) | |
| SMALLINT | NUMBER(05) | |
| DOUBLE | FLOAT(53) | |
| FLOAT | FLOAT(53) | Max Length is FLOAT(126) Default Length is 126 |
| REAL | FLOAT(21) | |
| FLOAT(N) (single) | FLOAT(21) | 1<=N<=21 |
| FLOAT(N) (double) | FLOAT(53) | 22<=N<=53 |
| ROWID | RAW(40) | |

**FIGURE 13.5**

*Final data type mapping.*

| | DB2 | Oracle | Oracle Data Type |
|---|---|---|---|
| CHAR NOT NULL | Empty String" | 1 Blank | VARCHAR2 |
| CHAR NULL | Empty String" | NULL | VARCHAR2 |
| VARCHAR NOT NULL | Empty String" | 1 Blank | VARCHAR2 |
| VARCHAR NULL | Empty String" | NULL | VARCHAR2 |

**FIGURE 13.6**

*Mapping of DB2 empty string to Oracle.*

- Indexes
- View
- Label
- Sequence
- Check Constraint
- View

The schema migration at DLD was done based on technology from FreeSoft by using a design repository for parsing the DB2 data model and creating the necessary DDL scripts for the Oracle data model. FreeSoft also generated the necessary DWNTIAUL and SQLLoader scripts to support the alternate loading scenario with Unloading and Loading the production data.

The DB2 database migration was done several times in the course of the project to accommodate structural data model changes. One of the key requirements was to avoid a frozen zone, which is a period where application changes could not be carried out.

### Note on SQL Developer

The Oracle SQL Developer automated database migration tool was not used for this project as Oracle had yet to realize a mainframe DB2 plug-in for this tool. Oracle offers a migration plug-in for DB2 on UNIX/LINUX as part of the Oracle SQL Developer.[4] SQL Developer v2.1 supports DB2 UDB v8 and v9, and a release for DB2 on z/OS v7 and v8 on z/OS will occur in 2010.

SQL Developer automatically converts the tables, triggers, stored procedures, and all other relevant objects in the source database to an Oracle database. Once the target Oracle database has been generated, SQL Developer migrates the data from the non-Oracle database to the target Oracle database. SQL Developer is completely metadata driven and based on Java EE technology. The tool uses a five-step process to automatically migrate the database schema and data.

1. Capture your source database and store in the Oracle SQL Developer repository in metadata tables.
2. Convert your captured model to an Oracle representation that is stored in the SQL Developer repository.
3. Generating SQL Scripts for your converted model.
4. Run the generation script to create the Oracle database schema and objects.
5. Move your data to Oracle using the automatically generated Oracle SQL Loader control files and scripts.

The SQL developer supports both online capture (JDBC connection directly to the source database) and off-line capture (no live connection required to the source database) of the source database models.

## Efficient Data Migration

Generally, we can distinguish between a database migration scenario that should use the SQL Loader and database migration that should use the Oracle Transparent Gateway for DB2 for each phase of a database migration.

- Determine optimal data load option. Perform a load/stress test with selected data as follows:
  - Unload DB2 data with IBM DSNTIAUL utility, Load data with Oracle SQL*Loader utility.
  - Use Oracle Transparent Gateway for DRDA for moving data from DB2 to Oracle database.
- Implement scripts for the unload and load process to reproduce the data load process:
  - Create batch job based on IBM JCL for unloading and creating control files for Oracle SQL Loader.
  - Create script with SQL statements for "Insert as Select" to move data across.
- Run tests to verify unload and load process, as applicable.
- Final sign-off test, document and archive deliverable.

In the case of DLD, a decision was made to implement the second scenario and to use the Oracle DRDA Gateway for loading the DB2 data. This process can be described as follows:

1. Migrate DB2 data model to Oracle data model, based on repository
2. Load data from DB2 to Oracle with Oracle Database Gateway for DRDA, based on "Insert as Select" commands
3. Synchronize Oracle data changes with DB2 database, based on Oracle Database Gateway for DRDA

This implementation allowed DLD to perform necessary tests on the Oracle database platform while synchronizing with the DB2 database on the production system. It also allowed DLD to minimize the switch-over to the new Oracle platform once all other acceptance tests had been completed.

### EBCDIC and ASCII Character Set

Data in the DB2 database on the IBM mainframe under the z/OS operating system are stored in the EBCDIC character set. The Oracle SQL*Loader can be invoked to convert EBCDIC to an ASCII character set during the database loading through SQL*Net protocol. Similarly, when using the Oracle Transparent Gateway for DRDA this EBCDIC to ASCII conversion is done through Oracle SQL*Net protocol as part of the DB2 to Oracle database connection.

The Oracle Transparent Gateway for DRDA solution for replicating data between Oracle and DB2 during the production rollout phase is shown in Figure 13.7.

**FIGURE 13.7**

*Using Oracle DRDA
Gateway for DB2 Data
Loading to Oracle database.*

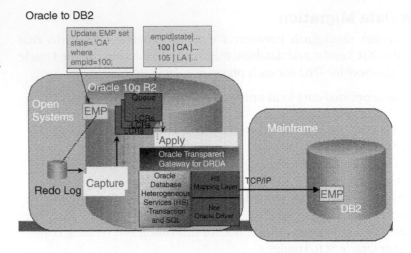

The LCRs in the Figure 13.7 are the Logical Change Records. The Oracle Transparent Gateway for DRDA is an Oracle product that resides in completely Open Systems and consists of

- Oracle Database Heterogeneous Services (HS): A process that is embedded in the Oracle database that makes non-Oracle database tables, like DB2, look like and act like Oracle database tables.
- HS Mapping Layer: A metadata repository that contains dictionary translation information and data type translations.
- Non-Oracle Driver: An Oracle embedded mainframe DB2 driver provided by the Oracle Modernization partner DataDirect Technologies.

## Application Porting

This section describes the re-platforming of one of the six core applications running on the IBM mainframe under DB2 and CICS. The task for DLD was to modify the source programs (i.e., COBOL) to make them access an Oracle database instead of the original DB2 database. The following issues had to be addressed:

- Convert DB2 ESQL to Oracle ESQL.
- Map DB2 built-in functions to equivalent Oracle functions/procedures.
- Verify, if any, operation against the EBCDIC character set that still works against the ASCII character set (e.g., COMP3 fields, alphanumerical sort).

The user interaction that is provided through 3270 emulation on PC client is not within the scope of this discussion.

### DB2 ESQL Syntax

The SQL commands used by DB2 (on any platform) differ from the Oracle SQL syntax in a number of areas, as shown in Figure 13.8.

FreeSoft used a tool-assisted manual process to enable the DB2-specific ESQL COBOL programs to work with Oracle COBOL ESQL programs:

- Process
  - Analysis of existing embedded SQL Syntax (e.g., DB2).
  - Changing ESQL Syntax to work with Oracle.

| DB2 | Oracle |
|---|---|
| **Syntax:** | **Syntax:** |
| `INSERT INTO [ table-name | view-name ]`<br>`  [ ( column-name [, column-name ]... ) ]`<br>`  [ OVERRIDING USER VALUE ]`<br>`  { VALUES`<br>`    { { expression | DEFAULT | NULL } |`<br>`      ( { expression | DEFAULT | NULL }`<br>`        [, {expression|DEFAULT|NULL }]...`<br>`      }`<br>`    } |`<br>`    fullselect [ WITH { RR | RS | CS } ]`<br>`              [ QUERYNO integer ]`<br>`  }` | *insert:*<br>`INSERT [hint] { single_table_insert |`<br>`multi_table_insert };`<br><br>*single_table_insert:*<br>`insert_into_clause { values_clause`<br>`        [returning_clause] | subquery };`<br><br>*insert_into_clause:*<br>`INTO dml_table_expression_clause [t_alias]`<br>`    [( column [, column]... )]`<br><br>*value_clause:*<br>`VALUES ( { expr | DEFAULT }`<br>`        [, { expr | DEFAULT }]... )`<br><br>*returning_clause:*<br>`RETURNING expr [, expr]...`<br>`    INTO data_item [, data_item]...`<br><br>*multi_table_insert:*<br>`{ ALL insert_into_clause [values_clause]`<br>`  [insert_into_clause [values_clause]]...`<br>`| conditional_insert_clause`<br>`}`<br>`subquery`<br><br>*conditional_insert_clause:*<br>`[ ALL | FIRST ]`<br>`WHEN condition THEN insert_into_clause`<br>`[values_clause]`<br>`[insert_into_clause [values_clause]]...`<br>`[WHEN condition THEN insert_into_clause`<br>`[values_clause]`<br>`  [insert_into_clause [values_clause]]...`<br>`]...` |

**FIGURE 13.8**

*DB2 to Oracle Mapping of ESQL.*

*(Continued)*

**FIGURE**
**13.8—Cont'd**

| DB2 | Oracle |
|---|---|
| | `[ELSE insert_into_clause [values_clause]`<br>`  [insert_into_clause [values_clause]]...`<br>`]`<br><br>***dml_table_expression_clause:***<br>`{ [schema .]`<br>`  { table`<br>`    [ { PARTITION ( partition ) |`<br>`        SUBPARTITION ( subpartition ) }`<br>`    | @ dblink`<br>`    ]`<br>`  | { view | materialized view } [@ dblink]`<br>`  }`<br>`| ( subquery [subquery_restriction_clause]`<br>`)`<br>`| table_collection_expression`<br>`}`<br><br>***subquery_restriction_clause:***<br>`WITH {READ ONLY |`<br>`      CHECK OPTION [CONSTRAINT constraint]}`<br><br>***table_collection_expression:***<br>`TABLE ( collection_expression ) [( + )]` |

- Modifying SQLCA/DA data structures for dynamic SQL.
- Modifying error handling to reflect Oracle error codes.
- Tool
  - The FreeSoft tool uses a COBOL and SQL language parser that has a metadata repository for making the DB2 SQL syntax changes to Oracle SQL syntax changes.

There are tools in the marketplace that can emulate Oracle ESQL calls written in DB2 ESQL. However, these tools were not used in this case because of the following benefits of making the changes at development time instead of using an emulation layer:

- Native development with Oracle pre-compiler
- Standard access for Oracle
- Performance is far better
- Native Oracle error handling
- No third-party emulation layer to pay for or support.

### DB2 Built-in Functions

There are a number of built-in functions that needed to be mapped to an equivalent functionality when migrating to an Oracle database. Figure 13.9 shows a

| DB2 | Oracle | Description |
|---|---|---|
| SUBSTR(str,index[,len]) | SUBSTR(str,index[,len]) | Returns a substring from str, starting at index and returns a length of len. |
| IFNULL(expr1,expr2)<br>COALESCE(expr[,expr])<br>VALUE(expr[,expr]) | NVL(expr1,expr2) | Returns the first argument that is not null. |
| UCASE(char)<br>UPPER(char) | UPPER(char) | Returns char in uppercase characters. |
| IFNULL(expr1,expr2)<br>COALESCE(expr[,expr])<br>VALUE(expr[,expr]) | NVL(expr1,expr2) | Returns the first argument that is not null. |
| LENGTH(char) | LENGTH(char) | Returns the length of the char string in number of bytes. |
| date('12/13/1989') | to_date('12/13/1989', 'mm/dd/yyyy') | Returns a type date value corresponding to the expression with which you call it. |
| month(date_expr) | to_number(to_char (date_expr, 'MM')) | Returns an integer corresponding to the month portion of its type DATE or DATETIME argument. |
| second(expr_expr) | to_char(date_expr, 'SS') | Returns the second part of the date expression. |
| year(date_expr) | to_char(date_expr, 'YYYY') | Returns an integer corresponding to the year portion of its type DATE or DATETIME argument. |

**FIGURE 13.9**

*DB2 to Oracle built-in function mapping.*

number of examples that had to be addressed during the migration of a built-in DB2 function and its equivalent Oracle built-in function.

The preferred approach that was chosen in the DLD project was to provide an Oracle function or PL/SQL procedure of the same name that emulates the exact functionality. The only required change was to modify the relevant ESQL command to invoke the appropriate function or PL/SQL procedure with input arguments, and to return the result to the calling application.

Oracle Consulting provided coaching assistance to DLD for identifying the affected source programs, making the necessary changes, and testing them against the target Oracle database.

### CICS Transaction Monitor

The core applications at DLD were operated by an external service provider on an IBM System z mainframe. This architecture involved user interaction based on a CICS transaction monitor: 3270 screens on mainframe and 3270 emulation on PC desktop.

In an intermediate step (as part of another project), DLD had ported these applications to a client-server architecture. The result was that applications were accessing the DB2 database on the mainframe. The user interaction was switched over to a separate dialog management system on a PC desktop that also had Web access. CICS usage was eliminated as a result of this project.

# PROJECT RESULTS

This section summarizes the project's results and focuses on the lesson learned. The new database and revised system were deployed successfully using the Oracle database. The data migration went as planned.

## Lessons Learned

This project was a multi-year effort, starting in the summer of 2005 and signed off to production in October of 2008. The following elements were essential to the successful completion of the project within the specified time frame and budget:

- Ensure that you establish a well-structured engagement model with clearly defined milestones
- Define the scope of the modernization project early in the project through the Oracle Modernization Discovery Workshop
- Gain an agreement on ownership of various roles and functions between client (DLD) project management and the delivery partners (Oracle Consulting Services, CSC, FreeSoft, and UC4)
- Engage specialized and highly skilled IT modernization partners to complete specific aspects of the modernization effort:
  - CSC: Legacy IT infrastructure assessment and analysis
  - FreeSoft: Mainframe DB2 to Oracle database migration
  - UC4: Migration of mainframe JCL and job scheduler to LINUX scripts and UC4 job scheduler
- Implement a steering committee with delivery partners to deal with milestones, issues, and reviews
- Use conversion tools for the database migration to minimize implementation time and maximize quality
- Revise operational process to fit the new target architecture, including development process

The most important lesson learned was that the project was ultimately about aligning technology and methodology with the people that were directly affected by this transformation.

Managing the transition to the target architecture was as important as managing the changes to the operational processes and user roles.

Finally, the project was about empowering the IT staff at DLD to leverage the Oracle technology in their day-to-day jobs.

# REFERENCES

1. *Oracle Maximum Availability Architecture and Best Practices.* http://www.oracle.com/technology/deploy/availability/htdocs/maa.htm.
2. FreeSoft International. www.freesoftus.com/en/.
3. *DB Migration Guide.* http://www.oracle.com/technology/tech/migration/db2_os390_conversion_guide.pdf.
4. *Free Migration Plug-in for DB2 Download.* http://www.oracle.com/technology/tech/migration//workbench/index_sqldev_omwb.html.

# CHAPTER 14

# MoDisco, a Model-Driven Platform to Support Real Legacy Modernization Use Cases

Gabriel Barbier, Hugo Bruneliere, Frédéric Jouault, Yves Lennon,
and Frédéric Madiot

## ABSTRACT

Presentation of a model-driven migration chain used by Sodifrance on its projects and of the Eclipse/MoDisco platform, a new model-driven framework to develop legacy modernization tools.

## CONTENTS

## INTRODUCTION

Legacy systems embrace a large number of technologies, making the development of tools to cope with legacy systems evolution a tedious and time-consuming task. To deal with the myriad of technological combinations found in modernization roadmaps, model-driven approaches and tools offer the requisite abstraction level to build up mature and flexible modernization solutions. This case study presents a two-phase discussion of model-driven modernization.

In the section Genesis of a Model-Driven Legacy Modernization Approach in this chapter we present the initial collaboration between AtlanMod and Sodifrance, which led to a model-driven legacy modernization approach. Then, in the section Process and Tools for Migrating Legacy Applications, we describe the current process and tools used by Sodifrance on its modernization projects. An illustration drawn from a real migration project, from VB6 to JEE, carried out for Amadeus Hospitality, is also included in that section. Finally, in the section MoDisco, a New Eclipse Platform to Support Model-Driven Legacy Modernization, we present a new Eclipse initiative capitalizing on this experience to deliver a model-driven platform for the development of legacy modernization tools.[1] An illustration of a knowledge discovery tool developed for WesternGeco to understand an existing application containing both Java and C# code is included in that section.

# GENESIS OF A MODEL-DRIVEN LEGACY MODERNIZATION APPROACH

In 1993, Sodifrance and Nantes University established a collaboration to work on semantic knowledge extraction from legacy systems. The goal of this collaboration was to transfer innovative work and ideas from Jean Bézivin's research team to a company able to industrialize the prototypes and solve industrial modernization problems encountered by their customers.

The research work of Jean Bézivin's team was to enable the representation of existing applications. When dealing with all the syntactical categories found in an existing program, they came to the conclusion that the precise, complete, and evolutionary expression of these categories, and of the various relations between them, needed a robust ontological framework. In 1993, they developed the sNets technology, a first implementation of typed, reflective, and modular semantic networks.[2] It was a minimalist representation for dealing with all kinds of models, metamodels, and meta-metamodels.

The sNets technology was immediately used by Sodifrance to develop a semantic discovery tool, named Semantor, to analyze any COBOL program and provide a fine-grained level of information about its internal structure and data (see Figure 14.1). The representation of this information, with typed nodes and links, could then be processed to discover control and data flows, represented in the same way. To help the user understand the programs analyzed, a

**FIGURE 14.1**

*COBOL source code and control flow displayed in Semantor.*

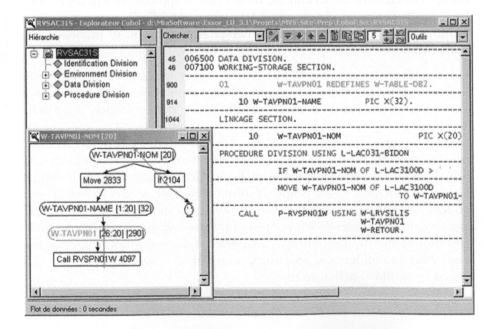

view of the program, synchronized with the source code, was provided to facilitate the understanding of the relationship between an element of the semantic network and its initial textual representation. In addition to this, graphical representations were automatically produced to facilitate navigation through this semantic network.

When faced with the need for evolution of a real program whose documentation is obsolete or missing, Semantor helps analyze the impacts engendered by a modification, especially on critical points or variables of the program. This allows the user to

- Take into account the secondary impacts via parent zones or subsidiary zones
- Take into account the impacts caused by redefined structures
- Select impact types: storage, test, computation, etc.
- Choose the number of propagation levels
- Select a propagation direction: forward, backward, or both
- Activate the interpretation of subprograms calls
- Indicate specific zones to be excluded or "mark" them as propagation breakpoints

This tool, now included in the Mia-Insight suite, has been used in numerous modernization projects, particularly for the two following project types: Year 2000 and Euro conversion.[3] Semantor has also been used in France to migrate COBOL programs from Bull's GCOS8 operating system to IBM's MVS. During this project, which ran 100,000 man-days, Semantor helped expose dependencies among the components, facilitating the step-by-step migration of the whole system.

In parallel, at the end of 1998, based on the experience gained in the rebuilding of another insurance company's contract management system where modeling and tailored code generators were successfully used, Sodifrance started developing its own model transformation technology. From this work, in association with Jean Bézivin, who brought his knowledge about early work at Object Management Group (OMG) on Meta Object Facility (MOF), two tools were created. The first was Scriptor-Generation, a template-based code generator for models; the second was Scriptor-Transformation, a rule-based, model-to-model transformation tool.

These tools, now grouped in the Mia-Studio suite, have been used by major companies to build tailored model-driven tools for producing their application systems. The type of applications produced with Mia-Studio vary from flight management systems written in C and ADA for avionics companies, to information systems based on JEE or .NET frameworks for companies in the banking, insurance, transportation, and administration sectors.

In 2002, Sodifrance was asked by one of its banking customers to migrate its client-server system written with the obsolete Cool:Gen technology to the JEE framework used to develop new applications. As this client had already adopted a model-driven architecture (MDA) process to produce these new applications, Sodifrance had the idea to link its legacy-analysis tools with its model-driven transformation tools to build a migration chain capable of automating the migration process.

On the basis of this successful experience, Sodifrance has now successfully carried out more than ten similar migration projects using this approach, capitalizing on a dedicated process and modular tools capable of confronting a wide range of source and target technologies.

## PROCESS AND TOOLS FOR MIGRATING LEGACY APPLICATIONS

### The Challenge

Many of the migrations performed by Sodifrance consist of transforming existing client-server applications to JEE or .NET environment. The technology of the source application is frequently based on a proprietary language no longer supported by its author. Examples of these languages, mainly created in the 1990s, are VB6, OracleForms, Forte, Cool:Gen, NSDK, Natstar, and PowerBuilder. Most of these languages are procedural as opposed to object-oriented.

The applications written in these languages are mostly based on a two-tiered architecture. The first tier (the server) is frequently a database containing stored procedures, or a mainframe application. The second tier (the client) is a collection of fat windows providing rich graphical components and embedding business processing and direct access to the server tier.

The challenge is to transform, simultaneously, the architecture of the application (from client-server to multi-tier), the paradigm used to structure the code (from procedural to object-oriented), and the implementation syntax(es). In addition, the target applications have to rely on patterns and frameworks that are generally different from one customer to another.

### The Approach

To solve the complexity of such transformations and facilitate reusability between similar projects, Sodifrance has progressively built a semi-automated migration chain based on model-driven engineering. The approach follows the Horseshoe Model as formalized by the OMG/Architecture-Driven Modernization (ADM) Task Force.[4] This model defines three synchronized steps that have to be combined to constitute a transformational path:

1. **Knowledge discovery of the existing solution:** This occurs at many levels of abstraction across varying degrees of scope as appropriate to the projects involved.
2. **Target architecture definition:** To create a transformation approach, analysts must create a target solution that serves as a framework into which existing solutions are mapped or transformed.
3. **Transformative steps that move the as-is state to the to-be state:** The approach ranges from the physical (e.g., a language migration) to the more abstract (e.g., business rule mapping to a rules-based environment).

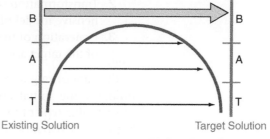

**FIGURE 14.2**
*ADM Horseshoe Model.*

Depending on business and IT requirements, the ADM Horseshoe Model (see Figure 14.2) includes a wide range of possible journeys from technical to business ADMs.

## The Migration Chain

### Overview

Sodifrance's current migration chain is based on models created by discoverers dedicated to each source technology. These models are transformed to produce the code of the target application. The transformations are performed by model-to-model and model-to-text engines driven by rules adapted to the particular context of each migration (see Figure 14.3).

The migration chain is composed of three main steps:

1. Extraction of a comprehensive model (the initial model) of the existing application from its assets (source code, configuration files, development repositories, etc.).

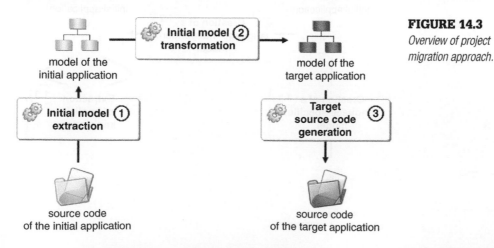

**FIGURE 14.3**
*Overview of project migration approach.*

2. Transformation of the model of the existing application into a comprehensive model of the target application (the target model).
3. Generation of the source code of the target application from the model of the target application.

In the case of migrations from client-server applications to JEE or .NET technologies, the initial and target models conform to two metamodels dedicated to this type of migration. To maximize reusability of the transformation between the two models, the client-server and multi-tier metamodels have been designed to be language-neutral and independent of any specific framework.

To avoid losing information during the transformation and to guarantee the generation of a complete application, the metamodels define both the concepts needed to fully describe the algorithms and the Graphical User Interfaces (GUIs). In addition, the client-server metamodel defines concepts such as fat window, whereas the multi-tier metamodel defines concepts such as class, Web page, MVC pattern, etc.

### Initial Model Extraction

To facilitate the creation of the initial model, this step has been divided into three sub-steps (see Figure 14.4):

1. A discoverer extracts information out of artifacts constituting the existing application to create an initial model conforming to the concepts of the implementation language.
2. A transformation translates this language-specific model into a language-independent model (the client-server model) to eliminate those concepts specific to the initial source language.

**FIGURE 14.4**

*Extraction of initial model.*

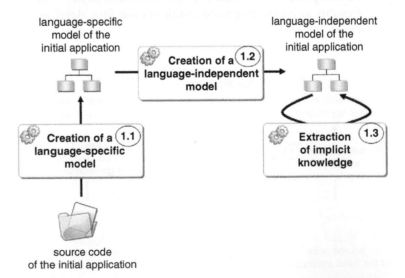

3. Implicit knowledge is deduced to enrich this model with information such as GUI navigation logic, control, and data flows; business versus technical data; and other useful information about the application environment.

### Initial Model Transformation

The second main step consists of transforming the client-server concepts into multi-tier concepts. It is during this step that the application is redesigned to identify business objects, data access components, and GUI navigation logic.

Several strategies involving cumulative transformations have been developed by Sodifrance to solve the principal cases encountered. When the transformation is too complex, or needs human expertise, tags are placed on the corresponding model elements to resolve them manually at the end of the transformation.

The result is a comprehensive model describing the complete target application with its presentation details, its business logic, and its access to databases and hosted services.

### Target Source Code Generation

The third step consists of generating the application source code from the target application model respecting the customer's technical choices (language, frameworks, design patterns, and coding rules). Apart from those cases where manual modifications are needed, because the target model is comprehensive, the regeneration is complete.

One of the main challenges in this generation is to manage the differences in the technical services provided by the source and target platform. There are two cases to be considered:

1. A technical component has no equivalent on the target platform, or existing components are too different, making the transformation too complex. The solution is to develop an equivalent component with the same level of service. An example of this would be a printing component that is often very specific to the initial environment.

2. The best practices of the target platform require a component to be used that has no equivalent on the initial platform (or it exists, but has not been used). One example of this is replacing direct accesses to a database by object-relational mapping such as Hibernate. This can imply a very complex transformation to fully respect the target component. Depending on the degree of this complexity, the number of occurrences, and the level of conformity to the best practices required by the customer, this transformation can be partially automated.

### *MDA Migration*

In most cases, the customers want to take advantage of the migration to industrialize the maintenance and future evolutions of the migrated application. Where they have already put in place an MDA process with modeling rules (or a DSL) and code generators tailored to their technical choices, the migration chain can be adapted and enhanced to integrate the production of UML models compliant with these code generators.[5]

These UML models are not complete representations of the application, but they contain the minimum information needed for the code generators to work. For example, most UML models contain neither specific business rules algorithms, nor the specific GUI design (position, size, and color of the widgets). It is for this reason that most generators exploiting UML models only generate file skeletons that have to be completed manually by the developers. To allow iterative work on models and files, these generators produce tags that identify portions where the developer can add his code. These fragments of code are preserved when the code is regenerated.

Rather than generating all of the code from the target model, this model is used to produce a UML model compliant with the modeling rules expected by the customer's code generator. All the code that cannot be produced by the UML generator (non-generated files and code fragments to insert into the file skeletons) is produced by a second generator using the comprehensive model. This code corresponds to the code produced manually in the customer's MDA process.

The last step consists of automatically integrating the code fragments into the file skeletons.

Once migrated, the application can evolve by modifying the model (for functional or design evolutions) or the code generator (for technical evolutions) and regenerating the code. Figure 14.5 shows the flow of the generation of a target application in an MDA migration.

The benefit of this approach is that, if the customer has already adopted an MDA process to develop new applications, the same process can be used to maintain the migrated applications. Figure 14.6 shows the conceptual flow of the maintenance process that would occur after an MDA migration has been completed.

## The Tools

For a given project, Sodifrance's migration chain is automated with three tools: a model discoverer, a model-to-model transformation engine, and a model-to-code generation engine.

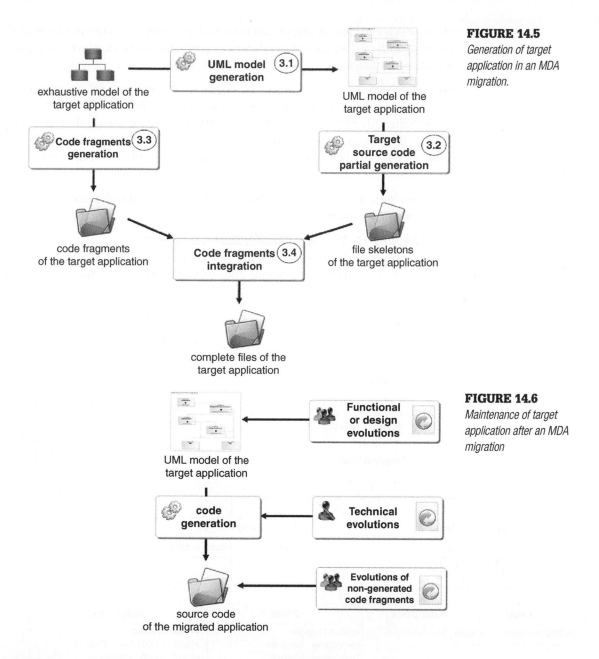

**FIGURE 14.5**
*Generation of target application in an MDA migration.*

**FIGURE 14.6**
*Maintenance of target application after an MDA migration*

## The Model Discoverer

A model discoverer is a tool that creates a model out of artifacts of the existing system. Most of these artifacts are files containing source code. These files are analyzed by a parser developed from the BNF grammar of the language used to develop the program. Sometimes models can be created by querying a database from which the table structures are extracted. In other cases, the model is built by using APIs to connect to a development environment from which the project structure is extracted.

In each case the result is a model conforming to a metamodel containing all the concepts needed to describe the existing application. In Sodifrance's migration chain, this metamodel is defined with MOF. Thus, the models provided by the discoverers can be serialized with XMI and exported for the use by the transformation engines. Figure 14.7 depicts a subset of one such metamodel for GUI representations.

Note in Figure 14.7 the various objects within this metamodel that are used to represent a GUI interface.

### The Model-to-Model Transformation Engine

To perform the required model transformation from the language-specific model to the target application and the UML models, Sodifrance uses

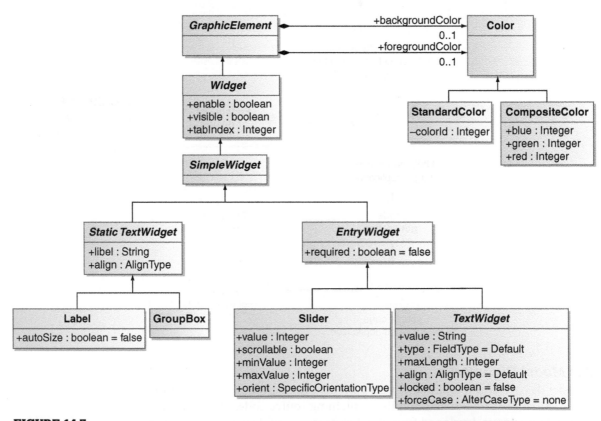

**FIGURE 14.7**

*Subset of Sodifrance's GUI metamodel.*

Mia-Transformation, the model-to-model technology provided by Mia-Software in its Mia-Studio tool suite. Mia-Transformation is a rule-based transformation engine and its dedicated editor used to define and maintain model(s)-to-model(s) transformation rules. Each rule is composed of a query, an action, a context, and sub-rules sharing the rule's context. The query and the action can be written using an inference syntax (similar to Prolog) or directly in Java.

Figure 14.8 depicts selected transformation rules for the transformation process. In the utilized migration chain, all the transformations are executed by the same tool with its own rule set organized in several reusable packages. The decomposition of the transformational path into several steps based on intermediate, language-neutral metamodels facilitates the reuse of transformation packages between migration chains dedicated to different source and/or target technologies.

### The Model-to-Code Generation Engine

The generation of target application artifacts was performed with Mia-Generation, the model-to-text technology provided by Mia-Software in its Mia-Studio tool suite.

Mia-Generation is a template-based generation engine and its dedicated editor used to define and maintain model-to-text transformation rules for any metamodel defined with MOF. Each template can define tags to separate generated

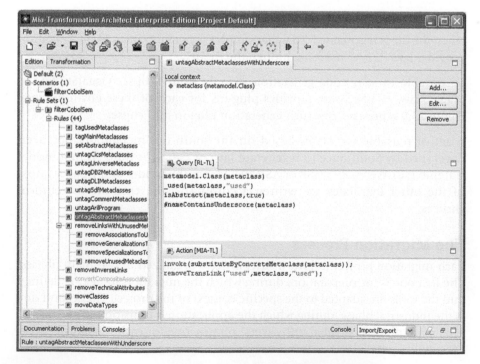

**FIGURE 14.8**
Edition of transformation rules with Mia-Transformation.

**FIGURE 14.9**

*Mia-Generation plug-in for Eclipse.*

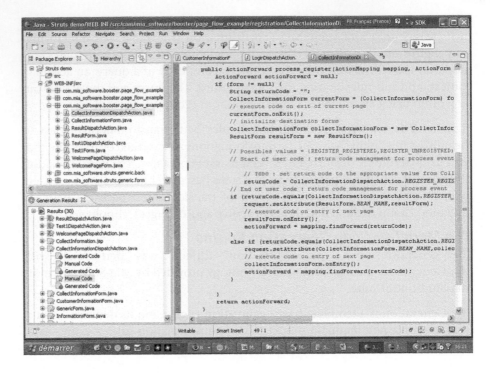

code from code added by the developer. These fragments of code are preserved when the file is regenerated. To write complex generation rules, Mia-Generation provides Java APIs to navigate through the model.

To be able to start code generation directly from Eclipse, VisualStudio, or MagicDraw, Mia-Software provides plug-ins for each of these environments. Figure 14.9 represents one such generation plug-in for Eclipse.

A set of reusable templates based on the multi-tier metamodel has been developed by Sodifrance to regenerate Java or C# algorithms from a model statement or Web pages (JSP or ASP.NET) from the model of the pages. Most of the other templates are written according to the customer's technical choices.

## The Migration Process

Each migration project follows a strict process organized in two main phases. The first one is the preparation, during which the migration strategy is defined and the tools are adapted to the specific context of the project. The second one is the industrial phase, during which the application is transformed and tested. This main phase is divided into several phases, one for each migration batch, executed in parallel.

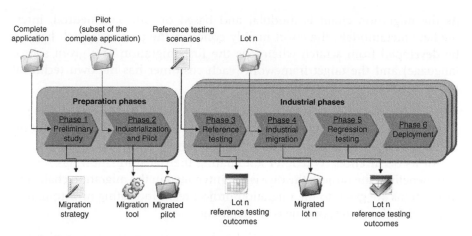

**FIGURE 14.10**

*Sodifrance's migration process.*

Figure 14.10 shows the overall migration process from preparation phases through the industrial (deployment) phases.

## Preliminary Study

This phase consists of analyzing the entire source application to be migrated to define the migration strategy. During this phase, the existing application's architecture is identified, the design patterns and the technical components used to implement the code are listed, and the dependencies between the main components are identified.

Based on the knowledge of the source application acquired, the target architecture is then defined in accordance with the customer's technical requirements. In the majority of cases, the customer has already defined an architecture and a framework for developing new applications in JEE or .NET environments. In such a case, the supplied framework is enhanced to support any new features needed by the application migrated. The main extensions concern graphical user components not available in the new framework and needed to reproduce rich functionalities of the existing application.

Finally, a migration strategy is defined to establish the way each concept of the initial application will be transformed. This strategy usually comes with technical prototypes validating the technical choices.

## Industrialization and Pilot Migration

This phase consists of adapting the tools that make up Sodifrance's migration chain:

- Discoverers
- Intermediate metamodels
- Model-to-model transformation rules
- Code generation templates
- Target framework

As the migration chain is modular and based on language-neutral, intermediate metamodels, the effort mainly concerns the parsers (which have to be developed from scratch when it is the first migration of a given source language) and the target framework (each customer has his own technical requirements).

Each time a new case is discovered that is not handled by the existing migration chain, a decision is taken whether or not to automate the transformation of this case. The two criteria used are the complexity of the case and the number of its occurrences. Whenever automating the transformation has no evident benefit to the project, the case is not integrated in the migration chain and instructions are given to the migration project team indicating how to manually modify the corresponding code fragment.

The new migration chain is then validated on a pilot application, which is a subset of the real application to be migrated. This phase is iterative, until the pilot is correctly transformed and all risks have been identified. Finally, once the pilot has been validated by the customer, a breakdown of the whole migration into migration batches is proposed to parallelize the migration process and facilitate the validation of each migration batch.

The following four phases — which included reference testing, industrial migration, regression testing, and deployment — were executed for each migration batch.

### Reference Testing
The reference tests are the result of test scenarios performed on the application before its transformation. The results of these initial reference tests are then compared to the results of the same testing scenarios performed on the migrated application.

### Industrial Migration
This phase consists of transforming the source code and configuration files of a migration batch. It begins by manually transforming the source application to handle any specific cases not covered automatically by the migration chain. Then the chain transforms the code. Finally, manual adaptations are made to the result to handle any other cases that have not been automated; for example, adapting the layout of the Web pages obtained from Windows screens.

### Regression Testing
This phase consists of executing the reference tests on the migrated application and comparing the results with those executed on the application before its transformation. The aim is to verify that the transformation has not caused unintended effects and that the new system still behaves like the initial one.

### Deployment

After the results of the reference tests have been validated by the customer, the application is deployed in the new environment. This phase is generally performed by the customer.

## Amadeus Hospitality: VB6 to JEE Migration

In 2008, Amadeus Hospitality (a subsidiary of Amadeus with 8,300 employees), the leader in IT solutions provided for the tourism and travel industry, asked Sodifrance to migrate one of their applications for hotel management from VB6 to Java Enterprise Edition (JEE).

### The Initial Application

The Amadeus Hospitality revenue management system (RMS) is a yield management application providing a fuller understanding of hotel customer behavior to help hoteliers in optimizing the profitability of their assets. It is deployed in more than 1,500 properties from 54 hotel chains. In 2000, a specific branch of RMS had been developed for Accor, one of their customers and a European leader in hotels and tourism.

The initial RMS version was developed in VB6, and was performing queries on an Oracle database. It was composed of 300 screens, 200 of them displaying charts (pie charts, bar charts, or line graphs). The VB6 code was composed of 306,000 source lines of code: VB6 code in 216 classes and 261 modules.

The Accor branch was composed of 100 additional screens (60 of them displaying charts) and an Informix database. Figures 14.11 and 14.12 show selected screenshots of the RMS application.

Amadeus Hospitality wished to migrate RMS to a new technical environment for two main reasons: the end of support for VB6 by Microsoft announced for 2008 and the possibility of opening up its information system and facilitating the integration of its partners. With this migration, it was also an opportunity for Amadeus Hospitality to merge the specific Accor branch into the main RMS branch.

### The Transformation

As JEE technology had been recently chosen at a corporate level, Amadeus Hospitality decided to select this technology for a new lightweight version of RMS based on a classic three-tier format organized in the following manner:

- Presentation tier: Screen-handling and user interaction management
- Business Logic tier: Business logic and application management
- Data tier: Data persistence and access to external components

The new architecture respects the following principles:

- Application of the model-view-controller pattern
- Externalization of accesses to data (database or external components) in the data access objects (DAO pattern)

**FIGURE 14.11**

*Screenshot of initial RMS application.*

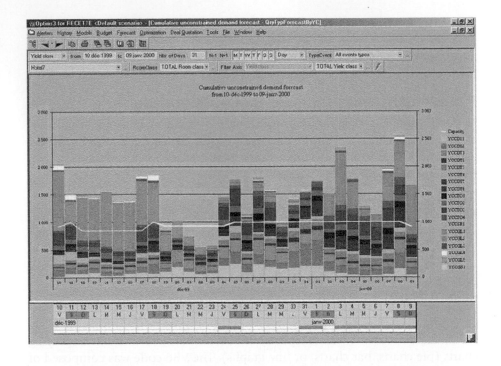

**FIGURE 14.12**

*Screenshot of initial RMS application.*

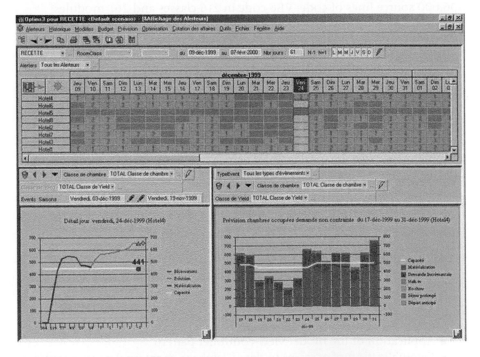

The new application has been implemented with four Java frameworks: JFreeChart (charts generation), WebWork (presentation layer), Spring (business and data access), and FOP (printing). The database, based on Oracle, remained unchanged for RMS, while the Accor branch database, based on Informix, merged into the Oracle RMS database.

To transform the existing application to this new architecture and technology, Sodifrance followed MDA with the tools and the process described earlier (apart from the production of a UML model, as Amadeus had not chosen to maintain the new application using an MDA process).

The transformation of the VB6 classes to Java classes has been relatively straightforward for the structure and the statements (see the sample VB6 translation in Figure 14.13). Figure 14.13 shows some of the selected VB6 source code that underwent migration.

Figure 14.14 depicts the resulting Java source code after the VB6 migration.

```
Dim oDim As cBaseDim
Dim oDefDim As cAnalysisAxis
  For Each oDefDim In AnalysisAxes
      If oDefDim.AxisType = AnaAxisTypStdAxis Or oDefDim.AxisType = AnaAxisTypSubInventory Then
          Set oDim = New cBaseDim
          Set oDim.AnaAxis = oDefDim
          mcolDims.Add oDim, CStr(oDefDim.Id)
          Set oDim = Nothing
      End If

  Next
  Set oDim = New cBaseDim
  Set oDefDim = New cAnalysisAxis
  oDefDim.AxisType = AnaAxisTypStdAxis
  oDefDim.Id = AnaAxisRoomTypeBar
  Set oDim.AnaAxis = oDefDim
  mcolDims.Add oDim, CStr(oDefDim.Id)
```

**FIGURE 14.13**

*VB6 sample.*

```
BaseDim oDim;
AnalysisAxis oDefDim;
for(int i=0;i<GlobalContext.getGestionCondVals_analysisAxes().size();i++)
{
    oDefDim = GlobalContext.getGestionCondVals_analysisAxes().get(i);

    if (oDefDim.getAxisType() == AnaAxisTypeEnum.ANA_AXIS_TYP_STD_AXIS ||
            oDefDim.getAxisType() == AnaAxisTypeEnum.ANA_AXIS_TYP_SUB_INVENTORY) {

        oDim = new BaseDim();
        oDim.anaAxis = oDefDim;
        mcolDims.add(oDim, StringUtil.parseString(oDefDim.getId()));
        oDim = null;
    }
}
oDim = new BaseDim();
oDefDim = new AnalysisAxis();
oDefDim.setAxisType(AnaAxisTypeEnum.ANA_AXIS_TYP_STD_AXIS);
oDefDim.setId(MConstants.ANA_AXIS_ROOM_TYPE_BAR);
oDim.anaAxis = oDefDim;
mcolDims.add(oDim, StringUtil.parseString(oDefDim.getId()));
```

**FIGURE 14.14**

*Translation of the VB6 sample into Java.*

Nevertheless, the transformation required the adaptation of the existing Sodifrance rules to take into account the specific Amadeus constraints. The following list contains some of the points for which adaptations have been made:

- User interface: The translation of the GUIs required a mapping between VB6 components and the equivalent Java components (including the mapping of corresponding APIs). Most of the target Java components have been selected from WebWorks, the framework chosen by Amadeus.

Figure 14.15 shows selected mappings from VB6 graphical components to Java.

**FIGURE 14.15**

*Subset of the mapping from VB6 graphical components to Java.*

| Library | Component | Number of utilisations | Technical solution |
|---|---|---|---|
| VB 6 | CheckBox | 117 | webwork checkbox |
| VB 6 | ComboBox | 51 | webwork combobox |
| VB 6 | CommandButton | 250 | webwork Input |
| VB 6 | Frame | 162 | webwork div |
| VB 6 | Image | 9 | webwork image |
| VB 6 | Label | 399 | webwork label |
| VB 6 | Line | 21 | Html hr |
| VB 6 | ListBox | 21 | webwork select |
| VB 6 | Menu | 2 | architecture complements |
| VB 6 | OptionButton | 41 | webwork radio button |
| VB 6 | PictureBox | 73 | Html image |
| VB 6 | Shape | 39 | case by case |
| VB 6 | TextBox | 115 | webwork textfield |
| ComCtl32 | ImageList | 20 | webwork div |
| ComCtl32 | ListView | 8 | Display of images in an html table |
| ComCtl32 | ProgressBar | 3 | Animated Gif |
| ComCtl32 | Slider | 4 | Architecture complements |
| ComCtl32 | TabStrip | 1 | webwork tabbedPane |
| Threed20.ocx | SSFrame | 19 | webwork panel |
| Threed20.ocx | SSCheck | 14 | webwork checkbox |
| Threed20.ocx | SSOption | 7 | webwork radio button |
| Threed20.ocx | SSPanel | 26 | webwork div |
| Timocx.ocx | DBList | 70 | Table |
| Timocx.ocx | DBCombo | 153 | webwork combobox |
| Timocx.ocx | DBEdit | 332 | webwork textfield |
| MSVBCldr.ocx | MSVBCalendar | 4 | webwork datepicker |
| InputDate.ocx | InputDate | 43 | webwork datepicker |
| Crystal | CrystalReport | 4 | FOP |

**FIGURE 14.16**

*Sample of navigation logic with WebWorks.*

```
<xwork>
    <include file="webwork-default.xml"/>
    <include file="config-browser.xml"/>

    <package name="default" extends="webwork-default">
            <action name="connect" method="connect" class="connect">
        <result>Login.jsp</result>
                    <result name="SUCCESS">index.jsp</result>
    </action>
    </package>

    <package name="login" extends="webwork-default">
    </package>

    <include file="xwork-optools.xml"/>
    <include file="xwork-optims.xml"/>
</xwork>
```

- Navigation: The navigation management has been implemented with WebWorks, which implements the MVC pattern. The logic of the navigation has been specified with XML files. Figure 14.16 depicts a sample of this logic.
  - Events management: In Java Web applications there are three technologies available for the handling of user events.
  - Form submission: The whole form is submitted. A new page is returned to the user. There is a latent period between actions.
  - JavaScript: The event is dealt with on the client side.
- Ajax: A flow is exchanged with the server in a way that is transparent to the user. This means that the user stays on the current page.

To maintain the user friendliness of the original client-server application, it was not advisable to systematically use the submission of pages function. Thus, to respect the general ergonomics of the new application, the migration of events has been systematized in the following manner:

- A click on a button, on a menu item: Form submission.
- Other events (value changes, enter/exit a field etc.) when the process connected to the event necessitates access to data on the server: Ajax.
- Otherwise, if the process is limited to the handling of graphic elements: JavaScript.
- Internationalization: Amadeus wished to maintain its existing method of internationalization management, which consists of displaying the different labels defined in the database depending on the user's language and the choice of the company to which he belongs. A caché system for labels has been developed to improve performance.
- Multi-database access: In the Accor version, a user with the necessary authorization can select the database from which he wishes to run the application. A mechanism for handling data sources has been put in place with the Spring Framework to make the use of one database or another transparent to the user.

- Running SQL queries: A generic mechanism to access data had been developed for the original application. This mechanism is based on SQL queries stored in ".sql" extension files. The same mechanism has been implemented with the help of a data access object responsible for:
  - Reading the desired query from the .sql file.
  - Interpreting it (analysis of any parameterized portions) to constitute the final flow.
  - Executing the query.
  - Recovering the final result and copying it into a transfer object.
  - Graph Printing: The default browser printing function cannot be used as the landscape orientation is not possible. To get around this problem, Sodifrance used the PDF format generated from the free library Java iText. For each graph, the user has the option to generate a PDF file in-line.
- Accessing distant components: Access to distant components (programs) was managed with a single OCX component written in C++. This component was used via a dedicated function (RemoteExecute) and by events raised depending on the context informing the caller (the VB6 program) with the result of its call. Rather than integrating the OCX component (or a recompiled version accessible with JNI), and given that no equivalent Java component exists with all the required mechanisms, the same component has been rewritten in Java.
- Data import/export: Data import and export were managed by a specific component developed by Amadeus to allow the user to upload the database by copying a bundle of data from an Excel or text file. To reproduce this functionality, Sodifrance explored the following two possible solutions:
  - Using an HTML/JavaScript table.
  - Using an Office Web Component.

The table below shows the advantages/drawbacks of each option:

| Solution | Functionalities | Portability |
|---|---|---|
| HTML/JavaScript | Partial | Yes |
| Office Web Component | Complete | Partial (needs Windows with Internet Explorer on the client workstation) |

The decision was made to use Office Web Component.

### The Migration Project

The migration project was completed by Sodifrance in 1,600 man-days with 10 engineers over a year. The preparation phase, composed of the preliminary study (study of the existing architecture, validation of the target architecture and specification of the transformation) and the industrialization (adaptation of the transformation chain), was carried out in 3 months.

The industrial phase was divided into three migration batches: two for the main RMS branch and one for the Accor branch. The reference tests were provided by Amadeus Hospitality as scenarios containing a total of about 3,000 unit tests, which have been replayed on the JEE version of applications to validate the transformation. The transformation of all the VB6 code (access to data, business rules, and interface) was 80% automated, while the definition of the screens (Forms) was only 50% automated, due to the necessity of redesigning them for a Web mode.

The new version of RMS is now composed of about 300,000 lines of code in 1,000 Java classes and 310 JSP (Java Server Pages). Figure 14.17 shows a screenshot sample from the migrated RMS application.

Figure 14.18 depicts a second screenshot sample from the migrated RMS application.

As required by Amadeus Hospitality, the new application has been tested with 100 simultaneous users and the performance is unchanged. The deployment of the final application was carried out by Amadeus Hospitality.

## MODISCO, A NEW ECLIPSE PLATFORM TO SUPPORT MODEL-DRIVEN LEGACY MODERNIZATION

In 2007, the European Community funded a new research project whose objective was to deliver open, model-driven solutions for complex systems engineering.[6] As developing complex systems requires integrating or transforming

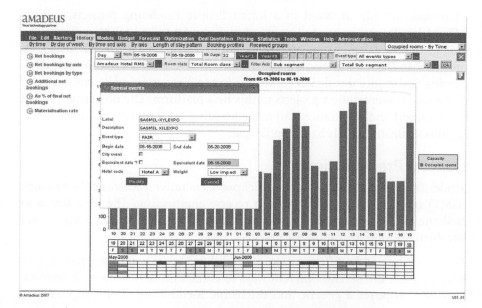

**FIGURE 14.17**

*Screenshot of migrated RMS application.*

**FIGURE 14.18**

*Second screenshot of migrated RMS application.*

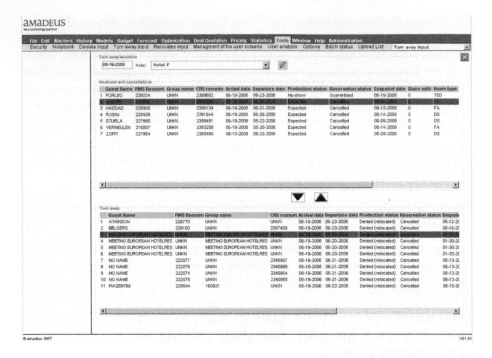

existing systems, Modelplex has planned to deliver solutions for knowledge discovery — how to create models out of existing heterogeneous systems to handle their complexity. Sodifrance and AtlanMod, the new INRIA laboratory created in Nantes by Jean Bézivin, were selected to lead this subject.

AtlanMod, already involved in a lot of Eclipse modeling projects such as ATL (Atlas Transformation Language, the model-to-model transformation language) and AMW (Atlas Model Weaving, a model weaving technology), proposed to launch MoDisco, a new Eclipse project dedicated to reverse engineering. Sodifrance decided to contribute to MoDisco to bring its experience of successful modernization projects to this new platform. The objective reached by AtlanMod and Sodifrance is to make MoDisco a reference platform for legacy modernization tools based on Eclipse.

## General Presentation

Model Discovery (MoDisco) is an Eclipse Generative Modeling Technology (GMT) component for model-driven reverse engineering. The objective is to facilitate the development of tools to extract models from legacy systems and use them on modernization use cases.

Because of the widely different nature and technological heterogeneity of legacy systems, there are several different ways to extract models from such systems. MoDisco proposes a generic and extensible metamodel-driven approach to model discovery. A basic framework, including implementations of OMG standards such as the Knowledge Discovery Metamodel (KDM) or the Structured Metrics Metamodel (SMM), and a set of guidelines are provided to the Eclipse contributors to bring their own solutions to discover models in a variety of legacy systems.

As an Eclipse component, MoDisco tools can integrate with plug-ins or technologies available in the Eclipse environment, especially those of the Eclipse Modeling Project, Eclipse Modeling Framework (EMF), model-to-model transformations, Graphical Modeling Framework (GMF), Textual Modeling Framework (TMF), etc.

## Discovery Principles

Principles of model discovery are based on a metamodel-driven approach. This means that every step is guided by a metamodel; thus, the very first step of a model discovery process is always to define the metamodel corresponding to the models to be discovered. This step is common to all types of systems.

Figure 14.19 depicts the metamodel-driven discovery approach as guided by the metamodel. The second step is the creation of one or many discoverer tools, referred to as "discoverers" in this chapter. These tools extract the required information from the system to build a model conforming to the previously defined metamodel. In some cases these discoverers can be partially generated from a description of the syntax of the files containing the information. In other cases, the discoverer reuses an existing component able to extract the information and translates this information into a model. The output of a discoverer is a model, in XMI format, for instance.

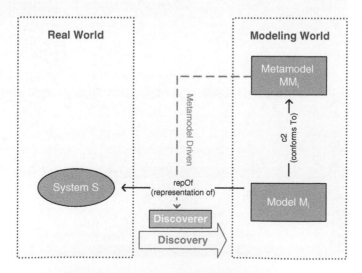

**FIGURE 14.19**

*Metamodel-driven discovery.*

## Architecture

MoDisco provides a platform supporting various legacy modernization use cases for various kinds of existing technologies. To facilitate reuse of components between several use cases, MoDisco has been organized in three layers:

- Use Cases layer: Contains components providing a solution for a specific modernization use case.
- Technology layer: Contains components dedicated to one legacy technology but independent from the modernization use case.
- Infrastructure layer: Contains generic components independent of any legacy technology.

Figure 14.20 shows each of these layers within the overall MoDisco architecture.

### *Use Cases Layer*

This layer contains components supporting legacy modernization use cases. The kind of use cases MoDisco could support is theoretically infinite. Nevertheless, the main ones are well identified:

- Quality Assurance: Verifying whether an existing system meets the required qualities (detection of anti-patterns in existing code and computation of metrics)
- Understanding: Extraction of information from an existing system to help understand one aspect of this system (structure, behavior, persistence, data flow, change impact, etc.)

**FIGURE 14.20**

*Overall architecture of MoDisco.*

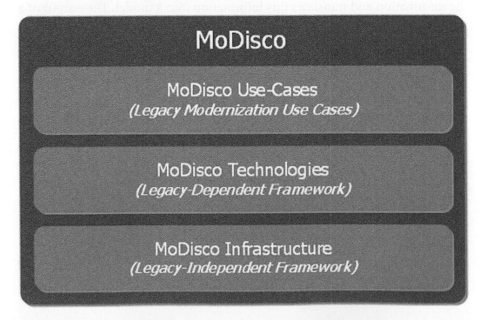

- Refactoring: Improvement of an existing system to integrate better coding norms or design patterns
- Migration: Transformation of an existing system to change the framework, language, or its architecture.

Figure 14.21 shows various MoDisco use cases within the MoDisco architecture. Other more specific use cases may be supported; for example, the extraction of business rules from programs to populate a business-rules engine or the modification of an existing system to better integrate with another system, etc.

### Technology Layer

The technology layer contains components dedicated to one legacy technology. These components can be reused between several use case components involving the same legacy technology. For example, a use case computing metrics on Java source code and another providing refactoring for Java applications could reuse the same component.

Use cases generally involve only one legacy technology (the one used to implement the existing system). Nevertheless, some use cases can involve several legacy technologies. This is the case when the existing system is heterogeneous and built with several languages. For example, when a system, implemented with Java, stores data into a relational database using JDBC, the use case may need MoDisco components able to analyze Java and SQL source code. Figure 14.22 depicts technology layers within the MoDisco architecture.

Each technology component is composed of, at least, a metamodel of the dedicated technology. This metamodel describes the elements required to support modernization use cases for the corresponding technology. Depending on the kind of use case, the metamodel can be complete (for refactoring or migration) or partial (for cartography or some quality analysis scenarios).

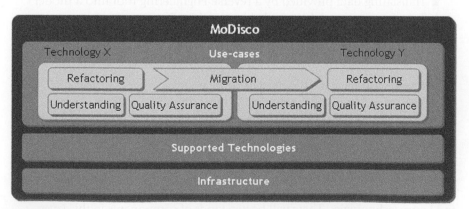

**FIGURE 14.21**

*Use cases layer of MoDisco architecture.*

**FIGURE 14.22**

*Technologies layer of MoDisco architecture.*

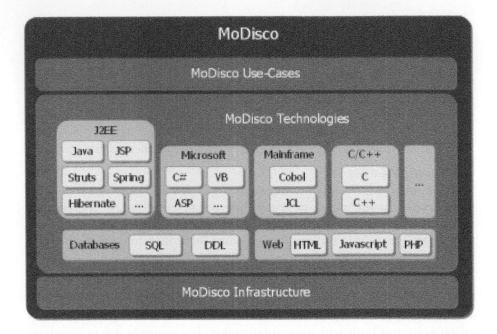

Ideally, the metamodel comes with a discoverer, a component that builds models conforming to the metamodel from artifacts of an existing system. Artifacts analyzed by discoverers are not necessarily source code files. There exist several other ways for a discoverer to find the information needed to create a model from an existing system:

- Analyzing parameter files
- Analyzing execution logs
- Unzipping an archive to access its contents
- Querying a database
- Using APIs to access a tool with which the system has been designed
- Translating data provided by a reverse-engineering tool into a model
- Transforming models provided by another discoverer

A MoDisco Technology component can come with utilities dedicated to its metamodel:

- Browsers to navigate the models more easily
- Viewers to represent the models graphically
- Computation of standard metrics
- Transformation to standard metamodels (ASTM, KDM, UML…)
- Generator to regenerate the initial artifact from its model

### Infrastructure Layer

The infrastructure layer aims at providing components independent from use cases and legacy technologies. There will be two kinds of components in this layer:

- MoDisco Knowledge components: Provide metamodels describing legacy systems independently from their technology. Like components of the technology layer, these components can come with discoverers or utilities. Examples of MoDisco Knowledge components are the metamodels from OMG/ADM:
  - KDM
  - ASTM (Abstract Syntax Tree Metamodel)
  - SMM
- MoDisco Technical components: Utilities to build or facilitate the use of all the other components. Examples of MoDisco Technical components are
  - Abstract discoverers from which concrete discoverers can be derived
  - A file-system metamodel describing the organization of files and directories
  - A model browser facilitating the visualization of MoDisco models

## Existing Components

MoDisco already contains several components for each layer.

### KDM

MoDisco contains a reference EMF implementation of the KDM, the OMG standard that ensures interoperability and exchange of data between legacy modernization tools provided by different vendors. This component belongs to the infrastructure layer of MoDisco.

### J2SE5 to Discover Java Applications

The J2SE5 metamodel is a reflection of the Java language as defined in version 3 of Java Language Specification from Sun Microsystems (JLS3 corresponds to JDK 5). It contains 101 metaclasses that allow the complete abstract syntax graph of a Java file to be described: the structure of a class (declarations of variables and methods), the body of each method (blocks, statements, and expressions), and the link between elements' usage and their declaration (superclass definition and the corresponding class declaration, variable setting and the declaration of the variable, method invocation and the declaration of the method, etc).

This metamodel comes with two additional components:

- A discoverer that populates a J2SE5 model from a Java project. This discoverer is based on the Eclipse Java Development Toolkit (JDT) component that provides an abstract syntax tree (AST) from a Java project. The role of the MoDisco discoverer is to translate this AST into a model conforming to J2SE5.

- A transformation to translate the J2SE5 model into a KDM model. This transformation supports the KDM Code package and part of the Action package: the structure of the Java classes and the signature of the methods are created in the KDM model and some of the statements contained within the methods (method invocations, for example).

**FIGURE 14.23**

*J2SE5 discoverers.*

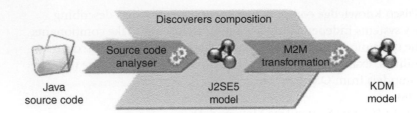

Figure 14.23 shows the overall transition from the Java source code to the KDM model. Combined with model-to-model and model-to-text transformation tools, the discoverer has already been used on several use cases:

- Quality Assurance: Control of specific coding rules
- Documentation: Generation of a specific UML model and HTML documentation (javadoc) taking into account a proprietary framework used to develop a JEE application
- Model Filter: Generation of partial UML models containing only typed dependencies between classes
- Migration from EJB2 to EJB3: Modification of the J2SE5 model to integrate the EJB3 concepts and regeneration of the source code
- Migration from Swing to GWT: Conversion of Swing APIs to Google Web Toolkit (GWT; a Java framework to develop rich GUIs for Web applications) APIs in the model generation of GWT files

The Model Filter use case, developed for the WesternGeco company, is described in the section Analysis of an Existing J2EE Application, a MoDisco Use Case on a Real Application. This component belongs to the technology layer of MoDisco.

### CSharp to Discover C# Applications

The CSharp metamodel is the reflection of the C# language as defined in version 2.0 of the C# Language Specification from Microsoft Corporation. It contains 81 metaclasses. Like J2SE5, this metamodel describes the contents of the methods.

This metamodel also comes with a transformation capability that supports mapping to the KDM. Work is in progress to contribute an open discoverer able to populate a C# model.

Combined with a proprietary discoverer (written in C) and ATL (the model-to-model transformation tool provided by INRIA/AtlanMod), this component has been used on the WesternGeco use case described in the section Analysis of an Existing J2EE Application, a MoDisco Use Case on a Real Application. This component belongs to the technology layer of MoDisco.

## Model Browser to Discover Model Contents

Each discoverer provides one or several models created by analyzing the artifacts of an existing system. These models typically contain a great number of elements, as modernization use cases need a very precise description of the systems they represent. Moreover, contrary to models created manually with a graphical modeling tool, models automatically created out of an existing system are not known beforehand. This is why it is crucial to provide a tool that helps explore this kind of model.

The MoDisco model browser is a feature-rich Ecore model browser. It can be used to browse and edit any Ecore model more easily than with the default Ecore editor.

The surface of the browser is separated into two panes: the left one displays a list of metaclasses, and the right one shows instances of the selected metaclass (i.e., model elements). At the top of each pane, a toolbar allows you to quickly change display options relative to that pane. The MoDisco generic model browser can be viewed in Figure 14.24.

Links can be followed between model elements by expanding the links tree nodes. Links appear for associations, aggregations, and the EMF container. The tree representing the model is infinite. Specific icons indicate the type of link (navigable or not, aggregate or not) and the number of instances attached via this link. The source of the link is always its parent in the tree, and the targets are its children.

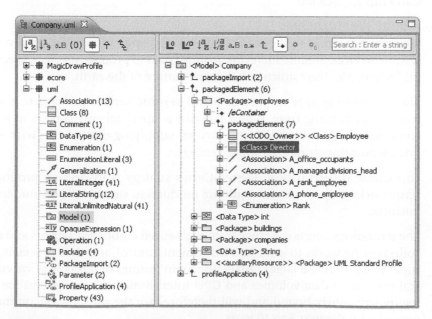

**FIGURE 14.24**

MoDisco generic model browser.

A toolbar allows the display options to be set (show links with no instances, show derived links, show link multiplicities, sort links by name, show a link to the container, show attributes in the tree, show empty attributes, sort instances by name).

The left pane displays all the metaclasses of the opened model with the number of instances for each metaclass. By right-clicking on a metaclass, its instances are displayed in the right pane. The browser additionally supports multi-selection of metaclasses.

Right click on a model element and select Browse to select this element's meta-class of this element in the left pane and display this model element among its siblings of the same type. You can also press Enter while an element is selected to trigger this action.

The MoDisco model browser currently provides one extension point for customizing the naming of instances and another one for specifying icons for model elements. More links will come in the future. This component belongs to the infrastructure layer of MoDisco.

## Analysis of an Existing J2EE Application, a MoDisco use Case on a Real Application

One of the first industrial use cases using MoDisco has been the understanding of a Large Scale Data Intensive Geological system for WesternGeco, a geophysical services company. As part of a research project funded by the European Community, Mia-Software has developed a tool to help WesternGeco understand this application.[6]

### About WesternGeco

WesternGeco works in the area of oil and gas exploration, offering advanced seismic services. Seismic surveying acquires data to produce images of geological features and their structure below the surface of the earth.

The company goal is to provide a full seismic service package to the oil companies, ranging from 3- and 4-D (time-lapse) seismic surveys to multi-component and electromagnetic surveys, supplying their clients with accurate measurements of subsurface geology.

To increase differentiation, WesternGeco's strategy is to develop proprietary seismic-related software and hardware products to support the seismic service business.

The technology covers the range from high-speed embedded sensors and data-collection networks to advanced instrument control and data processing on super-computers and large clusters. The main features of this type of system are real-time, large data volumes and CPU intensiveness. These systems are also highly technology bound and will therefore face the prospect of continuous upgrades for the next 5 to 10 years.

## Description of the Existing System

The system to be focused on in the Modelplex use case was the onboard Spread Management System, which boots up, controls, and monitors the spread instrumentation. The spread instrumentation is a very complex network of distributed computers, various devices, and sensor nodes (hydrophones).The time-lapse, or 4-D, seismic method involves acquisition, processing, and interpretation of repeated seismic surveys over a producing hydrocarbon field. The objective is to determine the changes occurring in the reservoir as a result of hydrocarbon production or injection of water or gas into the reservoir by comparing the repeated datasets. Figure 14.25 represents the functionality of a large-scale, data-intensive geological system.

To attain this goal, seismic acquisition has implied the development of a complex heterogeneous system:

- Data rate >100 MB/s
- Number of sensors >100,000
- Disk capacity >60 Tbyte
- Compute power >1 TFlop
- Network of computers >500

## Complexity of the Existing System

The complexity of the Spread Management System relies on five dimensions:

1. Size: The size of a deployed seismic spread is large. Each spread typically is composed of more than 100,000 sensors. The spread will also contain up to 1,000 distributed computers in various devices.
2. Heterogeneity: In the system as a whole (where Spread Management is a part), different technologies are used both at the hardware and software level. The set of used operating systems includes Embedded LINUX, LINUX, and UNIX. Programming languages include Java, C#, and C++ and communication mechanisms include CORBA, sockets, and Java RMI.
3. Distribution: The nodes of the spread managed by the Spread Management System are deployed in the sea along cables (streamers) that are towed behind a vessel. There are up to 1,000 distributed computers (nodes) in a spread of 10 cables. Each cable might be up to 12,000 m long.
4. Dynamicity: In case of some faults in the equipment, parts of the streamer (streamer section or node) have to be replaced *in situ* while the operation continues.

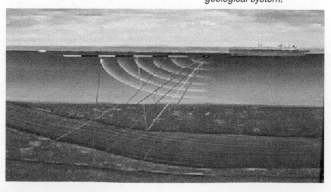

**FIGURE 14.25**
*Large-scale, data-intensive geological system.*

5. Autonomy: Each device is developed as an autonomous computer with no centralized logic. If one device dies it does not influence the other devices or the data traffic. There are multiple routing schemas. Autonomous devices also support better scaling by adding more transparent supporting devices to the network.

Figure 14.26 represents complexity dimensions of the Spread Management System.

### Problem Summary

In the case of legacy applications that are not modelized, with little or no documentation, the initial developers of these applications are no longer available. How can the knowledge of these applications be retrieved to support bug corrections and to develop new functionalities?

Two main constraints had to be taken into account:

- WesternGeco wished to turn the extracted knowledge into UML models
- The knowledge to be retrieved and the way to create a UML model from it could vary depending on specific needs

These constraints led us to design and develop a flexible solution, easily customizable, to extract specific points of view out of the existing system and to create specific UML representations.

### Architecture Overview

The solution put in place is a sequence of tools. The modularity of the migration chain facilitates the reusability of individual components and thus augments the flexibility of the global migration chain.

**FIGURE 14.26**

*Complexity dimensions of the application.*

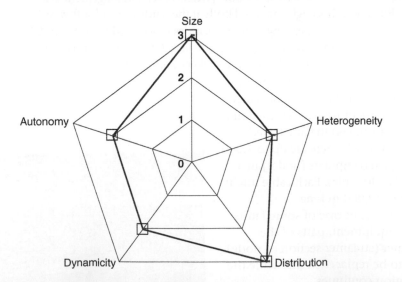

The standard migration chain is composed of a discoverer to extract a model from sources, and model transformations to bridge between different metamodels. To facilitate the reusability of components KDM was chosen as the pivot metamodel of the migration chain: rather than developing two transformations to UML (one from Java and another from C#), the KDM to UML transformation can be reused and connected to initial discoverers from Java or C#. In addition, KDM could be used as input to transformations to metamodels other than UML.

Figure 14.27 depicts the standard transformation chain from Java and C# to UML models.

The first version of the solution retrieves different dependencies between existing components. Therefore, to obtain a filtered model with dependencies from a selected element, the Java and C# discoverers were enhanced to obtain a KDM model with Action elements (elements related to the behavior of applications), and an additional transformation was inserted into the existing transformation chain. This transformation explores the KDM model to identify additional dependencies that are added to the KDM model. Based on KDM, it can be used with models coming from Java or C#.

Figure 14.28 shows the extended transformation chain from Java and C# to UML.

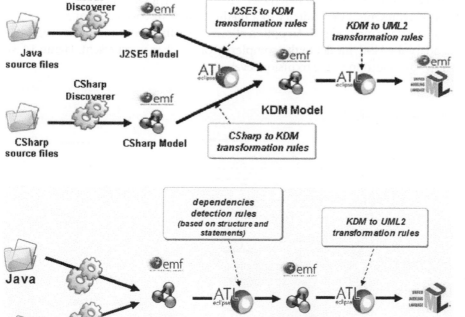

**FIGURE 14.27**

*Standard transformation chain from Java and C# to UML.*

**FIGURE 14.28**

*Extended transformation chain from Java and C# to UML.*

## Solution

The first version of the solution provided to WesternGeco supports two points of view, both represented with UML models:

1. To have a complete view of a legacy application, a full UML model is provided to show the structure of the legacy application. Modeling tools provide an automatic generation of class diagrams from this model (e.g., with Eclipse UML2Tool). Figure 14.29 shows an extracted UML model.

2. To visualize dependencies from an element, a model filter is provided and information extracted from intermediate models such as the KDM model. The main idea is to extract dependencies from the structure, but also from a profound analysis of the application. The KDM model is a detailed representation of the application, so we can explore all references to external elements and represent them as "Dependency" links in UML models. Finally, the UML model is optimal: it contains the strict minimum elements required to describe the dependencies graph of a Java or C# class selected in the development environment.

Figure 14.30 shows the results of the analysis from a Java class.

All dependencies are represented by attributes, associations, or UML dependencies named "local" or "method parameter." For example, a UML dependency named "local" represents a dependency in a method block discovered from a local variable or a static method call. An option allows the defining of a recursion-level filter to adapt the UML model to the complexity of the class to represent. Figure 14.31 shows the selection of the recursion level.

**FIGURE 14.29**

*Standard UML model extracted from Java or C# source code.*

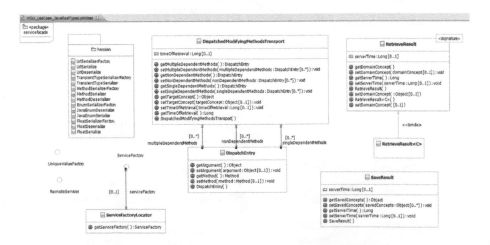

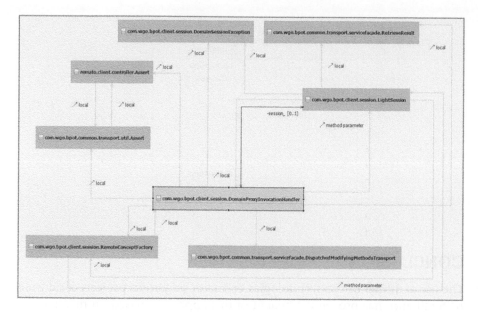

**FIGURE 14.30**
*Result of the analysis from a Java class.*

These tools have been delivered to WesternGeco to extract information from two applications:

- An application written in Java: 591 files for a total of 75,638 lines of code
- An application written in C#: 1196 files for a total of 341,326 lines of code

**FIGURE 14.31**
*Selection of recursion level.*

They are also available in the Eclipse MoDisco project as use cases. They demonstrate how to construct a discovery tool from existing discoverers and to customize it to fit specific needs.

All the sources of the plug-ins are available in the SVN repository of the Eclipse MoDisco project.

## Roadmap

To support new understanding needs, the standard migration chain can be easily extended with additional transformations or new discoverers. Based on open standards (Java, EMF, KDM, and UML) the initial components have been contributed to the MoDisco platform and the development of additional components can be undertaken with any tool compliant with those standards.

With the same approach, new components can be implemented to retrieve real type attributes when declared type is an interface.

Figure 14.32 depicts the retrieval of real type attributes.

**FIGURE 14.32**
*Retrieve real type attributes.*

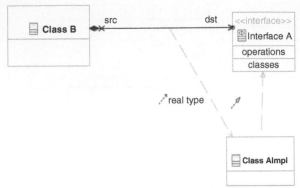

# CONCLUSION

The use of model-driven technologies on major migration projects conducted by Sodifrance has proven the benefit of this approach. Based on metamodeling standards, the tools used to extract the knowledge from existing applications, to transform this knowledge into new paradigms and architecture, and to regenerate the application according to specific technical platforms and patterns are more flexible and reusable. The new MoDisco platform will bring all these benefits into an open extensible framework containing model-driven, reverse-engineering tools and components. This platform will be use case oriented to deliver concrete tools for real-life software modernization scenarios.

# REFERENCES

1. Home page of MoDisco project (http://www.eclipse.org/gmt/modisco/).
2. Bézivin J. sNets: A First Generation Model Engineering Platform. In: *Satellite Events at the MoDELS 2005 Conference*, LNCS 3844; Springer; 2006:169–181.
3. Mia-Insight suite (http://www.mia-software.com/produits/).
4. Khusidman V Dr., Ulrich W. *Architecture-Driven Modernization: Transforming the Enterprise* (http://www.omg.org/cgi-bin/doc?admtf/2007-12-01).
5. Unified Modeling Language (http://www.uml.org).
6. *MODELPLEX — MODELling solution for comPLEX software systems, IST 34081* (www.modelplex-ist.org).

# A Guide to Moving Forward with Modernization

# CHAPTER 15

# Launching and Sustaining Modernization Initiatives

**William Ulrich**

The case studies that we have provided in this book are merely a snapshot in time. Some of the case studies were onetime projects while others are ongoing initiatives. In either case, executives must fund initiatives to maintain a sustainable modernization program. IT does not have an unlimited supply of funds to spend as it wishes and, as a rule, this means the business must continue the flow of project funding over an extended period of time. As a result, sustained business value must be demonstrated over time.

This chapter discusses various aspects of launching and sustaining modernization initiatives. This includes a discussion of pitfalls to avoid, modernization principles, tool and service strategies, where to start, and what to expect in the future from modernization.

## MODERNIZATION PITFALLS

More than a few modernization projects have been launched only to be canceled during the project or after initial implementation. In other cases, a project that was considered successful by IT was rejected out of hand by the business. These situations demonstrate that while the launch of a modernization effort is important, the sustainability and business adoption of these efforts are equally important. The following are some examples of common pitfalls that stymie or shut down modernization projects.

- Failure to communicate the value of a modernization project or longer term program to the business is the biggest risk to modernization sustainability. This is a very common situation that results in projects that are launched, partially delivered, and then canceled in a subsequent budgeting round. IT historically has not wanted and has not had the capacity to cost-justify modernization or other types of projects to the business. It has been easier for IT to fall back into its comfort zone and focus on IT cost cutting, which could actually result in less value to the business depending on the approach taken. Engaging the business early and often is a lesson learned in terms of sustaining support for modernization of IT architectures over the long term.

■ Viewing modernization as a tactic, as opposed to strategically, results in a situation where the visibility of these efforts never gains critical mass. Industry analyst firm Gartner Inc. stated that:

"IT modernization reinstates IT strategic planning at the heart of the CIO cabinet. Most CIOs will need to develop new skills and competencies in their management teams to deal with the significant challenges of IT modernization."[1]

In other words, management must view modernization strategically to really make a difference. Historically, however, modernization has been viewed in a tactical sense and focused on programmer productivity as the main benefit. Tactical thinking undercuts the real value of modernization, which should be architecture-driven, not driven by programmers or IT cost reduction. Tool vendors have magnified this problem by positioning tools at a very tactical level and not fully understanding or communicating the value of modernization as a transformative engine for IT and business architectures.

■ Selling modernization as a way to lower IT costs is a shortsighted approach that hinders modernization's visibility and curtails the use of modernization to strategic projects. As discussed in Chapter 1, selling modernization as an IT cost savings device will not get the attention of senior executives because the benefits of potential IT cost savings are limited when compared to the business benefits modernization can deliver. IT spending represents a very small relative percentage of revenue, typically less than 5%.[2] The non-IT side of a business, on the other hand, consumes 95% or more of the spending pie. Simple math tells us that there are significantly greater opportunities to save money on the business side than can be gained on the IT side through the effective and strategic deployment of IT resources. IT should, therefore, focus the power of modernization on establishing and sustaining benefits to the business. Applying the business architecture/IT architecture alignment approaches discussed throughout this book avoids the pitfall of focusing exclusively or too heavily on IT cost reductions.

■ A lack of coordination among teams that could benefit from modernization can significantly hinder sustainability of a modernization initiative. Limiting tool and service investments to a single project or area can also restrict the success and acceptance of a modernization program. In some cases, companies have had modernization tools in place for years, but have limited the use of those tools to a single area or even a single person. The result of this approach is that it dramatically restricts the potential benefits of modernization and denies the opportunities modernization can offer to areas that really need it. We have even seen situations where one area was attempting to procure modernization tools while another team already had similar tools installed and in use. In another case one area of a company dropped maintenance on a tool while another area of that same company was attempting to justify acquisition of that same tool. Having a centralized modernization center of excellence, which is discussed later in this chapter, goes a long way to addressing this issue.

# GUIDING PRINCIPLES OF MODERNIZATION

Establishing a set of modernization principles (generally accepted truths that guide one's actions) provides management, planning teams, IT architects, and project team guidelines for dealing with existing software architectures. Any project that directly or indirectly involves existing systems should consider and incorporate the following 15 modernization principles as a guide to action.

1. Any project that directly or indirectly relies on or contemplates modifying any existing software systems should have knowledge of those systems that is appropriate to that project.
2. Assessment of existing application and data architectures incorporates all systems that are directly impacted by the planned initiative and includes all interfaces to external systems or entities.
3. Depth and breadth of an assessment is directly proportionate to the amount of information required for a subsequent project phase.
4. Initial assessment activities focus on gaining a breadth of knowledge about the IT architecture.
5. Subsequent assessment activities focus on gaining a depth of knowledge about the application and data architecture.
6. Metric derivations of existing application and data architectures are essential to qualitative analysis of those environments and to modernization planning.
7. Functional and semantic redundancy and inconsistency is rectified across application and data architectures as appropriate to satisfy the need for modularity, cohesiveness, and consolidation within a given project or target architecture.
8. Business requirements are driven by the transition plan between the as-is and to-be business architecture.

9. Business architecture must be considered and incorporated into a modernization project as appropriate based on the impacts to the application and data architecture.

10. Modernization projects restricted to technical architectures will yield limited value to the business architecture and the business.

11. Software to be transformed into a model-driven, object-based, or services-oriented architecture must be cleansed of structural diagnostics, functional redundancy, semantic inconsistency, and other design and architectural pathologies.

12. Modernization disciplines are incorporated into planned and ongoing projects as is appropriate to the success of those projects.

13. Modernization projects evolve through a series of stages where each delivered stage provides demonstrable business and/or IT value.

14. Initial modernization project stages achieve early wins for frontline business users through the alignment of business processes, user interfaces, and shadow systems.

15. Later modernization stages achieve value through the alignment of application and data architectures with business capabilities, semantics, and governance structures.

These principles can be augmented with internal principles based on the evolution of modernization projects and teams. Be aware, however, that principles are descriptive and not prescriptive. In other words, principles guide one's actions and do not dictate how to achieve an end result.

Modernization principles should be considered and applied by management, planning teams, IT architects, project teams, business architects, and analysts responsible for working with IT. The responsibilities associated with these principles do not fall just on one party but are rather directed at all relevant and affected parties. If your enterprise establishes a modernization center of excellence, the center becomes the keeper of the modernization principles.

## SETTING UP A MODERNIZATION CENTER OF EXCELLENCE

A modernization center of excellence is an organizational unit that serves as the nerve center for modernization efforts within the enterprise. A center of excellence does not necessarily perform all modernization work, but this team does provide the support structure for successful modernization deployment.

Modernization work is typically coordinated within IT architecture teams, but this has led to the "borrowing" of personnel to assign them to modernization work on a part-time basis. Part-time commitment to modernization creates a situation where individuals have only cursory knowledge of modernization topics, a lack of vision as to how modernization can help the enterprise, and little vested interest in success.

The part-time commitment pitfall can afflict management as well as analysts and architects. For example, the head of enterprise architecture at one insurance company became a "drive-by" methodologist. In this role, he would subvert standard approaches, practices, and even naming conventions established by his team and outside experts based on whims of fancy. This part-time approach, which resulted from the lack of a center of excellence and no full-time modernization leadership, threw projects into chaos. The modernization center of excellence, coupled with a set of foundational modernization principles, addresses these issues. Such a center of excellence ideally has the following responsibilities.

- Establish and maintain a set of modernization principles.
- Work with executive teams to determine overall modernization strategy and options to support business and IT initiatives and plans.
- Maintain a centralized set of modernization skills to support management, planning teams, and project teams on an as-needed basis.
- Provide methodological and project planning support to assist with scenario identification and customization, plan development, project role definition and staffing, deliverable definition, and assistance with monitoring project progress.
- Coordinate efforts to develop, measure, and communicate return on investment value from a business and IT perspective. This role is essential and requires coordinating with project teams and project stakeholders.
- Serve as the knowledge center for in-house modernization tools and maintain an awareness of additional industry tool options. In addition to serving as a clearing house for tools and tool support, the center also provides tool integration as required based on the latest tool integration standards.
- Review and maintain a set of service vendor options and relationships for service-supported, in-sourced, and outsourced projects.
- Recommend project deployment options based on project requirements, constraints, and time frames. For example, the center would ensure that a project that is best completed as an outsourced effort is not taken as an in-house initiative.
- Provide modernization staff to fulfill project roles on an as-needed basis.

Enterprises that have not established a modernization center of excellence, regardless of what they call it, have had difficulty sustaining modernization programs. In these situations one-off projects, even if they were successful, were the beginning and the end of a given modernization effort. Long-term modernization benefits are best achieved if there is continuity from project to project and the center of excellence provides this continuity.

## MODERNIZATION TOOL/TECHNOLOGY STRATEGY

The number of false starts and re-starts that organizations have taken with modernization tools over the years can take its toll. Sometimes management sours on modernization and blames the tools or the vendor. It can take years to recover. Other times tools are deployed and lost in the organization infrastructure. To avoid this, management should establish a coordinated tool strategy that is driven by the types of projects that need to be completed, existing and target computing architectures, and the in-house versus outsourcing strategy pursued.

In-house tool functions needed to provide a minimum level of modernization support for an enterprise should focus on architecture analysis. Tool deployment on a given project can take several weeks or months if the tool is not already in-house and no usage procedures have been established. On the other hand, if it is merely a function of rolling the tool out to another team and applying established procedures to load a given application or applications into the tool repository, this time frame can be reduced to a week or so. The modernization tool or workbench needed to support ongoing assessment efforts should include the following features.

- Ability to analyze the main language environments, execution artifacts, database definitions, and user interface definitions
- Open repository that supports the analysis of these artifacts in a variety of ways
- Visualization capabilities to support the systems analysis from a variety of architectural perspectives
- Ability to customize visualization features to extend the baseline analysis capabilities
- The ability to produce and customize assessment metrics
- Standards-based exchange format so other tools can share IT architecture metadata as input to visualization, refactoring, and/or transformation efforts

These tool features provide a solid baseline for launching and sustaining a wide variety of modernization projects, as long as the methods and disciplines are clearly defined for a given project. If the tools are not coupled with adequate methodology and expertise, their value will be limited. Additional tool capabilities for refactoring and transformation could be licensed or brought in-house through service providers. These tools would have the following features.

- Ability to find and/or remove certain structural diagnostics
- Code slicing and code aggregation capabilities
- Code structuring capabilities
- Data definition rationalization and standardization
- Data definition extraction and data model creation
- Business rule extraction and transformation
- Transformation capabilities to model-driven architecture (MDA) or similar abstractions
- Appropriate testing tools to validate systems that have undergone modernization

The types of tools unlikely to be brought in-house are onetime transformation tools such as those used to move from one language and/or platform to another. These tools are typically owned and used by service providers and generally this work is done off-site. A service provider strategy should accompany a tool strategy as the two go hand-in-hand. A service vendor agreement may be used as an option to bring a tool in-house and test it out on a live project. This approach typically shortens the procurement cycle and gets project efforts moving more quickly.

## MODERNIZATION SERVICE PROVIDER STRATEGY

A service provider strategy can vary based on the types of projects, environments, and the ability of in-house personnel to perform modernization work. There are different types of providers and each has its own relative strengths and weaknesses. Some providers only perform certain types of work and many providers are specialists in a given area. In addition, some service providers carry their own toolset while others use tools that never leave the provider's "factory" environment. Other providers may have tool vendor relationships or may use whatever tools an organization has already installed. The following service options are available to support modernization projects.

- Tool providers often have a services team that helps with product installation, project setup, initial analysis work, and customization. These teams are not geared to work outside of the domain of their own technologies.

- Project-based service providers will work in-house on a project-by-project basis. In these cases, the provider fills all project roles including project management and project delivery. These providers are useful for well-defined, in-house projects but little or no skills transfer typically occurs.

- Off-site factory service providers have unique skills and tools that provide a variety of modernization options that range from analysis to refactoring to full-scale transformation. These providers are highly valuable for migration projects where in-house tools are not available and there is no need or desire to transfer these migration skills to in-house analysts. Relationships with these providers should be coupled with a strong on-site team that may include additional service providers.

- Service providers also offer support functions that create a "blended team" approach. The benefit to this approach is that the provider delivers certain skills while in-house personnel learn on the job. This approach is typically coupled with in-house tools, in-house project management, and vendor provided methodology or process support. Blended teams create a best-of-breed solution in many cases because everyone on the team is well suited to their respective roles.

- Specialty teams can perform a single set of modernization tasks; for example, there are firms that specialize in lift and shift projects that move the technical architecture from mainframe COBOL to Windows .NET COBOL. This work can be in-sourced as well as outsourced.

Any given modernization initiative may combine one or more of the previously listed service approaches. It is important to ensure that the right mix is applied to the right type of project. The center of excellence serves as a sounding board to ensure that the right service strategy is followed. The important consideration is to have a clear understanding of what is to be accomplished and ensure that the service provider takes its directions from you and not the other way around. Too often an enterprise will outsource accountability and knowledge of the work being done and this can only lead to problems.

## WHERE TO START

The question as to where an organization should start with a modernization effort is quite common. Much of modernization is common sense, assuming one has a foundational understanding of the general concepts, principles, disciplines, and scenarios. This foundation assumes that IT management and architects have educated themselves on the topic of modernization and engaged external resources to extend this baseline knowledge as required. Here are some areas to focus on when beginning your modernization journey.

### Assessing Requirements

Modernization is driven by specific business and IT needs. Determining requirements involves examining business and IT plans, identifying executive priorities, and examining the business and IT environment to see what needs to change. This process is not uncommon at most organizations, but the difference from an architecture-driven modernization point of view is that the requirements are viewed through a transformational perspective. All strategies should be viewed as an issue of how to get from where we are to where we need to go. This requires articulating not just the target business and IT architecture but exposing the as-is business architecture and IT architecture along with articulating a transition strategy to incrementally achieve the to-be version.

## Assessing Appetite

The knowledge of and appetite for modernization may be very low at your organization. This may require some education of management and architecture teams. On the other hand, moving forward with a modernization strategy may require soft-selling some of these ideas by building on small victories. Addressing user interface modernization can build small victories with the business communities. As this occurs, modernization analysts can begin looking at an SOA scenario or addressing consolidation concerns through modernization as a common sense way to meeting business challenges. The concept of modernization itself could remain as a behind-the-scenes concept. The best way to determine an approach is to assess the appetite for modernization without overselling it as a panacea.

## Building Support/Selling the Concept

Based on the appetite for modernization as a unique discipline, the center of excellence and other individuals promoting modernization will need to sell benefits. One approach is an honest assessment of the work done to date on IT projects, including project overruns and failures. This may be coupled with a portfolio management program. Highlighting past failures may be politically unpopular but can be a good way to communicate to executives that what has been tried in the past has not worked. Project transparency is one principle that modernization projects should adhere to and other projects should do the same. A second approach involves selling the idea of incremental value, which is beginning to hold sway with management over the "big bang" project theory.

Beyond these ideas, the best approach is to seek out planned projects or ongoing initiatives where modernization can play a role. This may involve a project that is in trouble because of a lack of understanding of the current IT architecture or a project where there is a clear need for a transition strategy. These cases are areas where the center of excellence can promote the use of modernization.

## Launching the Center of Excellence

A center of excellence could begin with one person taking on the role of modernization coordinator. Selling the concept of a center of excellence may take time if the modernization concept has not been sold to management. However, there still needs to be a centralized knowledge center because fully decentralized modernization efforts have been shown to be inefficient and ineffective, and have resulted in redundancies that undercut deployment efforts. Our recommendation is to begin small, set clear goals, define your roles well, and communicate how the center will support modernization efforts across the enterprise.

## Establishing a Baseline Assessment

Opportunities for pursuing modernization work rely in part on having a baseline understanding of the IT architecture as well as how IT architecture supports the business architecture. To communicate with and sell senior management, the IT architecture will need to map to business capabilities, which in turn must map to the organizational units that perform those capabilities. This high-level mapping does not require tools, but is the result of organizational knowledge derived from selected business and IT professionals.

The business may already have a capability model mapped to various business units. If so, this model can be used as a target for mapping functions supported by various applications and subsystems. Analysts should also develop a high-level data structure mapping that is restricted to major data stores that cross application boundaries and are core to the operational validity of a major application. This baseline assessment can be built using a simple database or, if available, a repository-based, architectural modeling tool.

The last step involves mapping major projects and initiatives to each application so that there is a good understanding as to what types of projects are either in the planning stage or in progress. This entire concept may be sold as a portfolio management effort or as fulfilling simple IT audit and accountability requirements. This knowledge base becomes the foundation upon which future modernization planning and analysis will build.

## Identifying Project Opportunities

One message has become clear as far as building management support. Go for the low hanging fruit that delivers the most value in the shortest time frame for the least amount of investment. IT traditionally has tried to make a big splash with large projects, big investments, and long delivery windows. We covered the relatively unsuccessful nature of these projects in Chapter 1. What may be counterintuitive to IT, but what has been proven to work is a concept that some organizations call a "quick win."[3] The quick win approach, also called the "rapid response" approach, relies on the concept of rapid response teams.[4]

Rapid response teams provide near-term value to immediate business requirements and deliver incremental value over a window of time that collectively add up to significant value. The overall strategy of launching quick win or rapid response teams is geared at rebuilding IT's relationship with the business, exposing and addressing frontline user requirements, creating the user-driven view of the target architecture, and driving deployed front-end solutions as requirements into backend architecture planning efforts.

Other projects have a natural fit for modernization. Architecture teams, for example, identify non-standard or obsolete languages, code generators, database engines, or platforms that are ideal modernization targets. The approach for addressing many of these projects involves outsourcing the migration/transformation effort. The center of excellence should target these potential projects by discussing the business and IT benefits of moving off of these obsolete technologies sooner versus later. Note that the mix-and-match use of modernization scenarios still applies to these outsourced migration projects.

Beyond the low hanging fruit and migration projects, additional modernization opportunities should focus on any planned or early stage projects that replace or interface with existing systems. Another indicator involves multiple projects that impact the same applications or an interconnected set of applications. High-level assessment results discussed earlier should help identify project opportunities. In addition, follow-up interviews assist with identifying where business and IT owners have an interest in applying modernization as an option. Note that modernization should not be forced on a project team or business unit. There are typically enough opportunities to apply modernization solutions within an enterprise where the owners are inclined to try different options.

## Procuring Project Funding

While the center of excellence may need to sell the benefits laid out in Chapter 1 to management on a case-by-case basis, a better option is to seek pre-funded projects that are ready to launch, but lack a strategy needed to achieve project objectives. In this way, the center of excellence is serving as a guide or mentor to project teams that are inclined to try modernization options as a way to achieve project goals. The project benefits and returns may already be in place and the modernization team can then ensure that the project approach and cost structure ensures appropriate returns on the investment in those projects.

When discussing project funding, planning teams should avoid the trap of pitting modernization against traditional solutions. As shown in some of our case studies (e.g., Chapters 7 and 9), projects can involve a hybrid of modernization, new functionality, new design, and even commercial-off-the-shelf (COTS) options. There may be multiple ways to achieve project objectives, and modernization should be considered as a portion of the solution where it can help achieve those objectives.

The basic way to determine how modernization can either curtail or reduce project costs, while ensuring that the project will ultimately succeed, is to evaluate the impact of applying various modernization tasks to certain stages of a given project. Consider the following sample questions as they apply to various project scenarios.

- Can a modernization assessment assist with understanding where and how to integrate, migrate, or deactivate existing application systems, subsystems, and data structures during the deployment of a COTS package and, therefore, lower the cost of deployment?

- Will migrating and transforming an application from the current environment achieve the same goals and reduce the costs, time, and/ or risks over a project that plans to rewrite that application using a Greenfield approach?

- Can a new application and data architecture design be populated and deployed more quickly and cost-effectively by capturing and reusing functionality from the existing application and data architecture than by other means?

These are just sample questions and should be posed to management and planning teams by the center of excellence. Moving modernization options into the executive suite, as directed by Gartner, requires moving beyond the overly simplistic either-or decision cycle that has dominated the modernization discussion in years past. When positioning modernization from a project perspective and from a cost justification perspective, focus on the ability of modernization to provide more cost-effective and efficient solutions to traditional IT challenges.

## Service Provider Analysis and Procurement

Most organizations lack in-house modernization expertise and need to bring in help for modernization planning and deployment efforts. Recognizing that not every service provider delivers the same types of service is an important step in starting down a successful road to architecture-driven modernization. For example, tool vendors are not good at strategic planning. Companies that perform off-site migrations are rarely interested in providing, nor are they equipped to deliver full service on-site support. Some service providers offer planning support while others offer implementation support. The trick is to know who to hire to perform certain tasks at various stages of modernization deployment. The general guidelines below are a good way to get started.

- Seek planning advice from individuals that have no vested interest in selling you a tool, helping with project implementation, performing off-site migrations, or providing ongoing in-house support. This avoids the conflict of interest in hiring a partner at a larger firm that recommends his team for all of your modernization needs.

- In addition to initial planning advice, other service providers can assist with the creation of an initial assessment across business and IT architecture boundaries. An assessment of this nature is analyst-focused, not tool-driven, and establishes a foundation for subsequent project planning and building an overall modernization strategy.

- If a migration initiative is planned, look at the various off-site migration service providers that can deliver those projects. Seek automated solutions over manual approaches and verify that the vendor is not building tools on your dime — unless this is a one-of-a-kind project.

- If you have project-specific needs and lack in-house expertise, but want to in-source a project with a defined starting point and ending point, look for full-service providers with expertise in the required tasks to be performed. Many times these service providers have their own tools or will recommend and deploy a third-party tool that they use on a regular basis.

- If you plan to perform ongoing assessment, refactoring, and transformation work in-house, look for a service provider with this expertise that can offer methodology support, training, and skills transfer. This is highly recommended, although each of these requirements should be clearly spelled out in the agreement. Skills transfer tends to take a back seat when project time frames and deliverables are on the line.

- If you have a near-term need to install and deploy a tool, work with the tool vendor's team to deliver a project-ready tool environment. As an alternative, certain tool vendors may also be able to recommend a third-party service provider to help with the project.

Note that some tool vendors have separate service teams that can actually provide full-service offerings that are not necessarily tied to a given tool. In addition, if business architecture analysis is required and the business has not performed work in this area, you may want to bring in this additional area of expertise to work with business teams. Finally, consider the service provider strategy discussed in Chapter 2 when looking at support for modernization projects. There is no "one size fits all" solution to modernization service options and the center of excellence will need to manage the vendor strategy.

## Tool Analysis and Procurement

When looking at how to get started with tool analysis and deployment, you will need to consider a range of options in the market and tie those options back to your project and service-deployment strategy. Assuming you have followed the service provider guidelines from the previous section, you should have a general idea of the tool and approach you want to pursue.

Assuming that you plan to perform in-house work that is either partly or entirely under the control of in-house teams, you will need a basic modernization workbench that fulfills the requirements set forth earlier in the section Modernization Tool/Technology Strategy. Consider the following approach for getting started.

- Determine the amount of in-house modernization assessment, refactoring, and transformation work to be completed across various application areas.

- If multiple substantive projects are envisioned and there is an off-the-shelf tool available to support project-related environments, identify tools to support those projects.

- Establish tool evaluation criteria to support the analysis and selection of a suitable modernization workbench. The center of excellence should establish a tool/vendor evaluation criteria that covers all major features and functions as well as platforms and technologies. Criteria should include "must have" product capabilities as well as "nice to have" capabilities to avoid having to re-evaluate tools using conflicting or inadequate evaluation criteria. The center of excellence also ensures that duplicate tooling is not being procured and that the most effective and efficient vendor relationships are established and maintained across various areas.

- Based on the evaluation criteria and a systematic analysis and selection process, identify the vendor and tool to be brought in-house.

- Establish a reasonable tool installation and deployment plan. The tool setup will take a week or so but initiating the tool and loading up information for a first-time project is likely to run 2–3 weeks or more depending on the situation. Verify that you have expertise on-site that has done initial project setup and tool population before. This is typically the tool vendor.

- Plan to address any installation or customization issues early and often with the vendor. Assign a tool support person from the center of excellence to broaden tool usage across application areas that can benefit from the tool.

The most important point is to not let the tool dictate your project plan or modernization roadmap. The tool is subservient to the tasks and subtasks contained within your methodology, which is driven by work plans that have evolved from one or more scenarios, which in turn are driven by business and IT requirements and strategy.

## Rolling Out an Initial Project

We recommend using the term "initial project" instead of the term "pilot." The term pilot implies that a test is being performed whereas initial project implies that real work is getting done. The goal of an initial project is not merely to test a tool, if there is a tool involved, but to exercise your judgment regarding scenario selection, project staging and staffing, cost justification, estimating capabilities, methodology, in-house team coordination and management, service provider support, and all other aspects of what would be involved in subsequent projects.

Lessons learned should be collected and managed through the modernization center of excellence. Having a centralized knowledge center becomes critical to ensure that the modernization benefits and lessons learned are shared accordingly. In addition, the cost justification process within an enterprise will have to be fine-tuned to incorporate modernization-based thinking. The center of excellence should be the knowledge and support center for planning and justification, just as they support tool, methodology, and related skills and disciplines.

## MODERNIZATION: WHAT TO EXPECT IN THE FUTURE

As modernization concepts evolve, organizations must continue to stay abreast of how to apply these advancements to existing systems. Unless an organization achieves a nirvana state of perfect architectures that reflect perfect designs and deployments, which is highly unlikely anytime soon, modernization will continue to be required to understand, refine, and retool existing systems. This means that modernization will become part of the overall project planning ecosystem. Under this concept, the following will become commonplace.

- All project planning sessions will consider modernization concepts as an integral part of any project that involves existing systems.
- Executives, management, and planning teams will seek to determine how they can deliver business and IT value more efficiently and effectively through modernization.
- Cost justification will seek to determine how understanding, migrating, and/or reusing existing systems functionality can benefit a project.

The future of modernization as an industry will reflect improvements in a number of areas as well as much wider acceptance. Given that the alternative to understanding and leveraging existing software assets is to not understand them and allow these assets to stifle business and IT strategies, common sense dictates that modernization concepts will only grow in acceptance and popularity. The degree of maturity of an IT organization will, therefore, evolve to include the ability to understand and modernize its valuable software assets as a common way of doing business.

# REFERENCES

1. Kyte A, Vecchio D. What the CIO Should Know and Do About IT Modernization. 2008: ID Number G00154885.
2. Ricadela A. InformationWeek 500: A Tough Climb This Year. 2002; http://www.informationweek.com/news/management/showArticle.jhtml?articleID=6503398.
3. Ulrich W. The Quick Win Team Interview With Juanita Lohmeyer. 2006; http://www.bpminstitute.org/whitepapers/whitepaper/article/the-quick-win-team-interview-with-juanita-lohmeyer-telus-communications.html.
4. Ulrich W. Synchronize Rapid Response Projects with Architecture Transformation. *Cutter Consortium Update*. 2003; http://www.systemtransformation.com/IT_Arch_Transformation_Articles/arch_synchronize.htm.

# Index

Note: Page numbers followed by *f* indicate figures.

**419**

Printed and bound by CPI Group (UK) Ltd, Croydon, CR0 4YY

03/10/2024

01040319-0013